CORPORATE PERSONALITY IN THE 20th CENTURY

Corporate Personality in the 20th Century

Edited by
CHARLES E. F. RICKETT
and
ROSS B. GRANTHAM

·HART·
PUBLISHING

OXFORD
1998

Hart Publishing
Oxford
UK

Distributed in the United States by
Northwestern University Press
625 Colfax
Evanston
Illinois
60208–4210 USA

Distributed in Australia and New Zealand by
Federation Press Pty Ltd
PO Box 45
Annandale, NSW 2038
Australia

Distributed in Netherlands, Belgium and Luxembourg by
Intersentia, Churchillaan 108
B2900 Schoten
Antwerpen
Belgium

Hart Publishing is a specialist legal publisher based in Oxford, England.
To order further copies of this book or to request a list of other
publications please write to:

Hart Publishing, 19 Whitehouse Road, Oxford, OX1 4PA
Telephone: +44 (0)1865 434459 or Fax: (0)1865 794882
e-mail: hartpub@janep.demon.co.uk

British Library Cataloguing in Publication Data
Data Available
ISBN 1–901362–83–3 (paper)

Typeset in 10pt Sabon
by Hope Services (Abingdon) Ltd.
Printed in Great Britain on acid-free paper
by Redwood Books, Trowbridge, Wilts

Foreword

It took over 30 years for what we would now regard as one of the central tenets of the Companies Act 1862 to reach the House of Lords for articulation. When it did in *Salomon v. Salomon & Co. Ltd.*, as a re-reading of the report of that case amply demonstrates, the point at issue—whether a closely-held company and the person who had set it up and sold his business to it were distinct—was regarded by the Law Lords as no more than a question of statutory interpretation, and a fairly straightforward one at that.

Contemporary comment regarded the decision as important, but there was nothing in the writing at the time which suggests that the case would become one of the cornerstones of the entire edifice of corporate law.

However, a cornerstone it has become, either desirably or calamitously, depending on the contrasting points of view expressed at the Seminar, the papers from which are collected in this volume.

What is undoubted is that the shadow of Aron Salomon has lain heavily across the extraordinary changes which have come about in corporate law over the century since the House of Lords decided his pauper's appeal, and the near-century since he died in penury.

It was, therefore, both appropriate and fitting that the Research Centre for Business Law at the University of Auckland should have organised the centenary celebration of the House of Lords' decision, the papers from which appear in this volume.

The papers were as diverse as they were incisive. The Seminar began with what might be described, with no disrespect, as a purist adherence to the doctrine of *Salomon* by David Goddard and Ross Grantham. That was followed by a penetrating analysis by Professor Ian Ramsay, commented on by Professor Tim Hazledine, on methods of regulatory control over companies reflective of the debate between prescription and laissez faire. Bob Austin then provided an interesting analysis of the current position as regards the respective liabilities of the companies within a corporate group, followed by a practical demonstration of how such liabilities may operate in practice from Andrew Borrowdale.

Then came a description from Joanna Gray of the current position in the United Kingdom as to the respective criminal liabilities of companies and their controllers—including an analysis of when companies may become the victims of their employees' acts, with a commentary from Bernard Robertson.

The second day's programme began with a scholarly presentation from Professor Dan Prentice as to the impact on companies and their controllers of insolvent trading, and an equally scholarly commentary from Tom Telfer. Finally, the Seminar was treated to an insightful analysis by Associate Professor Jennifer Hill of the varying roles ascribed to shareholders, with a commentary by Bob Austin.

The Conference was illuminating for all those whose fascination is corporate law. The contributions to the Conference deserve to be widely read, and this publication makes that wider audience possible. I recommend it to all who have an interest in corporate law—or in bootmakers!

Hon Justice Hugh Willliams,
High Court of New Zealand,
Auckland
8 January 1998

Preface

The decision of the House of Lords in *Salomon* v. *A Salomon & Co. Ltd.* has had a lasting influence on the development of modern company law. In July 1997, the Research Centre for Business Law at The University of Auckland hosted a two-day conference to celebrate the centenary of this seminal decision, and to reflect on the central doctrinal and practical issues facing modern company law. The papers presented at the conference, together with papers prepared subsequently, form the contents of the present volume.

We, and the Research Centre, are very grateful to all the essayists. Each one has given generously of their time and energy in producing these papers. The result is a volume that brings to bear on a range of issues affecting company law, the intellectual power and experience of a number of the Commonwealth's leading company lawyers. We are sure that readers will find much in their comments to stimulate thought and, we hope, further contributions to the debates about the nature and shape of company law in the modern world.

We would also like to express our gratitude to Richard Hart for his enthusiasm in publishing this volume, for his insightful suggestions, and for the help given us in the task of editing.

The Research Centre for Business was established at The University of Auckland in 1993, to promote research into all aspects of business and commercial law. As part of this function, the Centre organises lectures, seminars and conferences by resident and visiting experts. The Centre is grateful to the national New Zealand law firm of Chapman Tripp Sheffield Young and, in particular, to merchant bankers Fay, Richwhite & Co., for their very generous financial support in making possible the conference which led to this volume. Thanks are also due to the participants in the conference, from whose contributions in discussions the papers' authors greatly benefited.

Charles E F Rickett
Ross B Grantham
The University of Auckland
Chatham Islands Anniversary Day
1 December 1997

Contents

List of Tables

(all these Tables appear in Chapter 12)

Table of Cases

Table of Legislation

1

The Bootmaker's Legacy to Company Law Doctrine

ROSS GRANTHAM* and CHARLES RICKETT**

The century old decision of the House of Lords in *Salomon* v. *A Salomon &
Co. Ltd.*[1] is probably the most cited company law case in the jurisdictions of
the Commonwealth. The case is credited with having articulated the found-
ing propositions of company law, and it is accordingly treated by judges and
academics alike with a reverence bordering on the religious. In the decades
since their Lordships' speeches, however, company law has been the subject
of both continual and fundamental change. All Commonwealth jurisdictions
have undertaken significant revisions of their companies legislation, and in
many cases more than once. In the United Kingdom in recent times this has
been spurred on by the challenges and demands of European integration;
while in Australia and New Zealand, for so long content largely to adopt
English law, there has been a trend towards increasingly distinct and independent approaches to companies legislation. In Australia, the Corporations
Law represents an all-embracing, black-letter approach,[2] while the recent
New Zealand reforms reflect a more open-textured approach.[3]

   The centenary of *Salomon's* case provides a convenient opportunity to
review some of these developments in company law. The contributors to this
volume, who are leaders in company law scholarship from Australia, Britain
and New Zealand, and accordingly bring a number of differing perspectives
to the issues in question, pursue two principal aims. First, they seek to reassess
the importance and soundness of the base principles enunciated and applied
in *Salomon*. Secondly, they consider the inroads which have been made into
these principles in recent times, and appraise some of the continuing challenges to them which will need to be faced and met if the company is to continue to thrive as a unit of business endeavour into the next century.

---

* Senior Lecturer in Commercial Law, The University of Auckland.
** Professor of Commercial Law, The University of Auckland.

[1] [1897] AC 22.
[2] See, generally, J Green, " 'Fuzzy Law'—A Better Way to Stop 'Snouts in the Trough' " (1991)
9 *CSLJ* 144 and I Ramsay, "Corporate Law in the Age of Statutes" (1992) 14 *Syd LR* 474.
[3] The Companies Act 1993 (NZ) is relatively brief and relies, in part at least, on broader statements of policy.

I THE VICTORIAN COMPANY

When Queen Victoria ascended the throne in 1837, there were two principal legal vehicles for the conduct of large scale business ventures—the corporation and the joint stock company. A corporation existed either under a Royal Charter or by virtue of an Act of Parliament and, like its predecessors dating back at least two centuries, it was recognised as having a separate legal existence.[4] The joint stock company, on the other hand, was in law nothing more than a large partnership.[5] While it had shares that were freely transferable,[6] and a board of directors and constitution still recognisable as such today,[7] the joint stock company did not enjoy any legal identity separate from its "members". Accordingly, in regulating this form of "company", the courts employed the principles of partnership law.[8] The members, as partners, owned the assets and were jointly and severally liable for the debts incurred by the business. Without a Charter or an Act of Parliament to transform it into a true corporation, the joint stock company could be nothing but a partnership.

The application of partnership concepts created, however, a number of acute problems, which were much exacerbated by the rapidly increasing use during the nineteenth century of the joint stock company as the principal vehicle of business in an industrialised Britain. First, the principles informing partnership law were predicated upon a genuine relationship between the partners. Thus, the assumption reflected in the Partnership Act 1890 was of a venture undertaken actively by the partners together. The typical joint stock company, however, had hundreds, if not thousands, of members. The assumption of a personal working relationship between partners was simply stretched beyond breaking point when it was sought to be applied to a venture where there were so many "interested" people. Partnership law was out of its depth.[9] Secondly, the application of partnership law to a joint stock company posed

---

[4] *Halsbury's Laws of England* (4th edn), Vol 9, para 1209.

[5] L Sealy, "Perception and Policy in Company Law Reform", in D Feldman and F Meisel (eds.), *Corporate and Commercial Law: Modern Developments* (London, Lloyd's of London Press, 1996), 11–13.

[6] Although the creation of freely transferable shares was prohibited by the Bubble Act 1720, this did not prevent the creation of "companies" with shares that were, at least in substance if not formally, freely transferable.

[7] See A Du Bois, *The English Business Company after the Bubble Act 1720–1800* (New York, 1938), 291, and P Davies, *Gower's Principles of Modern Company Law* (6th edn, London, Sweet and Maxwell, 1997), 29.

[8] P Ireland, "The Triumph of the Company Legal Form, 1856–1914" in J Adam (ed.), *Essays for Clive Schmitthoff* (Abingdon, Professional Books, 1983), 31; M Lobban, "Corporate Identity and Limited Liability in France and England 1825–67" (1996) 25 *Anglo–American LR* 397, 401. This is perhaps most graphically illustrated by the fact that the leading text on company law in this period was Lindley's *Treatise on the Law of Partnership, including is Application to Companies* (London, Sweet and Maxwell, 1860).

[9] L Gower, "Some Contrasts Between British and American Corporation Law" (1956) 69 *Harv LR* 1369, 1372.

real difficulties for the successful integration of this legal form into the
general private law. For example, if a partnership was to be sued it was necessary to make all the partners party to the suit. While in a partnership of five
or six this presented no difficulty, discovering the identity of all the members
of a joint stock company, where the shares were freely transferable, was in
practice an insurmountable obstacle. Indeed, it was said that a joint stock
company could not, practically, be made to pay any debt which it chose not
to pay.[10]

The Companies Act of 1844 was enacted to deal with these problems.[11] The
reform pursued a twofold strategy. First, the position of the joint stock company was regularised. This was achieved by granting separate legal existence
to any venture which complied with the statutory machinery. Thus, no longer
was a promoter required to assume the expense and delay of procuring a
Charter or an Act of Parliament. The Companies Act itself conferred a separate legal existence upon those groups which met the Act's requirements.[12]
The second aspect to the reform was the restoration of the validity of the basic
premise of partnership law: the personal relationship between the partners.
This was achieved by articulating size requirements for both partnerships and
companies.[13] Partnerships were limited to a few partners, thus effectively
forcing large joint stock ventures to take on corporate form under the Act.
Companies, on the other hand, could not be established with too few members.

Apart, however, from regularising the position of the joint stock company,
the legislative reforms which began in 1844 seemed to have relatively little
immediate impact. As Sealy has commented, for the mid-nineteenth century
lawyer, the reforms did not affect the underlying nature of the company: "The
members of a company did not simply associate; in law, they associated as
partners."[14] Nevertheless, whether by design or oversight, the conferral on
many business ventures of the status of a corporation, and later, in 1855, of
limited liability, had implications well beyond the mere regularisation of difficulties associated with applying partnership law to large groups.

It was against this background, then, that *Salomon's* case fell to be decided.
The facts of the case are well known, and are recounted in detail in other
essays in this volume. In essence, the case concerned an attempt by the
liquidator of a company to recover from Mr Aron Salomon personally in
respect of losses incurred by the company. The basis of the liquidator's claim
was that the company was a fraud designed to shield Aron Salomon from his

---

[10] Lobban, n. 8 above, 404.

[11] Sealy, n. 5 above, 23; Lobban, n. 8 above; and Davies, n. 7 above, 38.

[12] It is worth noting in this respect that although we now tend to assume that the Companies
Act 1844 and subsequent Companies Acts created a separate legal entity, the Act itself states that
the "subscribers of the memorandum . . . shall be a body corporate . . .": see Companies Act
1985 (UK), s 13(3).

[13] Davies, n. 7 above, 38–9; Lobban, n. 8 above, 428.

[14] Sealy, n. 5 above, 23.

creditors. Thus, it was said that although there were seven subscribers, as required by the relevant Companies Act, six of them were "dummies" under Aron Salomon's control. The Court of Appeal upheld this argument. The Lords Justices were in no doubt that when Parliament had stipulated for seven subscribers, it had intended there to be seven "genuine" participants in the business.[15] In the House of Lords, however, their Lordships were equally clear that the liquidator's claim could not succeed. So was ushered in a new age in company law, fit for a new century, and Mr Aron Salomon, a bootmaker from Whitechapel in the East End of London, was assured of a place in legal history.

II THE NEW AGE

The House of Lords' decision is often credited with establishing that a company incorporated under the Companies Act is in law a distinct entity. However, while their Lordships do reaffirm this point, their decision is hardly the *fons et origo* of the distinct legal entity principle. The idea that a non-human entity could in law be treated as the subject of rights and duties had by 1897 already enjoyed long acceptance in English legal history.[16] It was, furthermore, a consequence clearly intended by the legislative reforms of 1844, over fifty years earlier. As we have seen, it was precisely because of the difficulties of dealing with groups of individuals as something different in law from merely a collection of legally distinct individuals that corporate status was extended to any group fulfilling stipulated statutory requirements. This is not to say, however, that *Salomon's* case does not deserve its place of honour at the very core of company law. It does, but the reason for that is that the case articulated two less transparent, but ultimately much more important, principles, the implications of which changed fundamentally the course of company law for the new century.

A Limited Recourse

If the status of the corporation as a separate legal entity with its own rights and duties was already well-established, the consequences of that status were less fully appreciated. In *Salomon*, the liquidator sought to make Aron Salomon responsible for the conduct of the company's affairs. In doing so, the liquidator raised for decision the issue whether control of a company entailed legal responsibility for its actions. In holding that the principle of limited recourse held good even where the individual's control of the company was

---

[15] See n. 27 below.

[16] See, generally, Davies, n. 7 above, Chap 2; and C Schmitthoff, "The Origin of the Joint-Stock Company" (1939) 3 *Univ Toronto LJ* 74.

absolute, the House of Lords established that the corporate form could be used legitimately to shield an "owner" of the business from liability for the conduct of that business.

Although labelled "calamitous" by one commentator,[17] the doctrine of limited recourse has, by and large, stood the test of time since its enunciation in *Salomon*. As Mr Goddard demonstrates, in the first essay in this volume, the doctrine promotes efficiency and is therefore, by one measure at least, justified. In his view, the bargaining process largely rules out externalisation by a company of the cost of production and, while there are concerns in respect of involuntary creditors, these concerns do not, in Mr Goddard's view, warrant a rejection of limited recourse. From a law and economics viewpoint, he argues that attempts to make directors and shareholders liable for torts committed in the course of the management of the company is inefficient. In a similar vein, Mr Goddard sees the development of liability of directors for reckless or insolvent trading as fundamentally subversive of the efficient balancing of risk and return which the doctrine of limited recourse achieves.

While almost certainly not in contemplation in 1897, the development of corporate groups has been one of the most dramatic legacies of *Salomon's* case.[18] In establishing that a shareholder is not responsible for the debts of the company, and also that a company may effectively have a single owner, their Lordships laid down the essential prerequisites for the development of the corporate conglomerates which are now such a dominant feature of business enterprise.[19] However, although a direct consequence of the decision, the development of corporate groups has raised serious questions about the extent to which the separate entity and limited recourse principles can legitimately be applied. In particular, where a corporate group is operated in effect as a single enterprise, with little or no respect paid to the legal boundaries between "separate" companies within the group, the subsequent reliance on those boundaries to defeat the claims of creditors, especially when the group as a whole is insolvent, looks at first blush like a rather unsavoury case of

---

[17] O Kahn-Freund, "Some Reflections on Company Law Reform" (1944) 7 *MLR* 54.

[18] For a discussion of the issues which corporate groups raise, see: P Blumberg, "The Corporate Entity in an Era of Multinational Corporations" (1990) 15 *Del J of Corp L* 283; P Blumberg, *The Multinational Challenge to Corporation Law* (New York, OUP, 1993), Chap 11; M Gillooly (ed), *The Law Relating to Corporate Groups* (Sydney, Butterworths, 1993); T Hadden, "The Regulation of Corporate Groups in Australia" (1992) 15 *UNSWLJ* 61; T Hadden, "Regulating Corporate Groups" in J McCahery, S Picciotto and C Scott (eds.), *Corporate Control and Accountability* (Oxford, OUP, 1993), 343; J Hill, "Cross Guarantees in Corporate Groups" (1992) 10 *CSLJ* 312; A Nolan, "The Position of Unsecured Creditors of Corporate Groups: Towards a Group Responsibility Solution Which Gives Fairness and Equity a Role" (1993) 11 *CSLJ* 461; D Prentice, "Some Comments on the Law Relating to Corporate Groups" in J McCahery, S Picciotto and C Scott (eds.), *Corporate Control and Accountability*, 371; C Schmitthoff and F Woolridge (eds.), *Groups of Companies* (London, Sweet and Maxwell, 1991).

[19] It is noteworthy that for much of the 19th century companies in America were forbidden to own shares in other companies: P Blumberg, *The Multinational Challenge to Corporation Law*, n. 18 above, 52.

technical law creating injustice. Does this expose a flaw in the basic tenets which underlie the decision in *Salomon*? In Dr Austin's essay, the argument is advanced that while the development of groups does not suggest a fatal flaw in the *Salomon* reasoning, it does highlight an important limit to its proper application. Dr Austin believes that while the justification for separate identity and limited recourse holds true as much for corporate shareholders as for individual shareholders, there is no basis upon which an intermingling of the assets of the members of a corporate group can be warranted. Where such intermingling occurs in practice, qualification of both the separate entity and limited recourse principles is merited, in order to defeat the frustration of legitimate creditor expectations, to circumvent an asymmetry of the legal and economic boundaries of the business, and to avoid the otherwise near impossible task faced by a liquidator.[20]

Despite the reverence with which *Salomon* is generally treated, there have in fact been, in the latter half of this century, some major inroads into the principles of separate entity and limited recourse. One of the most important examples of this is the imposition of liability on directors for the debts of the company. Professor Prentice explores in some detail the provisions adopted in most Commonwealth jurisdictions, whereby liability is imposed on directors for fraudulent, reckless and insolvent trading. While the limitation of liability enshrined in companies legislation is that of shareholders, the imposition of liability on directors for a company's debts nevertheless represents a serious challenge to the *Salomon* principles.[21] At its heart, *Salomon* established that whatever the responsibility of the directors to the company itself, creditors of the could look only to the company to satisfy their claims.

The difficult issue posed by this development is how it can best be justified. Although directors' liability provisions have been widely adopted, neither the legislatures nor the courts have managed any clear articulation of the the basis on which they may be explained. The most likely explanation given to date, and one that is also the least radical, is that such liability represents at least a logical, if not implicit, limitation on the principle of limited recourse.[22] As Professor Prentice argues, the liability operates as a mechanism to prevent the externalisation by the company of the costs of its business. From this perspective, and to the extent that considerations of efficiency provide the strongest basis for the principle of limited recourse, directors' liability can be seen as a logical limitation on this principle: it denies limited recourse where it would be inefficient to permit it. However, whatever the empirical evidence may reveal about externalisation, the crucial point is that, if directors' liabil-

---

[20] In New Zealand, this has taken the form of a statutory pooling of the assets of the members of a group: see Companies Act 1993, ss 271 and 272.

[21] These provisions are described in *Gower's Principles of Modern Company Law* as the "most extreme departure from the rule in *Salomon's* case yet achieved . . .": Davies, n. 7 above, 151.

[22] See, further, R Grantham, "The Judicial Extension of Directors' Duties to Creditors" [1991] *JBL* 1.

ity can indeed be justified as a logical limitation on the principle of limited recourse, then not only does it requires little further explanation, but it also defines what must be the proper scope and focus of any such limitation.[23] If directors' liability cannot, however, be justified in this way, but, rather, represents a direct encroachment on the limited recourse principle, then a much clearer and more compelling justification of the liability is needed and awaits elucidation.

A further, but no less threatening, development is the trend, which Ms Gray explores, towards utilising the criminal law as a tool of corporate governance. Thus, we now see, throughout the Commonwealth, the imposition of liability on the company for the unlawful actions of its directors and employees, as well as the imposition of criminal sanctions on directors and employees for the unlawful actions of the company. While a good case can be made from an instrumentalist point of view for subjecting companies to criminal liability (for example, the practical need to treat companies like individuals, the desirability of the burden following the benefit of such conduct, and the deterrent effect of penalising companies[24]), it is far from clear what aims are served by the imposition of such liability on directors and employees. This is a particularly pressing problem for company law, in view of the dramatic increase in regulatory complexity in all the Commonwealth jurisdictions over the last decade. Furthermore, such complexity shows no sign of abating.

The principles of separate identity and limited recourse, derived from *Salomon*, have stood the test of time. It is unwise, however, to infer success simply from survival.[25] What is more important is that the principles can be shown, as they are in the essays in this volume, to be inherently sound. This is not to contend, of course, that at the margins the separate entity and limited recourse principles do not require some refinement. They clearly do, but there is a real danger that in dealing with these marginal cases we might unwittingly embark upon a root and branch attack on them. It is essential, therefore, that in fine-tuning the content of our corporate law, we do so in a manner that does not destroy the very concept we seek to perfect. In that respect, the essays in this volume referred to above are of considerable importance. They remind us of the core, which is largely settled, while seeking to elaborate upon several penumbral but significant issues.

---

[23] Thus, for example, the extension of liability, in s 135 of the Companies Act 1993 (NZ), for reckless trading beyond the eve of insolvency is, on this basis, not appropriate.

[24] See, for example, C Wells, *Corporations and Criminal Responsibility* (Oxford, Clarendon Press, 1993); V Khanna, "Corporate Criminal Liability: What Purpose Does it Serve?" (1996) 109 *Harv LR* 1477; B Fisse and J Braithwaite, "The Allocation of Responsibility for Corporate Crime: Individualism, Collectivism and Accountability" (1988) 11 *Syd LR* 468.

[25] M Roe, "Chaos and Evolution in Law and Economics" (1996) 109 *Harv LR* 641.

B From Association to Corporation

As a number of the contributors to this volume note, the judgments in *Salomon* do not contain lengthy philosophical discussions of the nature of corporate personality. To conclude from this, however, that *Salomon's* only significant contribution to the law was its affirmation of limited recource is to sell the case short. Although ingeniously hidden beneath a reliance upon the literal wording of the relevant Companies Act,[26] the speeches of their Lordships represent a fundamental paradigm shift. In holding that A Salomon & Co. Ltd. was properly incorporated and did not constitute an abuse of the Companies Act, even though Mr Aron Salomon was the only active member of the business, their Lordships departed from the assumption that had formerly underpinned the legal understanding of the company.[27] As discussed above, the Companies Act 1844 was not seen as creating a new form of trading institution. Rather, it merely took the partnership that was the then joint stock form, and conferred upon it a separate legal existence. The existence of a genuine partnership was, therefore, a prerequisite to incorporation, both legally and historically. The Lords Justices in the Court of Appeal realised this. Their decision denying Mr Salomon the right simply to incorporate his business, using "dummies" to make up the required number of members, was thus an entirely predictable outcome.

From this perspective, therefore, the opposite decision reached in their Lordships' House was a radical reformulation of the corporate concept. It moved the legal model away from an association of individuals to something that more closely resembled the chartered corporation. Whether this paradigm shift was merely in response to changes in commercial attitudes, or whether it effectively led commercial opinion, is not clear. What is clear, however, is that it was a change of crucial importance, with several results.

---

[26] As Mr Goddard points out in his essay in this volume, their Lordships treated the matter as one of statutory interpretation. However, the real significance of their Lordships' speeches lies in their decision to approach matters from that perspective. In this respect, Michael Whincop's recent criticism ("Overcoming Corporate Law: Instrumentalism, Pragmatism and the Separate Legal Entity Concept" (1997) 15 *CSLJ* 411) of what he describes as the formalistic conception of the company presented in *Salomon* misses the point. In asserting the superiority of the modern law and economics approach to company law, Whincop treats *Salomon* as an exemplar of an arch-formalism which is unable to resolve complex legal issues. While a substantively formalistic approach may well be guilty of such a charge, no such charge can be levelled successfully against *Salomon*. Quite simply, it is not accurate to describe *Salomon* as having taken a formalistic approach to issues of substance. In any event, the Privy Council's approach in *Meridian Global Funds Management Asia Ltd.* v. *Securities Commission* [1995] 2 AC 500 also takes much of the wind out of Whincop's sails!

[27] See the contemporary note by Sir Frederick Pollock in the *Law Quarterly Review*, where he comments: "No one who knows anything of the earlier history of the Companies Acts can doubt, as a matter of fact, that such a decision as has now been given would have been impossible thirty or even twenty years ago. When the founders of company legislation spoke of seven or more persons being 'associated', they meant such an association as, without the help of the statute, would have made those persons members of an ordinary partnership": see (1897) 13 *LQR* 6–7.

First, it implied that shareholders were no longer the centre of the corporate universe. As Associate Professor Hill's essay recounts, a partnership conception accorded shareholders both ultimate ownership and ultimate control of the company. It was their very association that brought the company into existence, and it was their agreement, subject only to some very basic statutory requirements, that constituted and defined the company. The revision of the corporate model, from association to corporation, also redefined the role of the shareholders. The company was no longer a "they" but an "it".[28] In the steady subordination of the position of shareholders during this century, we have witnessed one major implication of this new paradigm being worked out.[29]

Secondly, the vision of the company adopted in *Salomon* has shifted the focus and function of corporate regulation. So long as the legal conception of the company was one of partnership, the focus of corporate law was, initially, to ensure that there was a genuine association and, thereafter, to facilitate the collective wishes of the associating members. It is this conception which explains not only the Court of Appeal's approach in *Salomon*, but also the infiltration of trust concepts into company law[30] and developments such as the unanimous consent rule.[31] Although the implications of the House of Lords' approach in *Salomon* for the structure of corporate law are, as Professor Ramsay's essay makes clear, still much in debate, there is no doubt that the paradigm shift from association to corporation has had a profound impact on the focus and content of company law this century. The change in focus is seen in the emphasis which the law now places on three issues in particular. These are, first, the regulation of relations between members and management, rather then merely between members and other members; secondly, the progressive loss of the members' ability to modify the constitutional arrangements; and, thirdly, the subordination of the contract of association, a process which has culminated in Canada and New Zealand in the complete abandonment of a contractual footing for the company.[32]

This paradigm shift has also had a significant impact on the content of company law. As long as the company remained an essentially private association it was both possible and proper to leave the regulation of the company to its members, subject only to a few minimum mandatory requirements. However, with the emphasis which *Salomon* placed on the institutional nature of the company and the associated attenuation of the members' interest to little more

---

[28] Sealy, n. 5 above, 26.

[29] Thus, for example, we have seen the board of directors raised from the position of a mere agent of the general meeting, to an organ of equal status with the general meeting, and now to the principal seat of power in the company (Companies Act 1993 (NZ), s 128). See, generally, Davies, n. 7 above, 183.

[30] Sealy, n. 5 above, 24.

[31] R Grantham, "The Unanimous Consent Rule in Company Law" [1993] *CLJ* 245.

[32] In the New Zealand Companies Act 1993, for example, in default of modification between the parties, the corporate constitution is entirely statutory (see s 28).

than a fungible investment, oversight by the members became increasingly unlikely and difficult. Thus, somewhat paradoxically given its *laissez faire* tone, the decision in *Salomon* effectively ensured that the State would end up playing a significant role in the regulation of the corporate form. Professor Ramsay's essay accordingly explores a major focus during this century, on identifying regulatory goals and determining how these goals might best be achieved. In this context, Professor Lowenstein, in the last essay in the volume, advocates the use of financial disclosure as a tool of corporate governance. As Professor Lowenstein notes, company law in most Western countries has sought (largely as a result of the influence of its illegitimate offspring, securities law) to make the management of companies more transparent by requiring, to a greater or lesser degree, the disclosure of corporate financial information. Thereafter, Professor Lowenstein suggests, the self-interest of the parties to the corporate enterprise can be trusted to cause those parties to pursue, more effectively and efficiently than any external regulator is able to, the goal of good corporate governance.

The theoretical dimension of company law is often dismissed as sterile. Although in recent years, particularly under the influence of the law and economics movement, interest in abstract theoretical conceptions of the company and company law has been rekindled, those involved with company law on a day-to-day basis—practioners, judges and law reformers alike—tend, perhaps understandably, to be more concerned with the detail of the law. However, a sound grasp of both the theoretical underpinning of the law and its historical development is essential if we are to understand why the law is as it is now, and to perceive how it might be refined without destroying its coherence. This volume of essays is an attempt to place key aspects of company law in a theoretical and historical perspective, and accordingly to lay bare the structural, theoretical and policy issues that are often overlooked in the quest for day-to-day solutions.

2

Corporate Personality—Limited Recourse and its Limits

DAVID GODDARD*

The legal personality of companies has been the subject of a great deal of comment and confusion, and quite a few strained metaphors. The company has been variously described as an efficiency instrument, a 9 to 5 body snatcher, and a body with the board as the brain and the workers as the arms and the legs. Even the phrase "legal person" involves a metaphor, which can on occasion occlude clear thought about substantive company law issues.[1]

The purpose of this essay is to explore the nature and practical significance of the legal personality of a registered company, and to provide an overview of how the concept has fared in the courts and in legislation from 1897 to the present day. I will use the tools of economic analysis of law, rather than anatomy or literary fancy. This may make my essay less entertaining than some ventures into this field: but it may also make it more useful.

I THE POINT OF *SALOMON* V. A *SALOMON & CO. LTD*.[2]—LIMITED RECOURSE WORKS

A What do we Mean by Legal Personality?

When I speak of the legal personality of a company, I refer principally to the legal rules that allow a company to enter into obligations, own property, and sue and be sued. The company does so in its own name, rather than in the names of, or on behalf of, its shareholders. They are not parties to its contracts and cannot be sued by its creditors. They do not have any right to its property—only a bundle of rights in relation to distributions of income and capital, and control of the company either directly (through votes of shareholders) or indirectly, via a board of directors.

* Partner, Chapman Tripp Sheffield Young, Wellington, New Zealand.

[1] For a brief survey of the confusion caused by the concepts of legal personality, and "lifting the veil", see N James, "Separate Legal Personality: Legal Reality and Metaphor" (1993) 5 *Bond L Rev* 217, and the various articles there referred to.
[2] [1897] AC 22.

Were one engaged in flights of literary fancy, reference to Mary Shelley's famous text on incorporation would be irresistible. One of the issues raised by Shelley's novel is whether the "monster" created by Dr Frankenstein is responsible for its own acts, or whether its creator is morally responsible for them. This is also a central issue of company law. The usual answer, given the prevalence of limited liability, is "not beyond the capital contribution each shareholder has made or promised to make". Not only can creditors of the company not sue the shareholders direct; they cannot normally sue the company, then look to the shareholders to put the company in funds to make up any deficiency. There are some exceptions to this principle, which we shall be examining in some detail. But it is true in virtually all cases.

The limit on the ability of creditors of the company to pursue claims against the company's owners above and beyond their capital contribution to the company is not an inevitable consequence of corporate personality. After all, unlimited companies can be formed in New Zealand and in many other jurisdictions—though they are rare, an important fact to which I will return. Indeed, in English legal history recognition of the legal personality of certain corporations preceded recognition of limited liability on the part of owners.[3] However, it is the combination of these features in virtually every modern company which is the distinguishing feature of that institution, from a practical and a theoretical perspective. So I shall refer to this bundle of attributes as "legal personality", as a form of shorthand, except where it is necessary to single out one or other of those attributes.

The organisers of this celebration of the centenary of *Salomon* originally requested an essay discussing the development of the law "from *Salomon* to *Meridian*".[4] I have taken some liberties with this request, as my primary thesis is that the two cases are about completely different issues, with no analytical connection, unless one falls victim to some of the more dreadful metaphors which the subject of corporate personality has sired over the last hundred years. This essay focuses on *Salomon* and the doctrine it establishes, properly understood, then proceeds to consider the fate of that doctrine in the cases and in legislation. Other contributors to this volume will have more to say about *Meridian* and the issues which that case raises.

B The Questions Posed by Legal Personality

Recognition of companies as separate legal persons from their owners, controllers and employees/agents gives rise to two fundamental questions:

---

[3] P Davies, *Gower's Principles of Modern Company Law* (6th edn., London, Sweet and Maxwell, 1997), Chaps 2 and 3, especially pp 38–46.

[4] *Salomon* v. *A Salomon & Co. Ltd.* [1897] AC 22 (HL); *Meridian Global Funds Management Asia Ltd.* v. *Securities Commission* [1995] 3 NZLR 7 (PC).

(a) When can acts or omissions in the course of a company's business result in liability of individual employees/controllers/owners? In other words, when does limited recourse *not* apply?

(b) When will the company be liable, whether in contract, tort (or other sources of non-voluntary civil obligations) or under the criminal law, as a consequence of the acts or omissions of individual employees/controllers/owners?

Salomon was concerned with the first of these questions. The issue was, in simple terms, whether limited recourse survived beneficial ownership of the company's shares, and control of the company, by a single natural person.

There is no necessary connection between this question and the question of attribution of acts and mental states of natural persons to the company, which was the subject of the Privy Council's advice in *Meridian*. However, the reminder of the Privy Council in *Meridian* that the purpose of the relevant laws must be the starting point for ascertaining how they should apply to companies is just as relevant in addressing the first of these questions. In this essay, therefore, I:

(a) review briefly the decision in *Salomon*;

(b) summarise the economic rationale for corporate personality, and in particular limited liability;

(c) describe some important developments in the law of limited recourse, as it applies to companies, over the last hundred years; and

(d) sketch some answers to the question whether those developments are to be welcomed, or whether (as I believe) there are respects in which the law has taken wrong turnings in this area, especially of late.

Other issues, beside the two fundamental ones I identified above, have arisen over the years as a consequence of the doctrine of corporate personality, mainly as a consequence of artificial distinctions drawn in statutes. I touch on some of these below, when discussing the topic so alluringly referred to as "the lifting of the corporate veil". But these cases have little to say to us beyond their special statutory context.[5]

C What did Salomon v. A Salomon & Co. Ltd. actually decide?

If we are to discuss what has become of *Salomon*, a good starting point is to clarify what that case decided. (Like many famous cases, it is rarely re-read—we all know what it says.) The case is an interesting tale of economic politics, and perhaps also religious prejudice—certainly, reading the case one

---

[5] As *Meridian* reminds us, when asking questions about the treatment of companies under a particular statute, the purpose of that statute will be the principal consideration, rather than any intrinsic aspect of the corporate form.

cannot, with Lord Macnaghten, "help thinking that the appellant, Aron Salomon, has been dealt with somewhat hardly in this case".[6]

So what exactly did *Salomon* decide, a hundred years ago?

Mr Aron Salomon was a leather merchant and wholesale boot manufacturer. He carried on business on his own account for many years, very successfully. In 1892 he formed a company, the shareholders of which were himself, his wife, a daughter and four sons. It was registered under the name "Aron Salomon & Company, Limited". Each held one share of £1 upon incorporation. (The company had a nominal capital of £40,000 divided into 40,000 shares of £1 each.)

The company purchased the business from Mr Salomon for some £39,000, to be paid partly in cash, and partly by the issue of debentures for the sum of £10,000. The price was on the generous side. A substantial part of the cash consideration was to be used by Mr Salomon to subscribe for 20,000 fully paid up shares of £1. The assets were transferred, and the debentures issued. The 20,000 shares were allotted to Mr Salomon. So he held 20,001 shares, and the remaining six shares were held by family members—apparently as nominee for Mr Salomon.

Mr Salomon assigned the debentures to a Mr Broderip as security for an advance of £5,000, with interest at 8 per cent. The debentures were subsequently reissued to Mr Broderip direct (but still by way of security for Mr Salomon's debt, with Mr Salomon retaining an equity of redemption).

The evidence showed that the beneficial owner of all the shares, and controller of the company as managing director, was Mr Salomon. The family did not intend to sell the business or permit outsiders to become involved in it—incorporation was not a precursor to parting with any interest in the business.

Before the sale the business had been very successful. But after the sale a series of events, including a succession of strikes in the boot trade, caused serious losses. In 1893, the year following the incorporation of the business, the company defaulted on its debentures and Mr Broderip sought to enforce his rights as debenture holder. A liquidator was appointed on the application of the unsecured creditors, and the liquidator proceeded to realise the assets of the business. After completing the realisation, the liquidator was left with assets which would discharge the claim of Mr Broderip and leave a balance of about £1,055 for payment to Mr Salomon as beneficial owner of the debentures, if the debentures were honoured. This would leave unsecured creditors for a total of £7,733 8s 3d without any dividend.

The liquidator sought to defend the claim by Mr Broderip against the company, claiming to have the agreements under which the business was sold to the company rescinded, to have the debentures delivered up and cancelled, seeking judgment against Mr Salomon for the sums paid by the company

---

[6] *Salomon v. A Salomon & Co. Ltd.* [1897] AC 22, 47.

under the agreements, and claiming a lien over the business and its assets for these sums. The grounds for this claim were that:

(a) the price paid for the assets exceeded their true value by £8,200 or more;
(b) the arrangements made by Mr Salomon for formation of the company were a fraud on the creditors of the company; and
(c) no board of directors was ever appointed or, if there was a board, it consisted solely of Mr Salomon, so there never was an independent board.

At trial, the liquidator gave evidence intended to show that the price paid for the business was excessive. However, he acknowledged that at the time of the transfer to the company the business was in a sound condition, and that there was a substantial surplus. No evidence was led supporting the allegation that there was no board, or that the board consisted solely of Mr Salomon. The evidence established that all the members of the company were fully aware of the terms on which the company purchased the business, and that they were willing to accept and did accept these terms.

The trial before Vaughan Williams J had an unusual result. His Lordship announced that he was not prepared to grant the relief sought by the liquidator in the name of the company. But he suggested that a different remedy might be open to the company, on the ground that the company was Mr Salomon's agent and nominee. He allowed an amendment to the counterclaim seeking a declaration that the company or the liquidator was entitled to be indemnified by Mr Salomon against the whole of the unsecured debts, judgment against Mr Salomon for that sum, and a lien for that amount upon all sums which might be payable to him in respect of his debentures or otherwise until the judgment was satisfied. The amendments also added allegations that the company was formed by Mr Salomon and the debentures issued in order that he might carry on the business, and take all the profits "without risk to himself"; and that the company was his "mere nominee and agent". The judge then granted those orders.[7]

The Court of Appeal upheld the trial judge, holding that the formation of the company, the transfer of the business and the issue of the debentures were a mere scheme to enable Mr Salomon to carry on business in the name of the company with limited liability contrary to the true intent and meaning of the Companies Act 1862, and to enable him to obtain a preference over other creditors by procuring a first charge over the company's assets by means of the debentures. Lindley LJ felt some difficulty in describing the company as Mr Salomon's agent, but instead characterised it as a trustee for him.[8]

---

[7] *Broderip* v. *Salomon* [1895] 2 Ch 323 (HC and CA).

[8] *Ibid.*, at 338, 340. The Court used strong language to describe the "scheme": Lindley LJ considered (at 339) that it did "infinite mischief", bringing the Act "into disrepute . . . by perverting its legitimate use". Lopes LJ considered (at 340–1) that if the scheme could not be defeated it would be "lamentable": "to legalise such a transaction would be a scandal".

Mr Salomon then mounted an appeal to the House of Lords, which, on 16 November 1896, delivered the famous judgments the centenary of which this publication celebrates. The decision was unanimous. Strongly worded speeches were delivered by Lord Halsbury LC, Lord Watson, Lord Herschell, Lord Macnaghten and Lord Davey, with Lord Morris concurring.

Their Lordships' speeches are more striking, on re-reading, for what they do not say than for their actual content. They are not profound analyses of the nature of corporate personality. They do not delve into the social and legal rationale for limited liability, let alone the economics of that institution. They read like a simple exercise in statutory interpretation. The company, they point out, was formed and registered in accordance with the statute. The statute did not say any more than that there must be seven shareholders—and there were. It contained no provisions as to the extent or degree of the interest held by such shareholders, nor in relation to their motive for becoming shareholders. Nor did the Act expressly prohibit forming a company so that a person could carry on his business in the name of a company. The policy identified by the Court of Appeal prohibiting "one man companies"[9] was to be found nowhere in the Act. As Lord Halsbury said: "If the Legislature intended to prohibit something, you ought to know what that something is."[10] Absent any guidance on the extent of any such prohibition, the only proper inference was that there was none.[11] Provided the statutory formalities were complied with, the company existed. It purchased the business under a valid contract which the board was authorised to enter into, with the approval of all members. "There was no fraud or misrepresentation, and there was nobody deceived."[12]

The House held that nothing in the Companies Act expressly or implicitly prohibited what had been done. The formal requirements had been met. The company was a real company. The creditors were its creditors, not Mr Salomon's. And the company had no claim against Mr Salomon—it was obliged to honour its debentures, validly issued to him.

Their Lordships had little time for the proposition that, though the company might have been validly formed, it was to be treated as a mere agent or trustee for Mr Salomon. As Lord Macnaghten said:[13]

"The company is at law a different person altogether from the subscribers . . .; and though it may be that after incorporation the business is precisely the same as it was before, and the same persons are managers, and the same hands receive the profits,

---

[9] Described by Lord Macnaghten as a "taking nickname, but [which] does not help one much in the way of argument": [1897] AC 22, 53.

[10] *Salomon* v. *A Salomon & Co. Ltd.* [1897] AC 22, 32.

[11] This approach did not, however, commend itself to the courts in the context of the capital maintenance rule, leading to more than a century of confusion before legislative intervention began to dispose of that confused piece of economically illiterate doctrine which, directed at entirely sensible ends, employed entirely unsuitable means.

[12] *Salomon* v. *A Salomon & Co. Ltd.* [1897] AC 22, 54 (*per* Lord Macnaghten).

[13] *Ibid.*, at 51.

the company is not in law the agent of the subscribers or trustee for them. Nor are the subscribers, as members, liable in any shape or form, except to the extent and in the manner provided in the Act."

The principles for which the decision stands can be briefly stated:

(a) ownership of the shares of a validly registered company is irrelevant to recognition of its separate legal personality, and to the limit on recourse to shareholders established by its memorandum of association; and

(b) control of the company by one person, or a small number of persons, is not of itself sufficient to ignore the statutory scheme and allow recourse to those controllers for the company's debts.

That is, *limited recourse works, in the absence of special factors above and beyond beneficial ownership of all shares and total control of the enterprise by one individual.* More metaphysical interpretations shed little light on practical issues, and lack any foundation in the prosaic speeches of their Lordships.

I believe that this decision is of great importance to company law today. In a situation where none of the creditors were, on the evidence, involuntary creditors it seems to me clearly right.

Others have described the decision as "shocking" and "calamitous".[14] Either they are reading too much into it, or they are wrong.[15] To explain why the members of the House of Lords who heard the *Salomon* appeal were better micro-economists than Vaughan Williams J, the members of the Court of Appeal, or Professors Kahn-Freund and Gower, I now turn to the rationale for corporate personality and limited liability, and explain why the creditors of Aron Salomon & Company Ltd. do not engage my sympathy.

II THE LIMITS OF LIMITED LIABILITY

A Why do we Recognise the Legal Personality of Companies?

In the field of commercial law, more than many other areas of law, we can say with some confidence that the economic benefits of an institution are co-extensive with its social benefits, and so with the policy rationale for its existence. The institution of the company, and the legal and administrative edifice that supports it, can be justified only by the economic benefits it creates. Absent those benefits, the institution's rationale is exhausted. And the same reasoning applies to features of the institution, as it does to the institution as a whole. If there is not a good economic reason for some facet of company law, it is probably unjustified and in need of reform.

---

[14] Davies, n. 3 above, 79; O Kahn Freund, "Some Reflections on Company Law Reform" (1944) 7 *MLR* 54.

[15] The remainder of this essay is an attempt to justify this rather blunt statement.

The facet of company law we are concerned with here is fundamental to the institution, distinguishing it from the law of partnership or, for example, the law of trusts. A business can be carried on by a sole proprietor, or by a partnership, or by a trustee for the beneficial owners of the enterprise. But only if the business is carried on as a company will the law treat the enterprise as a legal person in its own right, separate from its owners and managers, continuing unchanged as owners or managers change, and with no right of recourse on the part of creditors to the personal wealth of any of the current owners and managers (at least in normal circumstances).

There is an extensive academic literature on the economic rationale for separate legal personality and limited liability.[16] This essay can do no more than summarise its principal insights. In brief, the doctrines of legal personality and limited liability are practically important because they:

(a) enable the capital for a business venture to be collected from a number of investors, over time, while avoiding costs of transfer of the venture's assets when new participants are admitted, or existing participants depart;

(b) reduce the costs of transfer of the business venture (or interests in it)—instead of needing to transfer all the different assets of the business venture, all that need be transferred is the shares; and

(c) enable the business venture to be conducted on a standard form limited recourse basis.

B Corporate Personality to Reduce Transaction Costs

The first and second of these elements produce obvious reductions in transaction costs. They are achieved through the legal construct of separate legal personality on the part of the company, which owns property and carries on the business in its own name, while the ownership interest in the company (*not* in its assets) is represented by choses in action (shares). Ownership of shares may change—the ownership of the assets does not.

Note that limited liability is not required to achieve these savings—it is legal personality, pure and simple, which confers these benefits. A company where the owners were liable without limit for the debts of the venture would still achieve these efficiencies.

---

[16] For a convenient summary see F Easterbrook and D Fischel, *The Economic Structure of Corporate Law* (Cambridge, Mass., Harvard University Press, 1991).

C The Rationale for Limited Liability—Why is Limited Recourse Desirable as a Default Rule?

The third element requires further elaboration. It is less immediately obvious why a default rule providing for limited recourse is a desirable legal rule, producing social gains. It is possible to contract expressly for limited recourse with the persons with whom the business deals: this is common where a venture does not have separate legal personality. Trustees, for example, commonly enter into contracts which contain a provision limiting their personal liability to the assets of the trust available to them to discharge that liability. Large companies undertake projects financed by non-recourse lending—that is, where the lender can look to certain assets for repayment in the event of default, but not to the general assets of the company. If people can contract expressly for limited recourse, why provide for it in legislation?

This question can be answered in several ways.

(i) Limited Liability is the Efficient Default Rule—and Can Itself be Contracted Around

The first important point is that limited liability is not imposed as a mandatory rule. There are three senses in which it is not mandatory:

(a) businesses are not (for the most part) compelled to incorporate. Incorporating is moderately expensive. Owners of businesses are free to decide whether or not to form companies to operate the business;

(b) companies can be formed with unlimited liability. Although New Zealand law no longer provides for a separate category of unlimited company, the Companies Act 1993 still enables the company's constitution to provide for unlimited shareholder liability;

(c) it is possible to contract around limited liability—for example, by seeking personal guarantees from shareholders. This is almost universal practice when financial institutions lend to closely held companies. It is also common where significant commercial transactions are entered into with such companies—the shareholders are often expected to stand behind the company and its commitments. So all that registration as a company does is to reverse the "default rule"—instead of the law providing for unlimited recourse to those concerned in a business, unless this is varied by contract, the law provides for limited recourse unless that position is varied by contract.[17]

---

[17] Incorporation is the only method by which this reversal of the default rule can be achieved. In particular, simply publishing intended terms of trade which incorporate a form of limitation of liability, or including such a provision in a document filed in a public registry, will not be effective: see *Re Sea, Fire and Life Insurance Co.* (1854) 3 De G M & G 459.

The market is thus in a position to judge which arrangement is the more efficient. If limited liability posed significant risks for creditors, above and beyond those involved in dealing with natural persons of varying degrees of wealth (and honesty), we would expect to see the evolution of contractual terms designed either to reverse the default rule or to address that risk. The easiest term to adjust would be price—it costs little to charge one price to limited liability companies and another to individuals and firms. Or there could be different rules for payment—companies could be required to pay before taking delivery of goods, rather than being given credit. The owners of businesses would then need to assess whether the benefits of incorporating justified the cost of doing so, plus the additional cost of doing business with limited liability. If the cost of limited liability was high, we would expect to see few businesses incorporated, or perhaps a significant number of unlimited liability companies formed in order to take advantage of the transaction cost savings of corporate personality, without the trading disadvantages of limited liability.

Adam Smith is reported to have considered, presumably for this very reason, that, in ordinary trading undertakings, joint stock companies could not compete with private traders.[18] Yet (illustrating another important economic insight, that the value of an arrangement is normally better decided by voluntary choices over time than by executive fiat):

(a) incorporation of most forms of business undertakings as limited liability companies is today the rule, not the exception;
(b) in relation to certain substantial transactions with smaller companies, such as financing arrangements, reversal of the default rule through taking guarantees from shareholders is commonplace;
(c) in relation to the vast bulk of transactions in the normal course of business a distinction in terms of trade for limited liability companies is unheard of, even where relatively costly goods such as computers are supplied on credit. Other contractual techniques for addressing credit risk generally—such as retention of title clauses—are commonplace. But differentiation between firms with and without limited liability is not. My firm does not get better terms for most of its transactions—be they in relation to paper, computers, premises or human resources—than do companies, despite the personal liability of its partners.[19]

On reflection, the third of these observations is not especially surprising. What creditors are interested in is the creditworthiness of their debtors. Yet there is no necessary correlation between incorporation and creditworthiness,

---

[18] Davies, n. 3 above, 44 at n. 51, citing references to this view in the parliamentary debates on the Limited Liability Act 1855.

[19] Indeed other advantages of incorporation under our current law, such as the ability to grant floating charges, on occasion lead lenders to require borrowers to incorporate.

or lack of it. Many individuals are bad credit risks.[20] The best credit risks in the market, after sovereign States (or some of them), are large corporations. So adjusting the terms of trade used in a firm's general trading to draw a distinction between incorporated and unincorporated customers would be inefficient, and would be likely to result in loss of business to competitors not charging more on the basis of an economically irrelevant criterion.

Depending on the trade in question, different techniques will be used to identify good or bad credit risks, and to manage such risks. For a firm entering into many small transactions with a large number of customers—consider the supplier of daily newspapers—the answer may be to disregard entirely the creditworthiness of customers, and simply to diversify risk over a large number of purchasers, pricing to reflect a relatively predictable level of bad debts. Or the answer could be to refuse to give credit, but accept payment with credit cards which (for a fee, paid by the firm, in the form of a commission) transfer the credit risk to a bank which is better placed to manage it. Most hotels take this approach, accepting credit cards from individuals or companies, but not offering credit to any but the most substantial and regular customers with whom a relationship has been established. For a firm supplying computers, say, the answer may be terms of trade which retain title in the goods until paid for—this addresses the risk posed by uncreditworthy individuals, as well as companies. For still larger transactions, the answer may be to obtain credit references—or, again, to sell the credit risk to a bank by seeking payment by letter of credit or other form of irreversible credit.

In any but the largest transactions, detailed investigation of a counterparty's creditworthiness transaction by transaction simply does not pay. This, incidentally, is why Professor Gower is addressing the wrong question when, criticising the decision in *Salomon*, he observes:[21]

> "The only justification for [the result] is that the public deal with a limited company at their peril and know, or should know, what to expect. In particular a search of the company's file at Companies House should reveal its latest annual accounts and whether there are any charges on the company's assets. But the accounts will probably be months out of date and, in the case of a small or medium sized company, may be expurgated editions of those circulated to the members. Nor does everyone having dealings with a company have the time or knowledge needed to search the file. The experienced businessman with his trade protection associations can take care of himself, but the little man, whom the law should particularly protect, rarely has any idea of the risks he runs when he grants credit to a company with a high-sounding name, impressive nominal capital (not paid up in cash), and with assets mortgaged up to the hilt. Nor is it practical for the unemployed workman, who is offered a job with a limited company, to decline it until he has first searched the company's file."

[20] And natural persons also, in a very real sense, enjoy limited liability: see pp. 33–35 below.
[21] Davies, n. 3 above, 79–80.

Of course it is not practical for small businesses to investigate the credit-worthiness of each customer in detail. Nor is it for big businesses. But the local shop owner knows, as does the supermarket chain or large law firm, that if credit is given a proportion of the bills will not be paid each year. The choice is between the extra business that can be done by dealing on credit and the losses that will inevitably follow. And the shop owner also knows that there is no reason to suppose that the bad debts will come from limited companies, rather than natural persons. Both pose risks, yet neither's financial position is likely to be investigated in detail.

So the justification is not that potential creditors can and will discover the company's position by searching its file at the registry: it is that they can decide who they will deal with, and on what terms. Nor is it so much that those who *deal with companies* do so at their peril, and should know what to expect—though the label "Limited" is a fairly clear one, which I suspect few business people in New Zealand (large or small) do not understand. The point is that those who *give credit to their customers* do so at their peril, and should know what to expect. They have an entire armoury of techniques available to manage that risk, of which investigating the counterparty's creditworthiness is one of the more expensive and least attractive—so the fact that doing so in relation to companies is difficult and time-consuming (though perhaps less so than in relation to individuals?) is really quite irrelevant.

Nor, incidentally, does contemporary trade practice support any suggestion that the risks involved in dealing with companies are, at least for small to mid-sized transactions, greater than those involved in giving credit to natural persons. If dealing with limited companies systematically increased credit risks for their creditors, we would expect to see systematic distinctions in terms of trade. (Incidentally, smaller businesses still would not need to carry out complex and time-consuming investigations of corporate customers—they would simply follow larger businesses in modifying terms of trade in an appropriate, standardised, way.) The absence of such distinctions in the terms of trade of businesses, large or small, suggests that there is no systematically increased risk, or at least that it is so slight that the cost of managing it is not justified.

More generally, what Professor Gower overlooks, in common with many law-makers and judges, is that business is all about risk. Business people do not seek to eliminate all risk—quite the reverse. They actively seek to take certain risks, and to find the most appropriate way to manage other risks which result from business decisions. The decision to give credit is a deliberate choice to assume the risk of bad debts in order to increase levels of business. In most cases, the decision is not moreover to give credit to a particular company or person, but rather to give credit to all customers, or to certain classes of customer. The issue then becomes one of assessing the long run risk of dealing on credit terms with the relevant class of customers—reinforcing the irrelevance of debate as to whether it is practical or realistic to investigate the affairs of each individual debtor. Like any business risk, the decision to extend credit to some or all customers may or may not come off. If it does not, that no more engages our concern than any other business risk which, with the benefit of hindsight, the business's owners may regret.[22]

In summary, the predominance of the corporate form as a business vehicle and the fact that the default position of limited recourse is reversed in very few transactions numerically, and does not normally attract other pricing or contract term adjustments, suggest that:

(a) this is the efficient default rule in most commercial contexts;[23] and
(b) voluntary creditors, who are able to adjust contract terms for credit risk, have no greater complaint when a company fails than when an individual defaults. In such contexts, blaming the company's limited liability for their inability to recover is a red herring.

(ii) Limited Liability Reduces Monitoring Costs and Makes Securities Markets Possible

Another important benefit of limited liability lies in the effect of that rule on the need for investors to monitor the activity of the enterprise, and the wealth of other participants. If an investment in an enterprise brings with it unlimited liability for the debts of that enterprise, but I am not involved in its management on a day-to-day basis, I have a significant incentive to monitor the enterprise's activities, and in particular the likelihood of my being called on to meet its debts. This is obviously costly. If the amount for which I would be liable in the event of the enterprise failing depends on the ability of other investors to meet their share of its debts, I will also need to monitor their wealth if I am to assess accurately the risk I face.[24] This is likely to be even more costly, especially as the number of investors increases.

---

[22] In the course of discussion of this essay at the seminar, it was suggested that a person carrying on a business where credit is customary, such as a plumber, cannot in reality be said to make a choice to give credit. Assuming (for the sake of argument) that some trades or business activities necessarily entail giving credit, the choice of whether or not to engage in that activity taking into account its various incidents and risks—including the risk of giving credit—is still a real one. The hypothetical plumber can choose between employment (and little or no credit risk) and carrying on business on his or her own account, with all the advantages, disadvantages, risks and opportunities which that entails.

[23] Yet there is no other method by which it can be adopted as a default rule for a particular association—advertising, for example, will not do: see n. 17 above. This underlines the importance of incorporation.

[24] The need to monitor the wealth of other shareholders is substantially reduced if the liability of shareholders is proportional to their investment, rather than being joint and several: H Hansmann and R Kraakman, "Toward Unlimited Shareholder Liability for Corporate Torts" (1991) 100 *Yale LJ* 1879; D W Leebron, "Limited Liability, Tort Victims, and Creditors" (1991) 91 *Columbia L Rev* 1565. Even under this rule, however, wealth of other shareholders may be relevant to shareholder risk and share value, and the need to monitor the enterprise closely would be reduced, but not eliminated (with an associated increase in the cost of capital to reflect monitoring costs and/or the additional risk associated with not monitoring).

Similarly, assessing a market price for a share would require investors and analysts to investigate not only the position of the company, but also the wealth of its shareholders from time to time (unless it was improbable in the extreme that the company would fail and the shareholders incur liability—the value of Microsoft Corporation shares would still depend solely on expected cashflows to shareholders, one assumes). And shares would no longer be fungible—which is one of the key requirements for low cost markets in securities—since the value of a share may depend on who is selling it, and who remains as a shareholder.

Limited liability means that monitoring costs can be significantly reduced, and that shares are fungible, with a market price depending solely on the income stream generated by the enterprise. This means that large-scale efficient securities markets are possible, in which the price of a company's shares depends on the company's assets, and how those assets are employed. This in turn enhances managers' incentives to act efficiently, since otherwise:

(a) the market price will fall below the value of the assets if managed efficiently; and

(b) new investors will be able to acquire large blocks of shares at a discount, take control and achieve operational efficiencies. The market for corporate control depends on market prices reflecting the competence of current controllers, on low transaction costs in the market for shares, and on the absence of significant additional costs or risks associated with aggregating large blocks of shares.

The reduction in costs of monitoring and reduction in risk associated with investing in an enterprise also makes diversification possible for investors. Diversification is an important technique for managing risk and aligning investments to an investor's risk profile. Yet, if holding a stake in an enterprise inevitably entailed unlimited liability for the failure of that enterprise, diversification would involve costs and risks which made it an irrational strategy in many cases.[25] Investors would stick to one or two firms, and monitor them very closely indeed.

(iii) Alternative Regimes Would be Very Costly

Finally, administering a regime under which the liability of a company was unlimited would entail significant costs. There would need to be mechanisms for identifying which shareholders bore liability for particular events—the practical difficulty in tracing shareholders at the time of a wrongful act or series of acts is significant, yet if liability could not be traced back to prior holders it would be readily evaded and would become largely meaningless.[26]

---

[25] See Leebron, n. 24 above, 1595–600.

[26] See, for example, Hansmann and Kraakman, n. 24 above, 1896–9. The effect of uncertainty in incidence of liability on markets for capital would be significant, and leads these authors to

There would need to be mechanisms for tracing liability back through many layers of companies, including overseas companies, and through trusts (including unit trusts and pension funds) and other relationships. This tracing issue—and the costs of collection associated with such tracing—would be particularly acute in a country such as New Zealand where many large firms have foreign shareholders.

Providers of business capital would obviously seek to avoid unlimited exposure in various ways. One would be the provision of capital in the form of debt rather than equity—a rule which made shareholders liable for corporate obligations would produce an explosion of subordinated debt issues. To prevent this type of circumvention of an unlimited liability rule, there would need to be complex rules which distinguished between "real" debt and "equity disguised as debt"—a task which is hardly assisted by the elusive (if not illusory) nature of the distinction between debt and equity. Indeed, there would be a range of capital market transactions which could defeat the intended effect of such reforms, effectively reinstating limitations on liability through more costly holding structures and synthetic equity.[27] Another avoidance technique would be estate planning and divestiture (of the kind often engaged in by professionals compelled by law to practise with unlimited liability)—this is limitation of liability by another, more costly and therefore less efficient route.

The complexity of the rules required to make shareholder liability meaningful and the likely costs of administering such rules are striking. The gains from such rules would need to be compelling, to justify incurring those costs.

D The Costs of Limited Liability—Externalities

The social gains from limited liability described above—reduction in transaction costs with respect to aggregation of capital and transfers of ownership, and reduction in monitoring costs for investors—are very significant. However, as law and economics scholars remind us, they come at a cost. Shareholders get all the benefits from the firm's success—if a risky venture pays off, they get all the return. Yet if it fails, they do not bear the full cost of failure—creditors will bear some of this cost. The concern, from an economic perspective, is that this may lead to a form of moral hazard if

advocate a form of "claims made" liability. Yet this gives rise to difficulties of its own, not least as regards conflicts of interest between former shareholders and current shareholders in the administration of the litigation: see 1899. Yet another layer of complex and costly rules would be required to address these issues.

[27] See J A Grundfest, "The Limited Future of Unlimited Liability: A Capital Markets Perspective" (1992) 102 *Yale LJ* 387 for a discussion of the likely clientele effects of such reforms, and the various forms of instrument which could be used to obtain exposure to desired "risky" sectors without holding shares in such companies, and so assuming unlimited liability. As Grundfest points out, an attempt to devise regulatory responses to the wide range of possible mechanisms that could be developed to synthesise limited liability equity would be a massive, and almost certainly ineffectual, task.

shareholders are able to externalise the risk of their activities, to the extent that those risks exceed their capital contributions.

If there is a true externality here—with the costs of certain risky conduct not being met by those who engage in that conduct—we would expect to observe risk-taking in excess of socially efficient levels. The social cost of such activity lies in the losses associated with excessive—i.e. socially inefficient—risks, that would not have been taken if the full cost were borne by a risk-neutral investor.

In order to identify whether there are significant social costs associated with legal recognition of corporate personality, we need to examine the nature and extent of any externalities generated by that doctrine. If there are contexts in which such externalities are significant, an economically rational company law should seek to qualify those doctrines to reduce such costs to the point where the reduction in such costs is exceeded by the benefits foregone. While it is difficult—if not impossible—to quantify these benefits and costs, we should be able to shed some light on whether our company law responds to the real issues raised by corporate personality, and whether it does so in an appropriate way.

As Lord Buckmaster said in *Rainham Chemical Works Ltd.* v. *Belvedere Fish Guano Co. Ltd.*: "But in truth the Companies Acts expressly contemplate that people may substitute the limited liability of a company for the unlimited liability of the individual, with the object that by this means enterprise and adventure may be encouraged".[28] The issue—avoiding economic jargon—is whether we are getting too much enterprise and adventure for our own good! And if we are, in what circumstances ought it to be discouraged?

E No Externalities in the Case of Voluntary Transactions

(i) The Terms of Voluntary Transactions Internalise Risk to the Company

We have already discussed the position of voluntary creditors, and their ability to adjust terms to reflect risk. As a number of commentators have pointed out, there is no externality in the case of voluntary transactions—price and other terms reflect the risk of default, internalising it to the firm.[29] High risk

---

[28] [1921] 2 AC 465, 475.

[29] See, for example, Easterbrook and Fischel, n. 16 above, 50–2. The risk is internalised on average, across the range of firms with which the creditor deals. Thus, some companies will not bear the full costs of the risks which they pose, while others will pay the same price while posing a lesser risk. It is not rational for creditors to price separately for each and every firm with which they deal—distinctions will be drawn only if it is economic to do so. So some firms do externalise some risk—but it is externalised not to creditors, but rather to the other firms with which they are grouped for pricing purposes by those creditors. This is a common phenomenon in any insurance market—and limited liability can be thought of as a form of insurance—see pp. 29–30 below. An argument that this averaging was unacceptable because of the inevitable muting of incentives faced by particular firms would amount to an argument that all forms of third party insurance should be prohibited—a position few would advance.

debtors (whether incorporated or not) pay more for credit. And prices (and sometimes other terms) reflect the risk that the debtor will take on additional risk after credit has been extended.[30] Creditors can manage risk through a range of contractual and other techniques, including diversification and insurance (the cost of which becomes a cost of credit).

This is why *Salomon* is clearly right. The company's creditors knew they were dealing with a limited company. They had the ability to refuse to give credit or to fix the terms on which they were willing to do so. They could price to all customers for the risk of a proportion of bad debts—and undoubtedly many of them did. People who take a risk and who are paid to take it should not moan when the risk materialises. It is irrelevant to argue that they were not aware of the precise extent of the risk. Their lack of knowledge itself reflects a judgment that detailed investigation of the creditworthiness of every trade debtor or protection from loss in other ways (e.g. obtaining security or a guarantee) is more costly than simply taking the risk of a certain level of bad debts, and that it is cheaper to manage the risk through diversification over many debtors and over time. In many businesses, this is a rational judgement to make.

(ii) Risks Taken by Companies after Obtaining Credit

It is sometimes suggested that where a company engages in risky activity after credit is provided, that poses more of a concern since the price will not reflect the true risk of providing credit to the company in question. As many commentators have pointed out, so long as the company continues to return to the market for credit the need to avoid prejudicing the availability of such credit or increasing its cost creates an incentive not to engage in irrationally risky activities. But there is an "end game" problem. If the company is about to go out of business, and does not contemplate seeking further funding, the incentive to refrain from unduly risky activity is removed, especially where shareholder funds are negligible.

This end game problem raises questions concerning the incentives facing directors of a company on the brink of insolvency: but the issues do not concern protection of creditors, as some commentators argue. If directors systematically face perverse incentives of this kind, this is a form of moral hazard for which creditors will price (once again, on average). The cost of credit will reflect the risk that some firms, on the brink of insolvency, will take high risk gambles rather than closing down and realising such assets as remain for the benefit of creditors—just as the cost of car insurance reflects the cost to insurance companies of the moral hazard which such insurance poses.

---

[30] In some cases, debtors contract not to undertake new or additional risks without creditor approval—consider the normal terms of debentures and trust deeds constituting debt securities for issue in public markets, which typically restrict change of business or disposal or acquisition of assets beyond specified thresholds, or the incurring of certain types of competing obligations.

Particular firms may externalise this risk to some extent—but companies in general will not, and creditors in general will be no worse off.

This highlights an important point concerning rules imposing liability on directors for trading while insolvent—an issue to which I return below. There are reasons to believe that the cost to creditors of contracting with companies to avoid excessive risk-taking on the doorstep of insolvency and monitoring those contracts are such that all but the largest creditors (e.g. trustees for holders of debt securities) will not do so. Where there are many small creditors, who extend credit for short periods, it would not be in the interests of any one creditor to take such steps—and the cost of co-ordinating such action is itself disproportionate to the advantages obtained. So firms will continue to act in this (inefficient) way—and will pay for the privilege of doing so in the cost of credit. A law imposing liability on directors for insolvent trading to discourage such conduct will (if effective) improve creditors' recoveries—which will be reflected in the average cost of credit. So it is not creditors who benefit (at least, where creditors operate in competitive markets where cost reductions are competed away), but the companies to which credit is provided. The principal (long run) beneficiaries of insolvent trading rules are the companies whose cost of credit is reduced, rather than their creditors.

(iii) A Digression on the Social Value of Hard Decisions

I cannot resist a slight digression here. An obvious objection to the argument that creditors of Mr Salomon's company knew they were dealing with a limited company, and were free to contract accordingly, is that some of those creditors may not have made conscious decisions of the kind described. Indeed, some—even most—may have thought that they were dealing with Mr Salomon personally, or that Mr Salomon was required by law to stand behind the company.

If a person genuinely and reasonably believes he or she is dealing with an individual, not with the company, then that expectation should be given effect to. But the statutory requirements as to use of the company name in contracts and other written communications (currently set out in section 25 of the Companies Act 1993 (NZ)) should avoid any confusion on this point.[31] If the company's name has been used consistently in the transactions, and nothing has been done by the company's agents to engender confusion about who is being dealt with, that should be the end of the matter.

The second objection is more interesting. Creditors then—as now—may be ignorant of the law on shareholder liability. Indeed, they had every reason to be uncertain as to the position of Mr Salomon and other similar traders some

---

[31] The Australian legislation makes the position as to whom the creditor is dealing with clearer still, requiring the company to state its registration number in addition to its name on many documents including all contracts, invoices, orders, business letters and negotiable instruments: Corporations Law, ss 88A, 219.

101 years ago, since it was a novel issue on which the High Court and Court of Appeal were able to reach the conclusion that Mr Salomon was liable! It would certainly have been possible to argue that creditors had a "reasonable expectation" that Mr Salomon would be liable, and that some of them would not have given credit had they not believed this. Evidence from aggrieved creditors could have been called to that effect—and undoubtedly would be today, were a similar issue to arise. Certainly some creditors would have had their expectations defeated by the decision of the House of Lords. But the House was prepared to countenance this, in order to establish for the future what their Lordships saw as the right rule—and a clear rule that did not depend on precise degrees of control or ownership or the "particular facts of each case".

Looking at the benefits of such a rule, and its economic significance over the last hundred years, who can doubt that they were right to do so? The sound development of the law may from time to time require courts to treat parties harshly and defeat their expectations, in order to establish more appropriate expectations in the future and do justice to the community at large, prospectively. What is fair in the long run may seem unfair in the instant case—but justice is a long-term concept. I suspect our law would benefit if courts more often asked themselves what their decisions will mean for the community over the next hundred years, and weighed this against the temptation of contextual sympathy.

(iv) Incorporation as a Form of Insurance

It is worth pausing here to explore the question of incorporation from one more perspective. Lord Buckmaster's explanation of the rationale of company law is one that most of us would, if pressed, subscribe to: encouraging enterprise and adventure. We want to encourage businesses to take socially desirable risks—i.e. ones which, while they may involve a risk (even a substantial risk) of loss (even serious loss), nonetheless have a positive net present value.[32] Yet if a risk has a positive value, why would an unincorporated individual be reluctant to take it? Is incorporation merely a cloak for the taking of socially undesirable risks, with negative values, which individuals will not take unless they can enjoy the upside without paying for it?

The answer is twofold. First, individuals are typically risk averse. If they were not, the business of insurance would be far less extensive. Most of us prefer to pay insurance premiums in respect of our house, car and other significant assets (and be predictably a little worse off) than not to insure and take the risk of being either better off (we keep the premiums) or a lot worse off if disaster strikes. If business were left to risk averse individuals, many socially desirable risks would not be taken. In this sense, incorporation is very

---

[32] The New Zealand legislation is now, however, hostile to substantial risks of serious loss, to the potential detriment of commerce—see the discussion of s 135 of the Companies Act 1993, at pp. 58–59 below.

much like a form of "bankruptcy insurance", protecting the owner of the business from disastrous outcomes by limiting exposure to an excess equal to the company's assets.[33] So what we are doing is reducing risk aversion, to encourage the taking of socially desirable risks.

Are we reducing risk aversion too much? Has this "insurance" produced a form of moral hazard that may make all concerned worse off? The answer to this question is implicit in our discussion above: the insurance is purchased from voluntary suppliers, who give credit on terms which reflect the risk of non-payment. The owners of the business pay for this insurance, when they pay for credit. They pay less for credit when such insurance is not bundled with it—this is one reason why credit from a bank which holds shareholder guarantees (from shareholders of substance, at any rate) is likely to be cheaper than trade credit. The cost of any moral hazard is fully internalised to business owners, who bear it either directly (to the extent that losses are borne by them personally) or through the premiums they pay (indirectly, in the cost of credit).[34]

(v) When Should Voluntary Creditors be Able to Look to Owners or Controllers?

Should we ever be concerned, then, about voluntary creditors who have not contracted for recourse to owners or controllers of a company?

The answer is found in Lord Macnaghten's speech in *Salomon*, where his Lordship observed that in that case, there "was no fraud or misrepresentation, and there was nobody deceived".[35] If a controller or other agent of a company deliberately or carelessly deceives a creditor as to whom the creditor is dealing with or as to the creditworthiness of the company, and the information is material to the creditor's willingness to give credit, the person making the false or deceptive statement should be liable for the loss caused by their fraud or negligence.

Express misstatements are not too difficult to identify, and I imagine that my suggestion that they should attract liability is not in the least controver-

---

[33] For a discussion of incorporation as a form of insurance, and as a response to imperfections in insurance markets, see P Halpern, M Trebilcock and M Turnbull, "An Economic Analysis of Limited Liability in Corporations Laws" (1980) 30 *Univ Toronto LJ* 117. I differ below from a number of the conclusions reached in that article, however, primarily because the article places insufficient emphasis, in my view, on the pervasiveness of limited liability, the distortions in the market engendered by exceptions to limited liability of the type which they propose, the costs of alternative methods of limiting liability which are likely to be employed if such exceptions are introduced (such as asset divestiture), and the availability of alternative (non-distortionary) legal techniques for internalising risks.

[34] As with any form of insurance, some purchasers may engage in risk preferring behaviour once they have cover. But in general, purchasers have incentives to insure to the point of risk neutrality—and not beyond. The "average" behaviour generated by the rule is unlikely to be risk preferring—or the widespread use of incorporation would make everyone worse off, and would be unlikely to have flourished as it has.

[35] [1897] AC 22, 54.

sial. The difficult issue here is whether, simply by asking for credit, a person representing a company makes any implied representation as to its credit-worthiness.

The issue is one of actionable non-disclosure—and the law has always struggled to define the circumstances in which a duty to disclose may arise in the pre-contractual context. The law relating to guarantors is, in my view, a useful guide here—the question is whether the agent for the company knows (and so should disclose) that the company's ability to meet its obligations is outside the range of circumstances that would normally be encountered in a transaction such as that contemplated.[36]

It seems to me that it "goes without saying" that an agent seeking credit is representing that there are no aspects of the company's financial position out of the ordinary for transactions such as that which is contemplated, which he or she is aware of *and has not disclosed,* which make it impossible for the company to perform, or highly probable that it will not do so. Context will matter: a company seeking credit from a high risk lender (or trade creditor) need not disclose that its financial position makes recourse to normal bank credit impossible.[37] Note also that actual knowledge on the part of the agent is required: there is no other context I can think of in which the law requires a person to make unprompted disclosure of matters not known to that person, and imposes liability for failure to do so.

Directors who know that a company cannot meet its obligations as they fall due, and who nonetheless continue to carry on the business of the company by (*inter alia*) authorising employees to obtain goods or services on credit, similarly seem to me to be practising a deception on those creditors.[38]

From a purely contractual perspective, addressing the question whether a voluntary creditor has a good cause of complaint in relation to its dealings with the company, there are no other circumstances in which a voluntary creditor should be allowed to recover from controllers or owners, however deeply or vocally the decision to give credit to a company may be regretted after the event.

There is a further question, noted above, whether the moral hazard which limited liability creates for the controllers of near-insolvent firms can be

---

[36] See *Laws of New Zealand*, "Guarantees and Indemnities" (Lord Cooke of Thorndon (ed.), Wellington, Butterworths, 1993), paras 34, 35.

[37] As in the case of guarantees, where it is well established that a lender seeking a guarantee need not disclose expressly that the principal obligor's credit is unsatisfactory, that is implicit in the fact that a guarantee is being sought. There will be difficult boundary issues here, as in the case of guarantee cases, and the frequency with which the issues arise may justify spelling out the test in some detail in legislation.

[38] However, an express warning that the tacit assumption of solvency cannot be made should be sufficient to remove any liability. If the creditor is willing to proceed despite knowing that the risk of non-payment is high—presumably pricing to reflect that risk—then that creditor has no complaint if and when the risk materialises. There are creditors who are willing to lend at high margins to assist in corporate rescues—if they know the facts, they should get the protection they contract for, but no more.

remedied by imposing liability on those controllers for insolvent trading, at least in circumstances where transaction costs prevent direct contracting between the company and creditors in relation to such issues. If the cost of administering such rules were less than the cost of the risks that would otherwise be taken by such controllers, such rules would be desirable—though as discussed above, the long run beneficiaries of such rules would be the companies concerned, and not creditors as a class.

Thus, there is one situation in which creditors definitely should have a claim against controllers (where they have been misled), and another where there may be a case for liability (to discourage inefficient risk taking by controllers, despite the absence of any "wrong" to creditors in the sense of uncompensated risk). Later in this essay we shall, however, see some developments, both at common law and in statute, which go beyond either exception, and which create protections at once unnecessary and undesirable for voluntary creditors of companies.

F Externalities in Relation to Involuntary Creditors

Limited liability does (in principle) give rise to potentially significant externalities in the case of involuntary creditors—in particular, the victims of torts and other civil wrongs committed by the firm. Risk is shifted to such creditors without their having an opportunity to price for it or to negotiate security or other terms. If the enterprise does not have to pay this class of claimants for any increase in the risk which it imposes on that class, we would expect to see enterprises choose to engage in activities which create socially excessive levels of risk to involuntary creditors. There would be too much "enterprise and adventure".

Consider the operation of a factory producing pollutants as a by-product of its manufacturing activities. If the owners of the firm which operates the factory reap the benefit of additional profits from additional output, but their liability for harm caused is limited to their capital contribution to the firm, they have incentives to produce at an excessive, socially inefficient level.

There are, however, several observations that need to be made about the nature and extent of this moral hazard.

(i) No Externality where Corporate Assets Exceed Expected Liabilities

First, the moral hazard arises only where liabilities may exceed the enterprise's assets: up to that point, there is an incentive to take the same level of care as if the owners' liability were not limited.

(ii) Legal Techniques for Internalising Costs of Harm to Third Parties

Secondly, there are a number of techniques available to the law if it wishes to internalise the cost of such harm to those engaged in an activity. While also imperfect, there is reason to believe that they will in many cases be more effective than unlimited liability regimes.[39]

The most direct technique is to impose regulatory safety standards, enforced by inspection and compliance procedures. Another is to require either a minimum capital for a person engaged in that activity, or compulsory third party insurance as a condition of engaging in the relevant activity. Thus in Ontario, for example, no person may drive a vehicle without third party insurance in respect of injuries that may be caused by that activity. If a person insures, the cost of the insurance internalises the cost of harm that may be caused—and transmits, in the course of so doing, information about the reduction in risk associated with precautions such as driving a newer rather than an older car, or installing anti-lock braking, and so forth.[40] If the person does not insure, then that person may not engage in the relevant risky activity.

A similar approach could be taken to environmental liabilities, for example—it could be a condition of undertaking certain activities that environmental damage insurance be purchased up to a specified level.[41]

Where people purchase insurance, the cost of the risks they create is internalised through the premium paid for that insurance—the insurer, a voluntary creditor, is effectively substituted for the involuntary creditors as a source of pricing for risk and monitoring to reduce risk.[42]

(iii) Limited Liability is Pervasive—and is Not Confined to Companies

Thirdly, I deliberately referred above to *people* purchasing insurance, rather than solely to companies, because the problem of externalising harm for which there may be liability in tort or under other laws is not by any means confined to limited companies. An individual with assets which are less than the amount of his or her potential liability to others as a result of undertaking a risky activity faces precisely the same degree of moral hazard as a company with the same level of assets. As I have mentioned before, limited liability in

---

[39] See Grundfest, n. 27 above.

[40] Whereas in the same context in New Zealand, the existence of a flat rate ACC (accident compensation) premium paid by owners of vehicles set at a level which few cannot afford removes any signal about efficient levels of care or activity which might be transmitted by more appropriately priced insurance in conjunction with strict liability for harm caused.

[41] For example, in the United States the hazardous waste disposal industry is subject to "financial responsibility requirements" under the Resource Conservation and Recovery Act 1976—see the discussion in Hansmann and Kraakman, n. 24 above, 1928. For further examples, see Grundfest, n. 27 above, 421–2, especially n. 137.

[42] This is true whether the insurance is purchased under compulsion, or voluntarily.

respect of civil wrongs is pervasive in New Zealand, and is not confined to companies. In New Zealand as in most modern economies, civil liability is confined to the extent of a person's assets. If a person cannot pay her debts, she faces no sanction other than bankruptcy. Bankruptcy, which can be initiated by either the debtor herself or her creditors, is (among other functions) a process for limiting personal liability. The insolvency laws:

(a)   allow the bankrupt to retain certain basic items of property; and
(b)   provide for the automatic discharge of the bankrupt after a period of three years, absent special circumstances.[43] After this point, assets acquired by the debtor cease to be available to the former creditors, whose claims are extinguished. So in reality, we can say that every person enjoys limited liability, where the limit is that person's current assets plus their earnings (if any) for three years in excess of the level required for (modest) living expenses.

In addition, the social welfare system ensures that a bankrupt person will have access to sufficient income to provide for accommodation and a basic standard of living. An insolvent person in New Zealand today will not be deprived of the basics of life. This is another form of limitation of liability.

These comments may seem rather obvious. But if we are concerned about the moral hazard facing the owners of businesses whose assets are less than their potential liabilities, we need to bear in mind the fact that the very same moral hazard faces those carrying on business in their own name with a similar deficiency in personal assets. (Or, for that matter, going about normal daily life: many drivers on the roads today are incapable of meeting their potential liability for the damage they may cause to other vehicles and property, even in New Zealand where civil liability for personal injury by accident has been abolished.) Before expressing concern about the moral hazard caused by incorporation with limited liability, we need to identify how significant the *incremental* cost which it causes is likely to be, bearing in mind the pervasiveness of such moral hazard in our society already.

If we are sufficiently concerned about the risks a particular activity poses to third parties that we want to ensure all engaged in it take adequate precaution or face the full cost of failure to do so, the law should either regulate the activity directly or require all those engaged in the activity to have minimum net assets or to obtain adequate third party insurance. The requirement should apply to natural persons, overseas companies, and New Zealand companies alike.

The market will be distorted if we routinely disallow limited liability in such contexts, rather than adopting non-discriminatory techniques such as those described above, because different companies will face different cost

---

[43] Insolvency Act 1967 (NZ), ss 107, 114. It is very rare for a person not to be automatically discharged, though s 107 does provide for postponement of discharge in limited circumstances. And it is open to a bankrupt to apply for early discharge: ss 108–110.

structures in undertaking the same activity, which will be inversely related to their asset levels. Consider two taxi services—one owns a single car and is owned by an individual with few assets other than the taxi company. The other owns one hundred taxis. Each taxi is held in a separate company, with the shares owned by a parent company and the driver employed by the relevant subsidiary. If the law allowed victims of collisions to look through the subsidiary to the parent company, the larger firm would be at a competitive disadvantage to the smaller firm, other things being equal, because the expected cost of operating the business would be greater. Even though there may well be economies of scale in operating a taxi business, the cost of owning many cars would discourage such structures. Either driving without the necessary assets or insurance to meet claims should be prohibited or we should not worry about use of the corporate form to reduce costs of operation to the lowest level permitted by law. [44]

(iv) Incorporation does not Affect Personal Liability for Wrongs Committed by a Shareholder or Controller

Very importantly, where a tort is committed by an owner/controller against a third party with no relationship with the company, while carrying on the business of the company, the existence of the company does not shelter that person from liability. Suppose Mr Salomon had been out in his carriage, to see his bankers to negotiate an overdraft for the company. Returning to the office, he carelessly drove into a clerk waiting outside to serve a demand on him. The clerk could sue Mr Salomon himself or the company (which would be vicariously liable for his actions). Mr Salomon could not say "I was not me at the time, I was incorporated". So victims of torts perpetrated by real people can still sue those real people—they can disregard the presence of a company if they so wish.

The same is true where the owner or controller is a party to the commission of the tort because the owner has directed or procured the commission of the wrongful act, expressly or (it seems) impliedly, so as to be privy to the wrongful act. In such cases the owner is liable—incorporation will not protect the owner.[45]

---

[44] For a theoretical exploration of this issue, see Easterbrook and Fischel, n. 16 above, 57; J L Carr and G F Mathewson, "Unlimited Liability as a Barrier to Entry" (1988) 96 *J Pol Econ* 766.

[45] *Rainham Chemical Works Ltd.* v. *Belvedere Fish Guano Co. Ltd.* [1921] 2 AC 465 (directors not liable in negligence for explosion at munitions works operated by company, though liable on other grounds); *Performing Right Society Ltd.* v. *Ciryl Theatrical Syndicate Ltd.* [1924] 1 KB 1 (CA) (managing director not liable for breaches of copyright by band which played works, in circumstances where he did not select the works for performance and was not aware they were being performed); *Yuille* v. *B & B Fisheries (Leigh) Ltd.* [1958] 2 Lloyd's LR 596 (director liable in personal injury claim, as party to sending vessels to sea in an unseaworthy condition); *Wah Tat Bank Ltd.* v. *Chan* [1975] AC 507 (PC) (director who agreed terms with third party on which his company would convert goods consigned to lenders to the third party personally liable for conversions). See also *King* v. *Milpurrurru* (1996) 34 IPR 11 (Fed Ct Australia, Full Ct); *Green Cartridge*

In general, we can say that a person's civil liability for acting wrongfully *in person, in breach of non-voluntary obligations imposed by the general law* will not be reduced by the presence of a corporate entity. And since companies can only act through individuals, there will be few circumstances in which a tortious act by a company will not also entail liability on the part of some individual. If that individual is the owner of the company, or if the owner is a party to the tort (i.e. has directed or procured it), limited liability is irrelevant—the owner is fully liable.

(v) The Tort Liability of the Owner of an Unincorporated Business— Comparison

It is instructive to ask what circumstances would result in (imposed obligation) tort liability on the part of the owner of a business who did not elect to incorporate the business, and how these compare with the position of a shareholder or controller in an incorporated business. Personal wrongdoing is one example—but as noted above, Mr Salomon also would be liable in those circumstances. The owner might be a joint tortfeasor, having directed or procured the wrongful conduct—but again, Mr Salomon would also be liable. The last category of liability for our unincorporated owner is vicarious liability for acts of employees, in circumstances where the owner herself has not been negligent in any way, so is not personally liable. This is where the practical importance of limited liability lies: it is a shelter from liability on the part of *owners who are not at fault*. Shareholders can externalise tort liability imposed on them by law where the wrongdoing is not theirs but that of one or more employees whose conduct they have not directed or procured.

Of course, in these circumstances, the relevant employees will be liable. And they are in a contractual relationship with the employer. It is fanciful to suggest that employees are paid to take this risk and should insure against the risk of causing harm in the course of their employment—this does not occur in practice, and there are good reasons for this.[46] What does happen is that employers commonly—though not universally—insure against employee liability incurred in the course of employment.[47] Where there is insurance, the

Co. *(Hong Kong) Ltd.* v. *Canon Kabushiki Kaisha* (1996) 34 IPR 614; *Private Parking Services (Vic) Pty. Ltd.* v. *Huggard* (unreported, Supreme Court of Victoria, Batt J, 15 Feb. 1996) 1996 Vic Lexis 831.

[46] See, for example, D De Wees, D Duff and M Trebilcock, *Exploring the Domain of Accident Law: Taking the Facts Seriously* (Oxford, OUP, 1996), 347–8, describing numerous studies which suggest that asymmetric information problems and bargaining costs result in contractual risk premiums in wages which do not fully reflect the risk of injury in the course of employment—the same is *a fortiori* likely to be true in relation to the risk of liability to third parties.

[47] They do this not least because of the prospect that the employee will be held entitled to recover from the company under an implied indemnity for liability incurred in the course of performing his or her duties. Although this was rejected in England in *Lister* v. *Romford Ice & Cold Storage Co.* [1957] AC 555, where the employee drove negligently, it was suggested in that case that there is a right to indemnity in respect of liability arising out of an unlawful enterprise on

cost of operations is once again fully internalised to the company—there is no externality. So the class of case in which there is a true externality is reduced still further.

(vi) The Limited Effectiveness of Tort Liability as a Mechanism for Internalising Costs

The limited circumstances in which the owners of a business can in practice externalise costs of harm to third parties by incorporation direct our attention to a significant weakness in the case for unlimited liability. The ability of owners of a business to limit tort liability in respect of certain harms is only a cause for concern to the extent that the law of tort is itself an effective mechanism for internalising to a business the cost of harms which it causes to others. Yet there are many areas in which tort is of doubtful utility and where other regulatory mechanisms are employed to discourage excessive imposition of costs on third parties. In these areas (which in New Zealand include the entire field of personal injury), it is largely irrelevant that tort liability is limited by incorporation. And in other areas where tort is retained, its effectiveness as a deterrent is the subject of considerable debate.[48] If tort law does not, for various reasons, create appropriate incentives for businesses in respect of a particular type of risk, then the partial removal of such incentives is not a cause for undue concern.

The uncertain nature of the likely gains from introducing unlimited liability is underscored by the fact, discussed above, that it is only vicarious liability that is externalised by shareholders, i.e. the liability (in excess of corporate assets) that they would otherwise have had for wrongful acts by employees that they did not participate in or know of and approve.

The owners are not necessarily, in such circumstances, the least cost avoiders of the risk. Certainly, they might be able to do something about the risk—they could increase supervision or introduce ever more complex and costly compliance procedures—but the employees concerned may well be able to do so at less cost. Much of the case law on vicarious liability rules appears

---

which the employee has been required to embark without knowing that it was unlawful. That dictum has been followed in New Zealand: see *F* v. *Attorney-General* [1994] 2 ERNZ 62. And see the suggestions that there may be a more general right of indemnity, made by La Forest J in *London Drugs Ltd.* v. *Kuehne & Nagel International Ltd.* (1992) 97 DLR (4th) 261, 286–8.

[48] Some of the reasons why tort liability may be inappropriate or ineffective, even ignoring the question whether the cost of administering a tort system is justified by the reduction in accident costs it produces, are lack of full information concerning risks, precautions and their costs on the part of the relevant actors; limited means on the part of the persons on whom liability is sought to be imposed which reduce their effective exposure below the level of harm which may be caused; high discount rates in excess of the social discount rate; expectation of settlement of claims below the true cost of harm; and human attitudes to risk which appear to diverge in some significant respects from classical actuarial/probabilistic models (on this last point, see, for example, C R Sunstein, "Behavioural Analysis of Law" (1997) Chicago Working Papers in Law and Economics No 46, and the studies cited therein).

to be motivated primarily by the desire to compensate victims, where employees lack means. Yet the defendant having a deep pocket is not of itself a sufficient reason for imposing liability. In the absence of a good economic rationale for employer liability in such cases, we should not be overly concerned about use of incorporation to limit owner liability in this context. There can be no rational objection to the externalisation of a liability which should never have been internalised to the employer in the first place!

Posner suggests that one economic justification for vicarious liability is that typically employees have limited assets, so are not deterred by the threat of civil liability.[49] In the employment context, however, if the employer is made liable, employers (with greater assets) will take steps to avoid liability by exercising their ability to control and supervise the employee, to prevent wrongdoing by the employee. Employers can in turn create more appropriate incentives for employees by threatening them with disciplinary sanctions or dismissal, to which (the theory runs) they are more responsive than they are to threats of civil claims. This theory rests on some very broad assumptions about asset distribution and response to different types of sanction which will not always be well-founded. It also depends on some unstated assumptions about the increased risk that an employee will harm third parties while employed, as opposed to while he or she is not in employment. And the additional costs imposed on employers to create the relevant incentives add both to the cost of employment (which entails social costs) and to the costs of production (with resultant deadweight costs).

I strongly suspect that the benefits of vicarious liability as it stands today are negligible, if they exist at all. Indeed, it can be argued that such liability deters commercial activity to an undesirable extent by imposing costs on employment which serve little or no valid economic end, and so discourages socially beneficial "enterprise and adventure". Incorporation would then alleviate this over-extension of liability by partially restoring a more desirable liability regime.[50] Advocates for unlimited liability need to begin by making out a persuasive case for the social gains from vicarious liability—a step often omitted—before moving on to establish that such gains exceed the costs which their proposals entail. And they also need to establish—a challenge which is more difficult still—that the incentives for corporate employers to supervise and discipline employees described by Posner as the justification for vicarious liability will be significantly strengthened by liability in excess of corporate assets. It is only the marginal enhancement in such control, and the harm avoided as a consequence of that marginal enhancement, which can be weighed against the costs of their proposals.

[49] R Posner, *Economic Analysis of Law* (4th edn., Boston, Mass., Little Brown, 1992), 187.

[50] It is interesting to speculate on the extent to which misconceived extension of the doctrine of vicarious liability has encouraged growth in incorporations (over and above that which risk aversion in respect of exposure to voluntary creditors alone would produce), and the law's tolerance of limited liability even in the context of involuntary creditor claims, where the theoretical justification for it appears weakest. Perhaps two wrongs have made a right!

G Should Tort Creditors be able to Claim Directly Against Shareholders?

The discussion above demonstrates the very limited circumstances in which owners of a business are in fact able to rely on the doctrine of limited liability to externalise the costs of harm caused to involuntary creditors. One cannot but feel that the problem is overstated by some advocates for change to the law in this field, especially when seen in the context of the inherent imperfections of the tort system and the doctrine of vicarious liability. But the issue does undoubtedly exist: should the law respond by providing that tort creditors (and creditors in respect of other imposed obligations) can disregard the fact of incorporation, and pursue the shareholders of the company, if the company cannot pay?[51]

(i) Widely Held Companies

In the case of widely held companies, the partial removal of limited liability would be justified if and only if the social gain from any enhancement in incentives for owners and controllers of companies engaged in activities which cause harm to others[52] outweighed the total of:

(a) the costs of administering such a regime, including all the costs of tracing rules, liability fixing rules, enforcement rules, and liability reduction/avoidance mechanisms;

(b) additional monitoring costs incurred by shareholders; and

(c) costs caused by less efficient capital markets, and reduction of the ability to manage risk by diversifying investments.

While the outcome of this balancing exercise could be determined conclusively only by empirical studies, many of the elements are not readily measurable. In particular, it is difficult to assess the effectiveness of tort as a source of incentives, let alone the benefits from subtle enhancements to the tort system such as unlimited liability for shareholders. For practical policy-making purposes, one is driven back to an intuitive weighting of these factors. Given the certain costs involved in such reforms in respect of widely held companies, and the rather uncertain gains, it seems very unlikely that departure from the present regime is justified.

---

[51] Such reforms are strongly advocated by Hansmann and Kraakman, n. 24 above, and (somewhat more tentatively) by Leebron, n. 24 above. See also Halpern, Trebilcock and Turnbull, n. 33 above; and B R Cheffins, *Company Law: Theory, Structure and Operation* (Oxford, OUP, 1997), 505–7.

[52] At best, this would be an enhancement at the margin, given the many circumstances in which owners and controllers will not escape liability by virtue of incorporation. And there are good reasons to doubt whether such enhancements would occur at all in relation to widely held companies the shares of which are traded on public securities markets: see Grundfest, n. 27 above.

(ii) Closely Held Companies

In the case of companies with one shareholder, to take the polar extreme, the costs of such reforms seem much reduced—in particular, the concerns relating to monitoring costs and capital markets efficiency do not arise. Why does the law not provide that in the case of companies with one—or maybe even two or three—shareholders, the shareholders have unlimited liability to involuntary creditors? Would this not discourage socially excessive risk taking?

Even in the context of closely held companies, the gains from extending vicarious liability are uncertain. And the associated costs will still be significant, though less than in the context of widely held companies. All the costs of tracing rules and liability fixing rules will be present, as will the costs of limiting liability by other means. In addition, any rule which distinguishes between closely held companies and other companies will give rise to difficult (and administratively costly) boundary rules. A numerical limit on shareholders would not be appropriate, as evasion would be trivial. A limit based on capitalisation (presumably, before the relevant claim arose) would be equally arbitrary, and would pose the additional problem of possible fluctuations in the liability position of shareholders as the company's trading position changed. A purposive or discretionary test would make planning—and in particular, making decisions on insurance—uncertain and, as a result, more costly.

For these reasons, the case for an extension of liability is—at best—not proven. Where gains are uncertain, and costs all too certain, there is little justification for adding another layer of complex rules to our law books.

H Summary

In summary, there does not appear to be good reason for serious concern about the costs of limited liability, or any excessive risk taking which that doctrine may encourage:

(a) the gains from imposing unlimited vicarious tort liability on owners of companies are uncertain, and seem unlikely to be significant;

(b) the costs associated with the many complex legal rules required to implement a system of unlimited tort liability would however certainly be incurred, and would be appreciable;

(c) in small companies, owners actively involved in the operation of the company are unlikely to escape personal liability as a result of incorporation;

(d) in larger companies, any reduction in externalities brought about by removing limited liability is very likely to be outweighed by other costs;

(e) the problem of externalisation of involuntary creditor claims is not confined to limited liability companies. In circumstances where we have a particular concern about risks being externalised, as noted above, there are better legal techniques for addressing this concern which do not discriminate between different firms based on legal form; and

(f) there are significant complexities, arbitrary boundaries and costs associated with any attempt to address this issue by drawing a distinction between "large" and "small" companies.

I Criminal Liability—a Special Case of Imposed Obligations

One important and extensive source of non-voluntary obligations is of course the criminal law. We are all required to comply with the traffic laws, for example, whether we are currently driving on our own behalf or as employees of some other person. And one of the important functions of criminal law—though not its sole function—is to deter certain kinds of undesirable conduct. It does this by imposing sanctions for engaging in such conduct. Unlike civil law, criminal law has also solved (to some degree) the problem that pecuniary penalties do not deter those with no assets. Criminal courts have a range of sanctions available to them, including community service and imprisonment, to ensure that the criminal law has teeth even where defendants have no assets.

Companies have limited assets. They cannot be sent to prison. Does this mean that the corporate form can be used to externalise criminal liability? I believe it cannot, or at least not to any meaningful extent.

First, owners of a company cannot escape criminal liability for their own wrongs or for those to which they are parties. Incorporation does not shelter participants in crimes from liability.

Secondly, where the company's assets are sufficient to meet a fine imposed on the company, the owners are punished in the same way and to the same extent as a natural person who is fined. Indeed, the not infrequent specification of higher maximum fines for bodies corporate in New Zealand legislation creates the prospect of heavier penalties for the same wrong, deterring it more severely in the case of corporate defendants.[53]

Thirdly, in cases where the principal of an unincorporated business is not a party to an offence committed by an employee or agent:

(a) the employee or agent will be answerable for the offence. This will be true whether or not the business is incorporated. The incentives of the criminal law apply directly to the wrongdoer in either case; and

[53] Differential penalties tend to be justified as addressing the less risk averse attitude of companies in general, or as reflecting the scale of the conduct contemplated, or as a substitute for non-pecuniary penalties imposed on natural persons in more serious cases. The first consideration makes good sense. But surely scale of conduct is independent of legal form—and can be separately considered in the course of sentencing decisions. And the third factor makes little sense where an offence can only be punished by a fine, as is often the case.

(b) that owner will not as matter of general criminal law be liable. There is no vicarious liability for criminal acts as a matter of general criminal law. So there is no reason for concern about an incorporated employer/principal and its shareholders also being free from liability in such circumstances.

Specific statutes can reverse the general rule that an employer or principal is not liable for offences committed by an agent or employee to which he or she is not a party. An increasing number of statutes provide that, where a person commits an offence under the statute acting as the agent or employee of another (the principal), the principal is liable as if he or she had personally committed the offence unless he or she proves that:

(a) he or she did not know nor could reasonably be expected to have known that the offence was to be or was being committed; or
(b) he or she took all reasonable steps to prevent the commission of the offence.[54]

In almost all statutes where such a provision is found there is a corresponding provision in relation to the liability of directors and employees of companies. They are made liable where the act or omission which constitutes the offence occurs with their knowledge and consent, and they have not taken reasonable steps to prevent it. Consider, for example, section 340(3) of the Resource Management Act 1991 (NZ):

"(3) Where any body corporate is convicted of an offence against this Act, every director and every person concerned in the management of the body corporate shall be guilty of the like offence if it is proved:
(a) That the act that constituted the offence took place with his or her authority, permission, or consent; or
(b) That he or she knew or could reasonably be expected to have known that the offence was to be or was being committed and failed to take all reasonable steps to prevent or stop it."

Where the company is closely held, and the directors are also the owners, their position is analogous to that of the owner of an unincorporated business. Putting to one side the question whether such sweeping liability for principals is justified, in all the contexts in which it is currently imposed, it is clear that no advantage is obtained by incorporating a small business so far as criminal liability (and the incentives which it creates) is concerned.

The position appears to be essentially the same so far as larger businesses are concerned. Consider the position of a partner in a large unincorporated accounting firm, an employee of which commits an offence. A partner who was not involved in management of the firm, or the relevant part of it, would

---

[54] See, for example, Building Act 1991 (NZ), s 82; Crown Minerals Act 1991 (NZ), s 102; Maritime Transport Act 1994 (NZ), s 410; Resource Management Act 1991 (NZ), s 340; United Nations Convention on the Law of the Sea Act 1996 (NZ), s 10.

face no risk of liability. The question in relation to partners more closely connected with the offending employee (but who were not parties to the offence, as they did not authorise or consent to it) would be whether the requisite knowledge was present or steps were taken to prevent the offence. If the firm were incorporated, essentially the same issues would arise under provisions such as section 340(3)(b) of the Resource Management Act (section 340(3)(a) essentially restates the test for a manager to be a party to an offence under the general criminal law and appears to be, strictly speaking, unnecessary). An owner not concerned in management at all could not be liable. An owner with some role in management would be liable if he or she knew of the commission of the offence (or ought to have done so) and failed to take reasonable steps to prevent it. The burden of proof would be different. But the substance of the test for liability is the same.

In summary, incorporation does not, in general, enable owners of firms to escape criminal liabilities to which they would otherwise be subject.[55]

(i) Liability of Directors, as Opposed to Owners

The Resource Management Act 1991, like most such statutes, imposes liability on directors, rather than on shareholders. If we are seeking to prevent owners externalising costs by incorporation, is this a matter for concern? I believe it is not, for three reasons.

First, in many small companies, the sole director is also the owner—so there is no practical distinction. For the reasons described above, incorporation will not enable the owner/director to escape liability.

Secondly, where there is a separation of ownership and control, owners of unincorporated businesses not concerned in their management will not normally incur any criminal liability in respect of the acts of employees, since they will not know that offences are being committed and could not reasonably be expected to do so. So such owners will escape liability—though, admittedly, they bear the burden of establishing their lack of involvement, unlike passive shareholders.

Thirdly, and more generally, these statutes do not appear to be addressed to the concern that the assets of the company will be insufficient to meet a fine. Liability of directors is not made conditional on company funds being inadequate to meet the appropriate fine. The statute appears to permit a doubling up of liability for the same offence. If the fine imposed on the company is appropriately set, and the company is able to pay, the shareholders face the

---

[55] A survey of statutory provisions on this topic does, however, reveal a surprising diversity of approaches and drafting techniques, in an area where there is a strong case for consistent and principled formulations. In some cases (such as the Fisheries Act 1996 (NZ)), the position of a director appears to be worse than that of the owner of an unincorporated business! The question of criminal liability of principals, and of directors and managers, would benefit from systematic review—perhaps by the New Zealand Law Commission.

same costs as the owner of an unincorporated business. Why is this insufficient? The concern appears to be that the company's controllers do not have the same incentives to avoid the penalty as would a sole trader—there is an agency problem, which is only partially addressed in some cases through incentives based on director performance.[56] The imposition of personal liability appears to be intended to overcome reduced incentives for controllers whose personal wealth and reputation is not at risk in the event of breach, rather than externalities born of limited liability.

Imposing liability on directors creates precisely the reverse agency problem. Directors face personal sanctions if they take a risk of breaching the relevant legislation—yet the benefits from the activity which may result in a breach are derived not by them but by the owners. So we can expect to see either a requirement by those individuals that they be insured for such liability at the company's expense, internalising the cost to the company,[57] or levels of precaution taken at their direction which reflect their personal exposure but not the gains from breaches. That is, such rules are more likely to lead to over-precaution than to inadequate precaution. This topic itself deserves detailed exploration—but for present purposes, it is sufficient to note that the focus of such provisions on controllers rather than owners certainly does not suggest a need to qualify the basic limited liability rule.

In this context, incidentally, the prohibition in the Companies Act 1993 (NZ) on insuring directors and employees in respect of criminal liability appears to pass up an opportunity to internalise to companies the costs of omitted precautions and the benefits of precautions taken, even where compulsory insurance is not required. This rule requires careful re-examination.[58]

III DEVELOPMENTS IN THE LAST ONE HUNDRED YEARS

In this essay I will not attempt a systematic survey of the case law on *Salomon* over the last one hundred years. Such surveys are found in most company law texts, and they are not especially illuminating from the perspective of legal

---

[56] Shareholders can make a conscious decision whether to invest in a company, with one of the costs of the corporate form being precisely such agency problems. Various techniques such as performance-related pay may be used to address this—i.e. managers share in the business risks. Shareholders assume these risks voluntarily, so have no room for complaint absent actual misconduct. The cure for poor performance is, ultimately, dismissal. But the community at large has not agreed to assume this agency risk or to have the incentives created by the criminal law muted as a result of such structures. Hence direct liability for controllers.

[57] Where it is lawful to do so: in the case of criminal liability, however, insurance paid for by the company directly or indirectly is prohibited by s 162 of the Companies Act 1993 (NZ). The director's fees or salaries paid in certain contexts may however increase to enable self-insurance, in response to this prohibition.

[58] See, for a similar suggestion, R Cooter and T Ulen, *Law and Economics* (2nd edn., Illinois, Scott, Forseman, 1996), 405.

principle.[59] Instead, I will single out a few topics of particular interest, where significant doctrinal developments have occurred or have been threatened.

A Attempts by Voluntary Creditors to Use Tort to Circumvent *Salomon*

The single largest threat to *Salomon* posed by the development of the common law has emerged in recent years. That threat results from the development of tort liability based on "assumption of responsibility" and acceptance by the courts of concurrent liability in tort and contract. A number of jurisdictions have witnessed attempts by voluntary creditors of a company to recast their claim as a tort claim founded on an assumption of responsibility by the sole owner/director/employee of the company.

(i) Imposed Obligations and "Assumption of Responsibility" Torts

It seems to me, with respect to Lord Cooke,[60] that there is all the difference in the world between:

(a) obligations not to steal or damage tangible property—which are in a sense part of property law—and to avoid inflicting bodily harm intentionally or carelessly. We all owe such obligations to others at all times, whether or not we have met and dealt with each other. They are imposed obligations which we owe to those whom we have never met and with whom we have never previously dealt; and

(b) obligations which result from voluntary interactions, in the course of which one person assumes a responsibility to another, with or without payment for so doing.

In the former case, the presence of a contract or the interposition of a company (with a corresponding term as to limited recourse) in dealings between the parties or between one of the parties and the world at large should make no difference to personal obligations, absent actual agreement to that effect (express or implied). A person does not cease to owe these obligations to all other persons at all times simply because, when he or she goes to work, his or her employer is a company.[61]

---

[59] Some of the more interesting surveys are found in Davies, n. 3 above, chap 6; J H Farrar and M Russell, *Company Law and Securities Regulation in New Zealand* (Wellington, Butterworths, 1985), 48–52; and A Beck, "The Two Sides of the Corporate Veil" in J H Farrar (ed.), *Contemporary Issues in Company Law* (Auckland, CCH, 1987), 69.

[60] "An Impossible Distinction" (1991) 107 *LQR* 46.

[61] In this respect I share the difficulty of the majority in the Supreme Court of Canada in *London Drugs Ltd.* v. *Kuehne & Nagel International Ltd.* (1992) 97 DLR (4th) 261 in accepting the view of La Forest J that employees of a warehouse company were not personally liable for negligently damaging goods stored in the warehouse. I note that even La Forest J did not envisage personal liability being suspended for personal injuries, however, or for intentional torts, but only where a plaintiff has chosen to enter into a course of dealing with the company and

In the latter case, the central question must surely be: "Who has assumed this responsibility [to provide careful advice, etc]?" Normally, where the business (such as providing advice) is carried on through a company, it is the company, not the employee, which assumes that responsibility. And the recipient of the advice, etc., is a voluntary creditor of the company who has chosen to look to it and rely on it, on whatever terms may have been agreed. The default rule of limited recourse applies, absent agreement to the contrary. There is no externality here. So we should not have any concern about tort creditors where their claim is based on assumption of responsibility—they, like contract creditors, are voluntary creditors.

(ii)   New Zealand law threatens Salomon . . .

A number of tort claims of this kind have succeeded in New Zealand. The most extreme example is *Centrepac Partnership* v. *Foreign Currency Consultants Ltd. and Rutherfurd.*[62] A partnership had contracted with the defendant company to provide foreign currency advice and to act as their agent in foreign currency transactions. Mr Rutherfurd owned all but one of the company's shares, was a director of the company and provided the services as an employee of the company. In breach of instructions given to stay out of the market, Mr Rutherfurd committed the plaintiffs to several very unsuccessful transactions. They brought proceedings against the company in contract and tort, and against Mr Rutherfurd personally in tort. They succeeded against the company for breach of the agency contract, but not in tort.[63] They also succeeded in tort against Mr Rutherfurd. Gault J said:[64]

> "Guided by the Privy Council in *Yuen Kun-Yeu* v. *Attorney-General of Hong Kong* [1987] 3 WLR 776 at p 782 et seq, I have considered the relationship between Mr Rutherfurd and the plaintiffs and the foreseeability of damage determined on an

voluntarily assumed the risk of the company being unable to satisfy a judgment in contract or for vicarious liability (see 284, 285–6, 289–91). With much of his reasoning I am wholly and respectfully in agreement, however—in particular, as he says (at 277): "The plaintiff should not be able to use tort law merely to improve its contractual bargain." But I believe that the English Court of Appeal was correct in *Adler* v. *Dickson* [1955] 1 QB 158 in saying that obligations of this kind ought to be excluded by actual agreement, express or implied, and that exclusion of company liability does not in all circumstances necessarily imply exclusion of employee liability. If employee liability is excluded by contract between the company and a third party, however, the employee ought to be able to take advantage of this: in New Zealand the Contracts (Privity) Act 1982 achieves this sensible result. There will be difficult boundary cases, such as *Adler* or even *London Drugs*, where the question of implied exclusion may not be self-evident. However it is more illuminating to ask the correct question, even where it is difficult to answer, than it is to ask the wrong one!

   62   (1989) 4 NZCLC 64,940.

   63   Gault J followed *McLaren Maycroft & Co.* v. *Fletcher Development Co. Ltd.* [1973] 2 NZLR 100 on concurrent liability, an approach which would almost certainly not be taken today, since the decisions in *Rowlands* v. *Collow* [1992] 1 NZLR 178 and *Henderson* v. *Merrett Syndicates Ltd.* [1995] 2 AC 145 (HL).

   64   (1989) 4 NZCLC 64,940, 64,951.

objective basis. It is difficult to envisage a relationship outside contract reflecting closer proximity than that between the plaintiffs and Mr Rutherfurd in this case. He was engaged personally to provide (through the vehicle of his company) a consultancy service in foreign exchange dealings and in dealing on a regular basis on behalf of the plaintiffs. I have no doubt that any reasonable foreign exchange dealer, acting in those circumstances, would have realised that carelessness on his part would be likely to cause loss to his clients. Therefore I have no hesitation in finding that he owed to the plaintiffs a duty to act with skill and care in relation to their foreign exchange transactions.

To find a duty of care in this situation, in my view, does not involve lifting the corporate veil. The duty of care exists directly between the plaintiffs and Mr Rutherfurd. That applies notwithstanding the separate obligations existing in contract between Mr Rutherfurd's company and the client. It will not be in all cases in which a duty of care will be found to exist between a company director and the clients of the company. Each situation will depend on its own facts as in any case of negligence, and it is only where there is a sufficient degree of proximity and harm is foreseeable that the individual director personally will be held to owe a duty of care. The separate liability of a director or other employee of a company for torts committed by him is not excluded simply because the company is vicariously liable. Similarly the fact that the company may be liable in contract is no reason to exclude liability upon directors or employees for tortious acts."

Everything Gault J said is absolutely correct, if one is speaking of imposed obligations. If Mr Rutherfurd had run over the plaintiffs (pre-ACC) or set fire to their premises he would have been personally liable, and the company vicariously liable. But this was a case of reliance based on assumption of responsibility—by contract. The plaintiffs contracted with the company to provide certain services which Mr Rutherfurd would otherwise have had no obligation to provide. Who assumed a responsibility to provide those services? The company. And, conversely, the plaintiffs were agreeing to look to the company in the event of a breach, knowing that the label "limited" means limited recourse. That is its point. They were voluntary creditors of the company. The company's liability was primary, not vicarious—and Mr Rutherfurd, who had not agreed to undertake any responsibility to the plaintiffs other than "through the vehicle of his company", i.e. with limited personal liability, had no personal liability at all beyond the assets of that company.

Think of this case another way. Suppose Mr Rutherfurd had not formed a company, but contracted personally to provide the relevant services. Suppose the contract said "my liability is limited to $10,000, whether for negligence or otherwise, in the absence of dishonesty or fraud". The courts would give effect to this limitation.[65] There is no inconsistency between assuming responsibility and at the same time limiting liability. It seems to me that this is exactly what Mr Rutherfurd was doing when he interposed his company in his dealings with his clients: he was stipulating that his responsibility to them

[65] See, for example, *DHL International (NZ) Ltd.* v. *Richmond Ltd.* [1993] 3 NZLR 10 (CA); *George Mitchell (Chesterhall) Ltd.* v. *Finney Lock Seeds Ltd.* [1983] 2 AC 803 (HL).

would be limited to the assets of the company. There was no good reason to disregard that contractual term.

Similarly, in *Morton* v. *Douglas Homes Ltd.*,[66] Hardie Boys J held individual directors of a company which had negligently constructed four flats (with inadequate foundations) personally liable in respect of failures to take proper steps to ensure safe construction, where they knew of the need for special precautions, were responsible for supervision of the work and had not properly delegated responsibility for the work to a competent and reliable person. Addressing the question of principle, the judge said:[67]

"The principle of limited liability protects shareholders and not directors, and a director is as responsible for his own torts as any other servant or agent (see for example *Yuille* v. *B & B Fisheries (Leigh) Ltd.* [1958] 2 Lloyd's Rep 596, 619). His liability to the person injured is personal, and unaffected by any right of indemnity he may have against the company. Nonetheless, the separate corporate identity of the company must not be lost sight of, for the directors are not personally liable for the company's tort, except in the limited type of case discussed by Lord Buckmaster in *Rainham Chemical Works Ltd.* v. *Belvedere Fish Guano Co.* [1921] 2 AC 465, 476, namely where the company's wrongful acts were expressly directed by them. Apart from this kind of situation, whilst a director may be liable in negligence to a person with whom the company is dealing, it will only be where he personally, as distinct from the company, owed a duty of care, and failed to observe it. His liability then arises not by reason of his office of director but by reason of a relationship of proximity or neighbourhood existing between him and the plaintiff. It may well be that it is because he is a director that the relationship arises, but the fact that he is a director does not itself create the relationship.

In developing these allegations in their submissions, both Mr Fogarty and Mr Maling, supported as it happened by Mr Hancock, made it clear that they were basing their case not so much on any personal and direct involvement by the directors in the actual building operations, as on the knowledge they had of what was required to ensure the flats were safe, and the control they had to ensure that what was required was in fact done. It is thus on their respective roles as controllers, to use Speight J's expression, that reliance is principally placed. Those roles, it was submitted, became critical here because of the known state of the ground. Thus there is a fundamental distinction on the facts between this case and *Callagham* v. *Robert Ronayne Ltd.*, for that was a simple case of defective workmanship where there were no unusual circumstances to put the directors on their guard that particular care and procedures were required.

Mr Gallagher's reply was that this was in effect imposing liability on their directors by virtue of their office, making them as it were vicariously liable for what could at best be only the negligence of their company. As a test of that, he submitted that there could have been no claim against them had they been employees and not directors. But that is not necessarily so.

Directors play different roles in different companies. Where there are several directors, none of them exercising managerial functions, it would be most unlikely

---

[66] [1984] 2 NZLR 548.
[67] *Ibid.*, at 593.

that any one of them exercises a controlling role, so that liability in tort would be unlikely to arise except on a collective basis in the kind of situation to which Lord Buckmaster referred. On the other hand it may be very different where one of the directors is also the chief executive, or where the company is no more than an incorporated trader, or small partnership, and the directors exercise managerial control themselves.

The relevance of the degree of control which a director has over the operations of the company is that it provides a test of whether or not his personal carelessness may be likely to cause damage to a third party, so that he becomes subject to a duty of care. It is not the fact that he is a director that creates the control, but rather that the fact of control, however derived, may create the duty. There is therefore no essential difference in this respect between a director and a general manager or indeed a more humble employee of the company. Each is under a duty of care, both to those with whom he deals on the company's behalf and to those with whom the company deals in so far as that dealing is subject to his control."

Applying this test, each director was liable in respect of some of the company's failures, but neither was responsible for all. Questions of final authority, control and delegation were reviewed in detail.

Once again, it is helpful to take a wider, contextual view of these dealings. The plaintiffs were purchasers from the company (in respect of three flats), and subsequent purchasers (in respect of one flat). Two flats were sold while incomplete, with the company contracting to complete the construction work. It is difficult to see how it might be argued that the individual directors, rather than the company, had assumed responsibility for the quality or value of the flats. The decision can be justified, if at all, on the grounds that under New Zealand law there is an obligation imposed on every person concerned with the construction of a house to ensure that the house is properly constructed, which is not based on assumption of responsibility.[68] This would be an odd duty, which does not attach to other goods or products: but there is considerable judicial support for its existence, and it enables us to make sense of *Morton*.

(iii) . . . But the Court of Appeal Comes to the Rescue

Fortunately, the Court of Appeal has since set New Zealand law on the right track. In *Trevor Ivory Ltd.* v. *Anderson*,[69] the Court held, on facts very similar to those of *Centrepac*, that Mr Ivory was not personally liable. The plaintiffs owned an orchard in which they grew, among other things, raspberries. They obtained regular advice from Mr Ivory in relation to the orchard, having entered into a contract with his company, Trevor Ivory Ltd., for consultancy services. Mr Ivory provided advice in relation to spraying the orchard, which was acted on by the plaintiffs. The recommended spray killed

---

[68] Compare *Chase* v. *de Groot* [1994] 1 NZLR 613 (HC) and *Willis* v. *Castelein* [1993] 3 NZLR 103 (HC).
[69] [1992] 2 NZLR 517.

not only the target weeds, but also the raspberry plants. The trial judge held that the advice was given negligently and that the company was liable in contract and in tort. He also held Mr Ivory personally liable in tort.

Mr Ivory appealed. Cooke P, as he then was, held that there had been no direct assumption of responsibility by Mr Ivory to the plaintiffs. His Honour said:[70]

> "In this field I agree with Nourse J (as he then was) in the *White Horse* case that it behoves the Courts to avoid imposing on the owner of a one-man company a personal duty of care which would erode the limited liability and separate identify principles associated with the names of Salomon and Lee. Viewing the issue as one of the assumption of a duty of care, which is the way in which Mr Fogarty for the respondents rightly asked us to view it, I cannot think it reasonable to say that Mr Ivory assumed a duty of care to the plaintiffs as if he were carrying on business on his own account and not through a company.
>
> If the present case were in the personal injuries field, I might have been disposed in alignment with Willmer LJ in *Yuille* to have found a personal duty of care on Mr Ivory, on the basis of the very obvious risk to health in handling herbicides. We do not have that question in New Zealand since the Accident Compensation Act 1982. Where damage to property or other economic loss is the basis of a claim, it may well be possible to sheet home personal responsibility for an intentional tort such as deceit or knowing conversion. And of course if the individual defendant has placed himself in a fiduciary position towards the plaintiff, he will be personally liable for breach of fiduciary duty. But if an economic loss claim depends on establishing a personal duty of care, it is especially important to consider how far the duty asserted would cut across patterns of law evolved over the years in the process of balancing interests. Some discussion of that subject will be found in the *South Pacific* judgments to which I refer without repetition. In the instant case it is patent that the object of Mr Ivory in forming a limited liability company, an object encouraged by long-established legislative policy, would be undermined by imposing personal liability.
>
> Perhaps the contrary result reached in the High Court reflects partly the inculcated belief of many present-day lawyers that there is a clear and water-tight division between contract and tort, and that the two heads of liability should be considered quite separately. *Hedley Byrne*, now a quarter of a century old, may be cited to show that it can be a simplistic belief.
>
> Without venturing further into what some would see as unduly theoretical, if not heterodox, I commit myself to the opinion that, when he formed his company, Mr Ivory made it plain to all the world that limited liability was intended. Possibly the plaintiffs gave little thought to that in entering into the consultancy contract; but such a limitation is a common fact of business and, in relation to economic loss and duties of care, the consequence should in my view be accepted in the absence of special circumstances. It is not to be doubted that, in relation to an obligation to give careful and skilful advice, the owner of a one-man company may assume personal responsibility. *Fairline* is an analogy. But it seems to me that something special is required to justify putting a case in that class. To attempt to define in advance what

---

[70] [1992] 2 NZLR 517, at 523–4.

might be sufficiently special would be a contradiction in terms. What can be said is that there is nothing out of the ordinary here."

Centrepac was not expressly disapproved. However, Cooke P did note that the judge appeared to have considered solely the high degree of foreseeability, and thus proximity, without considering the wider issues of whether there are policy reasons for not finding a duty of care to exist, as restated in the recent decision of *South Pacific Manufacturing Co. Ltd.* v. *New Zealand Security Consultants & Investigations Ltd.*[71] His Honour also noted that *Morton* v. *Douglas Homes Ltd.* was at first sight an authority in support of the plaintiffs' case. However, he was "content to accept that on the particular facts there was an assumption of responsibility. Clearly the judgment was not intended to lay down a general rule in building negligence cases; and it would be unsafe to try to argue from one particular set of facts to another."[72]

Hardie Boys J agreed that "the test is or at least includes, whether there has been an assumption of responsibility, actual or imputed. That is an appropriate test for the personal liability of both a director and an employee."[73] His Honour continued:[74]

"It was the basis upon which the director was held liable in *Fairline Shipping Corporation* v. *Adamson* [1975] QB 180, (see p 189), where the assumption of responsibility was virtually express. It may lie behind the finding of liability in *Centrepac Partnership* v. *Foreign Currency Consultants Ltd.* (1989) 4 NZCLC 64,940. Assumption of responsibility may well arise or be imputed where the director or employee exercises particular control or control over a particular operation or activity, as in *Adler* v. *Dickson* [1955] 1 QB 158 (although there the issue did not arise, as it was a pre-trial decision on a different point of law). *Yuille* v. *B & B Fisheries (Leigh) Ltd.* [1958] 2 Lloyd's Rep 596 is another illustration. This is perhaps more likely to arise within a large company where there are clear allocations of responsibility, than in a small one. It arose however in the case of a small company in *Morton* v. *Douglas Home Ltd.* [1984] 2 NZLR 548, 593ff; but not in a case to which I made some reference in my judgment in *Morton*, namely *Callagham* v. *Robert Ronayne Ltd.* (Auckland, A 1112/76), 17 September 1979), a judgment of Speight J. It may be that in the present case there would have been a sufficient assumption of responsibility had Mr Ivory undertaken to do the spraying himself, but it is not necessary to consider that possibility.

   Where a director is said to have authorised, directed or procured the commission of a tort by his company, or indeed by an employee, the inquiry is rather different, and the cases in that area, such as *C Evans & Sons Ltd.* v. *Spritebrand Ltd.* [1985] 2 All ER 415 in the English Court of Appeal and *Kalamazoo (Aust.) Pty. Ltd.* v. *Compact Business Systems Pty. Ltd.* (1985) 5 IPR 213 in the Supreme Court of Queensland are not really in point, save as a reminder of the need for care in fixing directors with negligence."

---

71 [1992] 2 NZLR 282 (CA).
72 [1992] 2 NZLR 517, 523.
73 *Ibid.*, at 527.
74 *Ibid.*
75 *Ibid.*, at 532.

The third member of the Court, McGechan J, said:[75]

"When it comes to assumption of responsibility, I do not accept a company director of a one-man company is to be regarded as automatically accepting tort responsibility for advice given on behalf of the company by himself. There may be situations where such liability tends to arise, particularly perhaps where the director as a person is highly prominent and his company is barely visible, resulting in a focus predominantly on the man himself. All will depend upon the facts of individual cases, and the degree of implicit assumption of personal responsibility, with no doubt some policy elements also applying. I do not think this is such a case, although it approaches the line. While the respondents looked at his personal expertise, Mr Ivory made it clear that he traded through a company, which was to be the legal contracting party entitled to charge. That structure was negotiated and known. There was nothing like the persona superimposition so central to the decision in the *Fairline* case. There was no representation, express or implicit, of personal involvement, as distinct from routine involvement for and through his company. There was no singular feature which would justify belief that Mr Ivory was accepting a personal commitment, as opposed to the known company obligation. If anything, the intrinsic high risk nature of spray advice, and his deliberate adoption of an intervening company structure would have pointed to the contrary likelihood. On the present facts, I see no policy justification for imposing an additional duty of care. In this particular one-man company situation, and against the established trading understandings, I would not view such as just and reasonable."

In his recent Hamlyn lecture on the *Salomon* case, Lord Cooke of Thorndon identified the decision in *Trevor Ivory* as an example of the *Salomon* principle waxing, rather than waning.[76] The case is discussed under the heading "Taking *Salomon* further".[77] With respect, *Trevor Ivory* does not so much take *Salomon* further as hold its traditional ground (somewhat tentatively) in the face of a new foe. The Andersons were voluntary creditors of the company. They knew who they were dealing with. As Lord Macnaghten put it one hundred years ago, "there was no fraud or misrepresentation, and there was nobody deceived".[78] The Andersons were simply trying to use tort to improve their contractual bargain, to set aside the limited recourse term which applied by virtue of contracting with the company. But there is absolutely no ground, from a legal or an economic perspective, for permitting the contract to be rewritten in this way. The limited recourse term is just like an exclusion clause: and the courts have repeatedly held that tort claims based on concurrent liability should not and cannot be used to get around such clauses.[79] The same can be said, in equally unequivocal terms, about the use of tort to establish concurrent unlimited liability on the part of owners or controllers of the company.

[76] Lord Cooke of Thorndon, *Turning Points of the Common Law* (London, Sweet and Maxwell, 1997), 18.

[77] *Ibid.*

[78] [1897] AC 22, 54.

[79] See, for example, *Rowlands* v. *Collow* [1992] 1 NZLR 178, 191 (HC); *Central Trust Co.* v. *Rafuse* (1986) 31 DLR (4th) 481, 522 (SCC); *Henderson* v. *Merrett Syndicates Ltd.* [1995] 2 AC 145, 191 (HL).

Cooke P's judgment in *Trevor Ivory* is undoubtedly, in my view, one of the most perceptive recent judicial treatments of the relationship between the limited recourse nature of contracts entered into with companies and tort claims based on assumption of responsibility. The judgment identifies the critical factor: the term of limited liability represented by the interposition of the company. It also alludes to the distinction between cases such as *Trevor Ivory* and cases involving personal injury or intentional torts.

My one complaint is that the judgment does not go far enough into the territory described as "unsafe" and lay down a few general principles. Those principles flow direct from *Salomon*, and from the analysis set out above. The distinction identified by Cooke P in *Trevor Ivory*, between that case and personal injury cases, and by La Forest J in *London Drugs*,[80] between planned transactions and true "stranger cases", has a very simple foundation. As I have suggested above, the distinction is founded on a very important difference between imposed obligations, and obligations assumed voluntarily (e.g. in a "planned transaction"). Where the only source of obligations is their assumption in a contractual setting, the conclusion that the contracting parties are assuming reciprocal obligations and that persons not party to the contract continue with the normal imposed obligations but no others, is in most cases irresistible. The parties' dealings in *Trevor Ivory* make perfect sense as consensual dealings with an express limited recourse term. But surely the same is true of *Centrepac*, and also of *Morton* v. *Douglas Homes Ltd*. Conversely, in *London Drugs*, the employees damaged goods in breach of a general obligation imposed by law to refrain from carelessly damaging the property of others. The majority's decision, that the company's employees were not personally liable, seems clearly correct—just as it would be if the employees had stolen the goods in question. Far from anxiously considering the particular facts of each case, appellate courts could usefully set out some simple principles along these lines, to provide guidance to judges and advisers in this troubling field, and thus preserve the integrity of *Salomon*.

(iv) What Are the English Courts Doing?

Despite room for some nervousness about the "case by case" approach suggested in *Trevor Ivory*, one might think the New Zealand courts would, guided by the judgment of Cooke P, largely eschew finding an owner/director liable on the basis of "assumption of responsibility" tort. The Canadian courts seem similarly set on a course of respecting the terms on which the parties dealt: in addition to *Sealand of the Pacific* v. *Robert C McHaffie Ltd.*,[81] followed in *Trevor Ivory*, there have been subsequent decisions to similar effect, such as *Montreal Trust Co. of Canada* v. *Scotia McLeod Inc.*[82]

---

[80] *London Drugs Ltd.* v. *Kuehne & Nagel International Ltd.* (1992) 97 DLR (4th) 261.
[81] (1974) 51 DLR (3d) 702 (BCCA).
[82] Unreported, Ontario HC, Farley J, 29 Sept. 1994, 1994 Ont CJ Lexis 2871. As Farley J said

But despite citation of *Trevor Ivory*, the opposite result has been reached recently in England by the High Court and the Court of Appeal in *Williams* v. *Natural Life Health Foods Ltd.*[83]

In that case, the plaintiffs were franchisees of the defendant company, which marketed health food franchises. The plaintiffs purchased their franchise from the company following receipt of detailed advice and financial projections prepared by the company and its employees, which were held to be deficient in numerous respects. The company was in breach of a duty owed to the plaintiffs to ensure that the information and projections provided were reasonably and properly prepared, on the basis of the expertise and experience that the company professed to have.[84]

So far, so good. But the company was insolvent, and the plaintiffs also sought to establish breach of a duty of care on the part of its managing director (and, in substance, sole shareholder), Mr Mistlin. Mr Mistlin was held liable, on the ground that he had assumed a personal responsibility to the plaintiffs for the projections—even though he had few direct dealings with them and had never discussed the projections with them! This assumption of responsibility was justified primarily on the basis that it was Mr Mistlin's personal experience which the company was selling, and that Mr Mistlin "must have known that any potential franchisee would expect . . . the projections to have his personal stamp of approval, based on his experience at [his own shop]".[85]

Mr Mistlin appealed, with *Trevor Ivory* in the forefront of counsel's argument before the Court of Appeal. He lost. Hirst LJ considered that the reason Mr Mistlin was liable was that the knowledge and experience being marketed by the company was Mr Mistlin's knowledge and experience, derived in his personal capacity and not in his capacity as a director or officer of the company. His Lordship said:[86]

> "In other words the relevant knowledge and experience was entirely his qua Mr Mistlin, and not his qua director. Indeed I would go so far as to say that, in reality, Mr Mistlin held himself out as personally responsible for the only figures available to support the projections, as was indeed the fact.
>
> In my judgment this, coupled with all the other facts described above, takes this case out of the ordinary and gives it its special character which justifies the prima facie case upheld by the judge, even when making full allowance for the fact that this was a one-man company.

in that case: "In misrepresentation cases I would think the question (keeping in mind how corporations speak generally) is: 'Who is speaking?'" His Lordship concluded: "Given that the statements were made in [the directors'] capacity as officers and directors of [the company], it would not seem that there was any personal voluntary assumption of responsibility."

[83] [1996] BCC 376 (HC); [1997] 1 BCLC 131 (CA).

[84] Although the contract with the company contained certain exclusion clauses, the defendant did not attempt to argue that they were reasonable and thus effective under the Unfair Contract Terms Act 1977 (UK).

[85] [1997] 1 BCLC 131, 153.

[86] *Ibid.*

The case is thus somewhat akin to the *Fairline* case, and is distinguishable from the *Trevor Ivory* case not in principle, but because, as a matter of fact and degree, whereas the former lay (albeit narrowly) on one side of the line, this case falls on the other side.

I should emphasise that I have reached this conclusion solely on the particular facts of this case, and I do not think there is any risk of compromising the general concept of limited liability."

Waite LJ agreed with Hirst LJ. Sir Patrick Russell dissented, gaining "particular assistance from *Trevor Ivory*".[87] As Sir Patrick pointed out, Mr Mistlin "never stepped outside his function of managing director of the first defendant, nor did he do or say anything save in that capacity".[88]

The decision is irreconcilable with *Trevor Ivory*. Clearly Mr Ivory was marketing his personal expertise and knew that any advice given was expected to have his personal stamp of approval—whose else, indeed, could it have? This was not sufficient for Mr Ivory to be liable. The short point is that however the experience was obtained, whoever it may be who gathered it, it was being onsold by the company. In *Williams*, the company was selling expertise in operating health food shops—it is quite irrelevant that it was purchasing that expertise from an employee who acquired the expertise in another capacity.

The decision is also, in my view, irreconcilable with *Salomon*. The plaintiffs had chosen to deal with the company. They signed a contract with the company. They were voluntary creditors (who, moreover, had had legal advice on the franchise agreement). They should have been held to their bargain, rather than having a new one written by the court with a new, conveniently solvent, party.

Williams illustrates the danger of a case-by-case, "on the particular facts" approach to issues of general application. The plaintiffs inspired sympathy. The defendants did not. It is relatively easy to recite a list of facts, then say (with the High Court judge) "the totality of the evidence, as I have stated it, establishes that this is an exceptional case".[89] No principled basis for this "exception" was identified. Indeed Hirst LJ accepted that there was no distinction of principle from *Trevor Ivory*. Absent principle, how can distinctions—even of fact and degree—be drawn? The courts did not even mention the central issue—the limited recourse term implicit (if not explicit) in contracting to provide advice through a company.

I hope *Williams* is not good law in New Zealand. *Trevor Ivory* leaves room for similar conclusions to be reached, because it did not state clear principles or overrule *Centrepac*. Yet the actual decision in *Trevor Ivory* is founded on principle, not "fact and degree"—let alone narrow margins of fact and degree.

---

[87] *Ibid.*, at 155.
[88] *Ibid.*, at 156.
[89] *Ibid.*, at 153.

B Pooling of Assets of Companies in Liquidation

The rebuff of common law inroads on *Salomon* in cases such as *Trevor Ivory* is more than made up for by recent statutory attacks. One significant provision is section 271 of the Companies Act 1993 (NZ), which provides:

"(1) On the application of the liquidator, or a creditor or shareholder, the Court, if satisfied that it is just and equitable to do so, may order that —

(a) A company that is, or has been, related to the company in liquidation must pay to the liquidator the whole or part of any or all of the claims made in the liquidation;

(b) Where 2 or more related companies are in liquidation, the liquidations in respect of each company must proceed together as if they were one company to the extent that the Court so orders and subject to such terms and conditions as the Court may impose.

(2) The Court may make such other order or give such directions to facilitate giving effect to an order under subsection (1) of this section as it thinks fit."

Section 272 sets out guidelines for orders under section 271:

"(1) In deciding whether it is just and equitable to make an order under section 271(1)(a) of this Act, the Court must have regard to the following matters:

(a) The extent to which the related company took part in the management of the company in liquidation;

(b) The conduct of the related company towards the creditors of the company in liquidation;

(c) The extent to which the circumstances that gave rise to the liquidation of the company are attributable to the actions of the related company;

(d) Such other matters as the Court thinks fit.

(2) In deciding whether it is just and equitable to make an order under section 271(1)(b) of this Act, the Court must have regard to the following matters:

(a) The extent to which any of the companies took part in the management of any of the other companies;

(b) The conduct of any of the companies towards the creditors of any of the other companies;

(c) The extent to which the circumstances that gave rise to the liquidation of any of the companies are attributable to the actions of any of the other companies;

(d) The extent to which the business of the companies have been combined;

(e) Such other matters as the Court thinks fit.

(3) The fact that creditors of a company in liquidation relied on the fact that another company is, or was, related to it is not a ground for making an order under section 271 of this Act."

These provisions were introduced in 1980. They were based on recommendations in the Macarthur Committee Report in 1973.[90] That Report sets out a few vague concerns, in particular about "the case of a holding company

---

[90] Final Report of the Special Committee to Review the Companies Act, Mar. 1973 (1973 AJHR IV, H7 at 159).

which may seek to abandon its subsidiary",[91] and moves without further analysis to a recommendation that "the Court should be empowered, on the application of the liquidator of the subsidiary, to make an order that the holding company pay the whole or part of the subsidiary company's liabilities to its creditors".[92]

Where the affairs of the companies have been so commingled that it is impossible to know which of the companies in a group entered into certain transactions, or owned certain assets, joint liquidation seems clearly appropriate. But the criteria in section 272(2) seem surprisingly broad.

Contribution to an insolvent company's debts by a solvent related company is still more problematic. Where a parent company is called on to contribute to the debts of a subsidiary, in particular, the *Salomon* principle is clearly challenged. If the creditors of the insolvent company knew who they were dealing with, what is the case for contribution? How can it be relevant that the solvent company "took part in the management of the company in liquidation", if it did not commit any breach of duty to the company in so doing and is not liable for losses suffered as a result? If an individual shareholder who took part in the company's management would not be liable, why impose liability on a corporate shareholder?[93]

An economically rational case for contribution by a related company is made out only if, and to the extent that:

(a) creditors were led to believe they were giving credit to the surviving company, or that some assets of the surviving company were in fact assets of the insolvent company, and such representations were material to those creditors; or

(b) a parent company is a deemed director under section 126 of the Companies Act 1993, due to the control it exercises over a subsidiary's affairs, and is liable for losses caused by insolvent trading on the basis applicable to directors generally.

Sections 271 and 272 go far beyond these bounds, and require careful review if *Salomon* is to survive in the corporate group context.[94]

---

[91] *Ibid.*, at para 405.

[92] *Ibid.*

[93] Professor Ramsay's essay, Chap 12, notes the argument that some of the justifications for limited liability are weaker where the sole shareholder is a company. The justifications for giving effect to the default limited recourse term in dealings with voluntary creditors, where it has not been waived, are not affected in any way by the identity of the shareholder or shareholders. So far as involuntary creditors are concerned, it is correct that the arguments for limited liability are weaker for closely held companies than for widely held companies—but it seems immaterial that the sole shareholder is a company, rather than an individual. If the arguments for making shareholders of closely held companies liable without limit to involuntary creditors generally are not accepted, it is difficult to see the rationale for doing so where the shareholder is a company. In particular, generalised assumptions about the relative risk aversion of individuals and companies do not provide a rationale for so doing.

[94] A number of writers have commented on the special issues which *Salomon* is said to raise in the group context: see, for example, R Baxt, "The Need to Review the Rule in *Salomon's* Case

C Trading While Insolvent

Another set of provisions which has the potential to undermine the core *Salomon* principle is the liability imposed by statute on directors of companies which have continued to trade while insolvent. Under the Companies Act 1955 (NZ), in force before the 1993 amendments, liability could be imposed on a director or an officer of a company in liquidation, if the court so ordered, where:

(a) that person was knowingly a party to the contracting of a debt by the company and did not, at the time the debt was contracted, honestly believe on reasonable grounds that the company would be able to pay the debt when it fell due; or

(b) that person was knowingly a party to the carrying on of any business of the company in a reckless manner; or

(c) that person was knowingly a party to the carrying on of any business of the company with intent to defraud its creditors, or creditors of any other person, or for any fraudulent purpose.

Under the 1993 Act, the approach is somewhat different, and the exposure of directors greater still. Sections 135 and 136 provide:

> "135 Reckless trading
> A director of a company must not—
> (a) agree to the business of the company being carried on in a manner likely to create a substantial risk of serious loss to the company's creditors; or
> (b) cause or allow the business of the company to be carried on in a manner likely to create a substantial risk of serious loss to the company's creditors.
> 136 Duty in relation to obligations
> A director of a company must not agree to the company incurring an obligation unless that director believes at that time on reasonable grounds that the company will be able to perform the obligation when it is required to do so."

In my view, these provisions go far beyond the scope of any proper liability for failure to disclose risk. The existence of a substantial risk of serious loss to creditors (section 135) is a feature of many high risk businesses. Creditors can decline credit or can price accordingly. More importantly, if a creditor is aware of the risk and agrees to run it, where is the rationale for director liability?

as it Applies to Groups of Companies" (1991) 9 *CSLJ* 185; R Baxt, "Tensions Between Commercial Reality and Legal Principle—Should the Concept of the Corporate Entity be Re-examined?" (1991) 65 *ALJ* 352 and the cases and articles referred to therein. However, does not everything depend on how the group is administered and on whether the affairs of the separate companies are indeed separately conducted? Absent misrepresentation or deceit, why should corporate shareholders be less entitled to the benefits of limited recourse contracting with respect to defined parts of the group business? There is every reason to allow such arrangements, and no good reason to undermine them as a matter of general practice.

This objection applies even more strongly to section 136. Both director and creditor may know that the company may not be able to perform a contract—but the risk may be acceptable to the creditor, who knows that the company alone will be answerable for its failure to perform and may not have sufficient assets to pay damages. Why does the law intervene to impose liability on the director?

These provisions create a "substantial risk of serious loss" of the legal effect given to limited recourse by *Salomon*.[95] They preclude the very "enterprise and adventure" that the companies legislation seeks to encourage, and they ignore the fundamental precept that people can expect to be held to their contracts unless they have been deceived in a respect which is material to them, by express misstatement or by silence in circumstances where there was a duty to speak.

There is a case for a more limited ability to recover from directors where deceptions have been practised on creditors, expressly or by silence. There may also be a case for provisions imposing liability on controllers where a company trades on after insolvent liquidation is inevitable, taking excessive risks with creditors' funds, along the lines of the United Kingdom regime.[96] Even under that regime, which is considerably narrower than that of New Zealand, the absence of provision for contracting out is difficult to reconcile with the rationale for such rules.[97] If there is to be liability in this area, there is much to be said for a well defined statutory regime which balances risks and incentives, and provides safe harbours for managers, rather than leaving development of the law to broad brush obligations fashioned by the courts.[98] But the recent New Zealand reforms in this area are misconceived, and should be revisited.

D Director Liability for Failure to Keep Accounts

Finally, in this brief parade of provisions of the Companies Act 1993 (NZ) which may intrude on the *Salomon* principle, we find section 300, which provides:
   "(1) Subject to subsection (2) of this section, if—
      (a) A company that is in liquidation and is unable to pay all its debts has failed to comply with—

---

[95] For a more sanguine analysis of the effect of these provisions, see Hon Justice D Tompkins, "Directing the Directors: The Duties of Directors Under the Companies Act 1993" (1994) 2 *Waikato L Rev* 13. His Honour's approach is based on reading into these provisions some significant qualifications and glosses which are notably absent from the statutory language, and His Honour acknowledges that it would have been preferable for the statute to set these out expressly.

[96] See generally the discussion of these issues in Professor Prentice's essay, and Mr Telfer's insightful commentary on that essay, in this volume.

[97] For other criticisms, see Cheffins, n. 51 above, 537–48.

[98] As in, for example, *Kinsela* v. *Russell Kinsela Pty. Ltd.* (1986) 4 NSWLR 722; *Nicholson* v. *Permakraft (NZ) Ltd.* [1985] 1 NZLR 242; *Winkworth* v. *Edward Baron Development Co. Ltd.* [1987] 1 All ER 114.

(i)   Section 194 of this Act [which relates to the keeping of accounting records]; or

(ii) Section 10 of the Financial Reporting Act 1993 [which relates to the preparation of financial statements]; and

(b) The Court considers that—

(i)   The failure to comply has contributed to the company's inability to pay all its debts, or has resulted in substantial uncertainty as to the assets and liabilities of the company, or has substantially impeded the orderly liquidation; or

(ii) For any other reason it is proper to make a declaration under this section,—

the Court, on the application of the liquidator, may, if it thinks it proper to do so, declare that any one or more of the directors and former directors of the company is, or are, personally responsible, without limitation of liability, for all or any part of the debts and other liabilities of the company as the Court may direct."

What the law says here is, in effect, that directors must stop trading, not only if they know the company is insolvent, but also if they would have known this had proper accounting records been kept and proper financial statements been prepared. This provision troubles me, for two reasons:

(a) it goes beyond the normal subjective trigger of disclosure obligations, effectively imposing an obligation to know whether or not certain facts exist; and

(b) disclosure is not a defence: even if a creditor knows the company's affairs are a muddle, the directors may be liable for the debt. Should an accountant hired to sort out the company's defective records be able to obtain the benefit of this provision?

Imposition of liability for objectively misleading conduct now appears to be well entrenched in New Zealand law, under the Fair Trading Act 1986, which is of course based on provisions of the Australian Trade Practices Act 1974. If this law is defensible in commercial contexts, a question on which I entertain considerable doubt, it would be difficult to object to section 300 on the first of these grounds. And if there is to be director liability for insolvent trading, an objective requirement that the directors know the financial position of the company is an integral part of any such regime. So the first concern is not, perhaps, a significant one.

The court's discretion under section 300 (a palliative lacking with respect to sections 135 and 136) may enable consent to dealing with the company by a creditor with notice of the correct facts to be raised as a defence. However, it would be preferable for the provision to provide expressly that a creditor may contract out of the protection which section 300 provides.

E "Lifting the Veil"

I come, finally, to cases on "lifting the veil". It is not easy to know what is meant by this phrase. Most cases appear to be responses to the peculiarities of particular statutory regimes which the court is asked to apply to a company or group of companies to produce a surprising or unjust result. For example, *DHN Food Distributors Ltd.* v. *Tower Hamlets LBC*[99] is one of several cases concerned with compensation for the compulsory purchase of land, where a statute draws a seemingly arbitrary distinction between the compensation to be paid where the owner of land is in occupation of the land and where some other person is in occupation.[100] I do not believe that any general principle about corporate personality can be derived from such cases.[101]

All that can be said is, paraphrasing Lord Hoffmann in *Meridian*, that if the statute was intended to apply to a company "how was it meant to apply? . . . One finds the answer to this question by applying the usual canons of interpretation, taking into account the language of the rule (if it is a statute) and its content and policy."[102]

This approach is illustrated by the decision of the House of Lords in *Daimler Co. Ltd.* v. *Continental Tyre and Rubber Co. (Great Britain) Ltd.*,[103] where it was held that a company incorporated in England, all but one of the shares of which were owned by enemy aliens, could in substance be treated as an enemy alien if the persons in control of its affairs had that character. The special nature of the question whether a company is to be treated as an enemy alien, with the disabilities that that status engenders, obviously precludes an automatic and unthinking application of the "separate personality" doctrine as a complete answer. Rather, a substantive test, such as that outlined by Lord Parker,[104] must be adopted. Corporate personality is not being disregarded: an appropriate test for the character of that personality is, rather, being devised.

Nor is corporate personality disregarded when:

(a) a covenant in restraint of trade is enforced against a former employee carrying on business through a company: the prohibition must obviously as a matter of necessary implication extend to such a device;[105] or

---

[99] [1976] 1 WLR 852 (CA).

[100] See also *Smith, Stone and Knight Ltd.* v. *Birmingham* [1939] 4 All ER 116; *Woolfson* v. *Strathclyde Regional Council*, 1978 SLT 159 (HL).

[101] See Professor Ramsay's essay, Chap 12, for a study of Australian cases which tends to confirm the lack of any pattern or guiding principle in this field.

[102] [1995] 2 AC 500, 507.

[103] [1916] 2 AC 307.

[104] *Ibid.*, at 340.

[105] See *Gildford Motor Co.* v. *Horne* [1933] 1 Ch 935 (CA).

(b) equitable title to land is enforced by a decree of specific performance against a company formed by a reluctant vendor, to which he has transferred the land in an attempt to avoid performance. The company has notice of the purchaser's claim, and takes subject to that claim on normal equitable principles.[106]

In his recent Hamlyn Lecture, Lord Cooke suggests that:

(a) there is only one broad class of case where the cases on "lifting the veil" are consistent with the *Salomon* reasoning. "They are all cases where, under enactments such as those against fraudulent or wrongful trading, or on the permissible interpretation of an enactment or contract, or for the purposes of common law or equitable principles against fraud or oppression or relating to agency, it is necessary to look at what has happened in fact rather than form."[107]
(b) the sham or facade exception to *Salomon* is itself a sham—"unneeded and unsound".[108]

Certainly, it is difficult to see how any of these cases can be seen as an exception to *Salomon* in any meaningful way. None makes any inroad into the limited recourse rule. *Salomon* did not decide that a company is never to be identified with its shareholders or that the identity of the shareholders and controllers of a company can never be relevant to legal issues affecting the company. Such a rule would be plainly absurd. It was not enunciated by the House of Lords in *Salomon*. The exception industry is founded on a misconception.

The closest the House of Lords in *Salomon* came to providing support for that misconception is probably Lord Halsbury's reference to the company as "a real thing",[109] a phrase Lord Cooke took as the title of his Hamlyn lecture on *Salomon*. But one must always bear in mind the fact that, as Lord Hoffmann said in *Meridian*, "there is in fact no such thing as the company as such, no *Ding an sich*, only the applicable rules".[110] We should ask ourselves what those rules are, rather than allow ourselves to be captured by the legal equivalent of Dr Frankenstein's monster. Any "reality" the company enjoys is legal reality, nothing more, and the law can and must define the parameters of that "reality". It would not have had the same ring, but I cannot help wishing that Lord Cooke's lecture had been entitled "A really important default term"!

---

[106] *Jones* v. *Lipman* [1962] 1 WLR 832.
[107] Lord Cooke of Thorndon, n. 76 above, 13.
[108] *Ibid.*, at 17.
[109] *Ibid.*
[110] [1995] 3 NZLR 7, 12.

IV CONCLUSIONS

My conclusions are simple. First, *Salomon* is about limited recourse. The case decided that the limited recourse default term is not displaced where one person controls a company and has beneficial ownership of all its shares. Secondly, this default rule is of enormous practical importance—it is present in the vast majority of contracts entered into in commerce today. Thirdly, the *Salomon* rule is well founded in economic principle. Voluntary creditors of companies who deal on the basis of this default term, and who can address the risk it poses in many different ways, have no grounds for complaint. The only concern relates to imposed obligations (i.e. obligations to involuntary creditors). Yet even here:

(a) the problem is less extensive than is sometimes portrayed, since owners who personally breach such obligations, or who are parties to such breaches, do not escape liability. In particular, the problem is unlikely to arise in relation to smaller companies, where one or two owners are also the primary controllers and executives;

(b) the benefits of extending vicarious tort liability to owners of companies, in terms of enhanced incentives, are far from certain. Tort law is a blunt and unsatisfactory instrument for internalising costs in many contexts—and the economic benefits of vicarious liability are even less clear. The gains from "perfecting" the reach of tort liability, in the context of corporations, remain to be demonstrated;

(c) an unlimited liability regime would however give rise to some certain, and potentially significant costs, including the development and administration of complex rules in relation to fixing of liability, tracing through intermediate owners and enforcement of liability, and costs incurred by investors taking other steps to minimise liability (e.g. asset divestiture);

(d) there are also countervailing benefits from limited liability in terms of reduction in monitoring costs and efficiency gains in capital markets in all but the smallest of companies. These benefits are particularly significant in relation to larger companies whose securities are widely traded;

(e) the problem of externalisation of imposed obligation liabilities is not peculiar to companies. Limited liability is pervasive in our law, and is also enjoyed by natural persons. Where this is a particular concern, there are other ways of addressing the problem which are more effective and less distortionary than making inroads into limited liability.

The *Salomon* principle has come under attack, especially in more recent years. The New Zealand courts are (by and large) holding the line. The English position is less clear. It is essential, if the law in this area is not to undermine *Salomon* fundamentally, that the relationship between tort obligations of different kinds and incorporation should be stated as a matter of principle, rather than being addressed on a "case-by-case" basis. Tort claims based on assumption of responsibility should not be permitted to blur the line: *Centrepac* (and *Williams*) should be explicitly overruled.

On the legislative front, recent developments in relation to director liability and contribution by group companies go far beyond what is necessary or desirable. Once again, the statement of some underlying principles would enable much unfocussed concern to be cleared away, and sensible rules adopted.

On the whole, New Zealand law still gives effect to the *Salomon* doctrine. But both the legislature and the courts need to ensure that it does not die a death of a thousand cuts.

3

Commentary on Goddard

ROSS GRANTHAM*

There is a tendency in corporate law to dismiss the debate as to the nature of corporate personality as a sterile, metaphysical enterprise that is incapable of providing answers to real problems. The nature of the company, however, is important.[1] The theoretical underpinnings both "tilt"[2] the outcome of cases and establish the criteria by which we evaluate the utility and legitimacy of the corporate form. Mr Goddard's essay represents an important contribution to this debate. Dealing principally with limited liability, he employs the tools of law and economics analysis to demonstrate both the fundamental soundness of the *Salomon*[3] doctrine and the threat posed by recent developments, especially in the law of tort. There is much learning in Mr Goddard's essay, and much to agree with. However, two points can usefully be made.

I LIMITED LIABILITY

Mr Goddard's essay ranges an impressive array of arguments to demonstrate the efficiency, and hence legitimacy, of limited liability. I think, however, that the case he puts requires qualification in three respects.

First, in respect of voluntary creditors, the arguments resting on the consensual nature of the dealings are generally compelling. As the creditor is aware that he is dealing with a company, and of the risks associated with that, there is unlikely to be any systematic externalisation of the costs of the credit. Subject to deliberate misrepresentation, the price of credit will reflect both the cost of capital and the risk of default. However, at the margins this argument breaks down.[4] Where, for example, the company engages in excessively risky activity *after* the credit has been provided, the price necessarily falls below the

---

* Senior Lecturer, The University of Auckland.

[1] M Stokes, "Company Law and Legal Theory" in W Twining (ed.), *Legal Theory and Common Law* (Oxford, Blackwell, 1986), 161.

[2] M Horwitz, "*Santa Clara* Revisited: The Development of Corporate Theory" (1985) 88 *West Virginia L Rev* 173, 176, rejecting in the language of the Critical Legal Studies movement the claim of the American Realists that legal conceptions are infinitely "flippable".

[3] *Salomon* v. *A Salomon & Co. Ltd.* [1897] 2 AC 22.

[4] For a fuller account, see R Grantham, "Judicial Extension of Directors' Duties to Creditors" [1991] *JBL* 1.

true risk. The company thus externalises a portion of the cost of credit. While the need for future capital will normally restrain this externalising conduct, where the company faces insolvency such conduct is rational. There is no longer a need to instill confidence in lenders, and the limited liability of shareholders makes it logical for them to undertake an investment which is "riskier but alone offers the possibility, albeit remote, of a bonanza payoff that will prevent insolvency".[5] From this perspective, the recent inroads into limited liability in the form of wrongful trading liability[6] are a justifiable response to a market failure and the real question is whether the response is appropriately tailored to the risk.[7]

Secondly, in respect of corporate tort creditors, the arguments concerning limited liability are more finely balanced than Mr Goddard's essay might suggest.[8] In recent years, particularly in the United States, there have been several powerful arguments raised against limited liability in this context. Thus, Hansmann and Kraakman[9] demonstrate that in some circumstances limited liability encourages over-investment in hazardous industries. As the costs associated with such activities are borne by creditors, it is an attractive investment for shareholders.[10] It has also been suggested that limited liability in this context is undesirable because shareholders are better risk-bearers than the victims of torts: while shareholders can diversify their investment, individual tort creditors cannot.[11] Although it is true that at present the law shows no real sign of withdrawing limited liability in respect of corporate torts,[12] and while, as Mr Goddard points out, limited liability is an important prerequisite in the operation of capital markets, the case for limited liability in this context is by no means unassailable.

Finally, implicit in much of the law and economics literature is the normative assertion that allocative efficiency is *the* appropriate social goal. From this perspective, the efficiency of limited liability also serves to legitimate it. However, it is worth remembering that there are other more pluralistic

---

[5] J Coffee, "Shareholders Versus Managers: The Strain in the Corporate Web" (1986) 85 *Michigan L Rev* 1, 61.

[6] Companies Act 1993 (NZ), ss 135–136.

[7] In particular, whether liability for insolvent trading should exist, as it does in New Zealand, throughout the life of the company, or only where the company is in or on the verge of insolvency. The nature of the risk outlined here suggests creditors need the protection beyond that offered by market mechanisms only where the company is facing insolvency.

[8] For useful overviews of the competing arguments, see B Pettet, "Limited Liability—A Principle for the 21st Century?" [1995] CLP 125 and B R Cheffins, *Company Law—Theory, Structure and Operation* (Oxford, OUP, 1997), 507.

[9] H Hansmann and R Kraakman, "Toward Unlimited Shareholder Liability for Corporate Torts" (1991) 100 *Yale L J* 1879.

[10] Similar arguments appear in D W Leebron, "Limited Liability, Tort Victims, and Creditors" (1991) 91 *Columbia L Rev* 1565 and P Halpern, M Trebilcock and M Turnbull, "An Economic Analysis of Limited Liability in Corporation Law" (1980) 30 *Univ Toronto L J* 117.

[11] Leebron, n. 10 above, 1603.

[12] Compare, however, *Williams v. Natural Life Health Foods Ltd.* [1997] 1 BCLC 131 (CA). Noted by R Grantham, "Company Directors and Tortious Liability" [1997] *CLJ* 259.

conceptions of social welfare, notably those concerned with distributional issues.[13] From this perspective, the efficiency of limited liability is not necessarily an answer to the concerns over the moral and social legitimacy of limited liability.[14]

II CORPORATE PERSONALITY

Mr Goddard's essay identifies the two fundamental questions posed by the recognition of the company as a separate entity as being:

(a) When will the company's shareholders and controllers be liable for acts or omissions in conducting its business?
(b) When will the company be liable for the acts of individuals?

The essay is primarily addressed to the first of these and seeks to show that the law's response is efficient. However, I wish to focus on the doctrinal aspects of the law's answers to these questions. In particular, I want to suggest that many of the difficulties which are addressed in the latter part of the essay are due, in some measure at least, to a failure to recognise the doctrinal implications of introducing a fictional entity like a company into the legal and factual matrix.

First, there is a tendency to assume that substantive rules of law, both those specifically developed for companies and those of general application, can be applied to companies in the same way, with the same doctrinal tools and consequences, as when applied to individuals. However, despite the common law's tendency to endow the company with the full range of human characteristics, the law has not yet succeeded in breathing life into the *persona ficta*. As Lord Hoffmann put it, the company does not really exist and any "statement about what a company has or has not done, or can or cannot do, is necessarily a reference"[15] to human action.

The company's lack of corporeal substance has not, of course, prevented the application to the company of legal rules originally worked out for natural persons. It has, however, meant that there are differences in the way the rules are applied and in their consequences.[16] As Hart demonstrated,[17] legal rules which contemplate human characteristics, such as those of contract and

---

[13] See generally, the excellent overview in I Ogus, *Regulation: Legal Form and Economic Theory* (Oxford, Clarendon, 1994), 46.

[14] Pettet, n. 8 above, 143, 151.

[15] *Meridian Global Funds Management Asia Ltd.* v. *Securities Commission* [1995] 2 AC 500, 506.

[16] I pursue this theme more fully in "Illegal Contracts and the Powers of Company Directors", (1998) 114 *LQR* (forthcoming).

[17] H L A Hart, "Definition and Theory in Jurisprudence" (1954) 70 *LQR* 37. The decisions of the House of Lords and Privy Council respectively in *Re Supply of Ready Mixed Concrete (No 2)* [1995] 1 AC 456 (HL) and *Meridian Global Funds Management Asia Ltd.* v. *Securities Commission* [1995] 2 AC 500, reflect similar reasoning.

tort, can be extended to abstract legal conceptions like the company only by way of an analogy with natural persons. This analogy is driven by the practical need to extend such rules to the company, and is shaped by the policy and purpose of the particular rule at issue. The importance of this point is most clearly illustrated by the requirement of *mens rea* in criminal offences. While the company's inherent inability to form an intention was long seen as an obstacle to corporate criminal liability, it is now recognised that *mens rea* in a company need only be analogous to the guilty intent of an individual. Thus, *mens rea* finds its analogue in the company's status as employer,[18] or the intentions of its controllers,[19] or even in its corporate policies and culture.[20] When, therefore, rules are extended to companies, they do not, and cannot, operate in precisely the same way or with the same consequences as they do when applied to natural persons. The rules will apply in a "manner radically different from though still analogous to that in which such rules apply to individuals . . .".[21]

Secondly, as Mr Goddard's essay notes, one of the more serious threats to the principle in *Salomon* v. *A Saloman & Co. Ltd*[22] is the imposition of tortious liability on company directors and shareholders for acts or omissions undertaken in the course of the company's business. At a doctrinal level, the difficulty is that attempts to impose such liability pit the aims of tort law squarely against those of company law. Tort law imposes liability on the individual director or shareholder as the actual tortfeasor,[23] but company law places that liability exclusively on the corporate entity.

While there may be sound policy reasons why on occasion the company should be disregarded and liability imposed on directors or shareholders, much of the difficulty experienced by the courts in reconciling the tension between company and tort law is due to a failure to recognise that, *prima facie*, company law doctrines must necessarily be accorded primacy. While such a claim may seem imperialistic, such primacy is inherent in the very nature of company law. Despite our penchant for reification, the company is

---

[18] Thus, the company may be held liable for criminal offences by an application of the concept of vicarious liability: *Mousell Bros. Ltd.* v. *London and North Western Railway Co.* [1917] 2 KB 836; *National Rivers Authority* v. *Alfred McApline Homes East* [1994] CLR 760. See, generally, H A J Ford, R P Austin and I M Ramsay, *Ford's Principles of Corporations Law* (8th edn., Sydney, Butterworths, 1997), 683. The use of vicarious liability principles is not without its critics: R Welsh, "The Criminal Liability of Corporations" (1949) 62 *LQR* 345.

[19] *Tesco Supermarkets Ltd.* v. *Nattrass* [1972] AC 153 (HL). See, generally, P Davies, *Gower's Principles of Modern Company Law* (6th edn., London, Sweet and Maxwell, 1997), 229.

[20] It has been argued, though without judicial support, that the internal structure and culture of the company should satisfy the requirement of *mens rea*. Thus, a company might be held liable where its policies permitted or encouraged the crime. See J Gobert, "Corporate Criminality: New Crimes for the Times" [1994] *Crim L Rev* 722 and C Clarkson, "Kicking Corporate Bodies and Damning their Souls" (1996) 59 *MLR* 557.

[21] HLA Hart, n. 17 above, 53.

[22] [1897] 2 AC 22.

[23] Or as the one vicariously responsible.

merely a set of rules[24] which provides for the application of general principles of law, such as those of the law of torts and vicarious liability, in a manner different from that when applied to individuals. The primary purpose of this set of rules is to ensure that general principles of law, such as those of tort, are applied to a different entity and that the scope of their application is limited. Thus, although, necessarily, a director may be the actual tortfeasor or the individual responsible for a contract, the company law regime modifies the normal consequences of the director's actions. The responsibility for, and the legal consequences of, the tortious conduct or contractual undertaking do not sheet home to the individual. Where the company law regime applies, its essential function is to identify a different entity as the tortfeasor or contractor. To refuse to accept, therefore, as Thomas J did in *Dairy Containers Ltd.* v. *NZI Bank Ltd.*,[25] that these general principles are modified is not only to deny the primacy inherent in the rules of company law but it is to deny the company's very existence.[26]

Finally, discussions of corporate personality tend to be characterised by an either/or choice: either the corporation is an entity, distinct from its members, or the corporation is merely an aggregation of individuals.[27] Consequently, the company is either considered an entity for all purposes or it is disregarded for all purposes.[28] It is necessary, however, to remind oneself that the conception of the company as a distinct entity is a conclusion of law, not one of fact,[29] and one relevant only in its own particular context.[30] This means that while in some contexts the purposes for which the entity exists demands that its separateness be stressed, in others these purposes entail that we stress the role of the individuals joined in the common enterprise. In *Salomon*, for their Lordships to have stressed anything other than the separateness of the company would have been to frustrate one of the uses of the entity, the facilitation of limited liability.[31] Where, however, the entity concept is being used for purposes beyond those contemplated by the law, it is inappropriate to clothe the individuals with separate identity. This may be so because it is an improper one, as in *Gildford Motor Co. Ltd.* v. *Horne*,[32] or because a strict application would frustrate one or more of these purposes, as was perhaps

[24] *Meridian Global Funds Management Asia Ltd.* v. *Securities Commission* [1995] 2 AC 500, 506–7.

[25] [1995] 2 NZLR 30.

[26] See R Grantham, "Liability of Parent Companies for the Actions of the Directors of Their Subsidiaries" (1997) 18 *The Company Lawyer* 138.

[27] See, generally, A Beck, "Two Sides of the Corporate Veil" in J H Farrar (ed.), *Contemporary Issues in Company Law* (Auckland, CCH, 1987), 69.

[28] E Latty, "The Corporate Entity as a Solvent of Legal Problems" (1936) 34 *Michigan L Rev* 597, 600.

[29] *Ibid.*, 603.

[30] Hart, n. 17 above, 52–3.

[31] Hart, n. 17 above, 54–6; M Radin, "The Endless Problem of Corporate Personality" (1932) 32 *Columbia L Rev* 643, 665.

[32] [1933] Ch 935. The corporate entity was being used by the defendant to evade his obligations under a valid restraint of trade agreement.

the case in *DHN Food Distributors Ltd.* v. *London Borough of Tower Hamlets.*[33]

While there may be difficulties determining what an appropriate purpose is or what is implied by the pursuit of that purpose, the focus on the nature and function of the entity concept itself offers the prospect of an approach to a number of company law's persistent problems which is doctrinally coherent. In particular, it certainly seems more satisfying to impose liability on shareholders when the purported use of the entity is for purposes not contemplated by the law than the rather opaque assertions that the entity is to be disregarded because it is a mere facade,[34] or that justice requires it.[35]

[33] [1976] 3 All ER 462. Briefly, the case concerned a claim by the company for compensation in respect of the compulsory purchase of its factory. The right to compensation depended upon the claimant having an interest in the land. The land was, however, owned by the plaintiff's subsidiary. The Court of Appeal upheld the right to compensation on the basis that the company and its subsidiary were a single economic entity.

[34] This is the approach taken in *Adams* v. *Cape Industries plc* [1991] 1 All ER 929. See also Davies, n 19 above, 173.

[35] L Gallagher and P Ziegler, "Lifting the Corporate Veil in the Pursuit of Justice" [1990] *JBL* 292.

4

Corporate Groups

ROBERT P AUSTIN*

I INTRODUCTION

Salomon v. Salomon & Co. Ltd.[1] is one of the great pillars of nineteenth century British company law, along with such cases as *Ashbury Railway Carriage
and Iron Co. v. Riche*[2] and *Trevor v. Whitworth*.[3] But *Salomon's* case is more
than just a decisive turning point in corporate legal evolution, historically significant but no longer legally relevant. *Salomon* remains one of the most frequently cited cases in British Commonwealth company law, applied and
interpreted across a wide range of circumstances. This is because the decision
has come to be seen in very broad terms. Their Lordships held that Mr
Salomon's company had conducted business in its own right for itself, neither
as agent nor trustee, even though six of the seven incorporators were effectively nominees for the seventh. By extrapolation, their Lordships' decision,
rather than the text of the companies legislation itself, has been treated as the
source of the "separate entity" doctrine of company law.

In a narrow sense, *Salomon's* case has nothing to say about the legal personality of corporate groups. In a broader sense, modern corporate group
structures could not have evolved in Britain unless British company law first
adopted the proposition that an entity can have both a separate legal personality and a single effective owner and controller. In that sense, *Salomon's* case
is the starting point for an exploration of the law of corporate groups in
Britain, and in countries of the British Commonwealth which have been influenced by the British legal tradition.

II INROADS INTO *SALOMON'S CASE*

The corporate group structure raises a wide variety of legal issues, many of
them disconnected. There are, however, some broad themes. Laws which

* Partner, Minter Ellison, Sydney.
[1] [1897] AC 22.
[2] (1875) LR 7 HL 653.
[3] (1887) 12 App Cas 409.

require the consolidation of financial statements of parent and subsidiary entities are based on the principle that the financial position of a corporate group cannot properly be understood by examining each corporate entity separately. If the separate corporate entities are an economic unit, it is important to assess the financial position of the economic entity by eliminating inter-corporate operations and consolidating balance sheet, profit and loss and cashflow information. Laws about the use of tax losses within a corporate group also recognise the economic unity of the group, while certainly not (at least in Australia's case) disregarding the separate entities. Takeover and antitrust laws which are concerned to measure the acquisition of control or influence over another business entity will generally require the aggregation of the interests of all corporate group members, on the theory that the parent or group itself should be assumed to have the powers vested in any of the entities of the group.

Laws of all these kinds are interesting because they provide models for legal recognition of the significance of the corporate group, but at no stage do these laws challenge the separate entity doctrine of *Salomon's case* in its application in the group context. Typically, the laws assume that each entity has a separate legal personality which must be acknowledged in legal analysis; they then seek to overcome the consequences of applying the separate entity analysis in a given situation.

There is, however, a more specific and direct assault on the separate entity doctrine, in application to corporate groups. By the use of various techniques, courts and legislators have endeavoured to allow external creditors to recover debts from (or to prove in liquidation against) entities within a corporate group other than the entity with which they have contracted. These developments create a real exception to what is commonly regarded as the *Salomon* doctrine. The issues underlying the judicial and legislative developments are the subject of current debate in Australia and, I believe, elsewhere. It is therefore appropriate to consider these areas of controversy as part of this centenary celebration of the *Salomon* decision.

III THE CORPORATE GROUP CONCEPT

Any discussion of corporate groups must begin by establishing an agreed terminology. As Professor Eisenberg has pointed out,[4] the problems posed by corporate groups are so varied that, unless a common nomenclature is established, it is easy for commentators to talk past each other and even to confuse the real issues.

It is normal to confine the enquiry to corporations that are affiliated or connected in a manner that depends significantly on share ownership, rather than

---

[4] "Corporate Groups" in M Gillooly (ed.), *The Law Relating to Corporate Groups* (Sydney, Federation Press, 1993), 1.

affiliations purely by contract or interlocking directorates. Professor Eisenberg distinguishes between vertical corporate groups, consisting of a parent and one or more subsidiaries, and horizontal groups such as cross-ownership groups of which the Japanese *keiretsu* is the most famous example. Horizontal groups raise policy and legal issues which are well beyond the scope of this essay.

As far as vertical corporate groups are concerned, there is an important distinction between wholly owned and partly owned groups. In the latter case, the existence of the minority shareholding interests creates important issues of shareholder protection, whereas in the case of the wholly owned group the focus tends to be on creditor protection.

In this essay, I shall confine my attention to wholly owned groups, thereby excluding the minority shareholder issues which have caused such difficulty in the law of partly owned corporate groups.[5] I do so because the theme of this book is to reflect on the significance of *Salomon's case*, which was not a case about protection of minority shareholding interests. There is ample to consider if attention is confined to wholly owned groups.

IV REASONS FOR THE WHOLLY OWNED GROUP STRUCTURE

Corporate groups are formed for a multitude of reasons. However, as Professor Eisenberg observes,[6] it is very difficult to find *economic reasons* for the formation of wholly owned groups. Any economic goal that can be achieved by the creation of a wholly owned subsidiary could equally well be achieved by the formation of a division within a single corporate entity. Consequently, the reasons for formation of wholly owned corporate groups tend to be regulatory and historical.

Professor Eisenberg identifies some of the *regulatory reasons*. Where the group wishes to provide some managerial autonomy to a particular group business, running the business through a separate subsidiary may be a useful (though certainly not a necessary) way to emphasise the separation and autonomy of that business unit. In the case of a multinational group, the local law of a country in which the group wishes to do business may demand that the local business be conducted by a separate subsidiary. In some cases, there may be a tax advantage to be derived from operating through a separate subsidiary, and in other cases it may be possible to limit the influence of the regulator of a regulated business activity (such as banking or insurance) by

---

[5] See the chapters by M Gillooly ("Outside Shareholders in Corporate Groups" at 159), P Redmond ("Problems for Insiders" at 208), and R P Austin ("Problems for Directors Within Corporate Groups" at 133) in Gillooly (ed.), n. 4 above. For an excellent analysis of the creditor protection issue, see J Hill, "Corporate Groups, Creditor Protection and Cross-guarantees: Australian Perspectives" (1995) 24 *Can Bus LJ* 321.

[6] "Corporate Groups" in Gillooly (ed.), n. 4 above.

vesting that business in a regulated subsidiary and leaving the holding company outside the regulatory umbrella.

In some cases, the motivation for conducting a business through a separate subsidiary will be to circumscribe the group's exposure to the risks of the business. This is particularly so where there are high liability risks, such as risks of environmental or consumer liability. It should not be assumed, in such a case, that the group will deliberately undercapitalise the subsidiary which is engaged in risky business, compared with the likely capitalisation of a separately owned and self-contained business enterprise. The motivation of group management may be, more legitimately, to protect shareholders' funds of the parent from claims in excess of the properly capitalised value of the business of the subsidiary.

It must be remembered, too, that in many cases the corporate structure of a group is more a matter of *history* than planning. In Australia, groups frequently grow by acquisition rather than expansion. Once an acquired entity becomes wholly owned, it may be possible to run off the business to another part of the group, with the result that the acquired entity remains in the corporate structure as a shell waiting to be used for some other purpose. Winding it up may be pointless. In other cases, substantial assets and business operations are contained in the acquired entity, which can be transferred only at some considerable expense or with taxation disadvantages. Typically, in these cases, the acquired corporate structure is retained, even though operationally the business may be folded into a divisionalised management structure.

It is important to understand the factors which contribute to what will often appear at first blush to be a needlessly complicated group corporate structure. The external commentator who does not take time to understand the reasons for the structure can all too readily assume, unfairly, that it has been set up to defeat creditors or regulators, or for some equally unmeritorious reason. It is appropriate, in this context, to offer a few observations on group management structures and financial management, from the perspective of an Australian legal practitioner.

V MANAGEMENT STRUCTURES

The organisational structure of wholly owned corporate groups is anything but uniform. Much will depend on the size of the group as a whole and the geographical location and variety of its businesses. Business specialisation implies, where the group conducts more than one business, that there is a degree of decentralisation of management. But the synergies produced by combination are unlikely to be optimised unless management is centralised. In Australia, one often finds that these competing demands are reconciled by a management structure in which there are divisional units corresponding to the main business lines of the group, with divisional heads directly accountable to a small body of the group's most senior managers, including the chief executive.

An analogy has been drawn between the central management team and the external controlling shareholder of traditional legal theory, which intervenes to replace directors and officers who are not meeting the shareholder's targets for growth and profitability.[7] But in Australia, at least, one would expect the central management team to be much more actively involved than the traditional shareholder—involved in setting performance targets, taking major business decisions of concern to the divisions, actively reviewing performance and making staffing decisions. Central management teams tend to be highly interventionist, because of their own accountability to their board and the parent's shareholders.

VI FINANCIAL MANAGEMENT

The organisational structure for financial management of the corporate group is typically more complicated than the business management structure. While banking and corporate finance functions are likely to be centralised through the parent company's treasury operations, and budgets and budget projections will probably be set on a business divisional basis, financial reporting must take into account the separate corporate entities through which the business is conducted, in order to satisfy statutory reporting and income tax requirements. This means that some important decisions, including the funding of divisional businesses and transfer pricing within the group, are executed at a corporate entity level even if arranged at the central management or divisional level. The need to satisfy corporate entity requirements as well as business divisional requirements in financial management of the corporate group creates a special level of complexity and, if the group is not properly managed, can produce a chaotic picture of intermingling of the assets of separate entities and insufficient financial trails to permit the movement of assets within the group to be traced.

VII THE TENSION BETWEEN BUSINESS ORGANISATION AND CORPORATE STRUCTURE

In summary, the Australian position is that where the group has centralised senior management and a divisional business unit structure, there is an inevitable tension between the business organisational structure and the corporate structure, and the group's financial, taxation and overall treasury

---

[7] See T Hadden, R Forbes and R Simmonds, *Canadian Business Organisation Law* (Toronto, 1984), 118.

operations have to operate in an environment where they must pay regard to both the business divisions and the corporate entities.

Company law's requirement that a separate board be appointed to manage the business and affairs of each subsidiary within the group, though sometimes a salutary reminder of the different creditor interests which may be involved through the different parts of the group, is often seen as a troublesome inconvenience. The requirement of the law of directors' duties, that the directors must have regard to the separate interests of the group of which they are the directors, is likely to appear to the directors themselves to be totally divorced from a reality in which they sit on the board because they occupy middle management positions in a business division and are required to follow central management instructions.[8]

The centrally managed, divisionalised corporate group is the paradigm for the discussion which follows. The issues about creditor protection and management structure are clearly not unrelated.

VIII GROUP LIABILITY TO VOLUNTARY (CONTRACT) CREDITORS

Fundamentally, contract creditors are entitled to recover their debts from the entities with which they contract, and from no one else. This is the essence of the "separate entity" doctrine. As applied in *Salomon's case*, the consequence was that while the creditors of the leather and boot business had claims against the company which conducted the business, neither they nor the company had any direct claim against Mr Salomon, who was entitled to rely on the security granted by the company to him for the debt which it owed him. Applied to a corporate group context, this reasoning entails that creditors who contract with a subsidiary have no claim to recovery against other subsidiaries, or the parent, or the parent's shareholders.

This basic analysis has been confirmed, in the corporate group context, by the High Court of Australia in *Hobart Bridge Co. Ltd.* v. *Federal Commissioner of Taxation,*[9] where Kitto J approved a passage from the speech of Lord Sumner in *Gas Lighting Improvement Co. Ltd.* v. *Inland Revenue Commissioners,*[10] in which his Lordship rejected an invitation to disregard the corporate entity lying between the investor and the business:[11]

> "It is said that this was 'machinery', but that is true of all participations in limited liability companies. They and their operations are simply the machinery, in an

---

[8] See R P Austin, "Problems for Directors Within Corporate Groups" in M Gillooly (ed.), n. 4 above, 133, 140 ff. Compare Companies Act 1993 (NZ), s 131(2), which allows the directors of a wholly owned subsidiary, if expressly permitted to do so by the company's constitution, to act in a manner which they believe to be in the best interests of the holding company even though it may not be in the best interests of the subsidiary.

[9] (1951) 82 CLR 372 (HCA).

[10] [1923] AC 723.

[11] *Ibid.*, at 740–1.

economic sense, by which natural persons, who desire to limit their liability, participate in undertakings which they cannot manage to carry on themselves, either alone or in partnership, but, legally speaking, this machinery is not impersonal though it is inanimate. Between the investor, who participates as a shareholder, and the undertaking carried on, the law interposes another person, real though artificial, the company itself, and the business carried on is the business of that company, and the capital employed is its capital and not in either case the business or the capital of the shareholders. Assuming, of course, that the company is duly formed and is not a sham (of which there is no suggestion here), the idea that it is mere machinery for effecting the purposes of the shareholders is a layman's fallacy. It is a figure of speech, which cannot alter the legal aspect of the facts."

In England, it has recently been said that English courts have consistently adopted "a steadfast refusal to consider the possibility that a parent company may be liable for the debts of its subsidiaries".[12]

At a policy level, there is much to be said in support of the principle of limited liability.[13] Restricting personal financial liability to the level of the shareholder's investment in the company permits the shareholder to diversify his or her own investment portfolio, thereby reducing the risks of corporate investment and lowering the cost of capital. Limited liability enables the shareholders to externalise business risk. While this tends to encourage companies to take on too much risk, since the shareholders take all the benefits from the success of a risky project while they are able to share the downside risks with creditors, contract creditors are able to protect themselves by choosing not to contract or by charging higher rents, so that the cost of limited liability is thrown back onto the shareholders.[14]

IX QUALIFICATION TO THE SEPARATE ENTITY DOCTRINE

However, the crisp application of the separate entity doctrine to creditors dealing with corporate groups is neither without qualification nor without controversy. In Australia, the qualifications which must be made include:

(a) the possibility that the parent entity may be regarded, in the circumstances, as a shadow director consequently liable with the subsidiary's

---

[12] D Milman, in *Palmer's In Company*, Issue 2/97 (21 Feb. 1997), 2.

[13] See, in particular, R C Clark, *Corporate Law* (Boston, Mass., Little, Brown, 1996), 7-10; F H Easterbrook and D R Fischel, "Limited Liability and the Corporation" (1985) 52 *Univ of Chic LR* 89; S E Woodward, "Limited Liability in the Theory of the Firm'" (1985) 141 *J of Instit and Theoretical Econ* 601; compare J A Grundfest, "The Limited Future of Unlimited Liability: A Capital Markets Perspective" (1992) 102 *Yale LJ* 387.

[14] The argument for limited liability is less successful where the creditors are involuntary creditors such as tort claimants, who cannot take compensation from the shareholders for the cost of limited liability: see H Hansmann and R Kraakman, "Toward Unlimited Shareholder Liability for Corporate Torts" (1991) 100 *Yale LJ* 1879.

directors if the ingredients of insolvent trading liability under section 588G of the Corporations Law are made out;[15]

(b)   the further possibility that the parent entity may be liable for the subsidiary's insolvent trading if the ingredients of section 588V of the Corporations Law (which relate to the parent or any of its directors having reasons to suspect insolvency) are made out;

(c)   the factual possibility that the parent and the subsidiary may have entered into a deed of indemnity and cross guarantee in order to obtain relief on a group basis from complying with the accounting requirements of the Corporations Law at a subsidiary level.[16]

X   "LIFTING THE CORPORATE VEIL" IN THE CORPORATE GROUP CONTEXT

In a few cases there are suggestions that in the context of a wholly owned, centrally managed, group, it is appropriate to disregard the separate corporate entities and to treat the subsidiary as the *alter ego* of the parent, with the result that the creditors are treated as being in a contractual relationship directly with the parent. In some cases, the basis for lifting the veil in this manner is an articulated judicial view that the subsidiary is the agent of the parent on the facts.[17] The reasoning in some other cases suggests a more direct disregard of the separation of corporate entities, without reliance on any agency or trust principle.[18]

By and large, Australian courts have not shown much sympathy to the agency or trust analysis, and even less to the idea that separate corporate entities can be completely disregarded. However, there is some support for the concerns which underpin the "lifting the veil" cases in some judgments by Mr Andrew Rogers, formerly Chief Judge of the Commercial Division of the Supreme Court of New South Wales. Rogers J supported removing the significance of the separation of corporate entities, particularly in the context of liquidation, though by legislation rather than judicial fiat.

---

[15] See, in particular, *Standard Chartered Bank of Aust. Ltd.* v. *Antico* (1995) 13 ACLC 1381; compare *Dairy Containers Ltd.* v. *NZI Bank Ltd.* [1995] 2 NZLR 30.

[16] See Corporations Law, s 313; Australian Securities Commission class order ASC CO 91/211 (15 Apr. 1991); see J Hill, "Cross Guarantees in Corporate Groups" (1992) 10 *CSLJ* 312.

[17] The classic case is *Smith, Stone & Knight Ltd.* v. *Birmingham Corporation* [1939] 4 All ER 116; the cases are analysed in H A J Ford, R P Austin and I M Ramsay, *Ford's Principles of Corporations Law* (8th edn., Sydney, Butterworths, 1997), para 4.370.

[18] The principal English case is *DHN Food Distributors Ltd.* v. *Tower Hamlets London Borough Council* [1976] 1 WLR 852, where the judgment of Lord Denning MR is the only example of this approach. See D Sugarman and F Webb, "Three-in-one: Trusts, Licences and Veils" (1977) 93 *LQR* 170; D Powles, "The 'See-through' Corporate Veil" (1977) 40 *MLR* 337; D Hayton "Contractual Licences and Corporate Veils" [1977] *CLJ* 12.

XI THE *BRIGGS* CASE

In *Briggs* v. *James Hardie & Co. Pty. Ltd.*[19] the issue was whether the plaintiff, who had contracted asbestosis at work, could obtain an order to extend the statutory limitation period to permit his tort claim to proceed against his employer, a subsidiary, and its parent. The statutory question was whether there was "evidence to establish a cause of action".[20] The majority of the Court of Appeal of New South Wales said that the plaintiff need only show a possibility that the evidence existed.

Rogers AJA reasoned that in the present state of the law about piercing the corporate veil, it was not possible to say what evidence would ultimately suffice to make out a case. In the course of his reasoning, he reviewed the circumstances in which the corporate veil would be pierced in a group context. He rejected the argument that the corporate veil may be pierced where one company exercises complete dominion and control over another, as "too simplistic".[21] But he criticised the law as paying "scant regard to the commercial reality that every holding company has the potential and, more often than not, in fact, does exercise complete control over a subsidiary".[22] He found that Australian law did not permit an "enterprise approach" to liability relationships between the group and outsiders.[23] He suggested (as noted more fully below) that different approaches to piercing the corporate veil may be needed depending upon whether the claimant is a voluntary or involuntary creditor.

XII THE UNCERTAINTY ARGUMENT

One of the problems identified by Rogers AJA in the *Briggs* case is the sheer uncertainty of the law. In his view, Australian law had not fully worked out answers to such questions as whether, if control by the parent of the subsidiary's affairs is not itself sufficient, what degree of domination will justify lifting the corporate veil; the extent to which the subsidiary must have relied on the parent for facilities and management; or the extent to which under-capitalisation of the subsidiary is a relevant factor.

An obvious answer to his concern about the uncertainty of the law is to say that, in the absence of evidence of agency or trust or a sham, the correct Australian legal position is that the corporate veil will not be lifted on the basis of corporate group circumstances. Cases in which the corporate veil has

[19] (1989) 16 NSWLR 549.
[20] *Ibid.*, at 552.
[21] *Ibid.*, at 577.
[22] *Ibid.*
[23] On the enterprise/entity dichotomy, see A A Berle, "The Theory of Enterprise Entity" (1947) 47 *Col LR* 343; P L Blumberg, *The Law of Corporate Groups: Procedural Problems in the Law of Parent and Subsidiary Corporations* (Boston, Mass., Little, Brown, 1983), Chap 1.

been disregarded are, by and large, cases where doing so has conferred some benefit on the group companies (compensation, as in *DHN Food Distributors Ltd.* v. *Tower Hamlets London Borough Council*),[24] rather than cases where the lifting of the veil exposes an entity to liability.[25]

XIII   LAW VERSUS COMMERCIAL REALITY—THE QINTEX CASE

However, Rogers CJ's concern about corporate groups has not been confined to a concern about the uncertainty of the law. In his judgment in *Briggs*, he referred to the discrepancy between the law and "commercial reality" in the group context. He returned to this theme in *Qintex Australia Finance Ltd.* v. *Schroders Australia Ltd.*[26]

Schroders conducted foreign currency transactions on behalf of the Qintex group, without clearly identifying the subsidiary entity or entities on whose behalf instructions were taken. When a forward exchange contract resulted in a loss, the question was whether Schroders could appropriate amounts standing to the credit of a Qintex subsidiary to offset the loss, and that in turn depended upon whether Schroders had incurred the loss while acting for that subsidiary, or for some other subsidiary in the same group. Rogers CJ said:[27]

> "As I see it, there is today a tension between the realities of commercial life and the applicable law in circumstances such as those of the present case. In the everyday rush and bustle of commercial life in the last decade it was seldom that participants to transactions involving conglomerates with a large number of subsidiaries paused to consider which of the subsidiaries should become the contracting party . . . it may be desirable for Parliament to consider whether this distinction between the law and commercial practice should be maintained. This is especially the case today when many collapses of conglomerates occasion many disputes. Regularly, liquidators of subsidiaries, or of the holding company, come to court to argue as to which of their charges bears the liability . . . as well, creditors of failed companies encounter difficulty when they have to select from among the moving targets the company with which they consider they concluded a contract."

One commentator has greeted these remarks with cautious approval.[28] But another commentator, Fridman, has argued that the onus should lie with the creditor to ascertain which company in the group he or she is dealing with, and to ensure that the contract documentation reflects that understanding.[29]

---

[24] [1976] 1 WLR 852.

[25] An outcome not thought to be acceptable in *Adams* v. *Cape Industries plc* [1990] Ch 433: this thesis is developed, by reference to recent English cases, by Milman, n. 12 above.

[26] (1990) 3 ACSR 267.

[27] *Ibid.*, at 268.

[28] R Baxt, "The Need to Review the Rule in *Salomon's* Case as it Applies to Groups of Companies" (1991) 9 *CSLJ* 185, 186-7.

[29] S Fridman, "Removal of the Corporate Veil: Suggestions for Law Reform in *Qintex Australia Finance Ltd.* v. *Schroders Australia Ltd.*" (1991) 19 *ABLR* 211.

On this view, the key issue becomes whether the creditor has sufficient information about the companies and their creditworthiness to negotiate effectively with the correct entity. The creditor can rely on the company's published financial statements and, if they are misleading, sue the company or its directors for breach of the statutory duty to provide accurate financial statements or sue the auditors for breach of their duty of care.

Mr Rogers, as he had by then become, responded to this criticism extracurially by observing that litigation is not the answer to every problem, and a legislative solution to adjust the law to the commercial reality would be a better outcome.[30] With respect, this does not answer Fridman's point, which is essentially that if commercial creditors expect to be able to select the most wealthy corporate group entity as the entity to be made accountable for their debts, they have an unrealistic expectation which the law should not be required to satisfy.

XIV CREDITOR EXPECTATIONS

The idea that there is a discrepancy between creditor expectations and the legal outcome is perhaps understandable where the creditor is a retail or consumer creditor dealing with a well-known, branded corporate group. In the consumer context, however, the solution to the problem of creditor expectations is provided in consumer protection law, rather than in corporate law. It would be misleading conduct for the parent to acquiesce in a course of conduct which implied that the group's assets would support obligations to consumers, if this were not in fact the case.

It seems that the problem is with commercial creditors (such as Schroders) rather than with retail consumer creditors. Here, it is surely plausible to argue that it is open to the creditor, before extending credit, to clarify the identity of the other contracting party. A creditor who fails to do so must share some of the consequences of its conduct, which is inefficient and uncommercial as well as imprudent behaviour.

In the end, one wonders whether the *Qintex* case is merely an illustration of what happens when inexperienced foreign exchange traders fail to attend properly to their "back office" responsibilities. No one with inside knowledge of the workings of corporate groups would maintain that, in financial matters, the identity of the contracting entity is unimportant to the group's financial managers. If it is important within the group, then surely it ought to be equally important for those commercial parties with whom the group deals.

---

[30] "Corporate Groups—Problems for Outsiders" in Gillooly (ed), n. 4 above, 125.

XV THE ADMINISTRATION OF GROUP CORPORATE LIQUIDATIONS

There is, however, a basis for real concern in some of the observations made by Rogers CJ about corporate groups. Writing extra-curially since leaving the bench, he has referred to the problems which arise when the affairs of the group have been extensively intermingled.[31] Even if the creditor is careful to identify the subsidiary with which the contract was made, if that entity goes into liquidation there will be a delay while the liquidator sorts out the assets which are available for distribution to that entity's creditors. In all probability, several, and possibly all, group entities will be in liquidation, and a substantial part of the assets which would otherwise have been available to the group's creditors will need to be expended in ascertaining the facts and the applicable law which determine which group creditors obtain a distribution and which do not.

The level of complexity which a corporate group's affairs can present for the liquidator, necessarily unfamiliar with the group's operations before the commencement of the winding-up, can hardly be overstated. Where the group's financial affairs have not been administered with due regard to the corporate entities involved, through carelessness or impropriety, the difficulty is magnified enormously. Southwell J gave a graphic account of the difficulties confronting the liquidator of the Linter Group in the following passage from his judgment in *Linter Group Ltd. v. Goldberg*:[32]

> "Goldberg himself exercised almost total executive control over all companies. While he left management decisions of the various textile companies to their experienced managers, so far as group tactics and policy were concerned, Goldberg had the final say. He treated all units in the group as though they were beneficially owned by him. Some decisions were made by him (sometimes with the concurrence of his son-in-law Furst) without troubling to call meetings of directors. . . . The books of account were often treated as objects to be manipulated as the occasion demanded."

XVI "POOLED LIQUIDATION" UNDER AUSTRALIAN LAW

Confronted with the acute difficulties which liquidation of group companies will sometimes pose, liquidators are likely to explore all ways of avoiding separate liquidations of each group entity. In Australian law, one accepted mechanism for achieving this objective is to proceed by a scheme of arrangement under section 411 of the Corporations Law. A scheme of arrangement involves significant cost and time, and may therefore not always be thought an appropriate response to the problem. The historically separate provisions now

---

[31] "Corporate Groups—Problems for Outsiders" in Gillooly (ed), n. 4 above, 125.
[32] (1992) 7 ACSR 580, 589–90.

found in section 477 of the Corporations Law, which permit a liquidator to make a "compromise or arrangement" with creditors, are not available unless the court has evidence of consent by the creditors, and mere lack of objection is not sufficient.[33]

Liquidators have attempted to deal with problems in a group context by asking the court for directions under sections 479 or 511 of the Corporations Law, but so far without success.

In *Re Austcorp Tiles Pty. Ltd.*[34] a group of companies maintained only one bank account, and administered its affairs in such a manner that creditors were unsure of the identity of the company with which they had contracted. The liquidators jointly made an application to the court under section 479 of the Corporations Law for directions, seeking orders which would permit them to apply the funds of the companies to all the creditors of each of the companies on a *pro rata* basis. The court refused to make the orders, observing that in the absence of a scheme of arrangement, all that could be done was for each liquidator to make a distribution *pari passu* to the creditors of the entity concerned.

A similar answer was recently given by the Court of Appeal of New South Wales in *Wimborne* v. *Brien*.[35] In that case, half of the shares of the company in liquidation were owned by a husband, and the other half by his estranged wife. It appeared likely that when the Family Court proceedings between them were resolved, the company in liquidation and other companies would be transferred to the husband. The husband urged the liquidator to do nothing about the liquidation pending the outcome of the Family Court proceedings, but the wife urged the liquidator to proceed with the liquidation in the normal way.

The Court found that the liquidator was under a duty to the company as a separate entity, its members and creditors. There was no justification for the liquidator to purport to act in the interests of the "group" of which the company in liquidation formed part. Consequently, the liquidator had been justified in proceeding with the liquidation and incurring costs in doing so.

Although the liquidators in these cases failed to consolidate assets and liabilities on a group basis, a general principle appears to be emerging which may permit consolidation if, in the circumstances, the court has statutory authority to authorise it. The principle, said to be derived from bankruptcy law via some *obiter dicta* of Powell J in *Anmi Pty. Ltd.* v. *Williams*,[36] was recently formulated by Young J in *Dean-Willcocks* v. *Soluble Solution Hydroponics Pty. Ltd.*[37] as follows:

[33] *Re Austcorp Tiles Pty. Ltd.* (1992) 10 ACLC 62; see also *Re Trix Ltd.* [1970] 1 WLR 1421, but note also *Re BCCI (No 3)* [1993] BCLC 106 (reported as *Re BCCI (No 2)* [1992] BCC 715 and 1490).

[34] (1992) 10 ACLC 62.

[35] (1997) 23 ACSR 576.

[36] [1981] 2 NSWLR 138, 164.

[37] [1997] 13 ACLC 833, 839.

"The bankruptcy rule that where it is impracticable to keep the assets and liabilities of different companies in a group separate they may be consolidated if the consolidation is for the benefit of creditors generally [and] if no creditor objects, applies in a corporate winding up."

Young J was able to apply this principle to the facts before him because the companies were under administration at the time when their creditors resolved to wind them up. That being so, the court had jurisdiction under section 447A of the Corporations Law to make such an order as it thought appropriate about how the statutory provisions dealing with voluntary administration would operate in relation to the companies. The implication is that if the companies had not been under administration at the time of their winding up, there may have been no jurisdictional basis for applying the bankruptcy principle, notwithstanding the consent of creditors.

The message from these cases is that in Australia, and presumably in other countries which do not have any specific statutory authorisation, there is not yet any general ability to pool the assets of related companies for the purposes of efficient and speedy liquidation of a corporate group, in the absence of a scheme of arrangement or proceedings for administration. Consequently, there is no effective response to the administrative difficulties of litigation which were outlined above.

XVII THE NEW ZEALAND SOLUTION

There is a powerful argument for the view that procedures are needed to permit liquidators of failed subsidiaries to claim against solvent subsidiaries and a solvent parent, and if the result of those claims is to bring other entities into liquidation, to pool the group assets and creditor claims to permit fair and rateable dealing with all the group's creditors. That, in effect, is the solution adopted by New Zealand company law. Following provisions first enacted in the Companies Amendment Act 1980 (NZ),[38] sections 271 and 272 of the Companies Act 1993 (NZ) now provide:

"271(1) On the application of the liquidator, or a creditor or shareholder, the Court, if satisfied that it is just and equitable to do so, may order that—
(a) A company that is, or has been, related to the company in liquidation must pay to the liquidator the whole or part of any or all of the claims made in the liquidation:
(b) Where two or more related companies are in liquidation, the liquidations in respect of each company must proceed together as if they were one company to the extent that the Court so orders and subject to such terms and conditions as the Court may impose.
(2) The Court may take such other order or give directions to facilitate giving effect to an order under subsection (1) of this section as it thinks fit.

[38] See Companies Act 1955 (NZ), ss 315A–315C.

272(1) In deciding whether it is just and equitable to make an order under section 27(1)(a) of this Act, the Court must have regard to the following matters:

(a) The extent to which the related company took part in the management of the company in liquidation:

(b) The conduct of the related company towards the creditors of the company in liquidation:

(c) The extent to which the circumstances that gave rise to the liquidation of the company are attributable to the actions of the related company:

(d) Such other matters as the Court thinks fit.

(2) In deciding whether it is just and equitable to make an order under section 271(1)(b) of this Act, the Court must have regard to the following matters:

(a) The extent to which any of the companies took part in the management of any of the other companies:

(b) The conduct of any of the companies towards the creditors of any of the other companies:

(c) The extent to which the circumstances gave rise to the liquidation of any of the companies are attributable to the actions of any of the other companies:

(d) The extent to which the businesses of the companies have been combined:

(e) Such other matters as the Court thinks fit.

(3) The fact that creditors of a company in liquidation relied on the fact that another company is, or was, related to it is not a ground for making an order under section 271 of this Act."

A similar approach has been adopted in Ireland, and there are some similarities (and additionally, some important differences) with the German Stock Corporation Act 1965.[39]

The New Zealand courts are beginning to develop a jurisprudence regarding when the court will exercise its powers under these provisions.[40] Re Pacific Syndicates (NZ) Ltd.[41] is a good illustration of the complexity with which a liquidator may have to deal and the usefulness of the court's power. The problem in that case was that two related companies had solicited funds for contributory mortgages and had set up schemes, but had not set up the nominee companies which were to act as trustees for the scheme investors. Consequently the funds received under each scheme had been mingled in the same bank account. Additionally, a mortgage was granted to a director of one of the companies to secure an advance from that company's bank account;

---

[39] See the material cited in R P Austin, "Problems for Directors Within Corporate Groups" in Gillooly (ed.), n 4 above, 133, 134–5; see also D Sugarman and G Teubner (eds.), *Regulating Corporate Groups in Europe* (Baden-Baden, Nomos, 1990); F Wooldridge, *Groups of Companies: The Law on Practice in Britain, France and Germany* (London, IALS, 1981); T Hadden, *The Control of Corporate Groups* (London, IALS, 1983); U Immenga, "Company Systems and Affiliation" in *International Encyclopaedia of Comparative Law, Volume XIII (Business and Private Organisations)*, Chap 7, especially at 7–38 to 7–86.

[40] *Rea v. Barker* (1988) 4 NZCLC 64,312; *Re Grazing & Export Meat Co. Ltd.* (1984) 2 NZCLC 99,226; *Bullen v. Tourcorp Developments Ltd.* (1988) 4 NZCLC 64,661; *Re Pacific Syndicates (NZ) Ltd. (in liq)* (1989) 4 NZCLC 64,757; *Re Dalhoff and King Holdings Ltd. (in liq)* [1991] 2 NZLR 296 and (1991) 5 NZCLC 66,974.

[41] (1989) 4 NZCLC 64,757.

that director stated that he held the mortgage on behalf of scheme investors. The companies had brought an action to recover monies allegedly misappropriated from them, and their claim was settled by payment of a global sum. The liquidator of the companies obtained an order permitting the proceeds of the settlement to be pooled, on the basis that it was not feasible to apportion the fund between the two companies. This was clearly a much more satisfactory outcome than having to apportion on some more or less arbitrary basis and treat the claims of investors in the two companies separately.[42]

XVIII THE HARMER RECOMMENDATIONS IN AUSTRALIA

An approach similar to New Zealand's was recommended in Australia by the Harmer Committee.[43] The Committee recommended that the court should have the power to disregard the separate entities of related corporations so that, as in New Zealand, the winding up of the entities could proceed together as if they were one company. In exercising its power, the court would have regard to a number of matters, some going to whether it would be administratively convenient to allow liquidations to proceed together in view of the intermingling of the group assets. The criteria to which the court would have regard were similar to those set out in section 272 of the New Zealand Act, except that the administrative convenience of winding up the companies together would be expressly mentioned.

The Harmer proposals were subsequently attacked, principally by the Law Council of Australia, which objected on four grounds:

(a) the proposals would violate the separate entity principle;
(b) the proposals would interfere with project financing;
(c) the proposals would create uncertainty; and
(d) the proposals would complicate company accounts.[44]

The Law Council's criticisms might have been met without abandoning the proposal. The problem about company accounts could be addressed by clarifying the extent to which potential liability for the debts of a subsidiary should be disclosed as a note in the parent company's financial statements. It would be reasonable to say that, during the period before commencement of the subsidiary's winding up, the parent should be exonerated from disclosure of the potential liability, and users of financial statements who are concerned

---

[42] It can plausibly be argued that the criteria for the exercise of the court's discretion (s 272) are vaguely expressed and of limited relevance (see D Goddard, Chap 2). They could be redrafted to refer more directly to the practical problems of liquidating group companies, but the practical utility of the provisions is ample justification for their existence.

[43] See Australian Law Reform Commission, *General Insolvency Inquiry*, Report No 45 (Canberra, 1988), para 857.

[44] See J O'Donovan, "Grouped Therapies for Group Insolvencies" in Gillooly (ed.), n. 4 above, 86.

about the possible consequences of an insolvency of a subsidiary should turn to the group accounts to assess the financial position of the group overall.

XIX AN EXCEPTION FOR FINANCIAL SEGREGATION

As regards the argument about uncertainty, and consequently the difficulty in structuring certain transactions such as project financing transactions, a solution of a different kind might be developed. It could be sensible to create a specific exception to the court's power, which would allow a creditor's claims to be limited to a designated subsidiary or group of subsidiaries provided that those subsidiaries are financially managed in a manner which segregates their assets and liabilities from the assets and liabilities of the rest of the group, and that the segregation is documented in a manner which would permit a liquidator to trace the assets affected by it. In substance, the preservation of the separate entity doctrine in the liquidation of the affected subsidiaries would have to be "purchased" by adopting a regime of financial segregation and accounting.

The challenge will be to develop an effective regime of financial segregation which is not too restrictive but not too easily abused. It might be stated that the parent and other group entities could not be required to contribute to meet creditors' claims in the liquidation of a subsidiary if, during (say) the three years prior to the commencement of winding-up, the subsidiary has paid no dividends to its parent, has not entered into or repaid, or received payment of, any inter-corporate group loan, and has not engaged in any buy-back or reduction of capital.

XX INVOLUNTARY (TORT) CREDITORS

It may be possible, in the context of this exception to the court's power to require group entities to contribute to meet the subsidiary's debts, to assist the plight of tort claimants against a group subsidiary. The tort claimant's difficulty has been highlighted by Rogers AJA in the *Briggs* case,[45] and in academic literature.[46] The difficulty for tort claimants is that they cannot bargain through any contractual process to share the externalities of the enterprise risk with the shareholders of the entity against which they have a claim. Therefore, the shareholders (both in the corporate group context and outside that

---

[45] *Briggs* v. *James Hardie & Co. Pty. Ltd.* (1989) 16 NSWLR 549.

[46] See especially, Hansmann and Kraakman, n. 14 above; R C Downs, "Piercing the Corporate Veil—Do Corporations Provide Limited Liability?" (1985) 53 *UMKCLR* 95; B Welling *Corporate Law in Canada: The Governing Principles* (2nd edn., Toronto, Butterworths, 1991), 144–9; R Carroll, "Corporate Parents and Tort Liability" in Gillooly (ed.), n. 4 above, 91; and R Simmonds, "A Summing Up and Search for Solutions" in *ibid.*, 427.

context) have all the upside of the externalising of business risk which arises through limited liability, and in effect they are able to make an uncompensated transfer of business risk to the tort claimants. This will encourage corporations to take too much risk when the conduct of their business may generate tort liability.

In the *Briggs* case, Rogers AJA expressed some sympathy for the view that the parent's liability to tort claimants injured by the conduct of the subsidiary's business should depend on whether the parent has adequately capitalised the subsidiary or provided the subsidiary with insurance sufficient to cover foreseeable risks. A modification of this approach would be to give the court the discretion, along the New Zealand lines, to require the subsidiary to meet claims, including tort claims, in the liquidation of the subsidiary, but to add to the ingredients of the "financial segregation" exception which was suggested above, a requirement for the parent to show that at all times during the three years prior to the commencement of the winding-up, the subsidiary was either adequately capitalised to conduct its business or that it held sufficient insurance to cover the foreseeable risks of injury to third parties which would arise during the conduct of its business operations.

XXI   PARENT LIABILITY FOR INSOLVENT TRADING

It is a pity that the Harmer proposals were departed from in the legislation by which the Harmer Committee's report was generally implemented. Rather than authorising the court to amalgamate liquidations, the Corporate Law Reform Act 1992 amended the Corporations Law to expose the parent entity to liability for insolvent trading of its subsidiary. The subsidiary's liquidator may take proceedings for recovery against the subsidiary's holding company if the specific provisions of sections 588V and 588W of the Corporations Law are met. Broadly, liability may arise if the subsidiary is or becomes insolvent while trading.

The key component of the holding company's liability is that the holding company or one or more of its directors was aware that there were grounds for suspecting the subsidiary's insolvency, or "having regard to the nature and extent of the holding company's control over the subsidiary's affairs and to any other relevant circumstances", it is reasonable to expect that the holding company or one or more of its directors would be so aware. In other words, there are grounds for imputing an awareness of the subsidiary's plight to the holding company or its directors if it is reasonable to do so without having regard to the control relationship.

Section 588X gives the holding company some defences, essentially by permitting it to show that it had reasonable grounds to expect that the subsidiary was solvent, or that it reasonably relied on a competent and reliable person to inform it of the subsidiary's solvency, or that the awareness of a holding company director should be disregarded because of that director's illness or for some other good reason, or that the holding company took all reasonable steps to prevent the subsidiary from incurring the debt.

The new provisions cannot be seen as a solution to the problem identified by Rogers J. The statutory provisions seem to be focussing on a case where the parent and subsidiary are managed separately, as in the case of a local subsidiary of a foreign parent. The provisions are apt to deal with a local wholly owned group where assets of group entities are intermingled and the affairs of the entities are intricately intertwined. In such a case, it may be possible to prove the ingredients of holding company liability under section 588V. But the very complexity which creates problems in the liquidation of group entities will also generate problems in the proof of the ingredients of liability. The establishment of a judicial power to order that one entity contribute to the debts of the other and that liquidation proceed together is a much easier way of solving the problem.

XXII CONCLUSION

Interfering with the liability rules for corporate groups is a delicate enterprise. Just as limited liability itself is justifiable as an encouragement to entrepreneurial activity by the small business proprietor, so, equally, limited liability is an important encouragement for entrepreneurial activity in the corporate group. Without it, corporate group managers may be reluctant to expose the shareholders' funds of the parent entity to risky new business activity.

However, group entrepreneurship does not justify the intermingling of the assets and liabilities of group entities, nor the accumulation, layer upon layer, of intra-group transactions which can make the liquidator's task of unravelling the affairs of the insolvent subsidiaries either impossible or impossibly costly. A legislative model based on the New Zealand provisions would enable the courts to overcome some of the difficulties of corporate group liquidation, saving time and expense and ultimately improving returns for creditors. In order to limit the possible dampening effect that this could have on entrepreneurial activity, limited liability could be preserved where financial segregation and capitalisation/insurance of the subsidiary can be proved. In the Australian context, the need for reform of this kind is pressing. By limiting the reform to liquidation and providing an exception for financially segregated subsidiaries, the law would address the liquidator's administrative nightmare while allowing the principles of *Salomon's case* to continue to operate in the cases where, historically, it has proved so important.

5

Commentary on Austin

ANDREW BORROWDALE*

I INTRODUCTION

Goode's tenth (and last) principle of corporate insolvency law is that members of a company are not as such liable for its debts.[1] The future of this principle in the context of corporate groups depends, in New Zealand, upon the attitude of the courts to the pooling and contribution provisions contained in sections 271 and 272 of the Companies Act 1993 (formerly sections 315A–315C of the Companies Act 1955). As Dr Austin has already recounted, these provisions allow a court to order pooling of assets of related companies in liquidation and contribution by related companies to the assets of a company in liquidation.

There is no equivalent in Australia or the United Kingdom, but this does not exclude a pooling arrangement entered into by agreement between the various liquidators of companies within a group, as in the liquidation of the BCCI group.[2] The concept is borrowed from the United States, where it is known as substantive consolidation.[3] This is distinguished from procedural consolidation or joint administration where the bankruptcy proceedings of separate entities are consolidated for procedural purposes only, without affecting the substantive rights of creditors. The United States Bankruptcy Code does not expressly authorise the consolidation of separate estates, but a court may order consolidation by virtue of its general equitable powers.[4]

---

* Senior Lecturer in Law, University of Canterbury.

[1] R M Goode, *Principles of Corporate Insolvency Law* (London, Sweet and Maxwell, 1990), 22.

[2] For an account of the pooling agreements in that case see C Grierson, "Issues in Concurrent Insolvency Jurisdiction: English Perspective" in J Ziegel (ed.), *Current Developments in International and Comparative Insolvency Law* (Oxford, Clarendon, 1994), 577 at 608 ff.

[3] For a sample of literature, see B Weintraub and A N Resnick, *Bankruptcy Law Manual* (4th edn. by Resnick, New York, 1996), 8–86 ff; C Frost, "Organizational Form, Misappropriation Risk and the Substantive Consolidation of Corporate Groups" (1993) 44 *Hastings L J* 449; J S Gilbert, "Substantive Consolidation in Bankruptcy: A Primer" (1990) 43 *Vanderbilt L Rev* 207; C Grierson, "Shareholder Liability, Consolidation and Pooling" in E Leonard and C Besant (eds.), *Current Issues in Cross-Border Insolvency and Reorganisations* (London, Graham and Trotman, 1994), 205; E Hayes, "Substantive Consolidation under the Companies' Creditors Arrangement Act and the Bankruptcy and Insolvency Act" (1994) 23 *Can Bus L J* 444; and J Landers, "A Unified Approach to Parent, Subsidiary, and Affiliate Questions in Bankruptcy" (1975) 42 *U Chi L Rev* 589.

[4] *Re Auto-Train Corp. Inc.*, 810 F 2d 270 (DC Cir 1987), 276.

Consolidation is commonly ordered where the affairs of the companies in question are inextricably entangled, or at least so entangled that the cost of unravelling them is likely to absorb the assets in the liquidation.[5] Less commonly, consolidation may also be ordered on the basis that the creditors have dealt with the debtor companies as a single economic unit and did not rely upon the credit of a particular company within the group. In such cases, difficulty in separating the affairs of the companies may be only one factor in determining whether consolidation should be ordered. In an appropriate case consolidation may be ordered even where the affairs of the debtor companies are readily separated, as in *Re Flora Mir Candy*.[6]

The effect of consolidation is that intercompany debts and liabilities under guarantees are eliminated, the assets of the debtor companies are treated as common assets, and they are applied to the claims of creditors against any or all of the companies.[7]

The American courts have cautioned that consolidation should be used sparingly because of possible prejudice to creditors of a debtor company who have dealt solely with that company in isolation from others in the group.[8] This occurs where the likely distribution by company A within a group of companies would substantially exceed a distribution following consolidation of all companies in the group. The solution is to order consolidation of the debtor companies excluding company A.[9] Here the courts rely upon the doctrine of separate corporate personality, not for the usual purpose of shielding corporate participants (directors and shareholders) from liability, but to protect creditors. For this reason, Landers argues that the reliance by a creditor upon the credit of a particular entity should not be emphasised in considering whether consolidation should be ordered: the doctrine of separate incorporability was not designed as a protection for creditors.[10]

Consolidation is available in the United States between a solvent and an insolvent company. The non-debtor company is said to be "collapsed" into the debtor company. It appears to be only rarely ordered, and has the effect that all the assets and liabilities of the collapsed company are brought into the liquidation of the debtor company.[11]

II HISTORY OF THE NEW ZEALAND LEGISLATION

Sections 271 and 272 of the Companies Act 1993 potentially create a charter for New Zealand courts to discard the *Salomon* principle in relation to groups

---

[5] *Chemical Bank New York Trust Co.* v. *Kheel*, 369 F 2d 845 (2d Cir 1966), 847.

[6] 432 F 2d 1060 (2d Cir 1970).

[7] *Chemical Bank New York Trust Co.* v. *Kheel*, 369 F 2d 845 (2d Cir 1966), 847.

[8] *Ibid.*

[9] As in *Re Flora Mir Candy*, 432 F 2d 1060 (2d Cir 1970).

[10] Landers, n. 3 above, 640.

[11] Weintraub and Resnick, n. 3 above, citing *Re Moran Pipe & Supply Co.*, 130 BR 588 (ED Okla 1991), 593.

where some or all of the members of the group have been placed in liquidation. These provisions and their predecessors appear to have been little used. The starting point is section 24 of the Companies Special Investigations Act 1958 (now repealed), which provided for the pooling of assets in the liquidation of two or more companies to which the Act applied. That Act did not itself provide for liquidation of companies to which the Act applied, but merely imposed certain rules, such as the pooling of assets, on the liquidation of those companies in the usual way.

The pooling provision has not been carried over to the statute which replaced the 1958 Act, the Corporations (Investigation and Management) Act 1989. It has been said that a statutory manager has no role in a liquidation and it was inappropriate to re-enact a power in relation to the pooling of assets in a liquidation.[12] Further reasons include the following. The first is the enactment in 1980 of an amendment to the Companies Act 1955 itself to allow for pooling and contribution on liquidation. The second is that under section 52(3), a corporation under statutory management may be liquidated by order of the Governor-General in Council on such terms and conditions as are thought fit. Under section 38(2) the appointment of a statutory manager to a corporation has the effect that every subsidiary of the corporation is similarly placed in statutory management under the control of the statutory manager appointed to the parent. By section 40 an "associated person"[13] may also be placed in statutory management on the ground, *inter alia*, that the business and affairs of the corporation are so closely connected with the associated person that the statutory management of the former cannot effectively be carried on unless the associated person is placed in statutory management also. The result is that a statutory manager obtains control of the group and associated companies, and in an appropriate case may secure their liquidation on terms which include, *inter alia*, the pooling of assets.

The Companies Act 1993 takes over the pooling and contribution provisions found in the Companies Act 1955 since amendment in 1980, but with some differences. Sections 315B(2)–(5) of the 1955 Act do not appear in the 1993 Act. These include section 315B(2) ("In deciding the terms and conditions of an order under this section, the court shall have regard to the interests of those persons who are members of some, but not all, of the companies") and section 315B(3)(c) ("Nothing in this section or the order shall affect the rights of any secured creditor of any of the companies"). Presumably, provisions such as these have not been carried over into the 1993 Act because they are otiose: a court in the exercise of its just and equitable discretion under section 271 could not ignore the different interests of

---

[12] See *McDonald* v. *Australian Guarantee Corporation (NZ) Ltd.* (1989) 4 NZCLC 65,365, 65,376–65,377.

[13] For the definition of "associated person" see Corporations (Investigation and Management) Act 1989 (NZ), s 2(2).

shareholders who are not common to all companies in liquidation and could hardly upset the securities of secured creditors.[14]

III POOLING UNDER THE COMPANIES ACT 1993 (NZ)

The extent to which the pooling and contribution provisions of the Act will be used by New Zealand courts is unclear. It is suggested that there is a clear conceptual distinction between pooling and contribution. The rule in *Salomon's case* is twofold: a company is a distinct entity and therefore a shareholder is not liable for its debts. As the cases abundantly demonstrate, a court may readily disregard the first proposition, but will not do so in order to fix a shareholder with liability. A pooling order is an example of disregard of separate personality in order to divide an existing pool of assets among the creditors, while a contribution order is an example of disregarding separate personality by imposing liability upon a related company and so swelling the pool of assets available for the creditors of the company in liquidation. Yet this distinction is curiously submerged in the guidelines to which a court must have regard in deciding whether it is just and equitable to make a pooling or a contribution order.

Section 272(2) sets out the mandatory guidelines for a pooling order. These are:

"(a) The extent to which any of the companies took part in the management of any of the other companies:

(b) The conduct of any of the companies towards the creditors of any of the other companies:

(c) The extent to which the circumstances that gave rise to the liquidation of any of the companies are attributable to the actions of any of the other companies:

(d) The extent to which the businesses of the companies have been combined:

(e) Such other matters as the Court thinks fit."

By comparison with the American authorities, it is suggested that only the guidelines contained in section 272(2)(b) and (d) are truly relevant to the question of pooling. Conduct towards creditors of other companies (section 272(2)(b)) somewhat obliquely encompasses the factor that the impression is created among creditors generally that they deal with a single enterprise and not with a particular entity within the group. Combination of businesses (section 272(2)(d)) appears to refer to an objective circumstance—the extent to which the businesses have actually been combined. This is material not only

---

[14] For a discussion of the tension between the interests of secured creditors and others where a pooling order as to costs (as opposed to assets) is proposed, see *McDonald* v. *Australian Guarantee Corporation (NZ) Ltd.* (1989) 4 NZCLC 65,365, 65,380–65,381. In *Re Gulfco. Investment Corp.*, 593 F 2d 921 (10th Cir 1979), it was held that consolidation could not be used to strip a creditor of security.

to the difficulty of unravelling the separate businesses, but also to the impression given to creditors that the businesses are one.

It is difficult to see how the guidelines contained in section 272(2)(a) and (c) are relevant to pooling. The extent to which any of the companies took part in the management of the other companies is more relevant to contribution than pooling. It seeks to attribute responsibility to one company for the management of another. There is a clear distinction, it is suggested, between participation by one *company* in the management of another, and commonality of management of two or more companies. In fact, the courts will interpret this criterion as simply another facet of the single enterprise inquiry. In *Re Dalhoff and King Holdings Ltd. (in liq)*,[15] Gallen J considered an application for the liquidation of three companies, a parent and two subsidiaries, as if one company. The effect of pooling, if the order was made, was that the unsecured creditors in all three companies would recover 90 per cent of their debts, while shareholders would receive nothing. This was at the expense of shareholders in the parent, who would otherwise have received a dividend in the liquidation of 28 cents per share. Gallen J examined the criteria now set out in section 272(2). As to the first, the evidence was that separate board meetings were not called for each company and that the affairs of all three companies were considered at single meetings. Gallen J concluded: "In this case there was one inter-related group of companies which seems to have been operated by the management substantially as one entity."[16] Now this suggests that the businesses of the companies were combined, but does not mean that *one* company took part in the management of *another*. In fact, it would have been impossible to identify one company acting in the course of board meetings.

While some of the guidelines contained in section 272(2) in relation to a pooling order are not, it is argued above, quite apposite, in another sense these suggest a more liberal approach than that adopted in American law. The impossibility, or even difficulty, of disentangling the affairs of the companies in liquidation is not strictly a criterion to which the court must look. Rather it must have regard only to the extent to which the businesses of the companies have been combined. This is not necessarily the same test, although it subsumes difficulty of disentanglement. *Re Pacific Syndicates (NZ) Ltd.*[17] was a clear case for pooling on the grounds of the impossibility of separating the affairs of the two companies in liquidation, all parties, creditors and liquidators alike agreeing that pooling was desirable.

The American cases suggest that the most contentious issue in pooling cases is reconciliation of the interests of the separate creditors. *Dalhoff*, discussed above, is an unusual case in that it involved balancing the interests of creditors and shareholders. Section 315B(2) of the Companies Act 1955 required

---

[15] (1991) 5 NZCLC 66,959.
[16] *Ibid.*, at 66,965.
[17] (1989) 4 NZCLC 64,757, 64,767–64,768.

the court to have regard to the interests of persons who are members of some but not all of the companies. That provision has not found its way into section 272 of the Companies Act 1993. In *Dalhoff*, Gallen J said: "Clearly [section 315B(2)] is designed to ensure that no fraud is perpetrated upon the shareholders of one company by the activities of those of another."[18] It is submitted that this was not the direct aim of this provision at all. It was designed to protect shareholders who might be prejudiced through the collapse of their solvent company into the insolvent group, as in the case of the parent in *Dalhoff*. However, Gallen J considered that there was no evidence as between the shareholders of the three companies that one set of shareholders was preferred by management over the others. Accordingly he concluded that section 315B(2) did not apply. It is suggested that this reasoning is incorrect, and despite the lack of re-enactment of section 315B(2) in the 1993 Act, the prejudice to shareholders is still a relevant concern, as the American authorities affirm.

IV CONTRIBUTION UNDER THE COMPANIES ACT 1993 (NZ)

The true usurpation of the *Salomon* rule in relation to corporate groups is found in the power of the court to order contribution by a related company. The willingness of the courts to use this power is, it is submitted, constrained by two factors. The first is the commercial culpability of the related company. The second is the likely prejudice to creditors of the related company.

A clear case for ordering contribution occurs where a parent company strips a subsidiary by making a distribution to itself of the whole of the assets, leaving unsecured creditors of the subsidiary with only a shell against which to proceed. It is true that such a distribution may be recovered under section 56 of the Companies Act 1993 if the solvency test was not satisfied upon the distribution being made, and even at common law a dividend improperly paid out of capital was recoverable from shareholders who knew or ought to have known of the impropriety of the payment.[19] But there are two reasons why an order under section 271 is preferable. First, the action may be brought by an individual creditor, who accordingly is not reliant upon a possibly recalcitrant or uninterested liquidator. Secondly, the proceeds of recovery may, it is submitted, be ordered to be paid to the particular creditor who brings the proceedings, whereas any recovery under the distribution provisions accrues for the benefit of the creditors as a whole.

At the outer limit of cases in which a contribution order will be made must be *Rea* v. *Barker*[20] where the liquidators of company A joined a related company B to misfeasance proceedings seeking a contribution order on two

---

[18] (1991) 5 NZCLC 66,959, 66,969.
[19] *Hilton International Ltd. (in liq)* v. *Hilton* [1989] 1 NZLR 442, 459.
[20] (1988) 4 NZCLC 64,312.

grounds. It was alleged that B procured A to transfer to B orders without payment (A and B both manufacturing the same goods) and that, following liquidation, B refused to purchase A's stock which was in effect valueless unless
B purchased it. Reliance upon this latter ground in particular is drawing a
long bow, but Thorp J was prepared to dismiss a striking out application.
Doubtless, little can be read into this decision; by itself it cannot be taken to
evidence any indication on the part of the New Zealand judiciary to use the
court's contribution power to overcome the *Salomon* principle.

On the other hand, if there is such a willingness, legal advisers to corporate groups may well have to abandon previously secure bulwarks to corporate liability. The most obvious is the letter of comfort. The giving of a letter
of comfort falls squarely within the mandatory guideline contained in section
272(2)(b)—the conduct of the related company towards the creditors of the
company in liquidation. Certainly a court is unlikely to make a contribution
order which has the effect of enforcing a letter of comfort as if it were a guarantee, but it is quite possible that a court may fix the corporate author of a
letter of comfort with some portion of liability. Section 272(3) provides that
reliance upon the fact that the company in liquidation is related to the related
company is not a ground for a pooling or contribution order. Reliance upon
a letter of comfort, however, is in a quite different category.

As in the case of pooling orders, a court must be alert to the prejudice interested parties may suffer by an order of consolidation being made. For example, will a court order contribution if the likely effect is to tip the related
company into liquidation? Will contribution be ordered against a related company which is itself already in liquidation? This raises acute issues of conflict
between the interests of the separate creditors of the two companies, in contrast to the simpler scenario where a contribution order is sought against a
related company which is solvent and can afford to pay.

6

Corporate Personality, Limited Liability and the Protection of Creditors

DAN PRENTICE*

Most creditors of most companies are eventually paid,[1] and commercial life goes on as usual. In addition, most creditors who are not paid sums due will eventually proceed by some form of legal action, other than winding up, to obtain judgment and, if needed, execution.[2] Secured creditors, of course, are free to proceed against the assets subject to their security once there has been default.[3] Also of importance are non-judicial remedies, such as discontinuance of supply and reporting any default to a credit rating agency and thus impairing the other party's ability to acquire credit in the future.[4] However, inevitably there may be default by the corporate debtor which ultimately results in its being put into insolvent liquidation with the consequence that the unsecured creditors' claims will only be met in part. The question arises whether the asset pool available for the unsecured creditors can in some way be swollen to increase the dividend payable to the unsecured creditors. There are potentially three constituencies from which contributions may be sought: (i) creditors, (ii) shareholders and (iii) directors.

I RECOVERY FROM CREDITORS

It is not proposed to deal with this topic in any detail. However, it must not be overlooked that when a company goes into insolvent liquidation, there are a number of avoidance powers vested in the liquidator which, if successfully

---

* Allen & Overy Professor of Corporate Law, University of Oxford.

[1] If it were not so, the credit system would be radically different for companies; in fact it might not even exist.

[2] Thus, for example, in England and Wales there were approximately 18,000 petitions for winding up in 1995, whereas there were 895,301 warrants of execution against goods issued in the same year: *Judicial Statistics 1995*, Tables 2.7, 2.8 and 4.16.

[3] *Sowman v. David Samuel Trust Ltd.* [1978] 1 WLR 22.

[4] D Baird and T M Jackson, *Cases, Problems and Materials on Bankruptcy* (2nd edn., Boston, Mass., Little, Brown, 1990), 5.

invoked by him, result in the assets of the company being swollen. Thus, as far as United Kingdom law is concerned, the liquidator can challenge preferences,[5] transactions at an undervalue[6] and extortionate credit transactions.[7] Also, certain secured claims against the company can be transmuted into unsecured claims.[8] There are a number of important features of these provisions:

(a) On the whole, they deal with the inter-creditor fairness, and they are not designed to deal with the relationship between the company and its creditors; they simply underpin the collective nature of insolvency proceedings.

(b) Recovery may swell the assets available for distribution but it does so by returning to the company something that it previously owned.[9] There is, as it were, no new net gain to the company or its creditors.

(c) Where the avoidance powers are successfully invoked, the creditor who has to disgorge remains a creditor and is entitled to prove in the liquidation with other creditors.[10] What happens is that the preferred debt revives and the creditor is not precluded from proving.

(d) Inevitably, there is always the risk that action will not be taken by the liquidator to effect recovery for a range of reasons: the quantum involved may not make it worthwhile, the transaction may not be detected or the liquidator may not have the funds to finance proceedings.[11] What this entails is that the bringing of avoidance proceedings will be somewhat hit and miss and it will normally be the case that there will be little likelihood that such proceedings will greatly enhance the pool of assets available to satisfy creditor claims.

(e) The United Kingdom does not possess lender liability rules whereby a lender who irresponsibly (whatever that means) extends credit to the company can in some way be made liable for the company's debts or have its claim deferred.

---

[5] Insolvency Act 1986, s 239 (hereafter "the 1986 Act"): see *Re M C Bacon Ltd. (No 2)* [1990] BCLC 607. English preference law is debtor-driven in the sense that it is the intent of the debtor company that is relevant for determining preference. See generally D D Prentice, "Some Observations on the Law Relating to Preferences" in R Cranston (ed.), *Making Commercial Law: Essays in Honour of Roy Goode* (Oxford, Clarendon, 1997), 439.

[6] The 1986 Act, s 238.

[7] The 1986 Act, s 243.

[8] The 1986 Act, s 245 (defective floating charges—the effect of this is to give unsecured creditors a benefit for which they did not pay).

[9] This is even true of defective floating charges (the 1986 Act, s 245), since the invalidity of the charge entails that the asset is not appropriated to the security.

[10] This would normally apply to preferences. In the case of transactions at an undervalue, there will often be no underlying debt. The Australian legislation makes express provision protecting the right of a creditor who gives up a preference to prove in the winding up as though no preference had been conferred: see Corporations Law, s 588FI. Even if the preferred creditor is seen as a constructive trustee, he will not be any worse off even if he has to disgorge and pay compound interest. He is merely paying back the benefit he has received (see Prentice, n. 5 above, 444).

[11] The financing of liquidation proceedings raises important issues that will be addressed later.

II RECOVERY FROM SHAREHOLDERS

The next issue is whether it is possible to swell the assets available in a winding up to recover a contribution from shareholders. In the winding up of a company, a shareholder can be obliged to contribute only the amount "unpaid" on shares in respect of which he is liable as a past or present member.[12] It is by this simple mechanism that limited liability is brought about. The benefits of limited liability, at least as a matter of principle, have been well documented. As Hicks has stated,[13] "[t]o be a 'sleeping partner', without limited liability, would be exceedingly dangerous", and accordingly persons will invest in a firm with unlimited liability only where they can control the riskiness of the firm's activities and also monitor the wealth of their co-adventurers.[14] This combination would make it impossible for large aggregations of wealth to be assembled, at least in the private sector. Again, as Hicks states:[15]

> "Indeed, if there were no limited liability, such investments would hardly be made at all, except in the public sector. Thus it is not surprising that the building of railways was historically connected with the coming of limited liability."

Once the policy is determined that entrepreneurial activity is to be predominantly a matter for the private sector and not the public sector, limited liability becomes virtually inevitable. Limited liability also facilitates the transferability of shares[16] and greatly cuts down the costs of carrying on business in a collective form, in that shareholders will not need to monitor the wealth of the fellow shareholders which they otherwise would do in a regime of unlimited liability.[17] There are, however, risks associated with limited liability. This topic will be dealt with later.

There is a range of company law rules designed to ensure that the company receives what it should, in the form of either cash or non-cash consideration, in payment for its shares.[18] From early on, the courts considered that the creditor gave credit to a company's capital,[19] and various doctrines were

---

[12] See, for example, the 1986 Act, s 74(2)(d).

[13] A Hicks, "Limited Liability: Pros and Cons" in T Orhnial (ed.), *Limited Liability and the Corporation* (London, Croom Helm, 1982), 179.

[14] The reason for this is that persons who are not worth powder and shot and have nothing to lose may be willing to take risks that those with something to lose would be unwilling to take.

[15] Hicks, n. 13 above, 180.

[16] See S E Woodward, "Limited Liability in the Theory of the Firm" (1985) 141 *Journal of Institutional and Theoretical Economics* 601.

[17] See, generally, F Easterbrook and D Fischel, *The Economic Structure of Corporate Law* (Cambridge, Mass., Harvard University Press, 1991), Chap 2.

[18] See, generally, N Furey, "The Protection of Creditors' Interests in Company Law" in D Feldman and F Meisel (eds.), *Corporate and Commercial Law: Modern Developments* (London, Lloyds of London Press, 1996), Chap 9.

[19] *Re Exchange Banking Company (Flitcroft's Case)* (1882) 21 Ch D 519, 533–4 ("The creditor, therefore, I may say, gives credit to that capital . . .": *per* Jessell MR). It is questionable whether this makes any commercial sense at least if one is referring to the left hand side of the balance sheet.

developed to underpin this principle. It is proposed to deal only with those aspects of this development which are relevant to the primary focus of this essay.

First, no minimum capitalisation is required when a company commences life. While the market for credit might in theory operate to ensure that creditors dealing with an undercapitalised[20] company were adequately compensated, this will be highly unlikely in many cases,[21] and of course has no application to involuntary creditors.[22] There has been little interest shown in Commonwealth countries in minimum capitalisation requirements, something which is to be contrasted with continental Europe, where such requirements are the norm.[23] The one important exception is the capital adequacy requirement imposed on banks.[24] The problems with minimum capitalisation requirements are obvious. It is almost inevitable that the appropriate level of capitalisation (and it is not even clear what this means) will not be correctly estimated and will either be under-inclusive or over-exclusive.[25] Given this important and ineradicable difficulty, the route of minimum capitalisation as a means for protecting creditors is not an attractive one.

Secondly, there is no regulation of the corporate capital mix so that those setting up a company are free to finance the company by a mixture of secured debt and equity.[26] This means (as was the case with Mr Salomon) incorporators could themselves invest in the company in the form of secured debt so that, should the company be wound up, they would be in a position of priority according to the seniority of the security. Coupled with this, English law developed no doctrine of subordination to deal with this situation where a company capitalised in this way goes into insolvent liquidation. In many ways this is an attractive solution, since the claim of the subordinated creditor is not ignored, it remains enforceable and what is denied is his security or other advantage which the insider-creditor has received.[27] Nor, for that matter, have the courts developed any doctrines whereby "debt" contributed by members

---

[20] This merely means a company with inadequate capital for its purpose.

[21] A good example of a class of creditors who probably are not compensated for the risk of dealing with a company are pre-paying customers. It is arguable that such customers extend credit in much the same way as a person who supplies goods to be paid for later (see Cork Committee Report (1982, Cmnd 8558), at para 1052). It is to be doubted, however, that such customers do see themselves as supplying credit and may be in a weak position to protect their interests: see *The Protection of Consumer Prepayments: A Discussion Paper* (OFT, 1984), para 5.11.

[22] See pp. 104–105. English public companies must have a minimum capital of £50,000: Companies Act 1985, s 118.

[23] H-J De Kluiver, "Europe and the Private Company: An Introduction" in H-J De Kluiver and W van Gerven (eds.), *The European Private Company?* (Antwerp, Maklee, 1995), 21, 26–8. However, even there it is seen more as an "entrance fee" than as insurance for a company's creditors.

[24] See S Cresswell *et al.*, *Encyclopedia of Banking Law, Division B* (London, Butterworths, 1995), para 149.

[25] There are also technical difficulties in valuing non-cash considerations.

[26] Publicly listed companies in the United Kingdom are regulated as to their capital mix: see *The Listing Rules* (London Stock Exchange, London), para 3.16.

[27] See, for example, *Re Clark Pipe & Supply Co. Inc.*, 893 F 2d (5th Cir 1990) 693.

is treated as a matter of substance as equity ("phantom equity"), with the consequence that debt held by members could be subordinated to the claims of unsecured creditors. It is thus possible for members of a failing company to provide secured debt financing without the danger of this being categorised as equity.

Thirdly, although the courts developed the rule that shares could not be issued at a discount,[28] they developed no rules for valuing non-cash consideration.[29] The common law rule was that price was value, a perfectly defensible principle where the transaction is at arm's length, but much less defensible where the parties to the transaction were not independent of each other as normally is the case between a company and its promoters.

Fourthly, initially there were no obligations on the part of a company to take corrective action where the value of its net assets fell below the aggregate of its paid-up share capital and undistributable reserves or some such other capital benchmark.[30] This position has been changed by statute in the United Kingdom. Section 142 of the Companies Act 1985 requires the directors to summon a meeting of shareholders where the net assets of a public company are half or less of its called up share capital. The purpose of the meeting is to consider what steps, if any, should be taken to deal with the situation. This is Directive driven, by Article 17 of the Second Directive,[31] and it is a remarkably misconceived piece of legislation: (a) there are acute timing problems since it is often not crystal clear at exactly what point the net assets fall below the relevant benchmark; (b) it is unclear what business the shareholders' meeting is to transact since it is the duty of the directors to put forward and implement the necessary proposals to solve the company's difficulties; (c) the summoning of such a meeting can do unnecessary commercial damage to the reputation of the company; and (d) it would appear that a meeting has to be held even though it is not clear that the loss of capital is permanent.

Finally, when a company is in financial difficulty there is no obligation on the part of the members to invest additional sums in the company, nor can

---

[28] *Ooreguum Gold Mining Co. of India Ltd.* v. *Roper* [1892] AC 125. This is now a statutory proscription: Companies Act 1985, s 101. The "no discount rule" is hard to justify as a matter of principle in terms of creditor protection since creditors will always benefit no matter how deep the discount.

[29] *Re Wragg* [1897] 1 Ch 796, 811–14. There were exceptions to this where: (i) the consideration was a sham (*Re Wragg* [1897] 1 Ch 796, 815); (ii) where there was fraud (*Tintin Exploration Syndicate Ltd.* v. *Sandys* (1947) 177 LT 412); (iii) where the consideration on the face of it was manifestly inadequate (*Re White Star Line Ltd.* [1938] Ch 458); and (iv) where no attempt was made to place a finite value on the consideration received by the company (*Hong Kong and China Gas Co. Ltd.* v. *Glen* [1914] 1 Ch 527).

[30] See Companies Act 1985, s 264, which prohibits a dividend being paid in this situation in the case of a public company.

[31] 77/91/EEC; [1977] OJ L26/1 (Formation of Public Companies and Maintenance and Alteration of Capital).

they be compelled to do so.[32] Such a principle is the corollary of the principle of limited liability, and any legally enforceable obligation to contribute additional equity would subvert this principle.

III RECOVERY FROM DIRECTORS

A Introduction

Before dealing with the issue of directors having to contribute to the assets of a company which has gone into insolvent liquidation, a brief digression is needed on the risks associated with limited liability. This is a well-trodden path. There is debate whether limited liability results in uncompensated risk being imposed on creditors who deal with a company. Some argue that those dealing with companies are fully aware that the principle of limited liability will preclude recovery from members of the company, and therefore they will set the terms of the bargain with the company so as to ensure compensation for this risk.[33] Whether this in fact occurs could be answered by empirical evidence. Do unsecured creditors charge more when dealing with companies rather than unincorporated entities? Do employees of companies receive more than their equivalents in unincorporated concerns? Do banks charge more interest on secured loans to corporate as opposed to unincorporated concerns? Of course, even if the data indicated that both corporate and unincorporated entities were treated somewhat similarly, they would not necessarily refute the proposition that those dealing with companies were not compensated for the risk that was posed by the principle. For example, in the case of bank loans, the bank may extract a guarantee[34] from the directors and thus protect its interests.

   Even if one accepts that in consensual transactions persons dealing with companies are adequately compensated for the risk posed by limited liability, there are situations where this will not be the case. This is manifestly so with involuntary creditors, for example, tort victims or the State for environmental clean-up costs. More importantly, there are certain situations where even

---

[32] Companies Act 1985, s 16. Normally a member will be willing to do so where there are economic reasons justifying an additional investment, for example, a rights issue to cope with unanticipated liabilities. However, the greater the number of members, the less likely that such a rescue operation could effectively be mounted, partly because of the collective action problems, partly because the members will have different interests, and finally because the benefit to the member may be *de minimis.*

[33] R Posner, "The Rights of Creditors of Affiliated Corporations" (1976) 43 *Univ Chi L Rev* 499.

[34] It appears to be a common phenomenon that, at least in the case of the "one person" company, banks extract guarantees from the company's directors in connection with any borrowings. Of course, such a guarantee does not necessarily constitute a complete abrogation of limited liability, in that the quantum of liability is determined and not open-ended; liability under the guarantee cannot exceed the loan.

voluntary creditors will be subjected to uncompensated risk. Where a company is insolvent, the shareholders by definition cease to have any material interest in the assets of the company.[35] This point is neatly illustrated by the rule that in schemes of arrangement involving insolvent concerns there is no need to obtain the approval of the shareholders for the scheme.[36] In a situation of insolvency, the shareholders have a perverse incentive to continue the company in business since they have everything to gain and nothing to lose. Any additional loss will be at the expense of the creditors, and should the company trade back into solvency the gains will be appropriated by the shareholders. In other words, there is no downside risk but only upside advantage. Where the shareholders are also the directors, or there is considerable overlap, this incentive will be shared by the directors. Even if the directors are not substantial equity holders, they will have an incentive to continue to trade in order to retain their positions and the advantages that go with them. However, as against this they will have their reputations to consider, and this may encourage them to maximise the return to creditors by bringing the company's business to an end.[37]

B Common Law Liability of Directors

There are two techniques whereby the common law imposes obligations on directors. The first is to find an independent duty owed to creditors, and the second is to mediate the interests of the creditors through the company. *Williams* v. *Natural Life Health Foods Ltd.*[38] is a recent example of the first technique. There, the plaintiffs had been induced to enter into a franchise agreement for the operation of a health food shop. The figures as to its future profitability had been prepared negligently by the franchisor company, and it was on the basis of these figures that the plaintiffs entered into the arrangement. The plaintiffs sued the company in negligence alleging that the company owed them a duty of care which it had breached by giving them negligent financial advice. The company went into liquidation and the plaintiffs thereupon sought to obtain damages from M, the managing director and dominant shareholder of the company. The Court of Appeal upheld the judgment of the trial judge[39] imposing liability on M. The Court of Appeal recognised that to use the common law of tort to impose liability on a director could subvert the principle of limited liability. Nevertheless, it reasoned that there are

---

[35] *Ayerst (Inspector of Taxes)* v. *C & K (Construction) Ltd.* [1976] AC 167.

[36] *Re Tea Corporation Ltd.* [1904] 1 Ch 12.

[37] See R J Daniels, "Must Boards Go Overboard? An Economic Analysis of the Burgeoning Statutory Liability on the Role of Directors in Corporate Governance" in J Ziegel (ed.), *Current Developments in International Corporative Corporate Insolvency Law* (Oxford, Clarendon, 1994), Chap 23.

[38] [1997] 1 BCLC 131.

[39] [1996] 1 BCLC 288 (Langley J). See also D Goddard, Chap 2.

circumstances where a director could be found to have assumed a personal liability towards a person who was dealing with the company. However, such an assumption of liability should be tested against the principle that, by incorporating a one-man company, the person incorporating it makes it "plain to all the world that limited liability was intended".[40] For liability to arise it was necessary to show that the director had:[41]

> "assumed personal responsibility for the negligent misstatement made on behalf of the company. In my judgment, having regard to the importance of the status of limited liability, a company director is only to be held personally liable for the company's negligent misstatements if the plaintiffs can establish some special circumstances setting the case apart from the ordinary; and in the case of a director of a one-man company particular vigilance is needed, lest the protection of incorporation should be virtually nullified. But once such special circumstances are established, the fact of incorporation, even in the case of a one-man company, does not preclude the establishment of personal liability. In each case the decision is one of fact and degree."

A number of points can be made with respect to this development.

(a) The starting point is that incorporation is to be taken as a strong indicator that limited liability was intended and that the incorporators did not intend to be liable for the debts of the company. This would be so even though the corporate form is being used deliberately to obtain the advantages of limited liability in the face of future known risks.[42]

(b) The imposition of this type of liability will be rare and difficult to predict. In *Williams* itself, Sir Patrick Russell dissented, holding that there were no special or exceptional circumstances justifying the imposition of personal liability. The reason for such conservatism is limited liability; the majority in *Williams* considered that a disposition to find directors liable would subvert the principle of limited liability.[43] As Hirst LJ pointed out, this restrictive approach is particularly "needed" in the "case of a director of a one-man company".[44] It must also be remembered that companies enter into legal relationships by attributing to the company the acts of human agents[45] and the principle of attribution makes such acts the acts of the company and not those of the actor; something more is needed to show that the actor has assumed responsibility.

---

[40] *Trevor Ivory Ltd.* v. *Anderson* [1992] 2 NZLR 517, 524; see also 532 (*per* McGechan J). This case was cited extensively by the Court of Appeal in *Williams*. See also *Evans & Sons Ltd.* v. *Spritebrand Ltd.* [1985] BCLC 105, which evinces a more traditional attitude towards liability of a tortfeasor who is acting as a principal.

[41] [1997] 1 BCLC 131, 152 (*per* Hirst LJ).

[42] *Adams* v. *Cape Industries Plc* [1990] Ch 433, 544.

[43] [1997] 1 BCLC 131, 152 (*per* Hirst LJ); 154 (*per* Waite LJ).

[44] *Ibid.*

[45] *Meridian Global Funds Management Asia Ltd.* v. *Securities Commission* [1995] 2 AC 500; see R Grantham, "Corporate Knowledge: Identification or Attribution?" (1996) 59 *MLR* 732.

(c) The duty owed in this situation, which will normally be tortious but could be contractual where the court finds a collateral contract,[46] arises from the facts of the transaction and is not a duty arising from a director's status. It follows from this that any recovery goes directly to the plaintiff and is not mediated through the company to swell the assets available to the company's general creditors. This in no way constitutes a departure from the *pari passu* rule of distribution since "the assets" were never assets of the company but are damages (contractual or tortious) payable to the plaintiff, and there is simply no justification for channelling them through the company.

The second technique developed at common law for protecting the interests of creditors is to impose a duty on directors to consider the interests of the company's creditors. The conceptual apparatus for achieving this is relatively straightforward. Once a company goes into insolvent liquidation, the shareholders cease to have any interest in the assets of the company.[47] In insolvency, the shareholders "come last"[48] and as the company's assets are not sufficient to meet the claims of its creditors, the shareholders drop out of the picture. In this situation, the courts have held that the interests of the company are the interests of the creditors and the directors must act so as to maximise creditor welfare. There has been much dispute about the exact nature of this duty; it is not proposed to enter into this dispute here.[49] But a number of points need to be made.

(a) It is unclear if recovery will swell the assets available for the unsecured creditors or feed a charge, for example, a floating charge over all or substantially all of the company's assets. Given that the duty is owed to the creditors, a strong argument can be made that recovery should be in favour of the unsecured creditors, recovery by the company being merely mechanics and also being necessary to underpin the *pari passu* principle.

(b) Although the duty is said to be to the "creditors", the loss to the creditors is measured by the loss to the company. Thus loss caused by misfeasance,[50] the making of preferential payments[51] and the sale of assets to a company controlled by the selling company's shareholders so as to reduce the assets available for the vendor company's shareholders[52] have been seen as constituting breaches of duty to creditors. However, the measure of recovery was the loss to the company. There is no additional

---

[46] *Esso Petroleum Co. Ltd.* v. *Mardon* [1976] QB 801.

[47] *Ayerst (Inspector of Taxes)* v. *C & K (Construction) Ltd.* [1976] AC 167.

[48] *Soden* v. *British and Commonwealth Holdings Plc* [1996] 2 BCLC 207, 213.

[49] See R Grantham, "The Judicial Extension of Directors' Duties to Creditors" [1991] *JBL* 1; D D Prentice, "Creditor's Interests and Director's Duties" (1990) 10 *OJLS* 265. See also D Goddard, Chap 2.

[50] *Walker* v. *Wimborne* (1976) 50 ALJR 446.

[51] *West Mercia Safetywear Ltd.* v. *Dodd* [1988] BCLC 250.

[52] *Nicholson* v. *Permacraft (NZ) Ltd.* [1985] 1 NZLR 242.

obligation on the part of the directors to make any contribution to meet any loss to the company's creditors.

(c) Where directors have breached their duty to creditors, there can be no question of shareholder ratification of such breach. The shareholders as such have no role to play.

(d) The duty to the creditors must be mediated through the company. This is to ensure that the *pari passu* principle is observed and is given effect to. To treat the duty as being a free-standing duty to some of the creditors, for example, those who maintained the action, would undermine the *pari passu* principle. Mediation through the company also avoids multiplicity of actions.

(e) Finally, this type of action is arguably one that can be assigned to a third party to enable proceedings to be financed. Such an action would be sufficiently the property of the company and thus assignable by the liquidator to finance proceedings connected with the insolvency. This point will be developed later.

IV ENHANCING THE POOL OF ASSETS—DIRECTOR'S LIABILITY

In this section it is proposed to deal with those provisions that empower the court to order directors to contribute to the assets of a company which has gone into insolvent liquidation. As we have already seen, limited liability can provide a perverse incentive, particularly in the case of the owner/director company, to continue trading where the company is insolvent or on the verge of insolvency. In addition, the owners of the company will be indifferent to the riskiness of the activity, since the creditors will have no call on the individual wealth of the owners. Where the company is a public company, with a separation between shareholders and management, it has been argued that this perverse incentive may not be so acute. Managers will have less incentive to undertake risky ventures since their human capital is tied up in the firm.[53] It may also be that managers are reluctant to engage in the level of risk that the shareholders would consider appropriate because, *inter alia*, the fear of reputational loss should they get it wrong,[54] or disqualification under the Company Directors' Disqualification Act 1986.[55] There is a considerable grain of truth in all of this, but where managers are indifferent to reputation[56] or

[53] F Easterbrook and D Fischel, "Limited Liability and the Corporation" (1985) 52 *Univ Chi L Rev* 89, 107–8.

[54] R Kraakman, "Corporate Liability Strategies and the Costs of Legal Controls" (1984) 93 *Yale LJ* 857, 863–4.

[55] This has become a more significant regulatory device. In 1995 proceedings for disqualification were commenced against 1,145 directors; the figure for 1994 was 774: see Insolvency General Annual Report for 1995 (HMSO, London, 1996), 12.

[56] This is obviously the case where managers are fraudulent, e.g. Robert Maxwell. It would also be the case with respect to small companies where the manager lacks a transferable reputation.

do pursue a high risk strategy, then a perverse incentive will exist to try to trade out of the company's financial difficulties.[57]

One way of minimising any perverse incentive which a company may have to continue trading where it is in financial difficulties is to impose liability on the shareholders and/or directors with respect to losses incurred by creditors in circumstances where the company continues to trade at the expense of creditors since, the company being insolvent, the value of the shareholders' interest is zero. The value of continued trading to managers will, of course, not be zero since they will have a continued interest in receiving remuneration. This continued interest in remuneration is clearly recognised in the United Kingdom in cases arising under the Company Directors' Disqualification Act 1986 where the level of a director's remuneration is considered a factor to be taken into consideration in determining the unfitness of the director[58] to take part in the management of a company and the appropriate length of any disqualification order.[59]

As Mr Telfer points out in his courteous and perceptive commentary, there are legitimate reservations to be raised against provisions imposing liability on directors along the lines of either section 214 or sections 135 and 136 of the New Zealand Companies Act 1993. There are three points I wish to address:

(a) *Uncompensated Risk and the Market*: I agree completely that voluntary creditors have many mechanisms to protect themselves against, or gain compensation for, dealing with a company where its members enjoy limited liability. The problem is that they often fail to do so.[60] I simply do not think, for example, that pre-paying customers see themselves as extending credit, and they do not have the sophistication to ensure that there is a trust of their pre-payment.[61] Secondly, risk changes. The directors will be in a key position to assess the implications of such change, whereas the creditors in many situations[62] are not in a position to do so. Lastly, we talk somewhat glibly about risk assessment. In the case of

---

[57] See, generally, B Pettet, "Limited Liability—A Principle for the 21st Century?" (1995) 48 *CLP* 125.

[58] *Secretary of State for Trade and Industry* v. *Gash* [1997] 1 BCLC 341.

[59] *Re Cargo Agency Ltd.* [1992] BCLC 686, 690 (a director could not pay himself at the market rate where the company was just starting up); *Re CSTC Ltd.* [1995] BCC 173, 181 ("A director must bear in mind what a company can afford as well as what is the going rate for the job performed by the director if he were an employee elsewhere" (*per* Robert Reid QC)).

[60] Some creditors may have bargained for the risk of dealing with a company and any recovery from the directors in winding up in which they have a right of participation would result in their over-compensation (see T Telfer, Chap 7). This could be dealt with by permitting the court to award differential payments to creditors. Alternatively, parity of treatment for all creditors may simply be accepted as a second best solution in order to avoid the costs of trying to discriminate between creditors in a winding up.

[61] See n. 21 above.

[62] For example, creditors on a long-term supply contract, as opposed to short-term contactors who can bargain for up-to-date information. Also, at least as far as England goes, the published accounts are never up to date.

sophisticated financial creditors this no doubt occurs. However, in the case of unsophisticated trade creditors it is highly problematical the extent to which there is any assessment risk.

(b) *The Impact of Director Liability*: again, it is accepted that the threat of liability will affect directors' attitude to risk. The only way to avoid this is to abandon any attempt to impose liability on directors towards creditors. But there are arguments against such an extreme position. There will be a point at which directors appreciate that the *consequences* of their decisions can only result in insolvency. This may chill decisions at the margins, but it is a much higher threshold than current liability for misfeasance.[63] Also, the fact that shareholders may not as part of a hypothetical bargain agree to director liability rules is irrelevant. It is obvious that they would not agree to a rule, which could prejudice their interests, for the protection of creditors in a situation where they have everything to gain and nothing to lose.

(c) *Uncertainty and the Judicial Interpretation of Risk*: there is always the risk that judges will get it wrong. But at least as far as the United Kingdom is concerned, there is no evidence to suggest that they are unaware of the dangers of turning directors into the guarantors of the company's success.[64] The judicial task will be made more manageable if the conceptual apparatus for determining liability is drafted as precisely as possible. It must be conceded that this is not always the case.[65] Also, it is important that liability should be couched in terms of the *consequences* of a particular decision or decisions in the sense that the directors have to appreciate that the company cannot avoid insolvent liquidation.

The legislative response to directors continuing to trade when the company is insolvent or on the verge of insolvency has been to impose liability on directors for fraudulent or wrongful trading. It is proposed to examine these in turn, concentrating on the latter in greater detail.[66]

A Fraudulent Trading

Australia,[67] New Zealand[68] and the United Kingdom[69] have for well over the last half century provided that directors, responsible for reckless or fraudulent trading, can be ordered without limit of liability to contribute to the asset

---

[63] Of course, it might be argued that the misfeasance standard itself should be changed. This is another topic, but in England there has been no demand for any such change.

[64] *Re Sherborne Associates Ltd.* [1995] BCC 40.

[65] See T Telfer, Chap 7.

[66] I do not intend addressing the issue whether in certain circumstances "passive" shareholders who have benefited from the conduct of the directors should be held liable.

[67] Corporations Law, s 592(6).

[68] Companies Act 1993, s 380.

[69] The 1986 Act, s 213; Companies Act 1985, s 458.

pool should the company go into insolvent liquidation. Broadly these provisions apply where directors, or others who participated in the management of a company, did so in a reckless manner or so as to defraud the members or creditors. The court can make such order as it sees fit that the director contribute to the assets of the company. The shortcomings (in the sense of proving liability) of the "reckless" or "dishonesty" requirement, particularly the latter, have been well documented.[70] As was stated by the Cork Committee in 1982,[71] when commenting on section 332 of the Companies Act 1948:[72]

> "Section 332 not only creates a civil and personal liability; it also creates a criminal offence. The constituent elements of the two are identical. As a result the Courts have consistently refused to entertain a claim to civil liability in the absence of dishonesty and, moreover, have insisted upon a strict standard of proof. It is the general experience of those concerned with the administration of the affairs of insolvent companies that the difficulty of establishing dishonesty has deterred the issue of proceedings in many cases where a strong case has existed for recovering compensation from the directors or others involved."

In determining the quantum of recovery, the courts have held that the amount which the director is ordered to pay could contain a punitive element.[73] It is also clear that recovery cannot be ordered in favour of individual creditors; the action is brought by the liquidator on behalf of the creditors as a general body.[74] It probably follows from this that such cause of action would not be assignable, and this has a bearing on the funding of liquidation proceedings.[75]

B Insolvency Trading

Although the fraudulent trading provisions proved inadequate,[76] they did highlight the range of issues that arises in imposing liability on directors for incurring "credit" in circumstances where a company had no reasonable prospect of paying its debts when they fell due. These issues are:[77] (a) what are the trigger conditions for liability? (b) who is liable? (c) what (if any) defences are available? (d) who can seek relief and for whom is relief granted?

---

[70] The "reckless" requirement could be taken to import, and has been so interpreted, an objective requirement, namely, would the circumstances of the company's business have indicated to the ordinary prudent director that the carrying on of the business would cause loss to the company's creditors?: *Re Petherick Exclusive Fashions Ltd.* (1986) 2 BCR 177, 191.

[71] Cmnd. 8558, para 1776.

[72] This combined what is now s 458 of the 1985 Act and s 213 of the 1986 Act.

[73] *Re A Company (No 001418 of 1988)* [1990] BCC 526.

[74] *London & Sugar Overseas (Sugar) Co. Ltd.* v. *Punjab National Bank* [1997] 1 BCLC 705 (CA).

[75] See pp. 123–124 below.

[76] There is, however, still life in these provisions: see *Re A Company (No 001418 of 1988)* [1991] BCLC 17; *Re L Todd (Swanscombe) Ltd.* [1990] BCLC 454.

[77] Most of these issues are addressed in *General Insolvency Inquiry* (LRCA, Report No 45), Chap 7, which contains the best official discussion of these matters ("the Harmer Report").

and (e) what is the quantum of recovery? It is proposed to use primarily section 214 of the Insolvency Act 1986 for the purpose of illustrating these issues, but the solutions in other jurisdictions will also be referred to.

(i) What are the Trigger Conditions for Liability?

Section 214 applies where (i) a company goes into insolvent liquidation, and (ii) at some time before the commencement of the winding up the directors[78] concluded or ought to have concluded that there was "no reasonable prospect"[79] that the company could avoid going into insolvent liquidation. In determining whether or not the company's insolvent liquidation should have been foreseen by the directors, the directors will be treated as having the knowledge and skill of a "reasonably diligent person" having:[80]

> "(a) the general knowledge, skill and experience that may reasonably be expected of a person carrying out the same functions as are carried out by the director in relation to the company, and
> (b) the general knowledge, skill and experience that that director has."

It seems reasonably clear that in this standard sub-section (a) sets the floor (the objective standard), and sub-section (b) sets the ceiling (the subjective standard). For the purposes of section 214, the test of insolvency is balance sheet insolvency, namely, that the company's assets are insufficient for the payment of its debts and other liabilities and the expenses of the winding up.[81] This, of course, entails that a company may have been commercially solvent, that is able to pay its debts as they fell due, but nevertheless, the directors can still be held liable for wrongful trading. It also seems reasonably clear that debts and liabilities include present and future debts or liabilities, whether contingent or liquidated.[82] It would also cover liability in tort.[83] A number of points can be made with respect to the conditions that trigger liability.

(a) *"No reasonable prospect"*: the section applies where the director should have concluded that there was "no reasonable prospect" that the company could avoid insolvent liquidation. The standard to be applied in determining *when* liability should be imposed on directors for the consequences of a company's insolvency raises one of the most difficult problems in designing such legislation. It would be possible to make directors automatically liable (with or without defences) to contribute to the assets of a company should it go into insolvent liquidation. In other words, lia-

---

[78] The question of who is liable will be dealt with in greater detail herein.

[79] The 1986 Act , s 214(2)(a).

[80] The 1986 Act, s 214(4). This sub-section has now been treated as reflecting the common law standard of the duty of care of directors: *Re D'Jan of London Ltd.* [1994] 1 BCLC 561.

[81] The 1986 Act, s 214(6).

[82] Insolvency Rules 1986 (SI 1925), ("the Rules") r 13.12(3).

[83] The Rules, r 13.12(2).

bility would be strict. No proposals along these lines have been made. Leaving aside questions of fairness as between creditors,[84] such an approach would in all probability lead to the precipitate closure of otherwise viable concerns and, what may be the same thing, directors failing to take risky decisions that would otherwise be in the interests of the company's creditors and shareholders. It must also be remembered that premature closure of otherwise viable concerns imposes an unnecessary social cost. In addition, not to continue a concern which ultimately may prove profitable would prejudice creditors who are creditors at the time the concern is discontinued to the extent that the concern's assets are insufficient to cover its liabilities. What is required of directors where they appreciate that the company cannot avoid insolvent liquidation will be examined in greater detail when the issue of defences is dealt with.

(b) *Language of probability*: because the liability of directors is not strict, inevitably some language of probability will have to be used to determine when directors will be liable. Section 214 uses the terminology of "no reasonable prospect". This is to be contrasted with the Australian legislation, where the standard is more demanding in the sense that the possibility of director's liability is much wider.[85] Section 588G(1)(b) of the Corporations Law imposes liability where there are reasonable grounds for "suspecting" that the company is insolvent or will become insolvent by incurring a debt. Whether this will make a great deal of difference is impossible to predict, but in all probability it will be easier to show contravention of this provision.

(c) *Trading at creditors' expense*: the third point is that because directors do not necessarily have to bring a company's business to an end when it is in financial difficulties, this means that companies will trade at the expense of creditors. As was stated by the Cork Committee: "A company will not be under an obligation to show as a certainty that its debts will be paid. . . ."[86] It is inevitable that in some situations directors will make a reasonable decision to continue trading but the company nevertheless goes into insolvent liquidation. Overall, this may produce socially desirable results if the number of companies in difficulty that trade out of their difficulties outnumber those companies that fail to trade out of their difficulties.[87] However, it is arguably unfair to the creditors of the failed companies, if they are not adequately compensated for the risk they have run.

(d) *Different classes of creditors*: it may be that it is inevitable that a company will go into insolvent liquidation but that continued trading for a period of time will enhance the pool of assets available for creditors. During this

---

[85] For New Zealand, see T Telfer, Chap 7.

[86] Cmnd 8558, para 1800.

[87] This is somewhat simplistic. What is needed is some measurement of value comparing the failed companies with the successful ones.

[84] The fact that continued trading may cause loss to "new" creditors but "old" creditors may be paid off.

period of continued trading its creditors will change identity; some creditors will be paid off and new debt incurred. It is submitted that in this situation the directors would and should be liable for wrongful trading if they form, or ought to have formed, the opinion that the company could not avoid insolvent liquidation. As a matter of principle, it is wrong to allow directors to cherry pick between the company's creditors. It is also clear that this would be the position under the Corporations Law; an insolvent company would be incurring a debt when insolvent.[88] The position under United Kingdom law is less clear, but it is submitted that it is the same.

(ii) Who is Liable?

Section 214 imposes liability on directors, and for this purpose director includes a shadow director.[89] It is also clear that *de facto* directors are caught.[90] A shadow director is defined as a person in accordance with whose instructions the board is accustomed to act. In applying this definition, the matter has to be viewed through the eyes of the board of directors of the dominated company. Thus, even where the alleged shadow director issues detailed instructions, if those instructions are ignored by the board, the definition of shadow director will not be satisfied. Millett J (as he then was) has held that the terms *de facto*, *de jure* and shadow director are mutually exclusive.[91] While this will normally be the case, it is difficult to see that it should always be so. For example, it would be possible to have a *de jure* director who so dominated the board of directors (a Maxwell figure) that he would also be treated as a shadow. However, whether anything of significance flows from the dual status is to be doubted. There are two special situations where the issue of extended liability has created problems: the first relates to bank lending, and the second relates to corporate groups.

(a) Bank Lending

When a company is in financial difficulties, an obvious source of finance is bank borrowing, normally secured. There is no risk to the bank that it will be held liable for putting funds into the company in the form of debt rather than equity. Nor will the loan be treated as equity.[92] Propping up an insolvent concern, no matter how irresponsible, does not affect the creditor status

---

[88] S 588G(1)(b). This would also appear to be the position in New Zealand under the Companies Act 1993, s 136.

[89] The 1986 Act, s 214(7). See also Corporations Law, ss 588G(1)(a) and 60.

[90] *Re Hydrodan (Corby) Ltd.* [1994] 2 BCLC 180. An alternate director would only be caught provided he participated *qua* director in the company's affairs: see *Playcorp Pty. Ltd. v. Shaw* (1993) 10 ACSR 212.

[91] *Re Hydrodan (Corby) Ltd.* [1994] 2 BCLC 180, 183.

[92] These two consequences could follow in certain Continental jurisdictions. See, for example, H Rajak, *European Corporate Insolvency* (Chichester, Wiley, 1995), 242. See also D Fischel, "The Economics of Lender Liability" (1989) 99 *Yale L J* 131.

of a lender.[93] Normally banks do not appoint representatives to the boards of their debtor companies. A secured creditor has the right to police his security and the fact that he does so does not, and should not, entail that he becomes a shadow director. Where a company is in trouble, its bank may, *inter alia*, require it to[94] (a) appoint investigating accountants, (b) provide extra security, (c) reduce its borrowing, particularly where the company has exceeded its borrowing limits, and/or (d) call for management accounts and business plans as to how the company is to trade out of its difficulties. None of these should make the bank a shadow director. Even where the bank makes the adoption of a particular business plan a condition for extending additional credit, the status of shadow director will not arise, provided the directors retain a discretion to accept or reject.[95] Economically the company may have little option but to accept the bank's proposal, but this does not make it a shadow director since the directors retain a discretion to refuse and to put the company into creditors' voluntary liquidation or administration.

(b) *Parent–Subsidiary Relationship—Corporate Groups*

It is a truism that the corporate group is a feature of developed economies. One of the reasons for this in the United Kingdom is the ease of access to the corporate form—few impediments are placed in the way of obtaining corporate status.[96] Although the separate legal entity principle is the starting point, there is something commercially unreal in finding that a wholly-owned subsidiary is not subject to the stringent control of its parent. It is clear that in terms of strict company law principles, there are no legal objections to a subsidiary supporting the activities of its parent or other members of the group, in circumstances where the collapse of the group would prejudice the subsidiary's interests. If the directors of a subsidiary decide that the transaction is in the interests of the subsidiary, it is submitted that the parent would not be a shadow director.[97] In this situation, the directors would have brought independent judgement to bear on the matter and the fact that what they decided coincided with the parents desires would not make the latter a shadow director.

In *Re Hydrodan (Corby) Ltd.*, Millett J had to consider the application of the shadow director concept in the context of a parent/subsidiary relationship. In that case, H was a wholly-owned subsidiary twice removed from E plc. H had two corporate directors. It went into liquidation and the liquidator sought to make two of the directors of E plc liable under section 214, claiming that they were shadow directors. Millett J held that if E plc had given directions to

---

[94] P Fidler, "Banks as Shadow Directors" (1992) 7 *JIBL* 97, 99.

[95] Sir P Millett, "Shadow Directorship—A Real or Imagined Threat to the Banks?" [1991] *Insolvency Practitioner* 24.

[96] Companies Act 1985, s 1(3)(A), recognising the "one person" company. See, generally, T Hadden, "Regulating Corporate Groups: An International Perspective" in J McCahery, S Picciotto and C Scott (eds.), *Corporate Control and Accountability* (Oxford, Clarendon, 1993), Chap 18.

[97] *Equiticorp Finance Ltd.* v. *Bank of New Zealand* (1993) 11 ACSR 642.

[93] Self-interest would, of course, curb, if not eliminate, such behaviour.

the board of H and the directors were accustomed to act on such instructions, this would have rendered the company a shadow director.[98] More interestingly, he held that in this situation the directors of E plc would not be shadow directors, since they would be acting as the appropriate organ of the company and in so acting only rendered the company liable.[99]

In dealing with the issue of corporate groups, the Insolvency Act 1986 does not have a tailor-made provision. It simply applies the general provisions of section 214 which will require a liquidator to show sustained and pervasive successful interference with the management of the subsidiary by the parent, which has the effect of rendering the latter a shadow director. More importantly, it means that a parent company can abandon its subsidiary since such abandonment will not by itself result in liability. Take, for example, the facts in *Re Augustus Barnett & Son Ltd*.[100] In that case, a subsidiary had during the period when it was under the control of R, its parent, consistently shown a substantial deficiency in current assets. The auditors refused to sign its accounts on a going concern basis unless there was a letter of support from R. R issued such letters of comfort which were recorded in the subsidiary's accounts, and they provided the normal assurance that R was willing to provide the subsidiary with such financial support as was necessary to enable it to continue to trade at its current level of activity. On other occasions when suppliers became jittery, R indicated that it would continue to support its subsidiary. The subsidiary went into insolvent liquidation and the question arose whether R could be made liable under the then fraudulent trading provision.[101] The court held that: (a) R had not participated in the management of its subsidiary, and (b) the directors of the subsidiary had not been fraudulent, as they had in all good faith assumed that R would live up to its letter of comfort.[102] There was no serious argument in the case that R might have misled its subsidiary's creditors and that this would constitute a basis for piercing the corporate veil.[103] Although there appears to be no English case law dealing with this point, this would be a perfectly appropriate basis for piercing the corporate veil on the ground that the parent's conduct indicated an assumption of liability.[104]

The *Augustus Barnett* decision arguably would be decided no differently

---

[98] [1994] 2 BCLC 180, 184.

[99] *Ibid.*: "But if they did give such directions . . . acting as a board they did so as agents . . . (or more appropriately as the appropriate organ of the company . . .)." This follows from the application of the rules of attribution.

[100] [1986] BCLC 170 (noted D D Prentice (1987) 103 *LQR* 11). The facts are somewhat similar to those in *Deputy Commissioner for Corporate Affairs* v. *Coratti* (1980) 5 ACLR 119. See generally K Bennetts, "Expectations of Financial Support—Grounds for Avoidance of Directors' Liability Under Section 592, Corporations Law" (1991) 9 *CSLJ* 268.

[101] Companies Act 1948, s 332.

[102] Although this ultimately turns on its wording, a letter of comfort will not normally give rise to any liability: *Kleinwort Benson Ltd.* v. *Malaysia Mining Corp. Bhd* [1988] 1 WLR 799.

[103] Easterbrook and Fischel, n. 17 above, 58.

[104] See also D Goddard, Chap 2.

under section 214. R would not, on the findings of fact in the case, be a shadow director. The directors of the subsidiary might, although this is far from clear, be liable under section 214, in that their failure to obtain a binding legal commitment from the parent entailed that they had failed to take all reasonable steps to ensure that the creditors would be paid. In other words, the creditors have to be protected by a legally enforceable mechanism. In many ways, this is an unsatisfactory state of affairs since the parent by its conduct created the impression that it would stand behind the debts of its subsidiary.

There are at least two ways of dealing with this. The first is to make a parent automatically liable for the debts of its subsidiary (automatic liability). This probably would go too far in that it would completely negate the use of subsidiaries as risk-shifting devices. Provided a subsidiary is adequately capitalised and the parent does not make any misrepresentations as to support, the use of subsidiaries to provide a measure of protection for a group should not as a matter of policy be proscribed. Also, to have an automatic rule of liability would make it difficult for creditors to assess the degree of risk when extending credit to the parent or any subsidiary which the parent is supporting by, for example, a guarantee. Although, where a creditor is secured, this problem is greatly minimised as the creditor is protected to the extent of his security.

An alternative reform was that put forward in the Harmer Report. It proposed that a related company (which would include a parent) could be made liable to contribute to the assets of the company with which it was related where the latter company goes into insolvent liquidation. The court would have jurisdiction to make such an order where "it is satisfied that it is just".[105] In exercising its discretion the court would have to take into consideration:[106] (a) the extent to which the related company took part in the management of the company, (b) the conduct of the related company towards the creditors of the company[107] and (c) the extent to which the circumstances giving rise to the winding up of the company are attributable to the actions of the related company. It also qualified these proposals with the important caveat that mere reliance by the creditors of a company on the assets of the related company in entering into the transaction should not by itself give rise to any liability on the part of the related company. This model has much to commend it.[108] It has two important features. First, interference or involvement in management could trigger liability rather than the more stringent test for shadow directors where the complete domination of the subsidiary's board is required. The reality of the corporate groups is that a parent company can leave a

---

[105] The Harmer Report, para 335.
[106] *Ibid.*
[107] This would cover the type of holding out that took place in the *Augustus Barnett* case.
[108] The eventual legislation, ss 588V–588X, did not take the exact form recommended in the Harmer Report: see *Australian Corporation Law, Vol 2* (Sydney, 1991), paras 57, 384–57, 388. See also D Goddard, Chap 2.

measure of autonomy to the boards of its subsidiaries yet nevertheless have a significant influence on the management policy of the group.[109] Secondly, liability can arise where the parent creates a false impression of credit worthiness. To the extent that third parties are so misled in extending credit, a parent should be held liable.

(iii) Defences Available for Wrongful Trading

Section 214 provides defences for wrongful trading. A director will escape liability if he can show that he took "every step" with a view to minimising loss to creditors after he concluded, or should have concluded, that the company could not have avoided insolvent liquidation.[110] Although the section speaks in terms of "every step", the standard against which the director's conduct has to be measured is that of the "reasonable" director,[111] and accordingly the director will have to take every step that a reasonable director would have taken.

It is necessary to return to the circumstances in which liability can arise. Liability arises where the director concluded or ought to have concluded that there was no reasonable prospect that the company could avoid going into insolvent liquidation. The trigger event relates to consequences of continued trading and it does not require the insolvency to be brought about by a particular type of trading activity, for example, the incurring of debts.[112] The Australian legislation adopts the latter approach, and this appears to have given rise to a number of far from easy interpretative difficulties.[113] In many ways the United Kingdom solution is preferable. It makes it clear that involuntary creditors are caught and also it focuses on the right question, namely, has the directors' conduct in continuing to trade prejudiced the company's creditors? As we have already seen, debts and liabilities cover nearly every form of imaginable claim against the company[114] and it is to the deterrence of the incurring of these types of losses (and not just debts) that section 214 is directed.[115]

The directors must have concluded or should have concluded that the company had no reasonable prospect of avoiding insolvent liquidation.[116] Normally, the issue of what constitutes a reasonable prospect will arise only

---

[109] Compare, for example, *Standard Chartered Bank of Australia Ltd.* v. *Antico* (1995) 18 ACSR 1, 65–74 (dealing with the Corporations Law, s 556).

[110] The 1986 Act, s 214(4). This is the only defence. It has been held that Companies Act 1985, s 727, does not apply to s 214: *Re Produce Marketing Consortium Ltd.* [1989] BCLC 513

[111] The 1986 Act, s 214(4). See also pp. 112–113.

[112] For example, where the collateral of a debtor of the company is declining in value, the directors could be held liable for wrongful trading.

[113] See J Noble, "When Does a Company Incur a Debt Under the Insolvent Trading Provisions of the Corporations Law?" (1994) 12 *CSLJ* 297.

[114] See pp. 112–113.

[115] For a claim falling outside s 214, see *Re Kentish Homes Ltd.* [1993] BCLC 1375.

[116] The burden of proof is probably on the director.

where it is alleged that the directors should have concluded that there was no such prospect. If they had so concluded then, leaving aside the question of proof, which is made that bit easier by the fact that the liquidator has access to the company's books,[117] there can be no doubt that the directors will be liable to contribute.

Greater difficulties arise in determining what the directors ought to have concluded. A number of points can be made on this:

(a) First, as we have seen, the test will in part be objective; broadly the director will be deemed to have the knowledge and skill of a "reasonable" director.[118] Thus reasonable grounds will have to exist on which the directors have based their conclusions. As regards this, the normal rules of company law will apply and directors will be able to rely on the work product of subordinates unless they are put on notice that such reliance is misplaced.

(b) Secondly, in determining what information the directors ought to have known, directors will be assumed to have known the information which would have been revealed had the company complied with its statutory obligations to maintain proper books of account and to prepare annual accounts.[119]

(c) Thirdly, it is assumed that the directors carried out their duties. Section 214(5) provides that in determining whether a director has displayed a reasonable standard of competence in carrying out his functions for which he has responsibility, such functions will include "any functions which he does not carry out but which have been entrusted to him".

(d) Fourthly, the courts have recognised that the quantum of information and expertise possessed by directors will vary with the commercial sophistication and size of the company. As Knox J stated in *Re Produce Marketing Consortium (No 2) Ltd.*,[120] the "general knowledge, skill and experience . . . will be much less extensive in a small company in a modest line of business, with simple accounting procedures and equipment, than it will be in a large company with sophisticated procedures".

What constitutes a reasonable prospect is inherently elusive. In applying this test the court has to balance creditor protection against a policy which causes the precipitate termination of a company's business. What is clear from section 214 is that the legislature has accepted that in appropriate circumstances a company in financial distress can nevertheless attempt to trade out of its difficulties without the directors being necessarily liable should it fail to do so. The reasonable prospect requirement and the defence provided to directors

---

[117] Also, the liquidator has very powerful investigative tools at his disposal: the 1986 Act, ss 235 and 236. There is no privilege against self-incrimination in answering the questions of the liquidator: *Bishopgate Investment Management Ltd.* v. *Maxwell (No 2)* [1993] BCLC 1282. This may need to be altered in the light of *Saunders* v. *United Kingdom* (1997) 23 EHRR 313 (ECHR).

[118] The 1986 Act, s 214(4)(a).

[119] *Re Produce Marketing Consortium (No 2) Ltd.* [1989] BCLC 520, 550.

[120] *Ibid.*

are conceptually distinct, but nevertheless they are linked, since actions taken by directors to avoid loss to creditors could be equally applicable to both aspects of section 214.

Whether or not the defence is satisfied will very much depend on the facts of a given case. It is probably not a requirement that the steps taken by the directors must legally ensure that the creditors are protected, for example, by a bank guarantee, or the injection of fresh equity into the company. Vague assurances or expectations of support will not suffice.[121] It is unclear on what side of the line *Re Augustus Barnett & Sons Ltd.* would fall.[122] It is submitted that the reliance on the parent's letter of comfort in that case should not constitute a defence. It is simply much too easy for a parent to renege from such a commitment and the directors of the subsidiary will possess little leverage to compel the parent to live up to its commitments. The observations of Tamlerlin J (dealing with a different matter) are apposite for describing whether or not the defence has been established:[123]

> "The question is one of fact. Attention should be directed to whether a reasonable director or manager operating in a practical business environment would expect that at some point the company would be unable to meet a liability. The question involves consideration of the timing of revenue flow and debts incurred, and contingencies including the ability to raise funds. The conclusion ought to be clear from a consideration of the debtor's financial position in its entirety and generally speaking ought not to be drawn simply from evidence of a temporary lack of liquidity."

(iv) Anticipatory Relief

Obviously directors of a company in financial difficulties will be faced with a difficult decision, and it was to ameliorate this that the Cork Committee proposed that a procedure should be set up to seek anticipatory relief. Under this procedure the court would be vested with jurisdiction to declare that, no matter how events eventually turned out, the future trading sanctioned by the court could not give rise to a claim for wrongful trading.[124] This, of course, raises difficult questions of court competence to make such judgments. There was also a concern that there would be a conservative judicial reluctance to make such an order which would result in the precipitate closure of businesses. The Cork Committee, while recognising these difficulties, considered that the courts had the requisite competence. What was interesting were the types of orders that the Committee recommended that the court should be empowered to make. Two such orders proposed were: (a) permission to continue trading for a specified period, or (b) trading so as to complete existing

---

[121] See, for example, *Williams* v. *NCSC* (1990) 2 ACSR 131.
[122] See pp. 116–117.
[123] *Hawcroft General Trading Co. Ltd.* v. *Edgar* (1996) 20 ACSR 541, 548.
[124] Cmnd 8558, at paras 1798–1803. The application would be in Chambers and therefore there would be no publicity.

or prospective contracts, would not be wrongful.[125] The first of these deals with what is one of the most intractable problems in applying section 214, namely, what timing horizons should directors apply?[126] Given the uncertainty associated with this decision, a power in the courts to authorise trading for a specified period would probably be beneficial. The second example deals with a situation where continued trading would be wrongful, in that it is clear at the time the order is made that at the end of the day the company would inevitably end up in insolvent liquidation.[127] While continued trading in this situation may increase overall societal welfare (the continued trading will increase the asset pool available for distribution) it will do so at the expense of inter-creditor fairness, as certain creditors will be advantaged at the expense of others. It is questionable whether this is a principle that insolvency law should adopt.[128]

(v) Who can Seek Relief and for Whom is Relief Effected?

This raises a fundamental issue which is not always openly addressed by insolvency law. As we have already seen, there are many principles of insolvency law that result in the swelling of a company's assets in liquidation. The question arises as to the nature of such recoveries. If the relevant statutory provision merely establishes mechanics, then it is plausible to argue that the recovered assets, being assets vested in the company, remain subject to any security which the company has created over its assets. This, for example, is the position with respect to section 212 of the Insolvency Act 1986.[129] Where the section is perceived as creating a substantive right, it is more plausible to argue that the assets are recovered for the benefit of the unsecured creditors,[130] and thus not subject to any such security. Also, to the extent that the assets recovered are treated as having always inhered in the company, as the company's property, the right to such assets is assignable by the liquidator as a means of financing the liquidation.[131]

Section 214 vests the power to seek an order under the section in the liquidator. It is also clear[132] that what the liquidator is seeking to recover are "assets" which were never vested in the company; what he is seeking to obtain is a contribution from the directors for the purpose of satisfying the claims of

---

[125] *Ibid.*, para 1798.

[126] See, for example, *Re Sherborne Associates Ltd.* [1995] BCC 40.

[127] See pp. 112–113.

[128] Also, in many situations the liquidator can complete the contract.

[129] *Re Anglo-Austian Printing and Publishing Union* [1895] 2 Ch 891. This establishes a procedure for assessing damages against an officer of the company for breach of duty or misfeasance, and it is clear that it establishes no new cause of action but is merely procedural.

[130] This appears to be the position with moneys recovered as having constituted a preference: *Re Yagerphone Ltd.* [1935] Ch 392. Such recoveries may constitute assets for certain aspects of insolvency: *Katz* v. *McNally*, [1997] Bec 784.

[131] See p. 122 below.

[132] See *ibid.*

the company's creditors. Because of these two features, the courts have concluded:

(a) Any recovery swells the assets available for the unsecured creditors. In *Re
Oasis Merchandising Services Ltd.*,[133] the court held that potential recoveries under section 214 were not the company's property which the
liquidator could sell to a third party in order to obtain funding to bring
such proceedings. As the right to seek a contribution under section 214
only arose on liquidation, the contribution benefited the unsecured creditors.

(b) It follows from the above that section 214 recoveries do not form part of
the company's assets that could be charged by the company. The company can only charge assets with respect to which it is the beneficial
owner; as the right of action under section 214 is not one vested in the
company it could not charge it, or the proceeds arising from it.[134]

(c) The court has held that because section 214 payments form part of the
general assets available for unsecured creditors, payment from such assets
cannot be made to individual creditors.[135] This means that creditors who
are creditors before the date when the directors first became liable will
share with creditors who acquire this status when wrongful trading took
place. While this has implications for the financing of liquidations,[136] it
creates no unfairness since the wrongful trading will have affected the
ability of the company to satisfy the claims of all of its creditors.[137]

(vi) Quantum of Recovery

Where wrongful trading is shown to have taken place, the court has to determine the measure of recovery. In *Re Produce Marketing Consortium (No 2)
Ltd.*,[138] the court held that the purpose of section 214 was to compensate the
creditors for their losses suffered as a result of the wrongful trading, and
therefore the amount that the court should order the directors to contribute
should reflect this compensatory purpose. The amount that the directors
should be ordered to contribute is the amount by which "the company's assets
can be discerned to have been depleted by the director's conduct"[139] in continuing to trade after the date on which they should have appreciated that the
company could not avoid going into insolvent liquidation. It is, in other
words, a simple causation test. The fact that there was no fraud was not a

---

[133] [1997] BCC 282.
[134] For example, assets recovered as being void dispositions made after the commencement of
insolvency are chargeable: the 1986 Act, s 127; *Campbell* v. *Michael Mount PPB* (1995) 16 ACSLR
296; *Mond* v. *Hammond Suddards* [1996] 2 BCLC 470.
[135] *Re Purpoint Ltd.* [1991] BCLC 491, 499.
[136] See pp. 123–124.
[137] See, however, n. 84.
[138] [1989] BCLC 520, 552–3.
[139] *Ibid.*, at 553.

reason for fixing the amount at a nominal or minimal value although this fact could not be completely ignored. The liability of the directors was joint and several,[140] but the court could order one director to contribute to his fellow directors.[141] There is much to be said for joint and several liability at least being the starting point, as this will enhance the deterrent effect of the section. Under such a liability regime, directors will have an incentive to monitor the conduct of their fellow directors so as to avoid liability for their conduct. The maximum that the directors could be ordered to contribute under section 214 is obviously the net deficit in the company's assets. In other words, net loss to the creditors sets the maximum liability on the part of the directors. It follows from this that any sums recovered by the liquidator as, for example, preferences or transactions at an undervalue will go to reduce the maximum sum which the directors could be obliged to contribute under any section 214 order.

(vii) Miscellaneous

There are two matters that remain to be dealt with. The first relates to the financing of liquidation proceedings, and the second to the interrelationship of section 214 with the fraudulent trading section.

(a) Financing of Liquidation Proceedings

Although liquidation involves the carrying out of public policy functions, namely, the evaluation of the directors' stewardship,[142] it is inherently a "private process" in the sense that it is financed from the assets of the estate or by the company's creditors.[143] In many situations the latter source of funding will not be forthcoming.[144] Individual creditors who are owed small amounts will not consider it worth their while to contribute since the costs may exceed any gains. Any gains will be uncertain, and this is acutely so in predicting expected gains from litigation. Coupled with this, there are acute free-rider problems since many creditors will simply refuse to contribute to a fighting fund, knowing that they will benefit from any recovery, as the present position under English law is that the court lacks jurisdiction to award recovery

---

[140] Compare *Vinyl Processors (New Zealand) Ltd.* v. *Cant* [1991] 2 NZLR 416 where the court held that 5 directors should individually only be liable for one fifth of the amount that had to be contributed. It is submitted that such an order could be made under s 214.

[141] This is useful where the directors are not equally culpable.

[142] See Cork Report, Cmnd 8558, para 193. There is an obligation on the management of an insolvent company to "give an account of the reasons for the company's failure" and where appropriate "to submit their conduct of the company's affairs to impartial investigation".

[143] See generally G Moss and N Segal, "Insolvency Proceedings: Contract and Financing. The Expenses Doctrine in Liquidation, Administration and Receiverships" (1997) 1 *CFILR* 1.

[144] In the debates on the 1986 Act proposals were put forward for creating a fighting fund for liquidators out of the assets of the company: see HC Standing Cttee E, 20 June 1995, at 549.

in favour of particular creditors.[145] One way of dealing with these issues is for the liquidator to assign the company's cause of action and the assignee agrees to finance the proceedings in return for a percentage of any recoveries. The assignment provides the necessary financing, circumvents the collective action problem by eliminating the need for creditor agreement,[146] and eliminates the free-rider problem, in that all shareholders will finance the proceedings by the proportionate part of their claim which is enjoyed by the assignee should the action be successful.

The Insolvency Act 1986 empowers a liquidator to sell the company's property,[147] and property for this purpose includes any cause of action vested in the company at the time it goes into insolvent liquidation.[148] It has been held[149] that the rules relating to maintenance and champerty do not apply to such assignments since any such assignment is pursuant to a statutory power. This is not completely convincing,[150] but the principle has now been firmly established.[151] However, it is only causes of action vested in the company that can be assigned. The courts have held that a section 214 action is not vested in the company as part of its assets, it only arises on liquidation and is vested in the liquidator for the benefit of the creditors.[152] As a result, it cannot be assigned by the liquidator since it is not the company's property. In many ways this is an unfortunate ruling. A major problem with section 214 is arguably[153] an insufficiency of enforcement, an insufficiency that is attributable to lack of resources on the part of the liquidators to fund section 214 claims.

(b) *Interrelationship of Section 214 with the Misfeasance Section*

The second point relates to the interrelationship of section 214 recoveries with those also ordered to be made under section 212 of the 1986 Act. Section 212 establishes a summary procedure for actions against directors who have been in breach of duty to the company. Recovery under this section entails that a

[145] This is because recovery swells the asset pool which must be distributed *pro rata* among the creditors.

[146] The exercise of a power of assignment does not need either court or creditor approval: the 1986 Act, Sch 4, para 6.

[147] The 1986 Act, Sch 4, para 6.

[148] The 1986 Act, s 436 (property includes things in action).

[149] The cases are collected in *Norglen Ltd. v. Reeds Rains Prudential Ltd.* [1996] 1 BCLC 690.

[150] It would have been equally plausible to argue that only assignments that were lawful under the general law, for example, an assignment of a debt which carries with it the right to sue or an assignment to a creditor who would have a justification for maintaining the action, were included.

[151] There are two other reasons why assignments are made: (i) legal aid is available to an individual but not a company, and (ii) security for costs can be obtained against a company (Companies Act 1985, s 726) but normally not against an individual: see *Norglen Ltd. v. Reeds Rains Prudential Ltd.* [1996] 1 BCLC 690.

[152] *Re Oasis Merchandising Services Ltd.* [1997] 1 All ER 1009.

[153] There have been few reported cases involving s 214, and from this it might be inferred that it has little impact. As against this, however, it is clear that professional advisers do draw the attention of directors to the threat that s 214 poses.

director is returning to the company assets which he has misappropriated, or compensating the company for a loss that he has caused to it because of his misfeasance. As the assets recovered under this section are the assets of the company they are subject to any charge that the company has created over its assets.[154] There is no reason why a liquidator should not seek a remedy under both sections: section 212 compensating for loss to the company to the extent by which the company's assets were depleted by the director's breach of duty, and section 214 compensating creditors for their loss. Where the company has no secured creditors, recovery under section 212 will reduce the overall loss to creditors and therefore reduce the quantum recoverable under section 214. As we have already seen,[155] the maximum recoverable under section 214 is the net loss to the company's creditors.

Where a company has created security over its assets, recovery under both sections 212 and 214 create slightly more complex problems. To take an example. An order is made under section 212 obliging a director to repay £100,000 to the liquidator and an order for a similar amount is made under section 214. The director only has assets of £100,000. It is unclear whether the chargee scoops all because of the order under section 212,[156] or the recovery goes to the unsecured creditors because of the section 214 order. Probably the preferable solution is that there should be *pro rata* sharing.[157]

V CONCLUSION

Section 214 is the right start. It focuses liability on those who are in a position to determine whether a company is simply trading at the expense of its creditors. Also, the approach of imposing collective liability on directors is appropriate. However, its application to groups is unsatisfactory. Perhaps the major problem is insufficiency of enforcement. But this is a general problem as regards liquidation proceedings because often the liquidator will not have sufficient funds.

---

[154] See p. 121.
[155] See pp. 122–123.
[156] See p. 121.
[157] Compare *Re Unit 2 Windows Ltd.* [1985] 1 WLR 1383 (a case dealing with set-off where the creditor seeking to set off its debt against the company was the Crown being owed preferential and non-preferential debts).

7

Risk and Insolvent Trading

THOMAS G W TELFER*

The essay presented by Professor Prentice identifies directors as an important constituency from whom contributions may be sought to enlarge the asset pool for distribution to creditors. Although his essay raises a number of important issues, this commentary will focus in particular on the statutory liability of directors. As discussed in his essay, directors in England face personal liability under the Insolvency Act 1986 for wrongful trading. Creditors also benefit from statutory provisions in Australia[1] and New Zealand,[2] where director conduct is regulated by insolvent and reckless trading rules. Recent amendments in both these jurisdictions has placed a renewed emphasis on the issue.

Perhaps it is fitting on the centenary of *Salomon* v. *A Salomon & Co. Ltd.*[3] to re-examine the issue of director liability. Making directors personally liable marks a fundamental shift in company law. Professor Prentice, in an earlier work, described the English statutory innovation as "unquestionably one of the most important developments in company law this century".[4] Another author characterised the English wrongful trading provisions as "the most extreme departure from the rule in *Salomon's* case yet achieved".[5]

The common justification for the legislative protection of creditors is

---

* Senior Lecturer in Law, The University of Auckland, and Editor of the *New Zealand Law Review*.

[1] Corporations Law, Pt 5.7B, Div 4, ss 588G–588Y (Australia) as discussed by A Herzberg, "Duty to Prevent Insolvent Trading" in J Lessing and J Corkery (eds.), *Corporate Insolvency Law* (Queensland, Bond University, 1995), 8; B Mescher, "Personal Liability of Company Directors for Company Debts" (1996) 70 *ALJ* 837; J Schultz, "Liability of Directors for Corporate Insolvency" (1993) 5 *Bond L Rev* 191.

[2] Companies Act 1993, ss 135–136, as discussed in H Rennie and P Watts, *Directors' Duties and Shareholders' Rights* (New Zealand Law Society Seminar, 1996); M Ross, "Directors' Liability on Corporate Restructuring" in C E F Rickett (ed.), *Essays on Corporate Restructuring and Insolvency* (Wellington, Brooker's, 1996), 173.

[3] [1897] AC 22.

[4] D Prentice, "Creditors' Interests and Directors' Duties" (1990) 10 *OJLS* 265, 277. See also B Pettet, "Limited Liability—A Principle for the 21st Century?" (1995) 48 *CLP* 125, 133.

[5] P Davies, *Gower's Principles of Modern Company Law* (6th edn., London, Sweet & Maxwell, 1997), 151. McPherson J described the Australian insolvent trading provisions as a "far reaching transformation of the original 19th century concept of corporate trading limited liability": "The Liability of Directors for Company Debts" (1993) 1 *Insol LJ* 133, 141. He argues that "making one person liable for the debts of another is in legal terms, a revolutionary step".

that creditors bear an uncompensated risk in dealing with limited liability companies. This commentary questions whether an uncompensated risk exists and argues that there are sufficient market and contractual mechanisms which are available to restrain directors. However, even if it can be established that in some cases creditors are not adequately compensated for risk, one must consider whether the costs of regulation will outweigh the benefits of protecting against the possibility of uncompensated risk. As Professor Prentice's essay primarily focuses on the English provisions, I will examine the debate from a more general perspective and then raise some more specific issues that arise in the context of the New Zealand reckless trading rules.

I RISK-TAKING AND THE LIMITED LIABILITY COMPANY

The advantages of limited liability are well known and have been reiterated in Professor Prentice's essay.[6] The very nature of a limited liability company encourages directors to engage in risk-taking on behalf of shareholders. As shareholders are able to share in the potential gains in the growth of a company without having to risk more than their initial investment, investment is made on the basis that "those in charge will take risks in order to pursue and exploit potentially lucrative projects and ventures".[7]

Risk-taking, however, has been beneficial. As Sealy points out, the world's railways would not have been built, and today many information technology companies would not exist if directors were not willing to take risks. Similarly, a recent work on the evolution of the concept of risk notes that "the capacity to manage risk, and with it the appetite to take risks and make forward looking choices, are key elements of the energy that drives the economic system forward".[8]

However, creditors are at risk when lending to a limited liability company because the principle of limited liability "creates a perverse incentive for an

---

[6] Other sources discussing the advantages include Lord Cooke of Thorndon, "A Real Thing: *Salomon* v. *Salomon* [1897] A.C. 22, 33, *per* Lord Halsbury" in *Turning Points of the Common Law* (London, Sweet & Maxwell, 1997), 1, 11; F Easterbrook and D Fischel, *The Economic Structure of Corporate Law* (Cambridge, Mass., Harvard University Press, 1991), 41–4; B Pettet, n. 4 above, 141–52.

[7] B Cheffins, *Company Law—Theory Structure and Operation* (Oxford, Clarendon, 1997), 541. Easterbrook and Fischel note that shareholders "want managers to take projects with the highest mean returns, which may entail high risk. (No pain no gain).": Easterbrook and Fischel, n. 6 above, 99–100. See also Pettet, n. 4 above, 142. The American Law Institute's *Principles of Corporate Governance: Principles and Recommendations* (Minnesota, ALI, 1994), 135, recognises that "shareholders accept the risk that an informed business decision—honestly undertaken and rationally believed to be in the interests of the corporation—may not be vindicated by subsequent success".

[8] H Bernstein, *Against the Gods: The Remarkable Story of Risk* (New York, 1996), 3. L Sealy, "Directors' 'Wider' Responsibilities—Problems Conceptual, Practical and Procedural" [1987] *Monash Univ LR* 164, 181. See comments of Kirby P in *Metal Manufacturers Ltd.* v. *Lewis* (1988) 13 NSWLR 315, 317; *Hawkins* v. *Bank of China* (1992) 26 NSWLR 562, 575–7.

insolvent company to continue to trade".[9] Where a company becomes insolvent, shareholders have everything to gain and nothing to lose by the continuation of trade. If the company is able to trade out of its difficulties, the shareholders benefit in any gains. However, if its fortunes continue to decline, all additional losses will be borne by the creditors.[10] Limited liability, therefore, it is argued, shifts the risk of loss to creditors.

One way possibly to minimise the perverse incentive is to impose liability on the directors where the company continues to trade at the expense of the creditors.[11] In New Zealand, for example, directors will face the possibility of personal liability if they agree to the business of a company being carried on in a manner likely to create a substantial risk of serious loss to the company's creditors.[12]

II UNCOMPENSATED RISK AND THE MARKET

The creation of director liability assumes that creditors cannot take adequate steps to ensure their interests are protected. Professor Prentice has identified as a crucial issue "whether limited liability results in uncompensated risk being imposed on creditors who deal with the company".[13] Another author similarly argues that the underlying theme of insolvent trading legislation is to "define what risks the creditors of a corporation have not agreed to accept in their dealings with it".[14]

It is open to question that creditors suffer from an uncompensated risk. Some commentators have suggested that the market or consensually negotiated contractual terms may be sufficient to protect creditors against

[9] Prentice, n. 4 above; R Grantham, "The Judicial Extension of Directors' Duties to Creditors" [1991] *JBL* 1, 2–4. This point has also been made in the United States context: see S McDonnell, "*Geyer* v. *Ingersoll*: Insolvency Shifts Directors Burden from Shareholders to Creditors" (1994) 19 *Del J of Corp L* 177, 189–90; G Miller, "Corporate Governance in Chapter 11: The Fiduciary Relationship between Directors and Stockholders of Solvent and Insolvent Corporations" (1993) 23 *Seton Hall L Rev* 1467, 1484.

[10] D Prentice, "Directors, Creditors, and Shareholders" in E McKendrick (ed.), *Commercial Aspects of Trusts and Fiduciary Obligations* (Oxford, Clarendon, 1992), 81. For a discussion of the conflict between equity and debt in insolvency see, L Lin, "Shift of Fiduciary Duty Upon Corporate Insolvency: Proper Scope of Directors' Duties to Creditors" (1993) 46 *Vand L Rev* 1485, 1489–93; L Bebchuk and C Fried, "The Uneasy Case for the Priority of Secured Claims in Bankruptcy" (1996) 105 *Yale L J* 857, 873–4.

[11] D Prentice, Chap 6.

[12] Companies Act 1993, s 135.

[13] D Prentice, Chap 6; Pettet, n. 4 above, 146; D Wishart, *Company Law in Context* (Auckland, OUP, 1994), 174.

[14] J Dabner, "Trading While Insolvent—A Case for Individual Creditors' Rights Against Directors" (1994) 17 *UNSWLJ* 546, 574–5. Another author suggests that wrongful trading legislation ensures that management properly releases information about the company's financial situation in order that creditors can properly assess the risk and price of their loan contracts: L Flynn, "Statutory Liability for Culpable Mismanagement" in H Rajak (ed.), *Insolvency Law Theory and Practice* (London, Sweet & Maxwell, 1993), 135.

management decisions.[15] In other words: "Are not bondholders, creditors, lenders, and trade suppliers entitled to negotiate such creditor self protection provisions in indenture and other contractual arrangements with the corporation?"[16]

Creditors are aware that every contract involves a risk that the other party will not perform. That risk is a "normal one, a background presence in every transaction".[17] As Sealy notes, "creditors deal with a company as a matter of bargain, not of trust, and bargain involves risk".[18] Borrowers pay for the "freedom to engage in risky activities" and creditors are compensated for the risk of default by the interest rate charged. By voluntarily extending credit, "creditors must have found the risk return combination offered by the enterprise satisfactory".[19]

According to Professor Prentice, whether creditors are able to set the terms of the bargain to compensate for the risk could be answered by empirical evidence. For example, he asks whether creditors charge more when dealing with companies rather than unincorporated entities.

Cheffins notes that there appears to be little evidence that directly supports the proposition that creditors actually adjust interest rates when dealing with a limited liability company. However, he argues that creditors generally adjust interest rates in accordance with the risk that there will not be full payment. He suggests that banks, for instance, will charge higher interest rates for high risk corporate borrowers and that "creditors when they negotiate terms with debtors, take the impact of limited liability into account in much the same way".[20]

In addition to an adjustment in the interest rate, lenders are free to bargain for director guarantees or insist on other contractual terms which will reduce lender risk and increase the probability of repayment. Loan covenants may define the limits of total indebtedness, stipulate how funds are to be used, or restrict the ability of a company to change the nature of its business or sell

---

[15] For example, in reviewing the Australian insolvent trading provisions, DeMott stated, "it is not obvious why this statutory solution is preferable to private contract": see D DeMott, "Directors' Duty of Care and the Business Judgment Rule: American Precedents and Australian Choices" (1992) 4 *Bond L Rev* 133, 142.

[16] A E Stilson, "Re-examining the Fiduciary Paradigm at Corporate Insolvency and Dissolution: Defining Directors' Duties to Creditors" (1995) 20 *Del J of Corp L* 1, 61. In the United States, the issue of the directors' relationship with the company's creditors has arisen in the context of judicial developments. See *Crédit Lyonnais Bank Nederland* v. *Pathé Communications Co.* (reprinted in (1992) 17 *Del J of Corp L* 1099); and *Geyer* v. *Ingersoll Publications Co.*, 621 A 2d 784 (Del Ch 1992). Some authors have focused on the importance of the market and contract to control director conduct. See M Van Der Weide, "Against Fiduciary Duties to Corporate Stakeholders" (1996) 21 *Del J of Corp L* 27; Lin, n. 10 above.

[17] Flynn, n. 14 above. For a view that there are no externalities in the case of voluntary transactions, see D Goddard, Chap 2.

[18] Sealy, n. 8 above, 176.

[19] Easterbrook and Fischel, n. 6 above, 50–1; Lin, n. 10 above, 1501; R Posner, *Economic Analysis of Law* (4th ed., Boston, Mass., Little, Brown, 1992), 395.

[20] Cheffins, n. 7 above, 501.

assets. Further, creditors may insist on a minimum capitalisation or require the pledge of some form of security.[21] The threat of loan enforcement or the withdrawal of further financing may be enough to provide leverage sufficient to alter company behaviour.[22]

Not all creditors are in a position to insist upon such detailed loan agreements or demand security over all the company's assets.[23] The case of trade creditors is often advanced as a type of creditor which will not be able to protect itself through detailed contractual loan covenants.[24] If trade creditors insist on more protection than the market will bear, they risk losing customers.

However, a trade creditor is not always a weaker or smaller player than the corporate debtor. Some trade creditors may be major companies in their own right and be able to dictate the terms of trade. Reservation of title clauses are a means of protection available to trade creditors. In addition, trade creditors are often short-term creditors who can quickly respond to negative signals being sent by the financially troubled debtor or the reactions of other creditors.[25] Their options include cutting off supply, switching to cash terms of trade or charging higher prices. Companies, therefore, have an incentive not to mistreat trade creditors. Further, trade creditors have large customer lists which allow them to diversify the risk of default. Trade creditors who are uncertain about the prospects of a company's ability to pay in the first instance always have the choice of refusing to supply.[26]

The situation of employees is subject to debate. It is possible to claim that employees are consensual creditors. Their claim for a missed pay cheque may not be relatively large and the lack of payment is a vital signal of the firm's financial difficulties. Those who continue to work without pay will be aware of the risks they run. However, while their claim in the liquidation may be relatively small, the inability of employees to diversify their risks and the potential inability to transfer freely between jobs may mean that their losses are significant. This debate however is best addressed in the context of a

---

[21] R Posner, n. 19 above, 396; Cheffins, n. 7 above, 81. On the ability of creditors to protect themselves contractually in the United States, see Van Der Weide, n. 16 above, 46–7; Stilson, n. 16 above, 104; Lin, n. 10 above, 1506–7.

[22] L LoPucki and W Whitford, "Corporate Governance in the Bankruptcy Reorganization of Large Publicly Held Companies" (1993) 141 *Univ Penn L Rev* 669, 702.

[23] Grantham, n. 9 above, 2–3.

[24] See, for example, J Ziegel, "Creditors as Corporate Stakeholders: The Quiet Revolution— An Anglo-Canadian Perspective" (1993) 43 *Univ Toronto L J* 511, 530.

[25] On the importance of signals from other creditors see Lin, n. 10 above, 1503. See also G Triantis and R J Daniels, "The Role of Debt in Interactive Corporate Governance" (1995) 93 *Calif L Rev* 1073.

[26] Van Der Weide, n. 16 above, 49; S Schwarcz, "Rethinking a Corporation's Obligations to Creditors" (1996) 17 *Cardozo L Rev* 647, 663; Cheffins, n. 7 above, 82; Posner, n. 19 above, 398; J Mannolini, "Creditors' Interests in the Corporate Contract: A Case for the Reform of Our Insolvent Trading Provisions" (1996) 6 *Aust J of Corp L* 1, 34. However, on the practical problems facing trade creditors, see K Gross, *Failure and Forgiveness: Rebalancing the Bankruptcy System* (New Haven, Conn., Yale University Press, 1997), 168.

broad review of insolvency law. A study of preferred creditor priorities is particularly needed in New Zealand and the issue of employee claims should be reviewed in this larger context rather than within the narrow confines of director liability.[27]

Involuntary creditors are also problematic for the consensual model as noted in Professor Prentice's paper. Tort creditors are not able to contract in advance or avoid or monitor the risk. This issue has been the subject of a long debate. However, the solution of imposing personal liability for tort debts may operate to discourage investment in business enterprises. The issue, as in the case of employees, needs to be examined in a much broader perspective than that of director liability. Other possible solutions to this issue need to be explored, such as requiring companies to carry insurance or providing tort claimants with special priority in the liquidation.[28]

Specific contractual terms are only one mechanism which operates to reduce the risk of default. Other mechanisms, such as the ability to diversify a loan portfolio, may alleviate the consequences of default. Additionally, there are other elements which operate to constrain management behaviour. Before a contractual agreement is entered into, creditors have the ability to screen potential debtors by obtaining information which will be relevant to determining the probability of default. A company's financial statements and evidence of its past credit history will assist the creditor in determining whether to advance credit at all, and on what terms.[29] Creditors are not forced to lend to any particular enterprise. They are free to put their money in low risk investments rather than extend credit, for example, to a new high technology company.[30]

Once the loan has been advanced, the need for fresh infusions of capital will operate as another restriction.[31] If a company encounters financial difficulty, management will become dependent on the goodwill of creditors either to extend or to re-negotiate a loan, and "may not have a strong incentive to take action that will harm creditors' interests".[32] Debtors with a history of default will find it difficult to find suitable replacement credit. However, if a company has no interest in re-financing, this restraint will not be as strong.

---

[27] P Heath, "Preferential Payments on Bankruptcy and Liquidation in New Zealand: Are They Justifiable Exceptions to the Pari Passu Rule?" (1996) 4 *Waikato L Rev* 24; F H Buckley, "The Bankruptcy Priority Puzzle" (1986) 72 *Virginia L Rev* 1393; S J Cantlie, "Preferred Priority in Bankruptcy" in J Ziegel (ed.), *Current Developments in International and Comparative Corporate Insolvency Law* (Oxford, Clarendon, 1994), 414.

[28] For two authors who doubt the viability of disturbing limited liability for tort creditors, see B Pettet, n. 6 above, 152–9; Cheffins, n. 7 above, 506–8. Pettet's article contains references to the earlier American literature on this issue. See also D Goddard, Chap 2.

[29] Cheffins, n. 7 above, 74.

[30] Easterbrook and Fischel, n. 6 above, 50–1; Posner, n. 19 above, 395; Lin, n. 10 above, 1501.

[31] Easterbrook and Fischel, n. 7 above, 95.

[32] Lin, n. 10 above, 1508; Mannolini, n. 26 above, 31. As one author noted, "debtors who seek to borrow again need to avoid a reputation for imprudence": see C R Morris, "Directors' Duties in Nearly Insolvent Corporations: A Comment on *Crédit Lyonnais*" (1993) 19 *J of Corp L* 61, 66.

Professor Prentice has identified the perverse incentive created by limited liability which might cause management to continue to trade since it has everything to gain and nothing to lose.[33] However, the reverse situation may occur and, as Professor Prentice suggests, directors "will have their reputations to consider".[34] The employment market may operate to restrain managerial behaviour. "Rather than using wrongdoing as a way of gambling the company back to success, the managers may decide to avoid scrupulously any hint of wrongdoing for fear of inflicting irrevocable damage on their reputational capital in the managerial job market."[35]

Labour markets and social structures "create powerful constraints of their own" on managerial behaviour. As directors can envision unemployment and social ostracism "more visibly and painfully than they can visualise litigation over questions of corporate law, these extra legal constraints may be more powerful than constraints created by legal rules and the risk of personal liability".[36]

Professor Prentice suggests that labour markets will not operate as a constraint where managers are indifferent to their reputation. As an example he offers the case of fraudulent directors. While it is true that human capital issues will not have any impact on directors who set out fraudulently to misappropriate funds, it is also equally the case that no standard of insolvent trading provision will operate as a restraint on their conduct.

Other informal constraints may also operate. Fukuyama has identified the importance of trust within what he has called rotating credit associations. Where credit has been advanced within a tightly knit family or ethnic community, moral sanctions may be more significant than the legal consequences of default.[37]

Absent misrepresentation, in many instances creditors are able to take precautions which will compensate for the risk that default will occur. Protection is available either through specific contractual terms or through other market forces which will restrain management.[38] Is it legitimate for a creditor who was

[33] D Prentice, Chap 6.

[34] D Prentice, Chap 6.

[35] R J Daniels, "Must Boards Go Overboard? An Economic Analysis of the Effects of Burgeoning Statutory Liability on the Role of Directors in Corporate Governance" in Ziegel (ed.), n. 27 above, 557. See also Mannolini, n. 26 above, 32.

[36] DeMott, n. 15 above, 141; S Rose-Ackerman, "Risk Taking and Ruin: Bankruptcy and Investment Choice" (1991) 20 *J of Legal St* 277, 282. See also LoPucki and Whitford, n. 22 above, 713; Posner, n. 19 above, 399.

[37] F Fukuyama, *Trust: The Social Virtues and the Creation of Prosperity* (London, 1995), 10, 301.

[38] Goddard argues that ss 135 and 136 of the Companies Act 1993 "ignore the fundamental precept that people can expect to be held to their contracts unless they have been deceived in a respect which is material to them, by express missstatement or by silence in circumstances where there was a duty to speak": see D Goddard, Chap 2.p. 159. The relative impact of the market and the importance of contracting as a solution is of course subject to debate: see, for example, J E Parkinson, *Corporate Power and Responsibility: Issues in the Theory of Company Law* (Oxford, Clarendon, 1993), 113–36; D Millon, "Communitarianism in Corporate Law:

compensated for lending to a high risk company by way of a higher interest rate to recover from the directors personally under a reckless trading provision? In this instance, it is arguable the creditor has been over-compensated.[39]

If the focus is to be placed on whether or not there is any uncompensated risk, then is it not relevant also to examine the conduct of the creditor? Where a creditor had the opportunity to make further investigations before advancing the loan or chose to ignore obvious signals of insolvency can the creditor claim that there was an uncompensated risk for which the directors should be liable?[40]

It has been argued that regulation is required because the costs of contracting are too high, or that contractual terms will not always prevent management misbehaviour.[41] However, regulation to restrain management behaviour is not without its own costs. These costs might far outweigh the benefits of protecting against the possibility of uncompensated risk.[42] The 1962 United Kingdom *Report of the Company Law Committee* (Jenkins Report) considered this point. The *Report* considered it relevant, whether or not the imposition of further statutory regulations would:[43]

> "improve to an extent worthy of legislation the position of investors or creditors it was designed to protect; and if so whether its implementation would to any significant extent hamper or impede the company in the efficient conduct of its legitimate business, thus perhaps operating to the detriment of those very persons."

It is significant, therefore, to examine the possible consequences of imposing liability on directors.

III THE IMPACT OF DIRECTOR LIABILITY

The evaluation of corporate law from an economic perspective has recently been announced as part of the Australian *Corporate Law Economic Reform Programme*. Two key principles underpinning the *Reform Programme* are:

Foundations and Law Reform Strategies" in L Mitchell (ed.), *Progressive Corporate Law* (Boulder, Colo., Westview, 1995), 1. However, compare, S Bainbridge, "Community and Statism: A Conservative Contractarian Critique of Progressive Corporate Law Scholarship" (1997) 82 *Cornell L Rev* 856.

[39] Mannolini, n. 26 above, 52: M Byrne, "An Economic Analysis of Directors' Duties in Favour of Creditors" (1994) 4 *Aust J of Corp L* 275.

[40] Rennie and Watts, n. 2 above, 36; Byrne, n. 39 above, 17.

[41] For a review of this literature, see R Sappideen, "Fiduciary Obligations to Corporate Creditors" [1991] *JBL* 365.

[42] Mannolini, n. 26 above, 48; Byrne, n. 39 above. Wishart similarly posed the question whether the "transaction costs of creditors controlling or bearing the risk of certain events is greater or less than the total community costs of having a legal rule": D Wishart, "Models and Theories of Directors' Duties to Creditors" (1991) 14 *NZULR* 323, 336.

[43] United Kingdom, *Report of the Company Law Committee* (HMSO, London, 1962, Cmnd 1749), 3.

(a) cost/benefit analysis of the new legislative proposals as against the existing law; and

(b) the reduction of transaction costs for firms and market participants.

In addition, the review intends to include a discussion of directors' duties and,
in particular, "whether the current rules regulating company directors' conduct inhibit sound business judgment". The study has identified a crucial issue
in need of analysis.[44]

A regime which imposes director liability may result in decisions which are
biased towards less risky projects. Rather than adopting a course of action
which will result in a positive net present value, directors will be influenced
by the threat of liability and may decide to adopt a course of action which
has a lower positive net present value for the company.[45] Management exposure to personal liability "causes managers' incentives to diverge from the path
of wealth maximisation".[46]

The "liability chill" therefore imposes costs. Operating in a risk averse
fashion undermines the wealth creating capacity of the company. The costs of
refraining from "socially optimal levels of risk taking" must be taken into
account in assessing the merits of imposing director liability.[47] Easterbrook
and Fischel argue that "the social loss from reducing investment in certain
types of projects—a consequence of seriously modifying limited liability—
might far exceed the gains from reducing moral hazard".[48]

Where a company is involved in high technology, for example, a decision
whether or not to introduce a new product may involve risking the very existence of the company. Deciding to proceed may itself involve risk, given the
uncertainty in the constantly changing market. However, failure to introduce
the innovative product may "result in the certain death of the company" particularly in an industry where innovation is the custom.[49]

By opting for the safe and conservative policy choices "companies may
become stagnant" and ignore opportunities for new developments. Labour
intensive and job creating projects might be avoided in an attempt to minimise
financial obligations.[50] The New Zealand Law Commission recognized the
societal benefits of success in its 1989 Report:[51]

---

[44] Australia, *Corporate Law Economic Reform Programme* (Business Law Division, Treasury,
Canberra, 4 Mar. 1997); Australia, *Directors' Duties and Corporate Governance: Facilitating
Investment and Protecting Investors* (Treasury, Canberra, 1997).

[45] Daniels, n. 35 above, 564.

[46] Easterbrook and Fischel, n. 6 above, 100. Some commentators in Australia argued that the
new insolvent trading provisions would cause directors to "focus on defensive practices and their
own potential liabilities rather than on more legitimate concerns": see Dabner, n. 14 above, 561.

[47] Daniels, n. 35 above, 550, 562.

[48] Easterbrook and Fischel, n. 6 above, 50.

[49] Schwarcz, n. 26 above, 689.

[50] M Moffat, "Directors' Dilemma—An Economic Evaluation of Directors' Liability for
Environmental Damages and Unpaid Wages" (1996) 54 *Univ Toronto Fac L Rev* 293, 320.

[51] New Zealand Law Commission, *Company Law Reform and Restatement*, Report No 9
(Wellington, 1989), 52, 120.

"A company may be legitimately formed to embark on a speculative or very risky venture, or may undertake such a venture later. The chance of failure—and the prize for success—may be high. Indeed success may greatly benefit the community."

Directors fearing personal liability may not only avoid risky ventures but stop trading altogether.[52] Directors, therefore, may choose to put the company into voluntary liquidation rather than trying to trade out of their difficulties.[53] Cooke and Hicks argue that in the context of the English legislation a possible danger of the wrongful trading legislation is that "businesses will be closed down too early to avoid the risk of wrongful trading liability".[54] Schultz argues that in Australia directors may "be forced to bring to an end a company's business earlier than necessary in order to avoid personal liability".[55] Another author similarly concludes that section 588G of the Australian Corporations Law "may actually require the director to abort an existing project, or refuse to take on a new project, if there is some suspicion that the project will fail". The avoidance of risky projects will lead, it is argued, to a diminution of creditors' claims.[56]

The relationship between wrongful or insolvent trading and formal corporate rescue procedures is a further issue that needs to be addressed. In England and Australia, steps might be taken to place a company in voluntary administration.[57] This has the advantage of giving the company breathing space and discouraging individual creditors from initiating disruptive actions. It also might shield directors from civil claims for wrongful trading.[58] Directors may move towards the formal rescue procedures at an earlier date than required to protect themselves from personal liability.[59]

In Australia, it is a specific defence for directors to show that they took all reasonable steps to prevent a company from incurring the debt. Directors who invoke the voluntary administration provisions will be regarded as having

---

[52] In the United States context this has been raised by McDonnell, n. 9 above, 207.

[53] P Wood, *Principles of International Insolvency* (London, Sweet & Maxwell, 1995), 138.

[54] T Cooke and A Hicks, "Wrongful Trading—Predicting Insolvency" [1993] *JBL* 338, 350.

[55] Schultz, n. 1 above, 208.

[56] Mannolini, n. 26 above, 48.

[57] On the limited range of options available to directors, including the use of administrations, see F Oditah, "Wrongful Trading" [1990] *LMCLQ* 205, 211; United Kingdom, *Insolvency Law and Practice: Report of the Review Committee* (HMSO, London, 1982, Cmnd 8558), 400; L S Sealy, "Personal Liability of Directors and Officers for Debts of Insolvent Corporations: A Jurisdictional Perspective (England)" in Ziegel (ed.), n. 27 above, 492; V Finch, "Directors' Duties: Insolvency and the Unsecured Creditor" in A Clarke (ed.), *Current Issues in Insolvency Law* (London, Sweet & Maxwell, 1991), 96.

[58] R M Goode, *Principles of Corporate Insolvency Law* (2nd edn., London, Sweet & Maxwell, 1997), 210. A Keay, "Corporate Governance During Administration and Reconstruction Under Part 5.3A of the Corporations Law" (1997) 15 *CSLJ* 145, 147, 149.

[59] D Brown, *Corporate Rescue: Insolvency Law in Practice* (Chichester, Wiley, 1996), 5. Brown notes that administrators do not have the jurisdiction to commence wrongful trading actions: see 14, 35.

taken all reasonable steps.[60] However, formal rescue procedures are not without their costs, and the actual benefits of statutory reorganisation proceedings are the subject of an ongoing debate.[61] In New Zealand, there is no specific affirmative defence of this kind as there is no form of statutory voluntary administration. The New Zealand Parliament chose to adopt new reckless trading provisions outside a major review of insolvency law.[62] While Australian directors may be able to shield themselves from personal liability through voluntary administration, New Zealand directors face rather uncertain consequences and must await a proper integration of company and insolvency law reform.[63]

In addition to the costs of forgone investments, one must also consider the economic waste that results from defensive management.[64] In order to avoid liability, directors may spend an inordinate amount of time ensuring that their actions will not breach the required regulatory standards. Investigations and obtaining opinions as to the solvency of the company may distract directors from the fundamental strategic goals of the company.[65] The possibility of personal liability may result in directors spending corporate cash on "expert opinions and other self protective devices to a degree inconsistent with the shareholder's interests". In the context of wrongful trading provisions, directors may insist on obtaining "affirmative assurances of solvency, generated by internal or external experts in connection with many transactions".[66] Delay for more study may, however, turn out to be the worst decision.[67]

Finally, one should note that in some cases liability will deter talented individuals from accepting a position as a director. In the alternative, individuals

---

[60] See Corporations Law, s 588(H)(5)–588(H)(6) (Australia). See A Herzberg, "Duty to Prevent Insolvent Trading" in Lessing and Corkery (eds.), n. 1 above, 16. Dabner argues that the new insolvent trading provisions will "encourage boards of companies experiencing financial difficulties to more quickly appoint an administrator rather than attempt to trade through such difficulties": see Dabner, n. 14 above, 562; Schultz, n. 1 above, 208.

[61] Wood, n. 53 above, 138, 144. Wood notes that in some cases "forcing a director into formal proceedings is not usually the best way to save the business for the benefit of creditors". On the perverse incentives that are created by the effects of a reorganisation statute such as the American Chapter 11 regime, see B Adler, "Bankruptcy and Risk Allocation" (1992) 77 *Cornell L Rev* 439 at 473; B Adler, "Finance's Theoretical Divide and the Proper Role of Insolvency Rules" (1994) 67 *S Calif Law Rev* 1107, 1120.

[62] J H Farrar, "The Responsibility of Directors and Shareholders for a Company's Debts Under New Zealand Law" in Ziegel (ed.), n. 27 above, 546.

[63] On the issue of voluntary administration in New Zealand, see P Heath, "Voluntary Administration—Proposals for New Zealand" in Rickett (ed.), n. 2 above, 91; and T Telfer, "Insolvency Policy and the Proposal for Voluntary Administration in New Zealand" in *ibid.*, 120.

[64] Stilson, n. 16 above, 13–14.

[65] Moffat, n. 50 above, 306. Goode lists 12 points of survival for directors wanting to minimise risk of being found liable. Included in his list is a suggestion to obtain "outside professional advice on suitable remedial measures": Goode, n. 58 above, 210. See also M Hyde, "Directors' Liability" (1997) 141 *Sol J* 307.

[66] DeMott, n. 15 above, 139, 141. However, compare, H Glasbeek, "More Director Responsibility: Much Ado About . . . What?" (1995) 25 *CBLJ* 416, 448.

[67] Easterbrook and Fischel, n. 6 above, 99.

may accept positions on the condition that management adopts a conservative policy to ensure that there is no prospect of director liability.[68]

The standard of director liability has international repercussions as well. As Sealy notes, if the law sets unrealistic standards as the norm, directors may take their skills elsewhere and investments may be lost.[69] Given the relatively free economic movement between countries, it is no longer sufficient to consider company law solely from a domestic perspective.[70] Directors' duties must be measured in the broader international market.

IV   UNCERTAINTY AND THE JUDICIAL INTERPRETATION OF RISK

There are inherent difficulties when director conduct is to be measured against a statutory standard. Often management is required to make quick decisions, sometimes based on incomplete information. However, a decision may turn out to be a wrong one *ex post*.[71] But directors are hired for their particular skills and not for what hindsight they might have had. As Sealy notes, "their role is to live with risk, not to avoid it".[72]

However, directors are likely to find that their pre-liquidation decisions will be scrutinised "by various hostile constituencies armed with perfect hindsight".[73] Management will not only have to make a decision based on the financial information available to it at the time but will also have to consider how the decision will be perceived *ex post* in a subsequent lawsuit.[74]

Some have called into question the suitability of the judiciary to evaluate corporate decision-making. A court will have to reconstruct the business decisions years after the fact through the costly and in some cases inaccurate exercise of assembling testimony and documentary evidence.[75] Judges may develop a bias against business risks which will lead them to "rely on hind-

---

[68] Daniels, n. 35 above, 569; Moffat, n. 50 above, 306; McDonnell, n. 9 above, 209. On empirical evidence as to the potential effect of limited liability on directors and whether they might reduce the number of boards upon which they serve, see R Rao, D Sokolow and D White, "Fiduciary Duty à la *Lyonnais*: An Economic Perspective on Corporate Governance in a Financially Distressed Firm" (1996) 22 *J of Corp L* 53, 59; Dabner, n. 14 above, 561.

[69] L S Sealy, "Corporate Governance and Directors' Duties" (1995) 1 *NZBLQ* 92, 99.

[70] DeMott has argued that firms are increasingly able to practise regulatory arbitrage. A number of practices allow firms to transcend inhibitory elements of particular bodies of corporate law. See D DeMott, "Trust and Tension within Corporations" (1996) 81 *Cornell L Rev* 1308, 1336–7.

[71] D M Branson, *Corporate Governance* (Charlottesville, Va, Michie & Co., 1993), 338–9; Easterbrook and Fischel, n. 6 above, 98–9.

[72] Sealy, n. 69 above, 98.

[73] G Varallo and J Finkelstein, "Fiduciary Obligations of Directors of the Financially Troubled Company" (1992) 48 *Bus Lawyer* 239. One author argues that "the determination of what risks are unacceptable is carried out with hindsight, leading to the extension to business life of bureaucratic standards": L Flynn, "Statutory Liability for Culpable Mismanagement" in Rajak (ed.), n. 14 above, 149.

[74] McDonnell, n. 9 above, 206.

[75] Easterbrook and Fischel, n. 6 above, 98; Branson, n. 71 above, 339.

sight to evaluate too critically rapid decisions taken in light of uncertain events".[76] It is questionable whether or not courts will be equipped to assess and make business decisions for an insolvent company, particularly when the legislation requires an evaluation of directors' decisions to be made after the fact.[77] One author has questioned whether it is viable to leave the task of "assessment of reasonable risk in the hands of the judges". Given that reasonable risk-taking is a matter of assessment of the expectations of management, shareholders and creditors, not all judicial decisions will reflect the "realities of business".[78]

Beyond the issue of how management decisions are reconstructed and the competency of the judiciary to evaluate business decisions lies the important issue whether or not the statutory rules provide clear guidelines for directors. It is argued that "the utility of a statutory framework is measured in part by the certainty which it brings to the calculation of transaction costs".[79]

Professor Prentice quite rightly notes that "the standard to be applied in determining when liability should be imposed on directors for the consequences of a company's insolvency raises one of the most difficult problems in designing such legislation". In England the crucial phrase is "no reasonable prospect" which, according to Professor Prentice, is "inherently elusive".

Once a decision has been made to adopt a regime of director liability, Parliament should ensure "the availability of clear, crystallised safe harbours for diligent directors".[80] If legal rules are reasonably consistent and clear, company law participants will be able to ascertain a narrow set of possible outcomes and evaluate more consistently the costs and benefits associated with a particular strategy or course of action.[81] By way of contrast, a poorly defined standard clouds business judgement and leads directors to make decisions on the basis of avoiding liability.[82]

The dilemma for a company director who is unclear as to how a legislative standard will be interpreted has been aptly described by Cheffins. A director can "only speculate whether injecting more capital, cajoling other directors to

---

[76] Cheffins, n. 7 above, 543.

[77] Varallo and Finkelstein, n. 73 above, 254.

[78] Wishart, n. 13 above, 253. The business judgement rule in the United States in part is premised in part on the basis that courts are ill-equipped to "exhume and re-create business decisions": see Branson, n. 71 above, 338–9.

[79] D Pollard, "Fear and Loathing in the Boardroom: Directors Confront New Insolvent Trading Provisions" (1994) 22 *ABLR* 392, 396.

[80] Daniels, n. 35 above, 570; V Jelisvac, "A Safe Harbour Proposal to Define the Limits of Directors' Fiduciary Duty to Creditors in the 'Vicinity of Insolvency' " (1992) *J of Corp L* 144; Rao, Sokolow and White, n. 68 above, 61 (inconsistent application of standards by the courts will limit the efficacy of personal liability as a means of controlling agency costs; inconsistent application or unclear standards not only creates uncertainty but it may also increase the cost of financing).

[81] Cheffins, n. 7 above, 332. See this principle in operation in the context of reorganisation statutes: G Triantis, "Mitigating the Collective Action Problem of Debt Enforcement through Bankruptcy Law: Bill C–22 and Its Shadow" (1992) 20 *CBLJ* 242, 258.

[82] Rao, Sokolow and White, n. 68 above, 65.

take corrective action, tightening up accounting procedures, pursuing plans to achieve a turn around, consulting an insolvency practitioner, or putting the company into liquidation will be sufficient".[83]

V THE INTERPRETATION OF THE NEW ZEALAND COMPANIES ACT 1993

Uncertainty also surrounds the New Zealand statutory provisions, where the courts will be called upon to interpret the meaning of "substantial risk of serious loss to creditors" in section 135 of the Companies Act 1993. Directors may take some comfort in the preamble which places an emphasis on business risk:

> "a) To reaffirm the value of the company as a means of achieving economic and social benefits through the aggregation of capital for productive purposes, the spreading of economic risk, and the taking of business risks . . ."

The preamble also recognises the importance of encouraging "efficient and responsible management of companies by allowing directors a wide discretion in matters of business judgment".[84]

However, it is not certain that the importance of risk-taking and latitude in business judgments will have an overriding effect on the interpretation of the reckless trading provisions. These purposes must be balanced against the concluding words of paragraph (d) of the preamble which refer to the "protection for shareholders and creditors against the abuse of management power".

A Substantial Risk of Serious Loss

The difficulty with section 135 is that directors may not be able to predict with any certainty whether or not an adopted course of action will lead to liability.[85] The phrase "likely to create a substantial risk of serious loss" is problematic on a number of fronts. What is a substantial risk and what degree of

---

[83] Cheffins, n. 7 above, 542–3. On the problems of uncertainty in the new Australian provisions see, for example, Schultz, n. 1 above, 192. For a discussion of the difficulties and potential liability facing American insolvency practitioners in the context of advising insolvent corporations, see B Markell, "The Folly of Representing Insolvent Corporations: Examining Lawyer Liability and Ethical Issues Involved in Extending Fiduciary Duties to Creditors" (1997) 6 *J of Bankruptcy L and Pract* 403.

[84] Companies Act 1993, preamble. The importance of risk-taking was also recognised by the New Zealand Law Commission in its 1989 report. It recommended a replacement s 320 of the Companies Act 1955, as it was the view of the Commission that the existing s 320 went "too far in undermining the position of the company as a vehicle for taking risks": New Zealand Law Commission, n. 51 above, 52, 120. On the legislative history of s 320, see Rennie and Watts, n. 2 above, 31–4; M Russell, "The Companies Amendment Act 1980" [1981] *NZLJ* 131, 133; J Dabner, "Insolvent Trading: An International Comparison" (1994) 7 *Corp and Bus Law J* 49, 96–9.

[85] The Hon Justice D Tompkins, "Directing the Directors: The Duties of Directors Under the Companies Act 1993" (1994) 2 *Waikato L Rev* 13, 27. Tompkins states: "[T]he directors' duties spelt out in the Act should be clear and unambiguous. This section is not."

likelihood will be required?[86] The word "substantial" has been interpreted by courts in other contexts, however, with uncertain results. In *Terry's Motors Ltd.* v. *Rinder,* Mayo J stated that the word "substantial" was "an unsatisfactory medium for carrying the idea of some ascertainable proportion of the whole".[87] Similarly, Deane J in *Tillmans Butcheries Pty. Ltd.* v. *Australasian Meat Industry Employees Union* stated that "the word 'substantial' is not only susceptible of ambiguity: it is a word calculated to conceal a lack of precision".[88]

The New Zealand Court of Appeal has considered the meaning of "substantial" in the context of the Town and Country Planning Act 1953. In *Ashburton Borough* v. *Clifford,*[89] McCarthy J was of the view that substantial meant "considerable, solid or big and not merely unsubstantial". The other members of the Court, however, did not place a fixed meaning on the word and were content to allow it to be interpreted on the basis of common sense principles and on a review of all the circumstances.

While section 135 has yet to be reviewed by the judiciary in New Zealand, the provisions have nevertheless been discussed by a number of commentators. Criticisms of section 135 have focused on the fact that it has the potential to create liability for risks which are frequently faced by a number of businesses. The very nature of a limited liability company requires that there will be some risk to those who advance credit.[90] Deane notes that some businesses, such as new restaurants and small publishing businesses every day face substantial risks.[91] Watts argues that if one takes the view that "substantial" is taken to mean more than merely negligible, "nearly any business will involve directors in taking substantial risks of serious loss to creditors".[92] According to Watts, the "section is a virtual warranty of solvency".[93]

How one measures the risk of loss is an important factor. Deane argues that the provisions do not recognise the fact that there are two elements to business decisions. "The risk of loss is one. Equally important is the size of the prospective gains." Section 135, according to Deane, does not recognise the need for balance between risk and rewards. [94]

Justice Tompkins, in an article in the *Waikato Law Review*, disagrees and argues that Deane's concerns are not well founded. Justice Tompkins takes

---

[86] J Dabner, "Insolvent Trading: Recent Developments in Australia, New Zealand and South Africa" [1995] *JBL* 283, 305.

[87] *Terry's Motors Ltd.* v. *Rinder* [1948] SASR 167, 180.

[88] *Tillmans Butcheries Pty. Ltd.* v. *Australasian Meat Industry Employees Union* (1979) 42 FLR 331, 348.

[89] [1969] NZLR 927.

[90] Dabner, n. 86 above, 305. See also D Goddard, Chap 2.

[91] R Deane, "Besieged by Duties: Will the Companies Act Work for Directors?" (The Company Law Conference, 1994, NZ Law Society), 3.

[92] P Watts, "Company Law" [1993] *NZRLR* 268.

[93] Rennie and Watts, n. 2 above, 36. A similar view is taken of the Australian provisions. DeMott argues that the Australian provisions make directors contingent guarantors of the company's business: DeMott, n. 15 above, 141.

[94] Deane, n. 91 above, 3.

the view that in determining whether or not there is a substantial risk of serious loss, one must also examine the probability of gain:[95]

> "If a risk of loss is reasonably balanced by a prospect of gain, the risk could not be characterised as substantial. . . . The two words of emphasis in the phrase 'a *substantial* risk of *serious* loss' support the view that the court is unlikely to consider a director in breach of that duty if the risk of loss created is commensurate with the likelihood of profit."

A similar view is adopted by Gould, who argues that to succeed under section 135, a plaintiff would have to show that "the business as a whole was carried on in a manner in which the overall prospect of gain was not sufficient to balance the aggregate prospect of loss".[96]

Even if the risk of loss was reasonably balanced by the prospect of gain and the company fails, will the court with hindsight impose liability? Worse still is the case of the director who makes the calculation of gain versus loss and opts for the safer option to avoid personal liability. Whether it is open for the courts to balance the risk of gain remains to be seen. The specific wording of the legislation only refers to the risk of loss. Other specific interpretative issues also arise under sections 135 and 136.[97]

B Agreeing or Causing or Allowing

Under sections 135 and 136, a major issue to be resolved is whether personal liability will be imposed on a non-participating director. The former section 320 referred to any person who was "knowingly a party to a transaction". The earlier authority of *Re J E Hurdley & Son*[98] held that in order for liability to be imposed, it had to be shown that the member of the company "knew that the particular debts were being incurred".[99] Ostler J stated that "the object of the Legislature in using the word knowingly in the section was to protect such members of the company as have not taken an active part in its management".[100] Other cases followed this approach.[101]

---

[95] Tompkins, n. 85 above, 27.

[96] B Gould, "Directors' Personal Liability" [1996] *NZLJ* 437, 438.

[97] One issue that remains to be clarified is the phrase "the business". See the interpretation of the former s 320 and the phrase "any business" in *Re Nimbus Trawling Co. Ltd.* [1986] 2 NZLR 309; *Re Lake Tekapo Motor Inn* (1987) 3 NZCLC 100,157; Ross, n. 2 above, 185–6; A Beck and A Borrowdale, *Guidebook to New Zealand Companies and Securities Law* (5th edn., Auckland, CCH, 1994), 52. See also J Gooley, "Fraudulent Trading: Australian and New Zealand Experiences" (ALTA Conference 1993), 18.

[98] [1941] NZLR 686 (CA).

[99] *Ibid.*, at 734.

[100] *Ibid.*, at 745. See also P Howell and M J Whale, "Recent Developments in Insolvency Law and Practice" (New Zealand Law Society Seminar, 1987), 30; J H Farrar, "The Responsibility of Directors and Shareholders for a Company's Debts Under New Zealand Law" in Ziegel (ed.), n. 27 above, 532.

[101] *Re Pacific Wools* (1992) 6 NZCLC 67,824, 67,842; *Thompson* v. *Innes* (1985) 2 NZCLC 99, 463, 99, 470; *Rea* v. *Jordan Sandman Were Ltd.* (1992) 6 NZCLC 67,987, 67,993; Farrar, n. 100 above, 21.

However, in *Vinyl Processors (New Zealand) Ltd.* v. *Cant*, Hillyer J rejected the argument that the section protected external directors who had no particular knowledge of a specific debt. Hillyer J was of the view that the section could not operate if it only applied to an individual debt of which a director had personal knowledge. Knowledge of the particular debt was therefore not required as long as the debt was incurred in the "ordinary conduct of business". However, liability would not be imposed where management incurred extraordinary debts that directors would not expect.[102]

Under the new section 135(a) a director must not "*agree* to the business being carried on in a manner likely to create a substantial risk of serious loss to the company's creditors". Similarly, under section 136 a director must not "*agree* to the company incurring an obligation". Can someone agree to a course of action without having personally approved of it? "Agree" may in fact be narrower than "knowingly", and may mean that liability may fall "only on those who are actively involved in the decision".[103]

However, liability may be imposed on a non-participating director under section 135(b). A director must not "*cause or allow* the business of the company to be carried on in a manner likely to create a substantial risk of loss . . .". "Cause or allow" is much broader than agreement, but it remains to be seen whether personal liability can be imposed on a director who did not participate or have actual involvement in the decision.[104]

Australian jurisprudence on this issue may be useful for imposing liability on non-participating directors. Under the former Australian insolvent trading provisions, directors were given a defence if a debt was "incurred without the person's express or implied authority or consent". Directors who have conferred a general authority upon management to run the business, while remaining in total ignorance of the affairs of the company, will not be able to avoid liability.[105] In the recent case of *Standard Chartered Bank* v. *Antico* Hodgson J stated:[106]

---

[102] *Vinyl Processors (New Zealand) Ltd.* v. *Cant* [1991] 2 NZLR 417, 428–9. However, in *Re Wait Investments Ltd.* [1997] 3 NZLR 96, Barker J was unwilling to extend liability to a company secretary who "only knew about the transaction once the agreement had been signed" (at 366). Barker J distinguished the *Vinyl Processors* principle on the basis that the defendant was only a company secretary and not a director and did not have managerial role.

[103] Rennie and Watts, n. 2 above, 38; Ross, n. 2 above, 189; Beck and Borrowdale, n. 97 above, 53.

[104] Rennie and Watts, n. 2 above, 34: "In other words, does one permit something only when one is aware that it is going on and stands by?"

[105] I Trethowan, "Directors' Personal Liability for Insolvent Trading: At Last A Degree of Consensus" (1993) 11 *CSLJ* 103, 112.

[106] (1995) 38 NSWLR 290, 366. See also *Morley* v. *Statewide Tobacco Services Ltd.* (1992) 8 ACSR 305; *Group Four Industries Pty.* v. *Brosnan* (1992) 8 ACSR 463; *Byron* v. *Southern Star Group Pty. Ltd.* (1997) 15 ACLC 191; *Capricorn Society* v. *Linke* (1996) 14 ACLC 431; *Androvin* v. *Figliomeni* (1996) 14 ACLC 1,461; and *Neville Smith Timber Industries Pty. Ltd.* v. *Lennan* [1996] 2 Qd R 177. For an interpretation of the new Australian defence, see *Metropolitan Fire Systems* v. *Miller* (1997) 23 ACSR 699; compare *Metal Manufacturers Pty. Ltd.* v. *Lewis* (1988) 13 NSWLR 315. For a discussion of this issue in the context of *AWA* v. *Daniels* (1995) 13 ACLC 614, see J Cassidy, "Has the Sleeping Director Finally Been Laid to Rest?" (1997) 25 *ABLR* 102, 108.

"In the case of so-called sleeping directors, I think it is largely a question of fact in each case whether inactivity does or does not imply authority or consent. If the circumstances are that a director knows or should know that the company is incurring debts which it will not be able to pay as they fall due, and does not try to prevent this by persuasion, calling a meeting, etc, then authority by consent may well be implied. . . ."

The degree of participation may also be relevant in determining the quantum of liability.[107] In *Re Wait Investments Ltd.*,[108] the sole director of a company entered into an unconditional agreement to purchase a building for $1.635 million at the request of her husband, the manager of the company. Barker J found both the sole director, who had signed the agreement, and the manager liable under section 320. However, he held that the director's culpability was not as great as her husband's. Even though she was the sole director, she did not have any commercial expertise and did not manage the company's business. She relied entirely on her husband, who managed the company, and therefore was ordered to pay half the amount while her husband was required to pay the full amount of the loss. Barker J stated that "her moral culpability is less".[109]

C Section 136: Reasonable Grounds and Incurring an Obligation

Section 136 reads:

"A director of a company must not agree to the company incurring an obligation unless the director believes at that time on reasonable grounds that the company will be able to perform the obligation when it is required to do so."

The director's conduct will be measured on an objective standard. The director must believe on "reasonable grounds". Interpretations of the former section 320(1)(a) held that the subjective test, i.e. the belief of the director that the company would be able to perform, must be justified on an objective basis. The objective nature of the test—"on reasonable grounds"—"should be tested by the standard of an officer of the company of reasonable competence".[110] However, given the vast range of companies that operate in New Zealand, it is difficult to state with any certainty what "reasonable grounds" means.[111]

---

[107] A Beck, "Creditors and the New Age Company—For Better or Worse" (NZ Law Conference, 1996), 218.

[108] [1997] 3 NZLR 96.

[109] *Ibid.*, at 105; see also B Keene, "Single Transaction Companies: Risk Transactions" [1997] *NZLJ* 164.

[110] *Re Petherick Exclusive Fashions Ltd.* (1987) 3 NZCLC 99,946, 99,958; *Vinyl Processors (New Zealand) Ltd.* v. *Cant* [1991] 2 NZLR 417.

[111] For a similar criticism of the Australian provisions, see Mannolini, n. 26 above, 40. The reasonable business person is an "extraordinarily nebulous concept": see M Trebilcock, "The Liability of Company Directors for Negligence" (1969) 32 *MLR* 499, 511.

Criticisms of section 136 focus on the reasonableness standard which is imposed, with one author taking the view that it is an "onerous liability".[112] Where a particular type of business has a high failure rate, Deane queries whether such an at-risk business will be able to accept any credit where it might be difficult for directors to show that they did not have reasonable grounds for believing the business to have a high probability of long-term survival.[113]

Beyond the problems of imposing an objective standard, section 136 has inherited a problematic interpretation issue that has arisen in Australia. Under the Australian insolvent trading provision, liability may be imposed where a director "incurs a debt".[114] Professor Prentice has noted that, by way of contrast, in the English wrongful trading provision, "[t]he trigger event relates to consequences of continued trading and it does not require the insolvency to be brought about by a particular type of trading activity". He prefers the English model, which not only avoids interpretative difficulties of deciding when a debt has been incurred, but also "focuses on the right question, namely, has the director's conduct in continuing to trade prejudiced the company's creditors?".[115]

Professor Prentice has quite rightly identified a problematic area of the Australian provisions, and the same interpretative issue also arises under the New Zealand legislation. The courts must decide the important timing issue of when the obligation was incurred. The issue is crucial because the section requires an analysis of the director's belief at the time the obligation was incurred, and that such belief must be on reasonable grounds. The issue of when a debt has been incurred has been the subject of numerous decisions in Australia. However, despite the efforts of Hodgson J to set out some general principles in *Standard Chartered Bank,* there still remains some degree of inconsistency in the Australian courts' interpretation of this provision.[116] In New Zealand, we can look forward to similar litigation which will define "obligation"[117] and determine at what time guarantees, leases, extensions on

---

[112] Rennie and Watts, n. 2 above, 39.

[113] Deane, n. 91 above.

[114] Corporations Law, s 588G (Australia). The implications of the Australian cases on New Zealand law are discussed in Rennie and Watts, n. 2 above, 38–40.

[115] D Prentice Chap 6, p. 119

[116] J Mosley, "Insolvent Trading: What is a Debt and When is One Incurred" (1996) 4 *Insol L J* 155, 168. See *Standard Chartered Bank* v. *Antico* (1995) 38 NSWLR 290; J Noble, "When Does a Company Incur a Debt Under the Insolvent Trading Provisions of the Corporations Law?" (1994) 12 *CSLJ* 297. Noble concluded that such were the inconsistencies that it was "regrettable" that the new s 588G provision retained the ingredient of "incurring an obligation".

[117] The use of the term "obligation" in s 136, rather than "debt", is however significant. In some Australian cases it has been held that the failure to deliver pre-paid goods or services does not constitute the incurring of a debt. Liability was therefore not imposed. A narrow interpretation of "debt" has the potential to undermine the effectiveness of the Australian insolvent trading provisions. See P Grawehr, "A Comparison Between Australian and European Insolvent Trading Provisions" (1996) 14 *CSLJ* 17, 35. See also, for example, *Reed International Books Australia* v. *King & Prior Pty Ltd.* (1993) 11 ACLC 935; *Shepherd* v. *Australia and New Zealand Banking Group* (1996) 14 ACLC 987 (aff'd (1996–97) 41 NSWLR 431); Mosley, n. 115 above. However, the New Zealand courts may take a broader view of the situation when analysed under the term "obligation".

loans or contracts for the sale of goods were incurred. These rather technical issues distract from more important corporate governance issues.

VI THE HYPOTHETICAL BARGAIN

On balance one might ask whether or not the statutory regime would have been achieved by the company law participants if left to their own private bargains. If one adopts the view that the contracting process between debtors and creditors is imperfect and that gaps exist in the contractual documentation, the statute supplies the contractual terms that the parties would have bargained for under ideal circumstances.[118]

However, this interpretation is subject to challenge. From the perspective of a hypothetical bargaining model, Cheffins concludes that the English wrongful trading provisions cannot be justified on the basis that the parties would bargain for equivalent rules. For example, shareholders would be reluctant to bargain for a regime of director liability, as it would compel directors to shy away from taking "bold resolute decisions that are required to maximise profits". Shareholders invest money on the basis that "those in charge will take risks in order to pursue and exploit lucrative projects and ventures". Additionally, it is unlikely that directors would agree to increase their exposure and put their personal assets on the line.[119]

A similar conclusion can be reached from the perspective of a creditor. At first glance it may appear that creditors would contract for similar protection. Director liability increases the opportunity for recovery of debt and at the same time provides a deterrent against director misconduct.[120] However, directors of closely held companies will often have their interests tied to the fortunes of the company and will not have assets on which creditors might recover. Cheffins argues that as a matter of bargaining creditors do not always place a high priority on pursuing directors personally and seek other ways of reducing risk.[121]

Furthermore, it is unlikely that the parties would agree to a mandatory regime as it reduces choice and restricts the flexibility of loan agreements. In

[118] Cheffins, n. 7 above, 540–1; Mannolini, n. 26 above, 17; R Sappideen, "Fiduciary Obligations to Corporate Creditors" [1991] *JBL* 365, 382; Rao, Sokolow and White, n. 68 above, 55.

[119] Cheffins, n. 7 above, 264, asks "what rational actors would contract for if they had perfect information, did not face significant transaction costs, and could be fully confident that the agreements reached would be performed as arranged". On whether shareholders and directors would prefer such a rule, see 540–3. D Goddard argues that in the context of ss 135 and 136 of the Companies Act 1993, the provisions "preclude the very 'enterprise and adventure' that the companies legislation seeks to encourage . . .": see Chap 2. p. 59. See also D Goddard, "The 1993 Act Comes Into Its Own" (1997) 8 *CSLB* 95.

[120] On the deterrent effect of wrongful trading provisions, see J Dine, "Punishing Directors" [1994] *JBL* 325; and J Dine, "Wrongful Trading—Quasi Criminal Law" in Rajak (ed.), n. 14, above, 163.

[121] Cheffins, n. 7 above, 544.

some instances a creditor with a well diversified loan portfolio may prefer a risky strategy on the part of the company. Such a creditor may be confident prior to advancing the loan that they are adequately compensated for the risk. However, the mandatory nature of the statutory obligation may prevent the directors from engaging in that risk. One author argues that the inflexible nature of the Australian insolvent trading provisions do not resemble the result that the parties would have achieved through private bargaining and he suggests that parties be allowed to opt out of the statute.[122]

VII CONCLUSION

As the law cannot eliminate business risks, the central question is how best to achieve a balance "between protecting creditors and not discouraging a corporation's ability to innovate and take appropriate business risks".[123] The centenary of *Salomon* is perhaps an important time to examine the merits of the personal liability of directors. The legislative innovations have fundamentally altered the nature of company law. This commentary has questioned whether creditors truly require protection and asked whether the regulation is beneficial.

Perhaps a larger point has been lost in the debate over whether there is an uncompensated risk. If limited liability does shift the risk of loss to creditors, thus deteriorating their position, an equally important question to ask is whether this has been more than offset by the increased lending opportunities that the development of limited liability has offered since its inception in the nineteenth century.[124]

Additionally, in deciding to impose statutory liability one has to question whether or not the deviant director should be the paradigm for regulation. Parliament should avoid the temptation to regulate in response to notorious high-profile cases.[125] The comments of the 1926 United Kingdom Company Law Amendment Committee (Greene Report) may still have validity:[126]

---

[122] Mannolini, n. 26 above, 58. If directors had the ability to negotiate an exclusion of liability with their creditors, it can be argued that explicit negotiation of this issue would improve information flows to creditors about allocation of risks and increase the creditors' incentives to more closely monitor the companies activities. See D Halpern, M Trebilcock and M Turnbull, "An Economic Analysis of Limited Liability in Corporation Law" (1980) 30 *Univ Toronto L J* 117, 148.

[123] Schwarcz, n. 26 above, 673, 689. Company risk-taking raises hard policy choices (687): "[S]hould risk taking be encouraged where the success rate is low and the venture financed by creditors?"

[124] J B Baskin and P J Miranti, *A History of Corporate Finance* (Cambridge, OUP, 1997), 139.

[125] Daniels, n. 35 above, 571. See also discussion of this point in Dabner, n. 14 above, 552. Schwarcz argues that most business ventures "are not reasonably expected, even if unsuccessful, to have a dramatically negative impact on the corporation": Schwarcz, n. 26 above, 689.

[126] United Kingdom, *Company Law Amendment Committee* (HMSO, London, 1926, Cmnd 2657), 4.

"It appears to us, as a matter of general principle, most undesirable, in order to defeat an occasional wrongdoer, to impose restrictions which would seriously hamper the activities of honest men and would inevitably re-act upon the commerce and prosperity of the country."

The Report concluded that cases involving improper dealing divert attention away from the vast number of honest businesses and "create an exaggerated idea of the evils connected with limited companies and their activities".[127]

Further, a debate on the ideal regulatory standard to be adopted is in some ways unproductive. If a director is intent on engaging in misbehaviour, even the tightest of rules will not deter. As Sealy noted, the world share market crash of 1987 and the ensuing fall-out was not new. Companies have gone to the brink and left creditors waiting in line throughout history, both in jurisdictions with tough laws and in countries with lax ones. Sealy doubts "whether even a significant tightening up of the law on director's duties would have done much to prevent it from having happened on these occasions or from happening again in the future".[128] Regulation of risk, therefore, may be best left to the market.

---

[127] United Kingdom, *Company Law Amendment Committee* (HMSO, London, 1926, Cmnd 2657), 4. Anderson argues in the context of English law that public concern over fraud and insolvent companies "has achieved an exaggerated notoriety because it has been a feature in some very high profile cases": see H Anderson, "Insolvency and Fraud" (1997) 6 *Int'l Insol Rev* 1, 24.

[128] Sealy, n. 69 above, 99.

8

Company Law and Regulatory Complexity

JOANNA GRAY*

I INTRODUCTION

This is an appropriate moment in the history of company law to try to imagine what life would be like for the average British boot manufacturer one hundred years on after the decision in *Salomon* v. *A Salomon & Co. Ltd.*[1] It would be surprising nowadays to find a boot manufacturer who did *not* employ the corporate form, and any such company would be subject to a plethora of detailed statutory and regulatory obligations. These obligations arise not only under company law, but under many of the different areas of regulatory law which impinge directly on business activity. A Salomon & Co. Ltd. had, in the 1890s, no need of a technical compliance directorate to keep the company on the right side of health and safety, environmental, product standard, packaging and marketing legislation and regulation, and thus avoid the swingeing penal and quasi-penal sanctions that often attach to contraventions of such regulatory strictures. In fact Aron Salomon would most probably hang up his cobbler's last and cast around for another type of living, less hidebound by law, to pass on to his family.[2] This essay asks one very simple question. To what extent does company law doctrine reflect the growing role of regulation in business life?

There are many interesting legal and policy issues that arise around the related issues of corporate personality and corporate responsibility. One easily overlooked technique which regulatory laws often employ is an extension of the sanction of criminal liability so that it reaches beyond and behind the corporate veil to impose liability for regulatory contravention on a company's directors and officers, as well as on the company itself. In terms of regulatory efficacy, these types of what are subsequently referred to as "officer liability" provisions, are potentially useful weapons for enforcers of regulation and

---

* Senior Research Fellow, Institute of Advanced Legal Studies, University of London.

[1] [1897] AC 22 (HL).

[2] Suggestions that spring readily to mind include counselling, running a dating agency or religious sect and horse whispering.

framers of regulatory provisions. Officer liability provisions give such enforcers and framers a way of getting around the doctrine of corporate personality and pinning responsibility for the company's actions on those human actors behind the veil of incorporation who are responsible in the first place for the company's regulatory contravention. Thus these provisions represent a quite deliberate setting aside by the legislature, for policy reasons, of the principle that flows logically from the doctrine of separate corporate personality, that the company and only the company bears responsibility for its acts and omissions.

The second part of this essay examines the recent English Court of Appeal decision in *Re Attorney-General's Reference (No 1 of 1995)*[3] and its implications for company directors in a business world of increasing regulatory complexity. This decision sheds some light on judicial interpretation of these "officer liability" statutory provisions.

The third part of the essay then assesses the Court of Appeal's reasoning in the light of recent appellate case law on the responsibility of companies under criminal and regulatory statutes for acts and omissions of their officers and employees.

At first sight, these officer liability provisions may seem unrelated to the issue of corporate responsibility. The question for the law when considering corporate responsibility is: "In deciding, for the purposes of determining its liability under a criminal or regulatory provision whether a company has done or failed to do something, then, of all the actors who constitute the company 'de facto', whose acts are attributable to the company so that they can be said to be the acts of the company 'de jure' and thus determine the company's responsibility?"

As the cases after *Tesco Supermarkets Ltd.* v. *Nattrass*[4] show, there is no simple answer to this question, but the increasing sophistication with which the courts have begun to tackle it could, it is argued here, be usefully imported into the interpretation of the "officer liability" provisions considered in the first part of this essay. It is an immutable fact that, as regulation of all aspects of companies' conduct increases, the issues of:

(a) when is a company liable under a criminal or regulatory provision for the misdemeanours of its employees? and
(b) when are its officers liable under such provisions for the company's misdemeanours?

will continue to occupy the courts and the linkage between these two questions may become clearer.

---

[3] [1996] 1 WLR 970.
[4] [1972] AC 153 (HL).

II "OFFICER LIABILITY" PROVISIONS AND THE DECISION IN
RE ATTORNEY-GENERAL'S REFERENCE (NO 1 OF 1995)

In the complex regulatory world in which companies now do business, with a myriad of specific statutory criminal and regulatory offences in existence, directors can find that such offences can, if committed by the company, be visited upon their heads as well. The obvious rationale for this is that it gives the primary corporate offence extra "bite" and deterrent effect by looking through the corporate veil and fixing those officers who were responsible for the corporate offending with criminal or regulatory liability as well.

A Examples of "Officer Liability" Provisions

Some English examples of statutory provisions which put company directors at risk in this way include the following:

(i)   Section 733 of the Companies Act 1985:

"Offences by Bodies Corporate:
   (1) The following applies to offences under any of sections 21 [failure to comply with Part VI disclosure of interests in shares provisions], 216(3) [non-compliance with section 212 notice], 394A(1) [non-compliance with duty to make statement on ceasing to hold office as auditor] and 447 to 451 [non-compliance with and obstruction of company investigations].
   (2) Where a body corporate is guilty of such an offence and it is proved that the offence occurred with *the consent or connivance or was attributable to any neglect on the part of any director, manager, secretary or similar officer* of the body or any person who was purporting to act in any such capacity, he as well as the body corporate is guilty of an offence and is liable to be proceeded against and punished accordingly . . ." (emphasis added)

(ii) In like vein, section 432 of the Insolvency Act 1986, "Offences by Bodies Corporate", fixes a company's officers with liability for certain Insolvency Act offences:

"(2) Where a body corporate is guilty of an offence to which this section applies and the offence is proved to have been committed with *the consent or connivance of, or to be attributable to any neglect on the part of, any director* . . . he, as well as the body corporate is guilty of the offence and liable to be proceeded against and punished accordingly."

(iii) More sector-specific regulatory statutes adopt the same approach. For example, section 202 of the Financial Services Act 1986 states:

"(1) Where an offence under this Act committed by a body corporate is proved to have been committed *with the consent or connivance of, or to be attributable to any neglect on the part of . . . and director* . . . he, as well as the body corporate is liable to be proceeded against and punished accordingly."

Section 96(1) of the Banking Act 1987 does exactly the same thing with respect to corporate offences committed under that Act.[5]

These types of provisions can be seen as legitimate responses to the doctrine of separate corporate personality which, in their absence, would render many regulatory offences unable to reach and touch those individuals to whom the offending is "*de facto*", if not "*de jure*", attributable. It is interesting to note that all the provisions mentioned apply not just to directors and officers, but also to members where the affairs of the company are managed by those members.[6] These provisions are not intended to impose strict liability on the individuals concerned. Their liability is expressed to be fault-based, in that proof is required of their consent, connivance or causal neglect.

However, what if a company director is ignorant of the fact that an offence has been committed by his company? He is running the company in good faith, but in such a way as to mean the company has unwittingly strayed into business territory that is subject to specific statutory regulation (the very existence of which the director is unaware) and has thereby offended. Is that primary corporate offence to be visited on the directors through the operation of a statutory provision for secondary "officer liability", even if the director argues he did not "consent" to its commission by the company because he was unaware of the fact of its commission?

In other words, what meaning does the precept "ignorance of the law is no excuse" have in an era where it is, some business people would argue, all too easy to do business in such a way that offends against some or other specific statutory or regulatory edict. Should not the fact that the company is itself strictly liable for the offence be a sufficient deterrent without imposing an additional criminal liability on the ignorant officer for his "consent or connivance" in an offence which he was unaware was even being committed?

B *Re Attorney-General's Reference (No 1 of 1995)*

The question of what *mens rea* is required to prove "consent" in the context of these "officer liability" provisions received attention from the Court of Appeal in *Re Attorney-General's Reference (No 1 of 1995)*.[7] This appeal concerned the liability of directors of an unlicensed deposit-taking business.

Section 3(1) of the Banking Act 1987 stipulates that:

"[N]o person shall . . . accept a deposit in the course of carrying on a business which for the purposes of this Act is a deposit-taking business unless that person is an institution for the time being authorised by the Bank [of England] under . . . this Act."

---

[5] A trawl through health and safety and environmental regulatory legislation would provide many more examples.

[6] Companies Act 1985, s 733(3); Insolvency Act 1986, s 432(3); and Financial Services Act 1986, s 202(2).

[7] [1996] 1 WLR 970.

Section 96(1) stipulates further:

> "Where an offence under this Act committed by a body corporate is proved to have been committed with the consent or connivance of, or to be attributable to, any neglect on the part of any director, manager, secretary or other similar officer of the body corporate, or any person who was purporting to act in any such capacity he, as well as the body corporate, is guilty of an offence . . ."

The respondents, one of whom was a director and the other a deemed director of an investment and insurance brokerage company, had been charged with consenting to the offence of the carrying on by the company of an unlicensed deposit-taking business in contravention of section 3(1) of the Banking Act. The respondents were completely ignorant of the need for the company to have a licence and the trial judge therefore withdrew the section 3 charges from the jury on the grounds that the respondents could not have the requisite consent. He stated:[8]

> "the sole ground upon which I find there is no case to answer is that which was centred on the word 'consent' in s 96(1) of the Banking Act 1987 under which counts 1 and 2 are drawn. It does seem to me that a section 3 offence is indeed a strict liability offence, but that it is made otherwise where it concerns directors or persons purporting to act as directors; that is each of these defendants. In that regard I hold that a particular awareness must be proved, and . . . evidence adduced of a particular awareness of the director . . . including a lack of awareness of authorisation.
>
> That lack of awareness of authorisation . . . requires a specific application of the conscious mind to that point . . ."

The trial judge thought that the use of the word "consent" in section 96 of the Banking Act meant that Parliament required this specific *mens rea* on the part of the director charged, whereas the corporate offence was a strict liability one.

The Attorney-General referred two points of law to the Court of Appeal:

(a) On a charge against a company director of consenting to the acceptance of a deposit contrary to sections 3 and 96 of the Banking Act 1987, is ignorance of the law as to the requirement of the authorisation of the Bank of England a defence?; and

(b) What *mens rea* constitutes "consent"?

To the first of these questions, the Court of Appeal answered "No", and, in respect of the second, the Court held that proof that a defendant knew the material facts which constituted the offence by the body corporate and agreed to its conduct of its business on the basis of those facts gave that defendant sufficient mens rea to constitute consent.

The judgment of the Court of Appeal drives home to executive company directors the importance of continually subjecting the way in which they are

---

[8] These comments of the trial judge are extracted in the Court of Appeal judgment: *ibid.*, at 978.

conducting all the various aspects of the company's business to critical legal and regulatory audit. Lord Taylor CJ stated:[9]

"A director who knows that acts which can only be performed by the company if it is licensed by the Bank, are being performed when in fact no license exists and who consents to that performance is guilty of the offence charged. The fact that he does not know it is an offence to perform them without a licence, i.e. ignorance of the law is no defence . . . [The] suggestion that the director must have actively addressed his mind to the question of licences is wholly unreal. If the two directors, who were wholly responsible for the company's business activity, were ignorant of the need for a licence it can readily be inferred that they knew they did not have one. The concept of a director who is ignorant of the law requiring a licence, focusing his mind on the question of whether he has or has not obtained one is academic. Had anyone approached the defendant directors and asked: 'Have you a licence or authorisation from the Bank of England?' the ready answer would have been 'No', probably supplemented by 'I did not know I needed one.' There would have been no need for a search, an inquiry or a focusing of the mind. Since the question had not occurred to them they would know that the company did not have one."

C What Hope for the Blissfully Ignorant Art Director?

The Court of Appeal was at pains to point out that the effect of its ruling was not to create an absolute offence from section 96(1) of the Banking Act in respect of directors. Lord Taylor CJ stated:[10]

"There could, for example, in a company with a number of directors responsible for different limbs of the company's business, be a director who believed the licence had been obtained and was not therefore consenting to the offences committed by the company."

Thus, the Court of Appeal's analysis leaves room for a degree of exculpation in the case of a large functionally differentiated board of directors. Let us say, for example, the creative art director believed the necessary licence had been obtained by one of the more technical directors. This director could not be said to be consenting to the commission of the offence. However, what if such a director was just as ignorant of the need for a licence as the managing director and the rest of the board were? This in fact would more likely be the case in reality, since such a director would be more likely to leave all matters of legal compliance to his colleagues. The terms of the Court of Appeal's judgment seem to suggest that in this situation (which is, after all, more understandable and even desirable in that it would make for more efficient functioning of the board) the director would not be excused as he could not be said to have "believed the licence had been obtained . . .". Rather, he too was as ignorant of the law as the rest of the board, and was therefore just as

[9] [1996] 1 WLR 970, at 980–1.
[10] *Ibid.*, at 981.

consenting to the commission of the corporate offence within the meaning of section 96(1) as they were.

The Civil Division of the English Court of Appeal considered the effect of this type of "liability of officer" provision in *Richardson* v. *Pitt-Stanley & Others*.[11] Section 5 of the Employers' Liability (Compulsory Insurance) Act 1969 imposed criminal liability on any officer of a company who consented or connived in a company's failure to insure against liability to employees for personal injury. The case concerned an unsuccessful attempt to argue that section 5 also impliedly imposed civil liability on the company's officers who were in contravention of it, so that an injured workman could recover damages from such officers. The attempt failed, but the dissenting judgment of Sir John Megaw, who would have allowed for the existence of such a civil remedy, re-affirmed that, whereas the corporate statutory liability was absolute, that of the officers under section 5 was not and "relevant fault" must be proved:[12]

> "in order that the liability should exist, for the purpose of civil proceedings under . . . section 5, it is necessary for the employee to establish that the director in question consented to or connived at the failure to insure, or facilitated that failure by any neglect: in other words, there has to be shown a relevant fault on the part of the individual, other than the mere fact that he has general responsibilities as a director."

The only "relevant fault" which the Criminal Division of the Court of Appeal required in *Re Attorney-General's Reference (No 1 of 1995)* was that the defendant officer be proved to know the material facts which constitute the offence by the body corporate and to have agreed to its conduct of its business on the basis of those facts. This could quite easily cover less immediately involved directors who have only the most general of responsibilities for the area of business in which the corporate offence falls. That might be thought unfair and potentially inefficient in that this interpretation renders all directors potentially criminally liable for matters which are in practice far removed from their areas of knowledge, expertise and responsibility. Although the Court of Appeal might not have considered its decision to mean that it was imposing strict liability on such directors, those same directors could well be forgiven for thinking that it does.

This decision should serve to remind all company directors and officers, no matter what the demarcation of their area of responsibility for the company's business, of the importance of keeping a watching brief on legislative developments that do or could pertain to their company's overall business. This is not an easy task for the busy and stretched executive director who may quite justifiably feel that, by operating within a functionally differentiated board as he does, he should be able and entitled to rely on those of his fellow directors

---

[11] [1995] 2 WLR 26.
[12] *Ibid.*, at 37.

whose task it is to "know the law" and secure compliance with it to do so. Of course, to suggest that the Court of Appeal's decision should have been otherwise and should have perhaps recognised the reality of the way many boards allocate responsibility amongst their members is to run the risk of fragmenting the legal content of a company director's duties. Moving away from a unitary view of what constitutes a company director's responsibilities, at least for the purposes of applying these officer liability provisions, at first sight may seem to carry with it the danger of a return to the lax amateurism of the days of *The Marquis of Bute's Case*.[13] Another concern might be that if the courts were to take a more subjective view of the mens rea needed for this type of regulatory offence, then a board of directors might try to structure itself so that no one single individual on the board could ever be said to know sufficient of both the content of applicable regulatory law *and* the operations of the company to assume personal liability for consenting to or conniving in any regulatory contravention. However, it is suggested that the courts should and would see the Chief Executive and other senior executive officers as being in such a position, despite what they may claim to the contrary. Such an approach sits well with the view that the regulators themselves are beginning to take (in the financial regulatory sector at least) of "who should be seen to be responsible for what" when it comes to enforcement of regulatory standards.[14] To put it crudely, the buck has to stop somewhere with a real person, not just a corporate person, for sanctions for regulatory contraventions to have any sting in their tail. But the law ought to try as far as possible to "sting" the right person, i.e. someone who actually knew or whose job it was to know about the non-compliance and who can do something about it in the future. To sting the "wrong" person does not further the regulatory law's goals and will only create a disincentive for certain types of individual and function to be represented at board level. This could have deleterious wider and longer-term consequences.

---

[13] [1892] 2 Ch 100. The Marquis of Bute, having inherited the office of President of the Cardiff Savings Bank from his father when he was but 6 months old, and having attended just one board meeting in 38 years, was held not to be liable for lending irregularities within the bank's operation.

[14] A Consultation Document from the Securities and Futures Authority, *Proposals to Amend Guidance and the Rules in Relation to the Responsibilities of Senior Executive Officers* (London, SFA, Sept. 1996), created a stir of interest in that it sought, post-Barings, to make senior management responsible for compliance failures within their firms regardless of whether or not they were directly responsible. The Securities and Investments Board has now taken up this idea and is currently consulting to see if it would work more widely throughout the whole financial sector: see SIB Consultative Document, *The Responsibilities of Senior Management* (London, SIB, July 1997).

D Accessory Liability Provisions Versus Lifting the Corporate Veil the Old-fashioned Way

Another very recent decision of relevance and interest in the context of this centenary celebration of *Salomon* is the recent decision of Carnwath J in *Securities and Investments Board* v. *Scandex Capital Management A/S and Jeremy Bartholomew-White*.[15] The decision covered many points in respect of the system of authorisation and enforcement introduced by the Financial Services Act 1986, but what was especially interesting was the Securities and Investments Board's ("SIB") attempts to pierce the corporate veil of the first defendant company in order to fix the second defendant with personal liability for the many and various regulatory contraventions by the first defendant. The first defendant, Scandex Capital Management ("Scandex"), was a Danish company, now in liquidation, of which the second defendant, Mr Bartholomew-White, was managing director and in which he held one third of the share capital. Scandex had conducted foreign exchange trading for and on behalf of United Kingdom investors, had sent mailshots directed at investors into the United Kingdom, had made unsolicited calls offering forex trading services and had also made misleading statements about, *inter alia*, the level of commission Scandex was charging its clients. Significant losses were incurred by United Kingdom investors as a result of their dealings with Scandex. Scandex had been operating in Denmark on the basis of interim authorisation from Finans (the Danish investment business regulatory authority) under transitional provisions of Danish law implementing the Investment Services Directive ("ISD"), pending Finans' determination of its application for full authorisation to do investment business. This, it was claimed on behalf of the defendants, entitled Scandex to do investment business in the United Kingdom under the Euro-passporting provisions of the ISD, which are given effect to by section 31 of the Financial Services Act 1986. That argument was rejected by Carnwath J, with the effect that the company's investment business was therefore unauthorised and in contravention of the Financial Services Act 1986. There were other contraventions of specific regulatory provisions of the Act as well, but the basic one of interest here was the unauthorised doing of regulated investment business.

The SIB took enforcement proceedings against Mr Bartholomew-White (as well as Scandex) on the basis that he was personally responsible for Scandex's unauthorised investment business because that business should be treated as his business by a process of "lifting the corporate veil" and seeing through it in order for the court to say that it was he, not just Scandex, who had carried on unlicensed investment business. Relying on the few case law examples where the courts have characterised companies as mere covers or shams,[16] the

---

[15] Unreported, 26 Mar. 1997.

[16] *Gildford Motor Co. Ltd.* v. *Horne* [1933] Ch 935; *Jones* v. *Lipman* [1962] 1 WLR 832; *Re H* [1996] 2 All ER 391.

SIB argued that Scandex was nothing more than a strategic cloak for Mr Bartholomew-White's illegal forex dealing activities. However, in language which shows what a sea change has occurred over the past century in judicial thinking since the lower courts expressed such suspicion and hostility to companies in *Salomon*, Carnwath J ruled that the conditions for lifting the veil of incorporation were not satisfied for the purposes of giving the SIB summary judgment on this point and, indeed, were unlikely to be satisfied at any trial of this issue:

> "The cases in which the veil has been lifted are generally ones where the company is being used as a means of shifting responsibility from the person (company or individual) who would otherwise be liable or might reasonably be expected to be liable. That element is not present in this case. There was no reason to expect Mr Bartholomew-White to undertake investment business in his own name, and nothing unusual in him doing so through a company. He was fully entitled to organise his affairs in that way. Thus even if it were shown that he was the sole and effective mind of Scandex, I doubt whether that would be sufficient to establish the grounds for lifting the veil. It may well be established that Scandex was set up as a vehicle for avoiding the restrictions on investment business in the UK, but on the facts the restrictions being avoided were those applicable to Euro Currency [Mr Bartholomew-White's previous forex trading company which had been based in London] rather than to Mr Bartholomew-White as an individual. Furthermore it cannot be said that Scandex was clearly 'a one man company'. Mr Bartholomew-White was a one-third shareholder and only one of the directors. The evidence of the SIB appears to me consistent with the case of a major shareholder who also acts as managing director—a situation which is very common and has never been thought to justify lifting the veil."

So much for the SIB's attempt to lift the corporate veil in order to make Mr Bartholomew-White primarily liable for contraventions of the Financial Services Act. However, the SIB had markedly more success with that part of its enforcement action which was based on provisions in the Financial Services Act 1986 which enable action to be taken against those "knowingly concerned" in various contraventions thereof, including the most basic contravention of all—doing regulated investment business without authorisation.[17] Unfortunately, in the light of the discussion above of the Court of Appeal's decision in *Re Attorney-General's Reference (No 1 of 1995)*, Carnwath J did not settle the question of law as to the appropriate standard of knowledge required to establish that a person is "knowingly concerned" in another's contravention of the Financial Services Act. His Lordship did not need to address this question, as there was no difficulty in finding that Mr Bartholomew-White was knowingly concerned in Scandex's contraventions that took place after he had been put on notice of them by correspondence he received from the SIB. Thus, on the facts of this case, the provision clearly applied.

[17] The Court has power to make restitutionary orders against persons "knowingly concerned" in another's regulatory contraventions under ss 6(2) and 61(1), Financial Services Act 1986. See further *SIB v. Pantell SA* [1993] Ch 256 (CA).

Hence, the SIB managed to establish that Mr Bartholomew-White was "knowingly concerned" in Scandex's contraventions of investor protection legislation, and thus he was made subject to restitutionary orders to be used to compensate investors; although the SIB was unable to establish that he was actually party to the offending transactions and deeds himself on the basis that company law could not set aside Scandex's corporate veil.

This decision is a neat recent illustration of just how useful these types of accessory/secondary liability provisions are at getting regulation to bite when the rather tight strictures of case law prevent the lifting of the corporate veil to allow the particular regulatory law through to reach the "real" perpetrators. If enforcers reach a dead end with an appeal to courts to lift the veil, as is more than likely in most cases, they can often achieve the same result by using these statutory "officer liability" provisions.

III RECENT TRENDS IN CORPORATE REGULATORY AND CRIMINAL RESPONSIBILITY

I turn now to the separate but, it is argued, related question: "When is a company liable under a criminal or regulatory provision for the acts of its employees?" This question has spawned some of the most interesting recent appellate decisions[18] and theoretical literature in company law.[19] It is the uneasy co-existence of the doctrine of separate corporate personality and the need to establish *mens rea*/fault on the part of a company in so many criminal and quasi-criminal offences that gives rise to difficulty for the law.

However, as recent appellate case law has shown, there is nothing immutable about the doctrine in this context and the Law Lords have recently subjected it to some sophisticated analysis in decisions dealing with transmission of a company's employees' *mens rea* "upwards" to fix the company itself with responsibility under regulatory and statutory provisions.[20] The acts of the employee become those of the company, as liability moves in the opposite direction from that in which it travels under the "officer liability" provisions just considered, where the liability of the company becomes that of the individual officer.

When considering the question of corporate criminal/regulatory responsibility, Lord Hoffmann's reasoning in *Meridian Global Funds Management Asia*

---

[18] *El Ajou* v. *Dollar Holdings Plc* [1994] 1 BCLC 464 (CA); *Seaboard Offshore Ltd.* v. *Secretary of State for Transport* [1994] 2 All ER 99 (HL); *Meridian Global Funds Management Asia Ltd.* v. *Securities Commission* [1995] 2 AC 500 (PC); *Re Supply of Ready Mixed Concrete (No 2)* [1995] 1 AC 456 (HL).

[19] See, in particular, B Fisse and J Braithwaite, *Corporations, Crime and Accountability* (Cambridge, CUP, 1993); and C Wells, *Corporations and Criminal Responsibility* (Oxford, Clarendon, 1993).

[20] See, in particular, the analysis of Lord Hoffmann in *Meridian Global Funds Management Asia Ltd.* v. *Securities Commission* [1995] 2 AC 500; and *Re Supply of Ready Mixed Concrete (No 2)* [1995] 1 AC 456.

Ltd. v. *Securities Commission* seems entirely appropriate for the variegated statutory and regulatory climate in which companies now do business:[21]

> "[G]iven that [the rule in question] was intended to apply to a company, how was it intended to apply? Whose act (or knowledge or state of mind) was *for this purpose* intended to count as the act etc of the company? One finds the answer to this question by applying the usual canons of interpretation, taking into account the language of the rule (if it is a statute) and its content and policy."

This moves us away from an overly simplistic reliance on the "directing mind and will" approach to the liability of a company for the acts of its employees as seen in *Tesco Supermarkets Ltd.* v. *Nattrass*.[22] Organisation theory and practice have certainly moved away from this simple vertical "command and control" model of how a company functions. In an age of flatter corporate hierarchies, "empowered" front-line employees, and devolved decision-making, Lord Hoffmann's decision has considerable resonance in the real commercial world.

A A Company's Actions Speak Louder than its Words

The decision of the House of Lords in *Re Supply of Ready Mixed Concrete (No 2)*[23] is further evidence of this shift away from a formula for determining corporate responsibility based on a simple model of corporate organisation of vertically structured hierarchy, with an elite cadre exercising "command and control" and being the only people in the company capable of imbuing it with criminal responsibility.

The appeal arose out of breaches of certain injunctions that had been obtained by the Director-General of Fair Trading prohibiting further contravention of Restrictive Trade Practices legislation by four companies which were suppliers of ready mixed concrete. After the original injunctions had been obtained, all four companies had adopted compliance systems designed to ensure that there would be no further breaches of the legislation and had prohibited their employees from entering into illegal price-fixing and market-sharing agreements. However, despite the existence of these clear prohibitions, certain employees of the companies continued to meet in local pubs and carve up the Oxfordshire ready mixed concrete market between them, ostensibly on behalf of the companies that employed them. In enforcement and contempt proceedings in the Restrictive Practices Court, three of the companies admitted contempt and pleaded their internal compliance arrangements which were designed to prevent such illegal arrangements and practices as mitigation

---

[21] [1995] 2 AC 500, at 519. For the facts and an analysis of the *Meridian* decision and the issues raised therein, see S Robert-Tissot, "A Fresh Insight into the Corporate Criminal Mind" (1996) 17 *The Company Lawyer* 99.

[22] [1972] AC 153.

[23] [1995] 1 AC 456.

only. The fourth company, however, denied contempt, relying on its compliance prohibitions as a defence and disowning the actions of its non-compliant employee who, without the company's knowledge or authority, purported to make it party to the illegal arrangements. This argument did not impress the Restrictive Practices Court but succeeded in the Court of Appeal, and as a consequence two of the other companies which had at first admitted their contempt sought and obtained leave to appeal the original orders of the Restrictive Practices Court. These appeals were also successful, and it was against that decision of the Court of Appeal that the Director-General of Fair Trading appealed successfully to the House of Lords.

The comments of Lord Templeman are especially significant in the context of the present discussion of what the limits of corporate responsibility for the acts of its employees should be:[24]

> "The decisions of the Court of Appeal [in these two appeals] infringe two principles. The first principle is that a company is an entity separate from its members but, not being a physical person is only capable of acting by its agents. The second principle is that a company, in its capacity as supplier of goods, like any other person in the capacity of taxpayer, landlord or in any other capacity, falls to be judged by its actions and not by its language. An employee who acts for the company within the scope of his employment is the company. Directors may give instructions, top management may exhort, middle management may question and workers may listen attentively. But if a worker makes a defective product or a lower manager accepts or rejects an order, he is the company."

Companies are not protected from legal responsibility for the acts of their employees by the existence of quality control and preventive compliance systems designed to ensure that all employees act in such a way that legislation and regulation are never infringed. No matter how seemingly watertight and superior those controls are, if someone within the company subverts them and takes the company outside the law, the company cannot escape ultimate responsibility by pleading that it tried its best and its preventive systems ought to have worked. The simple fact is that they did not, and the task of the law here is to punish effective non-compliance no matter from where within the company it was generated. Lord Nolan makes this clear:[25]

> "The [Restrictive Practices] Act is not concerned with what the employer says but with what the employee does in entering into business transactions in the course of his employment. The plain purpose of section 35(3) is to deter the implementation of agreements or arrangements by which the public interest is harmed, and the sub-section can only achieve that purpose if it is applied to the actions of the individuals within the business organisation who make or give effect to the relevant agreement or arrangement on its behalf. This necessarily leads to the conclusion that if such an agreement is found to have been made without the knowledge of the employer, any steps which the employer has taken to prevent it from being made

---

[24] *Ibid.*, at 469.
[25] *Ibid.*, at 475.

will rank only as mitigation. Liability can only be escaped by completely effective preventive measures."

"By your deeds ye shall be judged" is the clear message to companies from both this decision and that of the Privy Council in *Meridian Global Funds Management Asia Ltd.* v. *Securities Commission*, with a much wider category of natural persons within the company now being seen to constitute the legal person of the company for the purposes of the company's responsibility under statutory and regulatory offences and controls. Although Lord Templeman's view of corporate organisation as evinced by his words extracted above is open to the criticism that it remains wedded to an overly simplistic vertical hierarchy based on a "command and control" theory of how business functions, at least the result of his decision is to recognise that the real *"de facto"* ability of a company to evade or break external legal controls resides as often as not at the interface between the company and the public (in the case of consumer protection legislation), or the environment (in the case of environmental protection legislation), or the factory floor (in the case of health and safety legislation). These places are exactly the focus of the law's design to protect and regulate the company's business, and are often a very long way away, in terms of the corporate culture and power structure, from the Head Office where the supposedly preventive compliance systems are promulgated.

It therefore seems entirely appropriate that the law on corporate responsibility has been moved along in this way from the position in *Tesco Supermarkets Ltd.* v. *Nattrass*.[26] The fictitious separate corporate person must now take responsibility for its employees' acts where its own systems of controlling those employees have failed. This may indeed seem harsh and the law should of course always be alive to the risks of designing its liability rules in such a way as to provide a gross disincentive to businesses to continue operating. Lord Nolan acknowledges this, but tosses the remedy into the lap of the legislature:[27]

> "How great a burden of the devising of such [completely effective] preventive measures will cast upon individual employers will depend upon the size and nature of the particular organisation. There are, of course, many areas of business life, not only in the consumer protection field, where it has become necessary for employers to devise strict compliance procedures. If the burden is in fact intolerable then the remedy must be for Parliament to introduce a statutory defence for those who can show that they have taken all reasonable preventive measures."

In the current climate of visible failures of compliance systems—particularly in the emotive and politically damaging area of retail financial services[28]—it

---

[26] [1972] AC 153 (HL).

[27] [1995] 1 AC 456, 475.

[28] Witness the mis-selling of personal pensions; Jardine Flemings' failure to control their Hong Kong fund manager, Mr Colin Armstrong, and his breaches of regulation at the expense of several Flemings unit trust funds; and Morgan Grenfell's recent failure of controls *vis-à-vis* unit trust management.

would be very surprising indeed if Parliament were even to consider introducing such an exculpatory defence for companies whose control systems fail.

B The Company as Victim

The artifice of separate corporate personality is also laid bare when one considers the company as "victim" rather than "perpetrator'. One is forced to ask questions, like "Did the company know X or was it deceived as to X?", in the context of deception and fraud offences, for deception operates on the state of mind of its victim, and of course ascertaining what and where is the mind of a company, as opposed to a natural person, is no easy task. Ascertaining where the corporate criminal mind is, and what is going on inside that mind for the purposes of the company's responsibility under criminal and regulatory offences, has created the interesting case law considered earlier.

The decision of the Court of Appeal in *R. v. Rozeik*[29] raises some of the same questions, but in the directly converse situation, in that it concerns the company as victim rather than as perpetrator. Of all the various actors who go to make up a company, whose knowledge should be attributed to the company for the purposes of its being said to be ignorant of or *sciens* to a deception? It is a truism to say that the same question of legal principle posed in different litigation contexts often yields different answers, and the decision in *R. v. Rozeik* bears that out.

The factual background to the appeal in *Rozeik* was commonplace enough. The defendant had been convicted of dishonestly obtaining by deception cheques from finance companies contrary to section 15 of the Theft Act 1968. It was alleged that the defendant had made dishonest applications for funds to finance companies using false information and false invoices relating to equipment hire-purchase agreements. The prosecution accepted that the branch managers of the finance companies may not have been deceived; indeed, they were probably aware that the defendant's representations were false. There was, however, no evidence put forward by the prosecution to show that the branch managers were acting in any way dishonestly or could be said to be a party to the defendant's fraud. At the defendant's trial, the judge had directed the jury to ignore the effect of the state of mind of these branch managers when deciding the question whether or not the companies were deceived. The jury was told simply to assume that the branch managers knew that the information supplied was false. The judge went further and directed that, quite apart from the branch managers, if *any* other employee or employees within the companies were deceived by the false invoices into doing something which resulted in cheques being obtained by the defendant then that was sufficient to find him guilty of "obtaining by deception" from the companies.

[29] [1996] 1 WLR 159.

The defendant appealed his conviction, basing his appeal on two grounds. The first ground was that the judge had misdirected the jury on the point of which persons within a company constituted the company's state of mind for the purposes of its being deceived. The judge was wrong to decide that persons within a company other than those responsible for making decisions to authorise the respective transactions were persons who could be deceived and whose deception could be attributed to the company for the purposes of section 15 of the Theft Act 1968. The second ground of appeal was that the trial judge had also been wrong to direct the jury to ignore the relevance of the fact that the branch managers most likely knew of the defendant's deception. In making that direction in those terms, the judge was effectively inviting the jury to assume the managers had acted dishonestly and were party to the defendant's fraud. This, the defendant argued, was a matter for the prosecution to prove (something it had not sought to do), not something which the jury should be invited to assume. So, since the branch managers' likely knowledge should not have been ignored by the jury, the defendant argued that it should be imputed to the companies which, therefore, could not be said to have been deceived for the purposes of section 15 of the Theft Act.

The Court of Appeal allowed the defendant's appeal, Leggatt LJ giving the judgment of the Court. Counsel for the defendant summarised his contention on attribution of knowledge for the purposes of a company being deceived thus:[30]

> "[W]here one employee is deceived by a representation but either the true position or the falsity of the representation is known to another employee in a position of equality or superiority to the employee deceived, the company cannot be said to have been deceived. . . . The offence is committed against the company, and not the individual employee, so if the company is fixed with knowledge of the true position it is not deceived."

This question obviously needed to be examined in the light of *Re Supply of Ready Mixed Concrete (No 2)*[31] and *Meridian Global Funds Management Asia Ltd.* v. *Securities Commission*[32] since they both concerned the attribution of acts and knowledge of employees to a company in order to fix it with liability as a perpetrator, and the Court of Appeal was now seised of the converse situation. So the Court of Appeal asked: "Whose state of mind represented the state of mind of the company for the purpose of ascertaining whether it had been deceived into entering into the hire-purchase agreements?" The answer was, evidently, the relevant branch managers *whose job it was* to process and approve these loan transactions. Nor could their knowledge that the invoices were false be attributed to the company, for if it could then the company could not possibly be said to have been deceived and the appeal

---

[30] [1996] 1 WLR 159, at 162.
[31] [1995] 1 AC 456.
[32] [1995] 2 AC 500.

must succeed. The Court of Appeal ruled that the trial judge was wrong to direct the jury to ignore the branch managers' knowledge and it agreed with the defendant's argument that such a direction should only have been made if the prosecution had proved that the managers were acting dishonestly and were privy to the fraud. Leggatt LJ explained the reason for the doctrine that the dishonest knowledge of a company's officers cannot be attributed to the company:[33]

> "The reason why the company is not visited with the manager's knowledge is that the same individual cannot both be party to the deception and represent the company for the purpose of its being deceived. Unless therefore it was proved that the managers were party to the fraud, with the result that their knowledge can be disregarded, their knowledge must be imputed to the companies, and the fact that other employees were deceived could not avail the companies."

The Court of Appeal also made some interesting comments on the defendant's contention that the trial judge had been wrong to direct that the deception of "any" employee within the company would suffice to constitute the deception of the company. The Court focused on the meaning of the word "obtained" in section 15 of the Theft Act 1968. From whom exactly was the cheque obtained? The Court of Appeal said it was not correct to say that the cheque had been "obtained" in this sense from a typist or an employee who had a mere clerical role in the process, but rather cheques could be obtained in the section 15 sense only from those who "had a responsibility to ensure that the cheques were not signed unless satisfied that the money should be paid",[34] in other words, the signatories of the cheques. "Who signed the cheques?" thus becomes a crucial question in a case like this one where the branch managers were most probably parties to the fraud. If it was an accomplice manger alone who signed, then there could not be said to be any obtaining by deception, but if an "innocent" signatory also had to sign the cheque, then it was possible to say that the cheque was obtained by deception.

So, where the cheques which were the subject of the indictment had been signed by the branch managers alone, the defendant's conviction was most certainly bad, and even where the cheques were signed by other "innocent" employees or co-signed by a manager with another "innocent" employee, the fact that the trial judge's direction to the jury had been overly wide, in that he said it was enough if "any employee" was deceived (and had therefore failed to focus the jury on the state of mind of the signatory), meant that the convictions in relation to those other co-signed cheques were unreliable too. Hence, all the defendant's convictions under section 15 of the Theft Act 1968 were quashed.

Should the law develop a different rule of attribution of knowledge to cover the "company as victim" situation from that rule which now prevails in the

---

[33] [1996] 1 WLR 159, 164.
[34] *Ibid.*, at 165.

"company as perpetrator" situation? Leggatt LJ explored this interesting and important question:[35]

> "Whether or not a company is fixed with the knowledge acquired by an employee or officer will depend on the circumstances. It is necessary first to identify whether the individual in question has the requisite status and authority in relation to the act or omission in point: *El Ajou* v. *Dollar Holdings plc.* . . . . It follows from this that information given to a particular employee, however senior, may not be attributed to the company if that employee is not empowered to act in relation to that particular transaction. An employee who acts for the company within the scope of his employment will usually bind the company since he *is* the company for the purposes of the transaction in question: see *per* Lord Templeman in *In re Supply of Ready Mixed Concrete.* . . . . The company may be liable to third parties or be guilty of criminal offences even though that employee was acting dishonestly or against the interests of the company or contrary to orders. But different considerations apply where the company is the victim, and the employee's activities have caused or assisted the company to suffer loss. . . . In cases in which the company is the victim the person or persons who stand for its state of mind may differ from those who do so in cases in which a company is charged with the commission of a criminal offence. The latter are less likely to represent what Viscount Haldane L.C. in *Lennard's Carrying Co. Ltd.* v. *Asiatic Petroleum Co. Ltd.* . . . . called 'the directing mind and will' of the company."

The range of employees and officers of a company who are able, in law, to make a victim of the company is therefore more restricted than those who are able by their acts, statements or omissions to constitute it a perpetrator. This appears to be a conclusion that can safely be drawn from the juxtaposition of this appeal with the decisions in *Meridian* and *Ready Mixed Concrete*. But what is especially interesting about what the Court of Appeal did in *Rozeik* was that it looked into the company's internal organisation and asked what were the functions and responsibilities of its various officers and employees; it then took those into account in designing an attribution of knowledge rule which would make sense of the particular offence of deceiving a company. Although the Court of Appeal there framed a narrower attribution rule than the House of Lords did in *Ready Mixed Concrete* and the Privy Council did in *Meridian*, the really important point to note is that in all three cases the judges were not afraid to examine the internal workings of the company and to ask: "who did what within the company?" and "what was the purpose of the legal rule in question?" Having ascertained answers to those question, then and only then did they go on to frame an attribution rule that gave the law in question efficacy and real meaning.

[35] [1996] 1 WLR 159, 164, at 164–5.

IV CONCLUSION

How are the two separate strands of company law considered in this essay related to each other? What has corporate criminal and regulatory responsibility (and its flipside of corporate victimhood) got to do with the problem of interpretation of officer liability provisions? In dealing with the former question, the courts have recently demonstrated a greater sensitivity and surer feel for the realities of the way statutory regulatory controls actually impact upon the corporate organisation. They have formulated legal principles of responsibility in such a fashion as to give legal controls maximum efficacy, and have given management the strongest possible incentive to make compliance systems substantively effective rather than simply literally correct. This "effects centred" approach could usefully be imported by courts faced with the problems of deciding whether an ignorant company director has the requisite mens rea for secondary responsibility for the illegal acts of the company under an officer liability provision. A re-examination of the comments of Lord Hoffmann in *Meridian Global Funds Management Asia Ltd.* v. *Securities Commission* extracted above reveal that he sees as integral to the process of ascertaining whose act/knowledge/state of mind is to be attributed to the company for the purposes of determining its responsibility under XYZ law the need also to ask the questions: what is XYZ law there to do? what policy objective is it designed to achieve? what effect is it supposed to have on the way in which companies do business?

Therefore, if this reasoning is applied to the questions tested in *Re Attorney-General's Reference (No 1 of 1995)*, it may point the way to a fairer basis for deciding what degree of fault or mens rea will suffice to render an officer liable for the offence of his company. The content of and policy behind the statutory corporate offence that is being visited upon an officer could first be examined. Then the extent of the knowledge or ignorance possessed by the officer charged of the state of the company's affairs which constitute the offence would be assessed. If, given the content and policy of the particular corporate offence, it is reasonable and efficient for the officer charged to leave all questions of legal compliance in the relevant area of the company's business to another officer or officers, then he should not be said to be consenting to the offence simply by virtue of the fact that he knew the company's business was being conducted in a particular way. It is time company law began to recognise the realities of doing business in an ever-changing regulatory climate and to appreciate that the way in which it attributes liability to officers should recognise the way in which those officers attribute tasks and responsibilities amongst themselves.

9

Commentary on Gray

BERNARD ROBERTSON*

In *Re Attorney-General's Reference (No 1 of 1995)*,[1] discussed by Ms Gray, the Court of Appeal applied a perfectly conventional test of *mens rea* to the infringement of a prohibition on unlicensed deposit taking. That is to say that the Court held that if a director knows of the facts that constitute the offence (or in the case of this offence, ought, but for neglect to have known) then it is irrelevant whether the director knew that it was an offence. This raises a number of questions with which I wish briefly to deal:

(a) Should there be a general defence of ignorance of the law?
(b) Should there be a narrower defence of legal or official advice?
(c) What do these offences and cases tell us about the rationale for corporate liability?
(d) What practical impact does the current state of the law have?

I SHOULD THERE BE A GENERAL DEFENCE OF IGNORANCE OF THE LAW?

The traditional rule, reflected in section 25 of the Crimes Act 1961 (NZ),[2] is that ignorance of the law is no excuse. This rule dates from a period when the criminal law consisted entirely of offences which would have offended moral sensitivities. In those circumstances it amounted merely to saying that one did not have to be a lawyer to be guilty of what every right thinking person would regard as an offence.

The state of the law at that time reflected the fundamental liberal principle that one could live as one liked, provided that one did not unilaterally and coercively transfer utility from another. The occasions when that was being done were generally obvious.

The question raised by Ms Gray is whether it is right to retain this rule when the criminal law has burgeoned into business regulation. In effect, the emphasis has changed from saying that ignorance of the law is no excuse to

---

* Barrister, Inner Temple and New Zealand and Editor of *The New Zealand Law Journal*.

[1] [1996] 1 WLR 970.

[2] "The fact that an offender is ignorant of the law is not an excuse for any offence committed by him."

making it an offence to fail to have a detailed knowledge of the law. In other words, if one does anything without first checking whether it is legal one is in peril.

That there is no moral or obvious content to the rule infringed in *Re Attorney General's Reference (No 1 of 1995)*[3] is demonstrated by the fact that the offence does not exist in New Zealand. In New Zealand, no licence is required to take deposits; rather, permission is required only to label onself as a "bank".

Since, however, one would hesitate to introduce a defence of ignorance of the law for crimes such as murder, rape and theft, this leads one to trying to distinguish between traditional criminal offences and "regulatory matters". This distinction is the subject of attention in writing on corporate responsibility, since many of the offences that companies will commit will be of the kind that we regard as "regulatory". From the left, the criticism is made that this is a distinction without a difference; the fact that matters such as health and safety at work offences do not appear in the criminal codes and are regarded as of lesser status is seen as evidence that the legal system accords higher priority to property owners' rights than to workers' rights, and so forth. Wells provides an extended version of this argument in her book.[4] At a more elevated level, this brings us back to the Hart–Devlin debate and the attempts by judges to distinguish between "mala in se" and "mala prohibita".

In an age dominated by legal positivism, the view put forward by Wells seems to have become the conventional wisdom, at least to the extent that those who feel uncomfortable with it find it difficult to argue against on any ground other than gut feeling. Gut feeling, however, may reflect the accumulated wisdom of a culture, and so it is here. The evolved criminal law was concerned to prevent unilateral and coercive transfers of utility. As transactions became more complex this extended to fraudulent transfers of utility, since these also offend against the basic principle that individuals enter into transactions to serve their own interests and it is by the pursuit of mutual interests that the general welfare is served. Regulatory offences, however, have not evolved from our dealings with each other. They have been imposed by Parliament specifically to interfere with our dealings. There is no reason, for example, why employees cannot negotiate for safer working conditions. Up to some point, which will be discernible by the parties but not by a third party regulator, avoidance of accidents will be in the mutual interests of both employee and employer. Beyond that point it may well be inefficient for both. Much environmental regulation likewise consists of interference in the ability of neighbours to negotiate with one another, provided that rights are clearly defined in the law of property and the law of tort.

---

[3] [1996] 1 WLR 970.
[4] C Wells, *Corporations and Criminal Responsibility* (Oxford, Clarendon, 1993).

This is not to say that developments in the real world may not necessitate the creation by Parliament of new offences to prevent unilateral transfers of utility, of which drinking and driving would be an example. But in the case of the offence in *Re Attorney-General's Reference (No 1 of 1995)*, the British punter's right to place deposits with someone who does not have to bear the expense of qualifying for a licence from the authorities has been removed.

There seems then to be a defensible difference between the two categories of offence. It is the distinction between laws which merely create a secure framework within which individuals can pursue their own interests and laws which are aimed at creating an ideal society. Those who deny any such distinction label themselves accordingly. If there is such a defensible distinction then it would seem possible to provide a general defence of ignorance of the law to "regulatory offences".

In New Zealand some, but perhaps not all, of the problems are avoided by the courts' willingness to create what Lord Reid in *Tesco Supermarkets Ltd.* v. *Natrass*[5] refused to create, namely, a category of offence for which demonstrated absence of fault or the taking of all reasonable precautions is a defence. Absolute liability is imposed in New Zealand only where the statute makes it plain that this is required.

II SHOULD THERE BE A NARROWER DEFENCE?

The alternative to a general defence would be a defence that one had genuinely taken legal or official advice, as advocated by Cameron.[6] The high water mark of the "ignorance of the law is no defence" rule must be the Canadian case in which a strip dancer relied on a court decision that her act was legal and was subsequently successfully prosecuted after a higher court overturned the decision.[7] The draft Canadian Criminal Code contains a defence of reliance on official advice or a court decision[8] and some Canadian decisions have effectively recognised such a defence.[9]

Definitional problems would be avoided, as it is hard to see that such a defence could apply to crimes such as murder, rape and theft. In fact, the mere taking of advice would be sufficient to demonstrate recklessness. But where the question to an adviser is "is this a legal way of carrying out this transaction?" or "what is the best legal way of carrying out this transaction?", actors cannot be said to have turned their minds to any particular risk.

There may well have to be restrictions on the defence. As a police officer dealing with people driving in Britain with foreign driving licences, I was

---

[5] [1972] AC 153.

[6] N Cameron, "Defences and the Crimes Bill" (1990) 20 *VUWLR* 57, 65–7.

[7] *The Queen* v. *Campbell* (1973) 10 CCC (2d) 26.

[8] Law Reform Commission of Canada, *Report on Recodifying Criminal Law* (Ottawa, The Law Reform Commission of Canada, 1986), 34–5.

[9] D Stuart, *Canadian Criminal Law* (3rd edn., Toronto, Carswell, 1987), 288–99.

frequently told that another officer had told the driver that he or she was within the law. Such advice will, of course, have been dependent upon the date on which it was given, the information which the driver gave the officer and the extent of the officer's ignorance of the law.

The defence could therefore be limited to written advice from a lawyer or official, or reliance on an extant court decision. A further control on the use of the defence would be the fact that it would constitute a waiver of legal professional privilege and enable investigation of what the client had told the lawyer and the lawyer's reasons for the conclusions expressed.

This may well seem a sensible solution to the evident unfairness of holding people liable for breaches of regulations whose existence they had no reasons to suspect. On the other hand, it may be regarded as a mere palliative for a problem that should not exist in the first place, and even as liable to exacerbate the problems discussed in Part IV below.

III WHAT DOES THIS TELL US ABOUT THE RATIONALE FOR CORPORATE LIABILITY?

The rationale most consistently given for corporate liability is that it forces shareholders to supervise the conduct of directors and directors to supervise the conduct of employees. The response to the inevitable failure of the criminal law to prevent all offences is to attempt to widen the classes of people who operate *in terrorem*. To some extent this may have been unneccessary, given the existence of the original corporate liability. Consent and connivance by a person in a position of authority may well be sufficient at common law to make one a party to an offence.[10] But the provisions discussed by Ms Gray also penalise negligence, not normally penalised by the criminal law. It is a short step from there to proposing absolute liability.

There are three main justifications for corporate liability. The first is supposedly a principled one, that justice requires that if individuals can be guilty of offences in given circumstances, then so should companies. On this argument there is clearly no requirement to visit liability on identified individuals; the whole point is that companies should be liable. The second justification is a pragmatic one; that for a variety of reasons it may be difficult, at any rate at reasonable cost, to identify and charge the individuals responsible for particular actions. The third justification is that corporate liability will force shareholders to supervise the most senior management properly.

Lord Hoffmann's discussion of corporate liability in *Meridian Global Funds Management Asia Ltd.* v. *Commerce Commission*[11] makes clear what we are then doing. According to Lord Hoffmann, there is no such thing as a com-

---

[10] See, for example, *Du Cros* v. *Lambourne* [1907] 1 KB 40 (owner of car sitting in front passenger seat of car while driver drove it recklessly); *Thomas* v. *Lindop* [1950] 1 All ER 966, 968 (licensee standing by while patrons drank after hours).

[11] [1995] 2 AC 500 (PC).

pany, merely a rule that says that when A or B do certain things, we say that the company is guilty. Provisions such as those Ms Gray has examined say that when the company is guilty certain people, call them C and D, may be guilty. So the position we have now reached is that when A or B do certain things, C and D are deemed to be guilty of criminal offences. This is simply vicarious or communal punishment designed to cause C and D to supervise A and B. The battle of principle over vicarious liability in the business world seems to have been lost long ago, but it is interesting to note that when politicians periodically suggest that parents should be held liable for their children's offending there is invariably an outraged response.

A detailed problem is caused in New Zealand by an apparent conflict between company and employment law. One of the effects of the Employment Contracts Act 1991 (NZ) was to extend the personal grievance procedure to classes of people who had not previously been covered by it, including individuals in positions of trust in large organisations. If such persons are dismissed or constructively dismissed without lengthy procedures and warnings they may well have a personal grievance. Yet company law may impose a duty on directors to act in a way that will be regarded as an unfair dismissal. Company directors are permitted to delegate their own duties only under strict conditions. In particular, section 130 of the Companies Act 1993 provides that directors are responsible for the acts of delegates unless they believe "on reasonable grounds at all times before the exercise of the power that the delegate would exercise the power in conformity with the duties imposed on directors of the company by this Act and the company's constitution".

In other words, the Companies Act requires directors to withdraw a delegation as soon as they suspect that it may not be being exercised properly. Such a withdrawal will very likely be construed as a constructive dismissal and it will be an unjustifiable dismissal if it is not preceded by numerous warnings. But merely to give such a warning may be to demonstrate that one is in breach of section 130 by continuing the delegation.

The same would apply to provisions imposing "officer liability". Directors who fail to subject dubious employees to vigorous supervision, or even to withdraw their delegated powers, may be found to be guilty of causal neglect. But either of those actions may well be interpreted by the employment tribunal or court as a constructive dismissal, exposing the company to damages and even to reinstatement of the employee. The next step would be to introduce "officer liability" provisions into employment law, thereby completing the vice in which directors find themselves.

IV WHAT ARE THE PRACTICAL EFFECTS?

The effect of corporate liability is to turn a purely private law duty owed by directors to shareholders into a public law duty and to inflict on shareholders some kind of public duty not shared by the rest of us, to ensure that others do not break the law.

This is in addition to the compliance costs suffered within firms, which can now be considerable. Ms Gray suggests that there is some recognition by judges that this burden may become intolerable, whereupon it is the job of the legislature to do something about it. Unfortunately, this does not address the real problem. It ignores the nature of international competition and focuses unduly on the position of currently established enterprises.

The question is not one of intolerable burdens, but of marginal burdens. A company in Britain or New Zealand may be competing today with companies in countries where property prices and taxation are lower and the labour market more flexible. On top of this, such a company now has to employ people to do nothing more than keep an eye on the government and forewarn the company of new legal developments. These costs represent a deadweight which companies abroad may not have to bear.

This is not to argue that British and New Zealand enterprises should be competing in the "high volume, low quality" end of the market with companies from elsewhere with lower labour costs. But whatever British and New Zealand companies do, such regulation will have a marginal effect on their profits, which in turn will have a marginal effect on investment, which in turn has marginal effects on jobs, and so on.

New Zealand businesses are only too well aware of these facts. In Europe, however, a wall has been erected round the thinking of businesses which seems even more impermeable than the thousand miles of sea which separate New Zealand from its nearest neighbours. Within that wall relative decline is inevitable and the matters we are discussing will assist that decline.

Within a market, we will not find that businesses complain unduly about regulation. This is because one of the most insidious effects of compliance costs is to protect large established enterprises which can afford to carry such overheads from competition by new entrants to the market and small operators. The question is not therefore whether such regulation is intolerable for particular institutions but whether it increases or decreases the general welfare. For the reasons explained above, this is a much more debatable question than seems conventionally to be assumed.

10

Changes in the Role of the Shareholder

JENNIFER HILL*

I INTRODUCTION

Revisiting *Salomon's case*[1] from a late twentieth century vantage point, one is struck by the simplicity of the case's scenario and message. Mr Salomon's clear role in Salomon & Co. Ltd. as "owner-shareholder" did not, according to the House of Lords, disturb the insulating effects of corporate legal personality.

The principle of corporate personality from *Salomon's case* has been applied beyond its close corporation origins to public corporations, and indeed to huge multinationals.[2] Nonetheless, as the twentieth century progressed, our image of the role of the shareholder underwent a series of critical shifts to reflect changes in the structure, composition and governance mechanisms of modern corporations. Indeed, in contrast to Mr Salomon's role, the most abiding vision of shareholders in public companies this century has been one of a dispersed and marginalised group, inevitably separated from their investment as a result of the division between ownership and control.[3]

This basic premise of shareholder vulnerability underpins and explains a wide array of doctrinal developments and debates in modern corporate law—matters as fundamental as the shift in division of powers between board and general meeting, free transferability of shares and the economic justifications

* Associate Professor of Law, The University of Sydney. My thanks to Janet Albrechtson and Theresa Kelly for their research assistance. Thanks also go to a number of friends and colleagues who discussed this project and provided valuable insights, or helped in other ways. These include Joanna Bird, Suzanne Corcoran, Lynne Dallas, Deborah DeMott, Christos Mantziaris, Ron McCallum, Richard Vann, David Wishart and Charles Yablon. Financial assistance for the project was provided by the Australian Research Council and the Law Foundation of New South Wales.

[1] *Salomon v. A Salomon & Co. Ltd.* [1897] AC 22.

[2] See K W Wedderburn, "Multinationals and the Antiquities of Company Law" (1984) 47 *MLR* 87, 92.

[3] See R Romano, "Metapolitics and Corporate Law Reform" (1984) 36 *Stan L Rev* 923; E S Herman, *Corporate Control, Corporate Power: A Twentieth Century Fund Study* (Cambridge, CUP, 1981), 9.

for limited liability. Dispersed shareholding patterns enhanced managerial discretion.[4]

Many of the fundamental assumptions about shareholder vulnerability which have characterised corporate law this century are themselves now outmoded.[5] They have been overtaken by further fragmentation, dispersing ownership to an increasingly wide group *à la* Clark's more recent evolutionary stages of financial capitalism.[6] The contours of share ownership in Australia today are very different from those earlier this century.[7] They have been reshaped in different ways, both by the inexorable rise of institutional investment and the trend towards privatisation and demutualisation.[8] Institutional investors particularly, with their expertise and highly diversified positions, seem a far cry from our familiar image of the hapless shareholder. Natural investors in large public companies are also better informed via the financial press and the continuous disclosure regime[9] than shareholders in earlier times. In spite of this, there has been little attempt to revise our legal conception of the role of shareholders in corporate governance, resulting in a disjunction between corporate theory and commercial reality.

This essay traces a number of visions of the role of shareholder which can be discerned at various times in corporate law. These images of the role of the shareholder overlap and recur in different forms, providing a richer and more complex picture of the shareholder's relationship with the company than that which emerged from the facts in *Salomon's case*. In some instances, these images are historically and progressively linked; in others, they are merely dichotomies inherent in corporate law. Against the backdrop of these evolving images, the essay then examines some contemporary developments concerning the role of the shareholder in the courts, under legislation and in the commercial realm. These developments include the controversial decision in *Gambotto's case*,[10] the strategy of using shareholder consent as a regulatory device and the implications of institutional shareholder activism. These examples demonstrate a tension and an ambivalence about the appropriate role of the shareholder in modern corporate law.

The message of this essay is a simple one. It is to argue that the underlying terrain in this area of corporate law has altered fundamentally and irrevoca-

---

[4] W Bratton, "The New Economic Theory of the Firm: Critical Perspectives From History" (1989) 41 *Stan L Rev* 1471, 1492.

[5] Scholarship this decade has challenged the inevitability of the received vision of shareholders. See, for example, B Black, "Shareholder Passivity Reexamined" (1990) 89 *Mich L Rev* 520; M Roe, "A Political Theory of American Corporate Finance" (1991) 91 *Colum L Rev* 10.

[6] R Clark, "The Four Stages of Capitalism: Reflections on Investment Management Treatises" (1981) 94 *Harv L Rev* 561, 562–8.

[7] See statistics on institutional shareholding in Australia and the UK cited by G Stapledon, "Disincentives to Activism by Institutional Investors in Listed Australian Companies" (1996) 18 *Syd L Rev* 152, 156.

[8] See Australian Stock Exchange, 1997 Australian Shareownership Survey, 2–9.

[9] See, for example, Australian Stock Exchange Listing Rule 3.1.

[10] *Gambotto v. WCP Ltd.* (1995) 69 AJLR 266.

bly, and it is important to address the issue of the shareholder's legitimate role in the corporation today. We need imagery, and ancillary legal doctrine, which makes sense in a modern commercial environment.

II VISIONS AND REVISIONS OF THE SHAREHOLDER

Many different images of the shareholder have at times underpinned corporate law debate.[11] The various ways in which shareholders can be characterised within the corporate structure have important implications for two major issues concerning the role of shareholders in corporations—first, the appropriate level of shareholder participation in corporate governance and, secondly, the status of shareholder interests, specifically whether they should be treated as paramount within the corporate structure. Participatory rights and status of interests are closely interconnected and provide a useful focus for examining the implications of different images of the shareholder in corporate law discourse.

A The Shareholder as Owner/Principal

The vision of shareholders as the "owners" of the corporate enterprise has an old and influential pedigree. The aggregate or partnership model of the corporation,[12] which was prevalent in the nineteenth century, assumed such a role for shareholders, just as it assumed a principal/agent relationship between the shareholders as owners and their agent directors. Although the contemporary nexus of contracts theory of the corporation again speaks of a principal/agent relationship between shareholders and directors, this modern reconstruction lacks the traditional hallmarks of agency that were implicit in the nineteenth century shareholder-centred view of the corporation. Thus, traditional corporate theory assumed that the role of directors was to carry out the will and implement the interests of shareholders,[13] and that within standard principles of agency law, shareholders had a formal right to control their agents.

The "shareholder as owner" vision under the aggregate theory was of great significance in the development of corporate law. In the United States, it was used to counter the view of the corporation as a creation of the State under the restrictive concession theory; rather, the aggregate model represented the

---

[11] See generally, J Hill and I Ramsay, "Institutional Investment in Australia: Theory and Evidence" in G Walker and B Fisse (eds.), *Securities Regulation in Australia and New Zealand* (Auckland, OUP, 1994), 289, 291 ff.

[12] See, for example, M Radin, "The Endless Problem of Corporate Personality" (1932) 32 *Colum L Rev* 643.

[13] See V Brudney, "The Independent Director—Heavenly City or Potemkin Village?" (1982) 95 *Harv L Rev* 597, 602.

corporation as a natural and, most importantly, private organisation, in which shareholders were akin to partners.[14] Early rules, such as vested rights, under which unanimous consent of shareholders was required for any fundamental corporate change, reflected this role for shareholders within the corporate structure.[15] Also, traditional tolerance by the courts of a low standard of skill and care in directors was based upon the assumption that the shareholders as principals should be more careful in selecting their agents.[16]

If shareholder assertion of ownership rights were the ideal, it was an ideal which bore an ever-decreasing resemblance to reality, with the growth of large public corporations at the turn of the century.[17] Indeed, some commentators doubt whether, outside the context of the close corporation, such as Mr Salomon's, shareholders ever occupied a position where they both owned and controlled the corporation, and view this "ideal" as itself another myth of corporate law.[18] If it is a myth, however, it is a tenacious one, with modern courts still sometimes relying upon it either to accord or to deny rights to shareholders.[19] The introduction in 1985 of a statutory provision dealing with shareholder inspection rights[20] provides such an example. Although at common law shareholder rights of inspection, in contrast to those of directors, were extremely narrow,[21] in one of the first decisions dealing with the new statutory provision, *Re Humes Ltd.*,[22] Beach J laid the groundwork for a remarkably liberal interpretation of the section. Citing United States authority, the judge included as justification for a generous right of access to shareholders the statement that "the books and property of the corporation really belong to the shareholders, and the reality cannot be overthrown by the fiction of law that a corporation is an artificial person or entity apart from its members".[23]

---

[14] See M Horwitz, "*Santa Clara* Revisited: The Development of Corporate Theory" (1985) 88 *West Va L Rev* 173, 204. The aggregate theory of the corporation was seen as hostile to both State regulation and the burgeoning management corporation. See Bratton, n. 4 above, 1489.

[15] See, for example, J MacIntosh, "Minority Shareholder Rights in Canada and England: 1860–1987" (1989) 27 *Osgoode Hall LJ* 561; Horwitz, n. 14 above, 200.

[16] See generally M J Trebilcock, "The Liability of Company Directors for Negligence" (1969) 32 *MLR* 499.

[17] See E S Mason, "Introduction" in E S Mason (ed.), *The Corporation in Modern Society* (Cambridge, Mass., Harvard University Press, 1960), 5, for the view that "those days are gone forever" when corporate ownership by shareholders could be taken seriously.

[18] See W Werner, "Corporation Law in Search of Its Future" (1981) 81 *Colum L Rev* 1611, 1612; J A C Hetherington, "When the Sleeper Wakes: Reflections on Corporate Governance and Shareholder Rights" (1979) 8 *Hofstra L Rev* 183, 194.

[19] For a modern use of the argument that the courts will not intervene to hold directors to account since the shareholders should themselves appoint directors of skill and good character, see *Re Enterprise Gold Mines NL* (1991) 3 ACSR 531. See further J Hill, "Protecting Minority Shareholders and Reasonable Expectation" (1992) 10 *CSLJ* 86, 102.

[20] Companies Code, s 265B (now Corporations Law, s 319).

[21] See *Burn* v. *London and South Wales Coal Co.* (1890) 7 TLR 118; *R.* v. *Merchant Taylors' Co.* (1831) 2 B & Ad 115; *Mutter* v. *Eastern and Midlands Railway Co.* (1888) 38 Ch D 92, 106; *Edman* v. *Ross* (1922) 22 NSWR 351, 358.

[22] (1987) 5 ACLC 64.

[23] *Ibid.*, 67.

B The Shareholder as Beneficiary

Increasing recognition of the separation between ownership and control in public companies—the fact that ownership of shares no longer carried the traditional incidents of property ownership—together with the triumph of the entity theory of the corporation, led to a revision of the image of shareholders in the early twentieth century. In the United States, a partnership model of the corporation became anachronistic in the light of the new commercial reality of management corporations, in which collective action problems for shareholders and managerial command of proxy machinery were seen as decisive in shifting control.[24] Under the entity theory, too, shareholder pre-eminence was by no means necessary or self-apparent, and it has been argued that the entity theory was influential in legitimating big business and centralised management at the time.[25]

The division between ownership and control thus implied both great power to managers and impotence of shareholders. Their newly perceived vulnerability was at the heart of Berle's characterisation of shareholders as "beneficiaries" for whom managerial powers are held in trust. The beneficiary classification, while treating the interests of shareholders as pre-eminent, deflated their rights of participation. This reflected the assumption that participation by shareholders in corporate governance was not feasible.

Although Berle and Dodd[26] reached very different conclusions to the celebrated question, "For whom are corporate managers trustees?", their shared axis was concern about the spectre of unbridled managerial power.[27] Berle's "minimalist version"[28] of managerial powers is as revealing for the choice of legal relationship as it is for choice of cestui que trust. Although not clearly distinguished in early English legal history, there are significant differences between the agency and trust relationship.[29] The powers, discretion and consequent third party liability of a "mere agent" are far narrower than those of

---

[24] See F Easterbrook and D Fischel, "Voting in Corporate Law" (1983) 26 *J Law and Economics* 395, n 1, quoting Berle and Means.

[25] See Horwitz, n. 14 above, 176, 223–4. Cf however Bratton, n. 4 above, 1511–13; D Millon, "Theories of the Corporation" [1990] *Duke LJ* 201, 240 ff.

[26] Dodd's response, which was to provide the grounding for the corporate social responsibility debate, viewed directors as trustees for a broader constituency, including groups such as consumers and employees as well as shareholders.

[27] See A A Berle, "Corporate Powers as Powers in Trust" (1931) 44 *Harv L Rev* 1049, 1073; E M Dodd, "For Whom Are Corporate Managers Trustees?" (1932) 45 *Harv L Rev* 1145, 1147; A A Berle, "For Whom Corporate Managers Are Trustees: A Note" (1932) 45 *Harv L Rev* 1365.

[28] See G Teubner, "Corporate Fiduciary Duties and Their Beneficiaries: A Functional Approach to the Legal Institutionalization of Corporate Responsibility", in K Hopt and G Teubner (eds.), *Corporate Governance and Directors' Liabilities: Legal, Economic and Sociological Analyses on Corporate Social Responsibility* (Berlin, NY, de Gruyter, 1985), 149 ff.

[29] R Meagher and W Gummow, *Jacobs' Law of Trusts in Australia* (6th edn., Sydney, Butterworths, 1997), 11–12.

a trustee.[30] The trustee analogy was used to justify the conclusion that directors should be subject to more stringent duties.[31]

Thus Berle's treatment of shareholders as cestuis que trust, rather than principals in an agency relationship, was an acknowledgment that shareholders had lost both *de jure* and *de facto* control of corporations.[32] With this basic premise, Berle's solution was to seek equitable controls over management's apparently absolute powers to ensure that those powers were harnessed for profit maximisation for shareholders.[33] Nonetheless, given the difficulties of enforcement of such managerial duties, shareholders would in practice still be "virtually helpless".[34] Notably absent from the debate was any alternative solution based upon restructured internal corporate governance.

In spite of the differences between an agency and trust relationship, it has been argued that the two models performed the same function of attempting to legitimate bureaucratic control, by portraying managerial power as constrained either by shareholder/principals in the agency context or by strengthened fiduciary dictates in the trust scenario.[35]

In the United Kingdom, terminology describing directors as "trustees" dates back to the mid-eighteenth century.[36] There is considerable academic debate whether directors were ever technically trustees in the early days of joint stock companies.[37] The language of "directors as trustees" has persisted in corporate law parlance,[38] in spite of an increasing divergence of their respective functions in the modern commercial world.[39]

Nonetheless, some recent Australian cases have expressly rejected both the terminology and implications of viewing directors as trustees. In *Daniels* v. *Anderson*,[40] for example, all members of the New South Wales Court of Appeal accepted that the trustee analogy was outdated and failed to reflect

---

[30] Meagher and Gummow, n. 29 above, 11–12. One of the hallmarks of true agency, lacking in the modern corporate setting, is that the agent is subject to "the continuous control" of the principal. See L L Dallas, "Two Models of Corporate Governance: Beyond Berle and Means" (1988) 22 *JL Ref* 19, 34–5, n. 42.

[31] See A I Ogus, "The Trust as Governance Structure" (1986) 36 *Univ Toronto LJ* 186, 194.

[32] See Dodd, n. 27 above, 1146.

[33] This approach was epitomised by the famous decision in *Dodge* v. *Ford Motor Co.*, 204 Mich 459, 170 NW 668 (1919). Cf Dodd, n. 27 above, who eschewed this paramount role for shareholder interests.

[34] See J L Weiner, "The Berle–Dodd Dialogue on the Concept of the Corporation" (1964) 64 *Colum L Rev* 1458, n 8.

[35] G Frug, "The Ideology of Bureaucracy in American Law" (1984) 97 *Harv L Rev* 1277, 1305.

[36] *Charitable Corporation* v. *Sutton* (1742) 2 Atk 400.

[37] Cf G Keeton, "The Director as Trustee" (1952) 5 CLP 11, suggesting these origins for the terminology, and L S Sealy, "The Director as Trustee" [1967] CLJ 83, refuting such claim. On this question, see also *Daniels* v. *Anderson* (1995) 16 ACSR 607, 748–9 (*per* Powell JA).

[38] For a recent example, see *State of South Australia* v. *Marcus Clark* (1996) 19 ACSR 606, 644.

[39] See, for example, R K Winter, *Government and the Corporation* (Washington, DC, 1978), 32–3; Sealy, n. 37 above, 86, 89.

[40] (1995) 16 ACSR 607.

commercial reality.[41] Clarke and Sheller JJA used this proposition to justify the existence of a common law action for negligence against directors; Powell JA, on the other hand, used it to support less extensive duties for directors than apply to trustees.[42] More recently, in *ASC* v. *AS Nominees Ltd.*,[43] while it was held that trust principles may have a ripple effect on the duties of directors in a trustee company, Finn J stated tersely that this was "not to reignite the arid debate on whether directors are trustees".[44]

Paradoxically, the Court of Appeal's decision in *Daniels* v. *Anderson*,[45] while purporting to reject a trustee model for directors, moved closer to the consequences of such a model in one significant way. Historically, a fundamental difference between the liability of directors and trustees was that a passive trustee would be personally responsible for failure to discharge the trust, while a passive director would generally not incur liability where delegation of powers had occurred.[46] The decision in *Daniels* v. *Anderson*,[47] together with developments in the area of directors' liability for insolvent trading,[48] blurred this distinction by curtailing the extent to which directors can legitimately delegate their responsibilities and rely upon the judgement of other corporate officers.[49]

The influence of both the shareholder as owner/principal and the shareholder as beneficiary converge in the terminology of the general meeting's role in curing directors' breaches of duty. Although sometimes treated as constituting a "waiver" of breach, implying an application of trust law under which a fiduciary may be protected from liability by obtaining the informed consent of the beneficiary,[50] many cases also refer to a resolution of the general meeting as "ratification" of the board's conduct, reflecting principles of agency law.[51]

---

[41] *Ibid.*, 656–8 (*per* Clarke and Sheller JJA); 750–1, 753, 755 (*per* Powell JA). See also L S Sealy, "Directors' 'Wider' Responsibilities—Problems Conceptual, Practical and Procedural" (1987) 13 *Monash Univ LR* 164, 165–6.

[42] See Keeton, n. 37 above, who criticises such divergence from trust principles as having led to a progressive decimation of directors' responsibilities.

[43] (1995) 18 ACSR 459.

[44] *Ibid.*, 470.

[45] (1995) 16 ACSR 607.

[46] Sealy, n. 37 above, 87–8.

[47] (1995) 16 ACSR 607.

[48] See generally J Hill, "The Liability of Passive Directors: *Morley* v. *Statewide Tobacco Services Ltd.*" (1992) 14 *Syd L Rev* 504.

[49] See *Daniels* v. *Anderson* (1995) 16 ACSR 607, 665–8.

[50] See P D Finn, *Fiduciary Obligations* (Sydney, Law Book Co., 1977), 51.

[51] Compare, for example, *Bamford* v. *Bamford* [1968] 2 All ER 655 (Plowman J) and *Winthrop Investments Ltd.* v. *Winns Ltd.* [1975] 2 NSWLR 666. See generally S Fridman, "Ratification of Directors' Breaches" (1992) 10 *CSLJ* 252.

C The Shareholder as Bystander

Given the factors which prompted Berle's characterisation of shareholders as cestuis que trust, it was perhaps inevitable that shareholders would eventually become "bystanders"[52] to decisions affecting their investments. This position was a by-product of the managerialist paradigm of the large corporation, which dominated corporate law for more than half a century, describing the firm as a power structure with management strategically placed at its core.[53] However, its roots were apparent as early as the 1860s when Charles Francis Adams Jr, describing tension between shareholder and management interests in the Erie Railroad, stated that the idea of inquiries by ordinary shareholders into the affairs of Erie was regarded by management as "downright impertinence".[54]

Much twentieth century corporate doctrine has restricted the participatory role of shareholders in corporate governance. It assumed the existence of a clear line defining managerial powers, carving out a domain which was constitutionally off-limits to shareholders. Thus, from 1906 it was apparent that, no matter what the position may have been under an earlier agency analysis of the relationship between shareholders and directors,[55] when managerial powers were vested in the directors under the company's articles of association, the general meeting was powerless to override decisions of the board,[56] even by unanimous shareholder agreement. In the United States, management's power was even stronger given that directors were generally protected from removal from office in the absence of "just cause". Management's power and discretion has continued to grow in the twentieth century. The old agency model continues, however, to inform the terminology of residual powers, which are often referred to as "reverting" to the general meeting, in spite of the fact that these powers are no longer viewed as having been delegated to the board by the shareholders.

The technical rules on company meetings have long reflected a managerialist paradigm. Not only were shareholders banished decisively from managerial decisions; cases such as *NRMA* Ltd. v. *Parker*[57] made it clear that shareholders in general meeting do not even have the power to communicate their views and opinions on management matters to the board. Shareholders' ancillary powers, such as the power to appoint and remove directors, were

---

[52] See R Buxbaum, "The Internal Division of Powers in Corporate Governance" (1985) 73 *Cal L Rev* 1671, 1683, who states: "To some degree the legislatures are responsible, but to a far greater degree it is the courts that are relegating shareholders to the questionable role of bystanders."

[53] See Bratton, n. 4 above, 1475–6.

[54] Quoted in n. 3 above, 6–7.

[55] See, for example, *Isle of Wight Rly Co.* v. *Tahourdin* (1884) 25 Ch D 320.

[56] *Automatic Self-Cleansing Filter Syndicate Co. Ltd.* v. *Cuninghame* [1906] 2 Ch 34. For the parallel shift in United States law, see Horwitz, n. 14 above, 214 ff.

[57] (1986) 4 ACLC 609.

attenuated by the practical difficulties of exercising such powers, management's superiority through proxy and agenda control[58] and judicial decisions which continued the oligarchical trend[59] of *Cuninghame's case* relying on a strong entity conception of the corporation. For example, in *L C O'Neil Enterprises Pty. Ltd.* v. *Toxic Treatments Ltd.*,[60] the court severely limited the circumstances in which shareholders could themselves convene a general meeting, thus, according to Kirby P's dissent, denying shareholders the means of "self help".[61]

A number of proposed reforms to the rules of company meetings under Australia's Second Corporate Law Simplification Bill[62] reflect an interesting retreat, however, from a managerialist paradigm relegating the shareholder to status of bystander. These provisions seem designed to facilitate greater involvement and "voice" for shareholders.[63] Clause 249F, for example, will reverse the decision in *L C O'Neil Enterprises Pty Ltd.* v. *Toxic Treatments Ltd.*,[64] by giving members with 5 per cent of voting rights an absolute power to convene a general meeting.[65] Clause 250S introduces a statutory right for members to ask questions or make comments on the management of the company,[66] in contrast to *NRMA* v. *Parker*,[67] which took the view that this was outside the role and function of shareholders. In spite of fears by the business community that these changes will lead to disruption of general meetings by small vocal minorities, the provisions may be too innocuous in practice to have a significant effect on shareholder participation in corporate governance.[68]

---

[58] See M E Levine and C R Plott, "Agenda Influence and Its Implications" (1977) 63 *Va L Rev* 561; *Re Dorman Long & Co. Ltd.* [1934] Ch 635, 657–8. For a modern statement of this phenomenon, see the recent comment by Ivor Ries that "Australia's Corporations Law, and most company articles of association, ultimately vest 90 per cent of the power over the choice of election methodology with established boards, who set the rules under which their members are elected. . . . Small shareholders, no matter how well organised and motivated, just ain't in the game when the big boys gang up": Chanticleer, "Big boys show how it's done", *Australian Financial Review*, 20 Nov. 1996, 52.

[59] See M Eisenberg, "Megasubsidiaries: The Effect of Corporate Structure on Corporate Control" (1971) 84 *Harv L Rev* 1577, 1602, who states: "Legally as well as practically, the board of directors is an independent power center within the corporation."

[60] (1986) 4 ACLC 178.

[61] *Ibid.*, 180.

[62] Second Corporate Law Simplification Bill 1996, Part 2G.2.

[63] The provisions are arguably consistent with a shift from "managed corporation" to "governed corporation". See J Pound, "The Promise of the Governed Corporation" [1995] *Harv Bus Rev* 89, and see further below under "The Shareholder as Participant in a Political Entity" and "The Shareholder as Managerial Partner (or 'The Collectivisation of Shareholder/ Management Interests')".

[64] (1986) 4 ACLC 178.

[65] See also cl 249Q, which permits dissenting shareholders to require the company to distribute resolutions and statements to other members in certain circumstances, at the company's expense.

[66] See also cl 250T, which allows members as a whole to question the company's auditor or representative if present at the AGM.

[67] (1986) 4 ACLC 609.

[68] The Parliamentary Joint Committee on Corporations and Securities (Report on the Draft Second Corporate Law Simplification Bill 1996, Nov. 1996, 20–5) pointed out, for example, that cl 250S and 250T do not entitle every member to ask questions or make comments, only "the

Yet another device by which shareholders were effectively excluded from participation in investment decisions was via the mechanism of the corporate group. This device enabled assets to be vested in a subsidiary and beyond the purview of the ultimate investors, thus replicating the original division between ownership and control.[69]

One variant of the bystander model, with benign consequences for shareholders, is the image of shareholders as *innocent* bystanders.[70] The assumption that shareholders are removed from decision-making power, and therefore lacking in any personal responsibility for corporate actions, has protected the inviolable status of limited liability in the public corporation context. In contrast, the courts have been more prepared to lift the corporate veil in close corporations with no division between ownership and control, where shareholders will be more directly "responsible" for corporate actions.[71] Hansmann and Kraakman's[72] proposal to impose liability for corporate torts on passive shareholders in public companies represented a radical break with this tradition. Their proposal avoided personal responsibility as a basis for personal liability; instead justification for liability was found in the benefits of the shareholders' role as residual equity owners and their efficiency as risk-bearers. On the Hansmann and Kraakman approach, wide dispersion and diversification of shareholding in public companies, the very features which had supported an innocent bystander model, were transformed into a justification for shareholder liability, under a risk-bearing efficiency rationale.[73]

Within the framework of a managerialist paradigm of the firm, the question whether the role of bystander was a satisfactory one for shareholders depended upon legitimation issues in the pro/anti-managerialist debate. For anti-managerialists, who argued that management held power without accountability and therefore without legitimacy, the further attenuation of shareholder participation in corporate decision-making merely exacerbated the central problem. Pro-managerialists, on the other hand, by-passed these concerns over legitimacy, stressing, as justification for their superior position

---

members as a whole". Also, the provisions do not impose any duty to answer the shareholders' questions. The Parliamentary Joint Committee considered that cl 250T should be strengthened by actually requiring that the auditor or representative be present to take questions at the AGM of a listed company.

[69] See Eisenberg, n. 59 above.

[70] Contrast, however, the view of Louis Brandeis that "a shareholder may be innocent in fact but socially he cannot be held innocent. He accepts the benefits of a system. It is his business and his obligation to see that those who represent him carry out a policy which is consistent with the public welfare."

[71] See, for example, Note, "Should Shareholders Be Personally Liable for the Torts of Their Corporations?" (1967) 76 *Yale LJ* 1190, 1196ff; R B Thompson, "Piercing the Corporate Veil: An Empirical Study" (1991) 76 *Cornell L Rev* 1036.

[72] H Hansmann and R Kraakman, "Toward Unlimited Shareholder Liability for Corporate Torts" (1991) 100 *Yale LJ* 1879.

[73] See generally J Hill, "Corporate Groups, Creditor Protection and Cross Guarantees: Australian Perspectives" (1995) 24 *Can Bus LJ* 321, 325–7; (1996) 38 *Corp Practice Commentator* 381, 385–7.

within the firm, the expertise of managers and their capacity for statesman-like conduct.[74]

D The Shareholder as Participant in a Political Entity

The corporation has sometimes been viewed as analogous to a system of private government,[75] with managerial powers approximating those of government authorities. Kirby J, for example, has called corporations "mini-democracies".[76] This image of the corporation is hardly a recent phenomenon. Hobbes, who found the rise of corporations threatening to the State's authority, noted with suspicion "the great number of corporations; which are as it were many lesser commonwealths in the bowels of a greater, like worms in the entrails of a man".[77] A political metaphor of the corporation has important implications for the role of shareholders, both in terms of their participatory rights and the status of their interests within a corporate commonwealth.

The origins of a political image of the corporation are not difficult to trace. Under liberal theory, the corporation occupied an equivocal and intermediate position within the State/individual dichotomy as a result of its group characteristic.[78] While through one lens organisations could be viewed as protectors of individual rights, they could also be viewed as more closely allied, or analogous, to the State itself. In the early phases of corporate law, special charters were obtained direct from the sovereign or State, combining public and private goals.[79] Even the real entity theory, which succeeded in displacing the concession model by recharacterising the corporation as "private" and separate from the State, mirrored representative democracy in its reliance on majority rule.[80]

Commentators have offered a range of justifications for viewing the corporation as a system of private government. For some, a political metaphor is

---

[74] Bratton, n. 4 above, 1476; Frug n. 35 above, 1282–3, 1328–34.

[75] See, for example, Mason, n. 17 above, 6–7; G Morgan, "Interests, Conflict, and Power: Organizations as Political Systems" in G Morgan (ed.), *Images of Organization* (Cal., Sage Publications, 1986), 141; E Latham, "The Body Politic of the Corporation" in Mason (ed.), n. 17 above, 218; K Brewster, "The Corporation and Economic Federalism" in *ibid.*, 72; H Steinmann, "The Enterprise as a Political System" in Hopt and Teubner (eds.), n. 28 above, 401; S Bottomley, "Taking Corporations Seriously: Some Considerations for Corporate Regulation" (1990) 19 *Fed L Rev* 203; J Pound, "The Rise of the Political Model of Corporate Governance and Corporate Control" (1993) 68 *NY Univ L Rev* 1003.

[76] "Justice Michael Kirby—Legal Departures" [1994] *Company Director* 19, 20.

[77] T Hobbes, *Leviathan* (1651) (New York, 1924), 218, cited in Latham, n. 75 above, 218–19.

[78] See generally G Frug, "The City as a Legal Concept" (1980) 93 *Harv L Rev* 1057; G A Mark, "The Personification of the Business Corporation in American Law" (1987) 54 *U Chi L Rev* 1441, 1445; P Selznick, *Law, Society and Industrial Justice* (New York, Russell Sage, 1969), 37–8.

[79] G A Mark, "Some Observations on Writing the Legal History of the Corporation in the Age of Theory" in L E Mitchell (ed.), *Progressive Corporate Law* (Colo., Westview, 1995), 67, 68–9.

[80] See Horwitz, n. 14 above, 218–19; M Hager, "Bodies Politic: The Progressive History of Organisational 'Real Entity' Theory" (1989) 50 *U Pitt L Rev* 575.

apt for its descriptive power, in that corporations have a structure and internal systems of authority common to all bodies politic.[81] According to Latham, where these essential elements exist, so too does a political system, "whether one calls it the state or the corporation".[82] On this analysis, legitimisation of control is a central concern of political institutions and corporations alike.[83]

Commentators have also focused on the political nature of decision-making within the corporation,[84] specifically the need for corporate managers to balance conflicting interests, as justifying the metaphor.[85] For Aristotle, politics were precisely this—the means to create order and common goals from divergent interests in society.[86] "Corporate governance", that shibboleth of the 1990s, itself has clear political overtones.[87]

Some theorists adopt a normative argument to the effect that persons whose interests are affected by decisions of either political or social institutions should be involved in the decision-making process. This approach presents the ideal of participatory democracy as a counterpoint to management-centred bureaucracies.[88] It also stresses the importance of "voice" over "exit", which is the primary focus for market-based theories of the firm.[89]

Yet another approach, akin to that of Hobbes, examines the relationship of corporations with the outside world, viewing their economic, social and political power as rivalling that of governmental bodies.[90] This approach focuses on large public companies with bureaucratic structures. It clearly underpinned the reasoning of the majority judges in the High Court of Australia decision, *Environment Protection Authority* v. *Caltex Refining Co. Pty. Ltd.*,[91] which denied corporations the protection of the privilege against self-incrimination.

---

[81] See Latham, n. 75 above, 220, who lists these essential characteristics as: (1) authoritative allocation of principal functions; (2) symbolic system for ratification of collective decisions; (3) operating system of command; (4) system of rewards and punishments; (5) institutions for enforcement of common rules. See also S Bottomley, "From Contractualism to Constitutionalism: A Framework for Corporate Governance" (1997) 19 *Syd L Rev* 277.

[82] Latham, n. 75 above, 220.

[83] L L Dallas, "Working Toward a New Paradigm" in Mitchell (ed.), n. 79 above, 35.

[84] See, for example, Dallas, n. 30 above, 25.

[85] See Steinmann, n. 75 above, 401, 402; Morgan, n. 75 above, 141.

[86] Morgan, n. 75 above, 142, 148.

[87] Bottomley, n. 81 above.

[88] Bratton, n. 4 above, 1497.

[89] See generally Pound, n. 75 above, who argues that a political model of corporate governance has now supplanted market-based theories.

[90] See, for example, Brewster, n. 75 above, 72, who states that "[w]e are bound to become increasingly uncomfortable when we contemplate the modern corporation as a power with many of the trappings of sovereignty". See also J E Parkinson, *Corporate Power and Responsibility: Issues in the Theory of Company Law* (Oxford, Clarendon, 1993), Chap 1; M Stokes, "Company Law and Legal Theory" in W E Twining (ed.), *Legal Theory and Common Law* (Oxford, Blackwell, 1986), 156, 176; P Blumberg, "The Politicalization of the Corporation" (1971) 26 *Bus Law* 1551.

[91] (1993) 178 CLR 477. See, generally, J Hill, "Corporate Rights and Accountability—The Privilege Against Self-Incrimination and the Implications of *Environment Protection Authority* v. *Caltex Refining Co. Pty Ltd.*" (1995) 7 *Corp and Bus LJ* 127.

In so doing, the majority judges stressed the great power and resources of the modern public corporation. Perhaps the most extreme version of this approach is represented by Gore Vidal's recent statement in the financial press that the United States is "governed by international corporations which [do] not take politicians seriously".[92]

Governments can be democratic or authoritarian. A persistent theme in the literature discussing the political dimension of the corporation is that, in spite of the appropriateness of the metaphor, it is only "make-believe democracy" which exists in the corporate commonwealth,[93] that corporations are in reality profoundly undemocratic systems of government.[94] Nonetheless, in spite of the inherent criticism of corporate power underlying much of this literature,[95] commentators such as Pound[96] have adopted the model optimistically, as a contemporary panacea for managerial failure. In Australia, too, Bottomley has advocated a political model of "corporate constitutionalism" as a blueprint for doctrinal changes to reflect a democratic ideal for companies.[97]

Successful theories are not only descriptive, but also influence policy outcomes. A political theory of the corporation has implications for shareholder participation in corporate governance. If directors are characterised as the "elected representatives"[98] of shareholders, this would suggest that, while not necessarily entitled to the full panoply of rights appropriate under an ownership model, shareholders are entitled to at least some level of meaningful participation in corporate governance.[99]

The implications of a political model are, however, variable, depending upon who count as "citizens" and the choice of legitimate interests to be considered in corporate decision-making.[100] Some models assume that the board of directors represents a single constituency of the shareholders, whose interests are pre-eminent.[101] From the perspective of status of interests, such a model differs little from a trust model or a contractual theory of the firm.

---

[92] "Vidal votes for chaos on his way to heaven", *Sydney Morning Herald*, 24 Jan. 1997, 3.

[93] Latham, n. 75 above, 225.

[94] *Ibid.*, 223; Morgan, n. 75 above, 141. See generally N H Jacoby, "Corporate Government: Autocratic or Democratic?" in N H Jacoby (ed.), *Corporate Power and Social Responsibility: A Blueprint for the Future* (New York, Macmillan, 1973), 165, 178, who disagrees with this common perception. On the dangers of accepting the metaphor of democracy where equality of power does not exist, in the different context of collective bargaining, see K Stone, "The Post-War Paradigm in American Labor Law" (1981) 90 *Yale LJ* 1509; K Stone, "Re-Envisioning Labor Law: A Response to Professor Finkin" (1986) 45 *Md L Rev* 978.

[95] For criticism of the model's moralistic overtones, see G Teubner, "Unitas Multiplex: Corporate Governance in Group Enterprises" in D Sugarman and G Teubner (eds.), *Regulating Corporate Groups in Europe* (Baden-Baden, Nomos, 1990), 67, 74.

[96] Pound, n. 75 above. Cf T A Smith, "Institutions and Entrepreneurs in American Corporate Finance" (1997) 85 *Cal L Rev* 1.

[97] Bottomley, n. 81 above.

[98] See Buxbaum, n. 52 above, n. 1.

[99] Professor Buxbaum describes this basic point as "a defensible if not an essential position" in corporate law: *ibid.*, 1672.

[100] See Mason, n. 17 above, 6.

[101] Jacoby, n. 94 above, 171.

Other political models, however, assume broader citizenship within the corporate commonwealth.[102] It is these models which stress that organisations have multiple constituencies and must create unified goals among people with diverse and conflicting interests.[103] The concept of industrial democracy and co-determination as a means to integrate workers' interests into corporate governance[104] is based upon a political model of the corporation, expanded to include employee interests.[105] Further extension to the model can take into account interests of others groups such as consumers, and even the "public interest".[106] This political model views the organisation as "a coalition of diverse stakeholders . . . with multiple goals".[107] Recent communitarian scholarship in the United States constitutes an explicit rejection of the primacy of shareholder interests, and a recognition of the vulnerability of non-shareholder constituencies within the corporation.[108] In keeping with this image, Philip Selznick has suggested the need for a transition from the idea of managing corporations to that of governing communities.[109]

A political model highlights the issue of power in the corporate realm, which is invisible under market-based contractual models of the corporation.[110] In highlighting the existence of power, it also recognises the need for checks and balances in decision-making and for accountability of management.[111] Where citizenship is interpreted to extend beyond shareholders and their interests, the focus of fiduciary duties will shift to improving the processes, procedures and fairness of managerial decisions.[112] This will have practical implications in suggesting that governance structures should be revised to provide for participation and representation of interests at the level where strategic decision-making takes place.[113]

---

[102] See, for example, Brewster, n. 75 above, who states that the modern corporation governs "a constituency whose interests are different from, and often at odds with, ownership" (72–3); A Chayes, "The Modern Corporation and the Rule of Law" in Mason (ed.), n. 17 above, 25, 41; P Selznick, *The Moral Commonwealth: Social Theory and the Promise of Community* (Cal., University of California Press, 1992), 346–7.

[103] Selznick, n. 102 above, 231; Steinmann, n. 75 above, 401, 402, 418; Morgan, n. 75 above, 142.

[104] See, for example, P L Davies, "Employee Representation on Company Boards and Participation in Corporate Planning" (1975) 38 *MLR* 254; D F Vagts, "Reforming the 'Modern' Corporation: Perspectives from the German" (1966) 80 *Harv L Rev* 23. See generally J Hill, "At the Frontiers of Labour Law and Corporate Law: Enterprise Bargaining, Corporations and Employees" (1995) 23 *Fed L Rev* 204, 218–21.

[105] See Morgan, n. 75 above, 145–6; Mason, n. 17 above, 6; P L Davies and K Wedderburn, "The Land of Industrial Democracy" (1977) 6 *Ind LJ* 197, 200–1.

[106] See Steinmann, n. 75 above, 411–14.

[107] Morgan, n. 75 above, 154.

[108] D Millon, "Communitarianism in Corporate Law: Foundations and Law Reform Strategies" in Mitchell, n. 79 above, 1. See generally "New Directions in Corporate Law", Special Issue, (1993) 50 *Wash and Lee L Rev* 1373ff.

[109] Selznick, n. 102 above, 237, 289 ff.

[110] Teubner, n. 95 above, 71–2, 74; Dallas, n. 30 above, 26.

[111] Bratton, n. 4 above, 1497–8.

[112] See, for example, F K Kubler, "Dual Loyalty of Labor Representatives" in Hopt and Teubner (eds.), n. 28 above, 429, 441–2.

[113] Steinmann, n. 75 above, 423.

According to some political commentators, a hallmark of advanced liberal governments is a tendency to govern, not directly, but by harnessing the "regulated and accountable choices of autonomous agents",[114] thereby creating a form of private government. In emphasising the self-regulatory nature of large corporations,[115] the political metaphor can redirect attention to matters such as internal justice systems,[116] "corporate cultures"[117] and the way in which corporations, like governments, can interact with, and mould, the behaviour of constituents.[118]

Due to its historical connection with the now defunct concession theory of incorporation, a political model of the corporation is sometimes dismissed as equally *passé*.[119] Nonetheless, a political model is able to accommodate a number of important contemporary changes in the commercial world better than many other models. It is therefore worthy of renewed attention.

Many of the classic distinctions and categories in the corporate context, which supported an image of the corporation as "private" and shareholder-centred, have become increasingly blurred. Thus, the boundaries between "public" and "private" enterprise are less clear-cut in the late twentieth century,[120] particularly in view of the modern tendency of governments to transfer a greater range of "public services" to the private sector.[121] The distinctiveness of share capital itself has diminished, blurring the line between debt and equity.[122] Also blurred is the traditional boundary between shareholders and employees, given that behind the shareholding facade of superannuation funds lies a vast proportion of the country's working population.[123]

[114] N Rose, "Government, Authority and Expertise in Advanced Liberalism" (1993) 22 *Economy and Society* 283, 298; P Ewick, "Corporate Cures: The Commodification of Social Control" (1993) 13 *Studies in Law, Politics, and Society* 137, 139.

[115] Selznick, n. 102 above, 231; J Black, "Constitutionalising Self-Regulation" (1996) 59 *MLR* 24.

[116] See B Fisse and J Braithwaite, *Corporations, Crime and Accountability* (Cambridge, Cambridge Univeristy Press, 1993), 81.

[117] See J Hill and R Harmer, "Criminal Liability of Corporations—Australia" in H Doelder and K Tiedemann (eds.), *Criminal Liability of Corporations* (The Hague, Kluwer, 1996), 71, 86–9.

[118] For interesting contemporary scholarship on the interlocking relationship between government and governed, see G Burchell, "Liberal Government and Techniques of the Self" (1993) 22 *Economy and Society* 267; Rose, n. 114 above: B Cruikshank, "Revolutions Within: Self-government and Self-esteem" (1993) 22 *Economy and Society* 327; P Ewick, "Corporate Cures: The Commodification of Social Control" (1993) 13 *Studies in Law, Politics, and Society* 137.

[119] The model is also at odds with the economic "nexus of contracts" model of the corporation favoured by the current Australian government. See P Costello, "Is the Corporation Law Working?" (1992) 2 *Aust J Corp L* 12; Treasurer's Office, Canberra, Corporate Law Economic Reform Program, Mar. 1997.

[120] Mason, n. 17 above, 16–19; Frug, n. 78 above, 1128 ff.

[121] Mason, n. 17 above, 16–17; Ewick, n. 118 above, 139.

[122] See Dallas, n. 83 above, 35–6; Mason, n. 17 above, 3, where he states: "The equity owner is joining the bond holder as a functionless rentier."

[123] See R Buxbaum, "Institutional Owners and Corporate Managers: A Comparative Perspective" (1991) 57 *Brooklyn L Rev* 1, 28–9.

E The Shareholder as Investor (or "The Shareholder as Bystander and That's The Way it Ought to Be")

The contractual theory of the firm,[124] which views the corporation as a nexus of contracts, provides a sharp contrast to political models of the corporation. Whereas political models with broad citizenship focus on the resolution of conflicts of interest within the firm, the very concept "within the firm"[125] is meaningless to contractual theorists, who deconstruct the firm into a series of private exchanges between resource holders.[126] Collective aspects of the organisation itself dissolve under this relentlessly individualistic approach.[127]

Many commentators have lamented the gradual attenuation of shareholder participatory rights, viewing it as a sad evolutionary fact which should either be reversed or compensated for by external controls.[128] Law and economics theorists, however, focusing on the capital-raising function of public corporations and the shareholder's role as investor,[129] have seen a restricted participatory role as unproblematical. According to Manne, for example, "if the principal economic function of the corporate form [is] to amass the funds of investors, qua investors, we should not anticipate their demanding or wanting a direct role in the management of the company".[130] In other words, the fact that shareholder participatory rights are limited is not a cause for angst;[131] far from representing the evisceration of shareholder power, it is perfectly natural and consonant with the structure and nature of the corporation.

At first blush, the contractual theory of the corporation appears very different from a "shareholder-as-owner" model. Under the contractual theory, shareholders are not "owners".[132] They are merely one group of resource

---

[124] For a lucid exposition of the contractual theory of the corporation, agency theory and the efficient capital markets hypothesis, see H N Butler, "The Contractual Theory of the Corporation" (1989) 11 *Geo Mason U L Rev* 99. See also F Easterbrook and D Fischel, *The Economic Structure of Corporate Law* (Cambridge, Mass., Harvard University Press, 1991), Chap 1.

[125] Steinmann, n. 75 above, 401, 407; Bottomley, n. 81 above.

[126] M C Jensen and W H Meckling, "Theory of the Firm: Managerial Behavior, Agency Costs and Ownership Structure" (1976) 3 *J Fin Econ* 305.

[127] For criticism of this side of the contractual theory of the corporation, see Teubner, n. 95 above, 67, 70 ff.

[128] See generally Werner, n. 18 above; Romano, n. 3 above.

[129] See R Buxbaum, "Corporate Legitimacy, Economic Theory, and Legal Doctrine" (1984) 45 *Ohio St LJ* 515, 526, describing the transformation of the shareholder from "king of the corporation to king of the market".

[130] H Manne, "Our Two Corporation Systems: Law and Economics" (1967) 53 *Va L Rev* 259, 260–1. For a recent parallel argument that institutional investor passivity is a natural result of economic evolution, see T A Smith, "Institutions and Entrepreneurs in American Corporate Finance" (1997) 85 *Cal L Rev* 1.

[131] See, for example, R Winter, "State Law, Shareholder Protection, and the Theory of the Corporation" (1977) 6 *J Legal Stud* 251. See also Mark, n. 79 above, 71, who states that, according to contractarians, "[t]he putative abuse of shareholders . . . is largely mythical".

[132] Butler, n. 124 above, 107.

holders, on an equal footing with other groups such as managers, creditors, employees, customers.[133] Nonetheless, the apparent difference between the two models is ultimately superficial. While the contractual theory deprecates shareholder participatory rights in corporate governance, it resurrects shareholder interests to pre-eminence,[134] through the guiding principle of "profit maximisation". With its minimal participatory rights, but primacy of shareholder interests, the contemporary contractual theory most closely resembles, paradoxically, a trustee/beneficiary model.[135] But, while the trustee model assumed that direct shareholder intervention was impossible, contractual theorists generally view intervention as inappropriate and unnecessary, since the constraints of the market will force managers to act "*as if* they have the shareholders' interests at heart".[136] Indeed, Easterbrook and Fischel deride proposals for greater participatory rights for shareholders, viewing shareholder apathy as the response of rational investors in business entities.[137]

The image of shareholders under a contractual theory as "investors" who invest "in the investment, not in the corporation"[138] treats share ownership as a fungible within the market-place for stock. Under this analysis, the hub of shareholder protection should be located outside the corporation, in ensuring a fair and open market, offering shareholders ease of entry and, crucially, exit. The "Wall Street Walk" is seen as a more efficient way to deal with unsatisfactory management than intervention in corporate affairs.[139] Relying on this approach, it has been argued that shareholders exchanged corporate control for marketability of their shares.[140] In this way, management's control is legitimated as stemming from a voluntary, consensual arrangement with shareholders. By rendering the corporation itself essentially "private" through the device of contract, little scope is given for government intervention to protect shareholders.[141] Rather, protection should occur through regulation of the

---

[133] F Easterbrook and D Fischel, "Voting in Corporate Law" (1983) 26 *J L and Economics* 395, 396.

[134] See, for example, J Macey, "An Economic Analysis of the Various Rationales for Making Shareholders the Exclusive Beneficiaries of Corporate Fiduciary Duties" (1991) 21 *Stetson L Rev* 23. See generally W Bratton, "The 'Nexus of Contracts' Corporation: A Critical Appraisal" (1989) 74 *Cornell L Rev* 407, 427 ff; Dallas, n. 30 above; Millon, n. 25 above, 229–31.

[135] See Frug, n. 35 above, 1311.

[136] Butler, n. 124 above, 122.

[137] Easterbrook and Fischel, n. 133 above, 396. See also Winter, n. 131 above, 263.

[138] Buxbaum, n. 129 above, 526.

[139] In other words, in clear contrast to a political model of the corporation, "exit" is seen as more important than "voice" for shareholders under a contractual model: Steinmann, n. 75 above, 408.

[140] See W Werner, "Management, Stock Market and Corporate Reform: Berle and Means Reconsidered" (1977) 77 *Colum L Rev* 388, 397; Hetherington, n. 18 above, 200–2.

[141] Bratton, n. 4 above, 1480. For criticism of the power of the contractual model to privatise and legitimate the corporation, see Buxbaum, n. 129 above, 520; Millon, n. 25 above; G Teubner, "Enterprise Corporatism: New Industrial Policy and the 'Essence' of the Legal Person" (1988) 36 *Am J Comp L* 130, 131.

securities market, specifically by mandatory disclosure rules.[142] Takeovers are relied upon to ensure the accountability of management.[143]

This model of shareholders has given important insights into the effect of a stock market on the expectations of shareholders. It is reflected in a number of restrictive judicial decisions, where in determining whether a shareholder has a "proper purpose" or has been harmed "*qua* shareholder" under a statutory provision, the courts have limited this to interference with the shareholder's economic interests.[144]

F The Shareholder as Cerberus

A number of recent developments in Australian corporate law appear to cast the shareholder in a new role. This image of the shareholder is one of guardian or monitor of managerial decision-making. This role manifests itself at both a procedural and substantive level. Broad procedural monitoring is reflected, for example, in the Australian Investment Managers' Association (AIMA) guide for recommended corporate practice.[145] The principles of good corporate governance contained in this guide are remarkably detailed, and affect matters such as the composition of boards, appointment of non-executive directors, and key board committees and performance evaluation.[146] Recent lobbying by the AIMA for greater disclosure of director and executive remuneration also falls within this category of procedural monitoring.[147]

Under Australian corporate law, monitoring also applies to specific management decisions. By ensuring that certain questionable managerial actions are referred to the shareholders in general meeting, various provisions of the Corporations Law and the Stock Exchange Listing Rules use shareholder consent as a regulatory device and transform shareholders into monitors. This function for shareholders is consistent with a political model of the corporation. Under the related party transaction provisions of the Corporations Law,[148] for example, shareholder monitoring promotes corporate self-

---

[142] See generally M Blair and I M Ramsay, "Mandatory Corporate Disclosure Rules and Securities Regulation" in Walker and Fisse (eds.), n. 11 above, 264.

[143] Werner, n. 140 above, 403–4. However, the efficacy of takeovers as a reliable constraint on managerial powers is questionable from both a theoretical and practical perspective. See generally, Hill and Ramsay, n. 11 above, 295–6.

[144] A classic example is *State ex rel. Pillsbury* v. *Honeywell Inc.* (1971) 291 Minn 322, 191 NW 2d 406.

[145] Australian Investment Managers' Association, *Corporate Governance: A Guide for Investment Managers and Corporations* (2nd edn., Sydney, July 1997).

[146] Cf the much-vaunted, but far from onerous, ASX Listing Rule 4.10.3, which came into effect on 1 July 1996 and avoids any prescriptive rules on content, merely requiring that an entity disclose in its annual reports its main corporate governance practices, if any. See generally AIMA, *Corporate Governance Statements by Major ASX Listed Companies* (Sydney, Mar. 1997).

[147] See J Hill, "Remuneration Disclosure in Australia", AIMA Research Paper, No 1/1996.

[148] Corporations Law, Part 3.2A. On self-regulatory strategies in corporate governance generally, see W Bratton and J McCahery, "Regulatory Competition, Regulatory Capture, and Self-Regulation" (1995) 73 *NC L Rev* 1861.

regulation and seeks to ensure that shareholders have participation rights in transactions where there are dangers of conflict of interest, or self-dealing, by the company's controllers. Effective shareholder monitoring of such transactions can arguably benefit all groups within the corporate enterprise.

This role for shareholders can also be viewed as akin to that of Cerberus, guardian of the underworld. In assessing the suitability and effectiveness of shareholders in this role, it is well to remember that Cerberus occupies an ambiguous role in Greek mythology. Cerberus is generally regarded as fearsome. However, since the dog's main function was to bark at the dead (who, as shades, could not be frightened or harmed anyway), its role might appear largely ceremonial. Furthermore, stories abound of Cerberus failing in its guardianship duties *vis-à-vis* the living. In the Æneid, for example, the Sybil ensures that Æneas can pass into Hades by the simple device of tossing a cake soaked in honey and a sleeping drug to the dog;[149] Orpheus, searching for Eurydice, lulls the dog to sleep with his lyre.[150] We are not told whether Cerberus' multiple heads created additional collective action problems.

The metaphor of Cerberus is a revealing one in the corporate context. Traditional assumptions about shareholder passivity in public companies make the question of their fitness for a guardianship and regulatory role under Australian corporate law a relevant and important issue.[151]

G The Shareholder as Managerial Partner (or "The Collectivisation of Shareholder/Management Interests")

Another possible vision of shareholders in the age of large institutional investors is an image of shareholders as full-scale partners with management in the control of corporations and in corporate decision-making. In the post-takeover period, a number of scholars have supported this model, which overlaps with a shareholder-centred political view of the corporation, on the basis that it constitutes a desirable reassertion of owner control and managerial accountability to shareholders, which has been lacking for much of the twentieth century.[152] Under this model, the wheel has come full circle—shareholder interests are entrenched and made dominant by strong participatory rights in the management of corporations. Shareholders and board members are reconnected under a scheme of shared power.[153] The potential

---

[149] D Rosenberg, *World Mythology: An Anthology of the Great Myths and Epics* (London, 1986), 145. Heracles, by covering himself in a protective lion skin, also succeeded in carrying the monster off from its post in the Underworld: 32.

[150] M Grant, *Myths of the Greeks and Romans* (London, 1962), 267.

[151] See further below under "Shareholder Consent as a Regulatory Device—The Shareholder as Cerberus".

[152] See, for example, Pound, n. 63 above; Pound, n. 75 above.

[153] Pound, n. 63 above, 90. For sceptical views about the likelihood of this form of governance occurring, see J E Fisch, "Relationship Investing: Will It Happen? Will It Work?" (1994) 55 *Ohio St LJ* 1009; Smith, n. 130 above.

resurrection of the role and interests of shareholders is clearly viewed as a "return to Eden" by some scholars.

The image of shareholders as partners in management has both a descriptive and normative limb. The descriptive limb points to the increasing influence of institutional shareholders, which has challenged traditional assumptions about shareholder passivity and lack of influence.

A number of diverse developments in the Australian commercial world suggest greater co-ordination between institutional shareholders and closer ties between the institutions and corporate management. First, the growth of institutional investors, fanned by the introduction of the Superannuation Guarantee Charge, has altered the traditional pattern of widely dispersed shareholdings.[154] The formation of the Australian Investment Managers' Association in 1990 decreased the difficulties of collective action and effectively created a coalition of shareholder interests. In Australia particularly, market capitalisation and equity turnover is highly concentrated in the top fifty listed companies,[155] making reliance on the Wall Street Walk, the standard form of relief under an investor model of the shareholder, more difficult for institutions with large shareholdings. In a number of matters, shareholders have acted collectively, and there have been recent moves by the Australian Securities Commission to ensure that collective action by institutional investors is not constrained by the restrictions on acting in concert under the Takeover Rules.[156] In the corporate sector, the growing power of institutions is reflected in the creation of the position of shareholder liaison officer within many companies. A final commercial development, which, more than any other, may guarantee the pre-eminence of shareholder interests, is the rise of pay-for-performance remuneration, which can tie managerial reward to profit-maximisation for the benefit of shareholders. These developments suggest a novel "collectivisation" of shareholder and management interests.

The normative argument claims that a model of shared power between shareholders and management is desirable because it provides greater legitimacy for the exercise of managerial power and ensures that management will maximise corporate performance for the benefit of shareholders.

Nonetheless, there are a number of dangers inherent in a model of the shareholder as managerial partner and in the "collectivisation" of institutional shareholder and management interests. In Australia, it is both interesting and disconcerting that this shift to the collectivisation of shareholder and management interests has occurred precisely at a time when there has been an unprecedented "decollectivisation" of labour interests through new systems of

---

[154] See, generally, Parliamentary Joint Committee on Corporations and Securities, Inquiry into the Role and Activities of Institutional Investors in Australia, Issues Paper, Canberra, Nov. 1994, Chap 2. See also Hill and Ramsay, n. 11 above, 298.

[155] Hill and Ramsay, n. 11 above, 294.

[156] See ASC Draft Policy Issues Paper, Collective Action by Institutions, 26 Nov. 1996; Chanticleer, "ASC arms the institutions", *Australian Financial Review*, 26 Nov. 1996, 64; A Deans, "Case for Collective Action", *Australian Financial Review*, 10 Feb. 1997, 52.

enterprise bargaining.[157] Many labour lawyers are concerned about the effects of decollectivisation on worker interests. There is as yet little recognition of the extent to which changes within the commercial realm, which have strengthened the interests of shareholders, increase employee vulnerability. The recent controversial announcement of the proposed closure of BHP's steel factory in Newcastle arguably reflects the development of closer ties between shareholders and management, since it was suggested in the financial press that institutional pressure had been a powerful influence on management's decision.[158] Concern for shareholder interests by BHP management was certainly far less pronounced a decade ago.[159] A message from contemporary developments is that it is dangerous to have governance structures where shareholder and management interests are collectivised and labour interests are not.

Another danger of a model elevating institutional investors to managerial partners is that the interests of powerful institutional investors may, or may not, be congruent with the interests of other shareholders.[160] Indeed, one of the basic tenets of corporate law is that shareholders may vote in their own best interests, a proposition which assumes that shareholders' interests may diverge.[161] There also exists the danger of entrenchment of managers through alliances with institutional investors.[162]

III VISIONS OF THE SHAREHOLDER IN RECENT AUSTRALIAN CORPORATE LAW DEVELOPMENTS

A *Gambotto* and the Vision of the Shareholder as Owner (or *"Plus ça change, plus c'est la même chose"*)

In the early 1960s, a leading corporate law commentator stated that the days of viewing shareholders in public companies as owners with proprietary rights

---

[157] See R McCallum, "Crafting a New Collective Labour Law for Australia" (1997) 39 *J Ind Rel* 405.

[158] Contrast the reporting of the proposed closure in the *Sydney Morning Herald* and *Australian Financial Review*: "BHP's real target: 8,000 jobs", *Sydney Morning Herald*, 30 Apr. 1997, 1; "BHP's rescue operation: Investors welcome radical surgery for ailing division", *Australian Financial Review*, 30 Apr. 1997, 1.

[159] In this respect, see National Companies and Securities Commission, *Report on the Cross Investments between The Broken Hill Proprietary Company Ltd. and Elders IXL Ltd.* (Australian Government Publishing Service, Canberra, 1986).

[160] For dangers in this regard, see, for example, E B Rock, "Controlling the Dark Side of Relational Investing" (1994) 15 *Cardozo L Rev* 987; Fisch, n. 153 above, 1036, 1038 ff; D DeMott, "Agency Principles and Large Block Shareholders" (1997) 19 *Cardozo L Rev* (forthcoming).

[161] See DeMott, n. 160 above, contrasting the constraints which would apply to large block shareholders if they were characterised as agents for other shareholders, with the current legal position where no such fiduciary relationship is presumed to exist.

[162] See P Conard, "Beyond Managerialism: Investor Capitalism?" (1988) 22 *JL Ref* 117, 119.

were "gone forever";[163] no longer could anyone take this image of the shareholder seriously. The High Court of Australia, however, in *Gambotto v. WCP Ltd.*,[164] showed that it takes the image of shareholders as owners seriously indeed.

Few decisions in recent Australian corporate law have provoked more commentary and controversy than *Gambotto*. The outcome of the decision was that an amendment to the company's articles of association, enabling a person holding 90 per cent or more of the company's shares to acquire compulsorily the remaining shares, was held to be invalid. The traditional test of validity for a resolution altering a company's articles had been to ask whether the resolution was passed "*bona fide* for the benefit of the company as a whole".[165] The majority judges in *Gambotto* however imposed a more stringent test for alterations to the corporation's articles involving expropriation of shares or "valuable proprietary rights attaching to shares".[166] According to the majority, an alteration to permit expropriation would be justified only if for a proper purpose, in that significant detriment or harm to the company would result from the minority's continuing share ownership.[167] The goal of the majority shareholders in *Gambotto*, namely to reduce the company's taxation liability by approximately $4 million did not satisfy this test of validity.[168]

The decision in *Gambotto* surprised many commentators, given a number of key factual features of the case. The first of these was the small shareholding of the dissenting minority. Industrial Equity (through wholly-owned subsidiaries) owned 99.7 per cent of issued shares in WCP Ltd. Of the 50,590 shares in minority hands, the dissenting shareholders owned only 15,898. Secondly, the approach of the majority judgment in the High Court of Australia enabled a small minority in the case to withstand a buy-out of their shares at a price considerably above a valuation report, which itself was conceded by minority shareholders to be both independent and fair.

---

[163] Mason, n. 17 above, 5–6.

[164] (1995) 69 ALJR 266.

[165] *Allen v. Gold Reefs of West Africa Ltd.* [1900] 1 Ch 656, 671.

[166] The judges in the majority considered that a different test would apply where no expropriation of shares or proprietary rights attached to shares was involved. In those circumstances, they stated that an alteration to the articles would be valid, unless *ultra vires*, beyond any purpose contemplated by the articles, or oppressive: see (1995) 69 ALJR 266, 271.

[167] Additionally to the proper purpose requirement, the expropriation must not operate oppressively on minority shareholders: *ibid.*

[168] According to the High Court, the majority cannot expropriate the minority "merely in order to secure for themselves the benefit of a corporate structure that can derive some new commercial advantage by virtue of the expropriation" (*ibid*). Only McHugh J, while agreeing that the majority shareholders bore the onus of establishing that the amendment was not oppressive, considered that the restructuring of the company for the purpose of achieving tax savings was a proper commercial objective. Nonetheless, McHugh J thought that the majority had failed to discharge the onus of showing that the transaction was not oppressive, in terms of fairness of price and disclosure (279).

Thirdly, the decision undercut traditional principles of majority rule and free alterability of the articles,[169] effectively giving minority shareholders a veto right for corporate reconstructions, unless the majority shareholders could show that that expropriation was necessary to avoid serious detriment to the company. The court's approach effectively reverts to the old nineteenth century concept of vested rights, the inflexibility of which majoritarianism was designed to overcome. Finally, the case involved shareholding in a public company, not a closely-held company. The courts are rightly wary of "freeze-outs" in the context of closely-held corporations, where members may be particularly vulnerable to oppression since the corporate business will often constitute their livelihood and valuation of shares may be more difficult where no market exists.[170] Shares in public corporations are treated to a much greater extent as fungibles, in accordance with an image of shareholders as investors.[171] The judgments in *Gambotto* fail however to distinguish between oppressive conduct in these two contexts.

The decision in *Gambotto* is underpinned by an image of shareholders as owners of the corporation, with full-blown proprietary interests. According to the joint judgment of Mason CJ, Brennan, Deane and Dawson JJ, the freedom to alter the articles of association is to be interpreted against the backdrop of these proprietary rights, and is constrained by them.[172]

The High Court decision in *Gambotto* has received much attention precisely because its outer limits are so unclear, as are the full implications of a proprietary model of shareholder rights. It has been asked, for example, whether deference to the proprietary nature of share ownership would prohibit the introduction of an anti-greenmail article, designed to ensure that individual shareholders cannot force a buy-out of their shares at a price or on terms not available to other shareholders. Would such an article interfere with members' proprietary rights?[173]

Gambotto is also radically out of step with the United States approach in this area, where the basic presumption is that minority shareholdings are *prima facie* defeasible, subject to a requirement of entire fairness and the ability of the court to examine the buy-out price through the appraisal remedy.[174]

---

[169] For strong criticism of this aspect of the case, see M Whincop, "*Gambotto v. WCP Ltd.*: An Economic Analysis of Alterations to Articles and Expropriation Articles" (1995) 23 *ABLR* 276.

[170] See Hill, n. 19 above.

[171] See S Fridman, "*Gambotto v. WCP Ltd.*: An Analysis of the High Court Decision" (1995) 6 *Butterworths Corp L Bulletin* 4, 6–7.

[172] Mason CJ, Brennan, Deane and Dawson JJ rejected the respondents' argument, that an alteration to the articles allowing expropriation will be *prima facie* valid unless the minority shareholder discharges the onus of proving either improper purpose or oppression, on the basis that such approach "tilts the balance too far in favour of commercial expediency and fails to attach sufficient weight to the proprietary nature of the share": see (1995) 69 ALJR 266, 272.

[173] See D DeMott, "Proprietary Norms in Corporate Law: An Essay on Reading *Gambotto* in the United States" in I M Ramsay (ed.), *Gambotto v. WCP Ltd.: Its Implications for Corporate Regulation* (Centre for Corporate Law and Securities Regulation, Melbourne, 1996) 90, 96.

[174] *Ibid.*, 97; V. Mitchell, "The US Approach Towards the Acquisition of Minority Shares: Have We Anything to Learn?" (1996) 14 *CSLJ* 283.

The High Court's adherence to property rules, under which the holder of entitlements is given veto rights, is in marked contrast to the greater reliance on liability rules in the United States, which allows enforced trade for an objectively determined price.[175] This divergence is a clear reflection of the different images of the shareholder underpinning each approach.[176]

Implicit in the High Court's characterisation of shareholder rights as proprietary in *Gambotto* is the view that shareholders' rights are predominant within the corporate structure and coextensive with the interests of the company itself. The majority judges took the view that advancing the interests of the company as a commercial entity was not a valid justification for the expropriation of minority shares. McHugh J, in contrast, thought that the realisation of tax savings was a "legitimate business objective", capable of sustaining expropriation, thereby recognising the interests of the corporation as an ongoing commercial enterprise.

There is a tension between the approach of the majority in *Gambotto* and that adopted in a number of other developing areas of corporate law, such as takeovers. Although Australian case law has traditionally taken the view that directors faced with a takeover must act for the benefit of the shareholders as a whole, rather than the corporation as a commercial entity,[177] several recent cases support a broader conception of the corporation's interests than simply the interests of its shareholders. In the takeover context, this has been welcomed by some on the basis that the old shareholder-centred model of the corporation is "a relic of a less complex age" and is "out of step with the world of business dealings, economics, and even industrial law".[178]

B Shareholder Consent as a Regulatory Device—The Shareholder as Cerberus

As discussed earlier, a number of statutory provisions use shareholder consent as a regulatory device, to screen conduct which would otherwise be prohibited. It is in this context that shareholders are treated as monitors in legitimating certain corporate conduct.

Corporate regulation lies across a broad spectrum. Duty-based controls, such as fiduciary duties imposed to constrain managerial discretion, are dependent upon judicial monitoring to ensure compliance.[179] As in other fields

---

[175] DeMott, n. 173 above, 97; G Calabresi and A D Melamed, "Property Rules, Liability Rules, and Inalienability: One View of the Cathedral" (1972) 85 *Harv L Rev* 1089, 1092.

[176] See, generally, D Burgman and P Cox, "Reappraising the Role of the Shareholder in the Modern Public Corporation: *Weinberger's* Procedural Approach to Fairness in Freezeouts" [1984] *Wis L Rev* 593, 624 ff.

[177] See, for example, *Ngurli Ltd.* v. *McCann* (1953) 90 CLR 425.

[178] S Corcoran, "Managers and Majorities in Takeover Regulation" in Walker and Fisse (eds.), n. 11 above, 759, 765–6.

[179] Parkinson, n. 90 above, 73.

of law, both "crystal" and "mud" rules (or rules and standards) are used as regulatory techniques.[180] Crystal rules are those with clear, sharp, determinate boundaries, directives which define *ex ante* whether conduct is or is not permissible and allow for little discretion in the decision-maker.[181] No such clarity exists with mud rules, or standards. Their hazy penumbra requires the *ex post* exercise of judicial discretion based upon an array of specific factual and contextual matters, as well as social values.[182] Standards are often perceived to promote substantive equality and fairness, as opposed to the formal equality under crystal rules.[183] In many situations, the distinguishing features of rules and standards are blurred, with regulation comprising hybrids of the two.

Corporate law has long struggled with the difficulty of using crystal rules to define and quarantine transactions which are clearly detrimental to the corporation from those which are commercially justified. The familiar uncertainty as to scope of the "financial assistance" prohibition is a good example of this difficulty.[184] The Jenkins Committee, for instance, while recognising that the open-ended language of the section gave rise to uncertainty and could possibly catch unobjectionable conduct, nonetheless recommended against a more crystalline formulation of the rule, stating that it would not be "wise to attempt any more precise formula for describing the sort of transaction which may be the means of giving financial assistance".[185] The reason for this is that the more determinate and certain is the rule, the more easily it may be evaded.[186] It is a feature of rules that they often suffer from over- or under-

---

[180] See C M Rose, "Crystals and Mud in Property Law" (1988) 40 *Stan L Rev* 577. See also D Kennedy, "Form and Substance in Private Law Adjudication" (1976) 89 *Harv L Rev* 1685, 1687–713; M Kelman, A *Guide to Critical Legal Studies* (Cambridge, Mass., Harvard Univeristy Press, 1987), Chap 1. In the corporate law context, see D DeMott, "Oppressed But Not Betrayed: A Comparative Assessment of Canadian Remedies for Minority Shareholders and Other Corporate Constituents" (1993) 56 *LCP* 181, 220–1; J F Williams, "The Fallacies of Contemporary Fraudulent Transfer Models as Applied to Intercorporate Guaranties: Fraudulent Transfer Law as a Fuzzy System" (1994) 15 *Cardozo L Rev* 1403, 1452 ff.

[181] According to Sullivan, "[r]ules embody a distrust for the decisionmaker they seek to constrain": see K M Sullivan, "Foreword: The Justices of Rules and Standards" (1992) 106 *Harv L Rev* 24, 64.

[182] Kennedy, n. 180 above, 1688.

[183] Williams, n. 180 above, 1454. For other relative merits and demerits of rules and standards, see Sullivan, n. 181 above, 62 ff; Kelman, n. 180 above, 40–5.

[184] See generally, R P Austin, "The 'Financial Assistance' Prohibition" in R P Austin and R Vann (eds.), *The Law of Public Company Finance* (Sydney, Law Book Co., 1986), Chap 8. See also D Harding, "Section 67 of the Companies Act—Present and Proposed Law" (1978) 10 *Comm L Assoc Bull* 1.

[185] *Report of the Company Law Committee* (HMSO, London, 1962, Cmnd 1749), para [180].

[186] See Sullivan, n. 181 above, 62–3; M Horwitz, "The Rule of Law: An Unqualified Human Good?" (1977) 86 *Yale LJ* 561, 566. On the other hand, the rules on a company giving financial assistance in connection with the acquisition of its shares are nowhere near as muddy as they might be. These transactions could be dealt with under normal fiduciary duty principles. Instead, the legislature has targeted financial assistance specifically, on the basis that such transactions are particularly prone to abuse.

inclusion, while standards side-step this problem by conferring greater discretion on the decision-maker.[187]

The use of shareholder consent as a regulatory device under Australian corporate law cuts an uneasy path through the twin poles of regulation by crystal and mud rules. The trigger for the introduction of the related party transaction provisions, for example, was the perception that broad fiduciary duties *per se* had been dismally inadequate as a constraint on managerial powers in the 1980s. By prohibiting certain types of conduct which are prone to abuse, subject however to consent by the general meeting, the related party transaction provisions cure the problem of over-inclusion under crystal rules, through the mechanism of shareholder consent. From this perspective, the shareholders can be seen as adopting a legislative function by defining more narrowly the conduct which is offensive. Viewed from the perspective of mud rules or standards, the shareholders may be regarded as exercising the role of decision-maker. Thus, the critical use of discretion based upon contextual and factual considerations to assess the transaction, which would in the case of standards reside in the court, shifts to the shareholders in general meeting. On either analysis, the shareholders' role as a screening device for questionable transactions is a significant one.

Although in recent times most attention has focused on shareholder consent under the related party transaction provisions, general meeting approval is used as a regulatory device in a number of other sections of the Corporations Law and the Stock Exchange Rules. In relation to the financial assistance prohibition, the technique was recommended by the Jenkins Committee in its 1962 Report as a way to fine-tune the scope of the prohibition;[188] however it was not introduced into the Australian provision until almost twenty years later.[189] The technique was also introduced in 1989 in conjunction with the reforms enabling companies to purchase their own shares under share buy-back schemes.[190]

Shareholder consent also has a powerful role as a monitoring device under the ASX Listing Rules. It applies in a number of specific circumstances, which could be subject to abuse: where the company issues more than 10 per cent of its capital within a twelve-month period;[191] issues capital otherwise than *pro rata* to its directors or their associates;[192] acquires or disposes of assets for

---

[187] Sullivan, n. 181 above, 58–9.

[188] *Report of the Company Law Committee*, n. 185 above, para [178]. The Jenkins Committee also recommended the filing of a statutory declaration of solvency by the directors.

[189] The shareholder consent provision was originally introduced as s 129(10) of the Companies Code and is now contained in s 205(10) of the Corporations Law. See generally Austin, n. 184 above, Chap 8.

[190] Part IV Division 3A Companies Code; now Part 2.4, Division 4B Corporations Law.

[191] See ASX Listing Rule 7.1.

[192] See ASX Listing Rule 10.11.

consideration in excess of 5 per cent of shareholder funds;[193] or sells its main undertaking.[194]

The related party transaction provisions therefore follow a tradition in Australia of utilising shareholder consent in a guardianship role. The basic structure of the provisions is as a follows. Part 3.2A enacts a broad prohibition against a public company or its child entity conferring a financial benefit on a related party of the public company.[195] The general prohibition is subject to a number of exceptions.[196] Additionally, infringing transactions which are not salvaged by any of the specific exceptions may be legitimised via approval by ordinary resolution of the general meeting.[197] As with an increasing number of shareholder consent provisions, judicial decisions and reform proposals, the approval must be given by disinterested members.[198]

The reliance on disinterested shareholders brings into focus a key difference between viewing shareholders as monitors and the image of shareholders as owners. If monitoring by shareholders is seen as an alternative form of corporate regulation, a requirement that the decision-maker be disinterested is of fundamental importance. If, however, a private model of the corporation is adopted, with the shareholders regarded as owners, this requirement becomes less relevant. The latter model accounts for a number of strongly majoritarian nineteenth-century decisions, such as *North-West Transportation Co. Ltd.* v. *Beatty*,[199] holding that since a share was personal property of the member, the right to vote could be exercised as a member pleased, even in the member's own interests.[200]

While the majority judges in *Gambotto* used the rhetoric of property entitlement for shareholders, they appeared to balk at the full implications of that model, leaving open the question whether interested shareholders could vote on a proposed amendment of articles to allow expropriation, if the expropriation were otherwise for a proper purpose.[201] On the High Court's own reasoning it would appear that, provided a proper purpose for the alteration

---

[193] See ASX Listing Rule 10.1.

[194] See ASX Listing Rule 11.2.

[195] Corporations Law, s 243H.

[196] See P F Hanrahan, "Transactions with Related Parties by Public Companies and Their 'Child Entities' Under Part 3.2A of the Corporations Law" (1994) 12 *CSLJ* 138, 150 ff.

[197] See Corporations Law, s 243Q (shareholder approval of the financial benefit itself); and s 243R (shareholder approval of a contract to give a financial benefit).

[198] Corporations Law, ss 243ZB and 243ZF. Independent shareholder approval is also required under various ASX Listing Rules (see, for example, Listing Rules 10.1 and 10.11) and is relevant in other contexts, such as schemes of arrangement and reductions of capital. See generally E Boros, "The Implications of *Gambotto* for Minority Shareholders" in Ramsay (ed.), n. 173 above, 82.

[199] (1887) 12 App Cas 589, where a defendant director was able to use his majority shareholding in general meeting to approve certain actions which he had taken as director.

[200] On the tension between this principle and the doctrine of fraud on the minority, see generally, F G Rixon, "Competing Interests and Conflicting Principles: An Examination of the Power of Alteration of Articles of Association" (1986) 49 *MLR* 446. See also MacIntosh, n. 15 above, 599 ff.

[201] *Gambotto* v. *WPC Ltd.* (1995) 69 ALJR 266, 272.

to the articles were established, majority shareholders could themselves, as holders of property rights, vote in their own self-interest.[202] Yet this conclusion would be out of step both with modern requirements of disinterested voting and with the High Court's own pro-minority shareholder stance in *Gambotto*.

The shift towards disinterested shareholder voting reflects another major development identifiable in contemporary corporate law—namely, the "proceduralisation" of corporate law. The courts have become increasingly reluctant to interfere with the substance and outcomes of corporate decision-making, but have shifted their focus to issues of fairness in the decision-making process itself.[203]

The extent to which shareholder consent provides a serious constraint on managerial decisions under the related party transaction provisions is unclear. The contours of a number of the exceptions to shareholder consent, such as the "reasonable remuneration" exception,[204] are vague and malleable, and it has been argued that the "arm's length terms" exception[205] offends the spirit of the Companies and Securities Advisory Committee's original proposal, in that it should be the *potential* for conflict in such situations which is offensive, whether or not the transaction is made on commercial terms.[206] It certainly appears odd that the shareholders' role, rather than being to discriminate between commercial and uncommercial transactions within the gamut of transactions which are vulnerable to abuse, should be restricted to approving those which are on their face uncommercial. Nonetheless, it may be that many of the prophylactic effects of the provisions are invisible, since we cannot know the extent to which the mere threat of a general meeting vote may deter management from proceeding with questionable transactions.

Irrespective of the scope of transactions subject to shareholder approval under Part 3.2A of the Corporations Law, the question remains whether the shareholders in general meeting are in this, and in the other instances where their consent is used as a legitimating device, able to fulfil that function, or whether, like Cerberus, they will be imperfect guardians at best.

C Institutional Investors as Players in the Corporate Governance Game— The Goodman Fielder Fracas and the Coles Myer Meleé

Under the most pervasive twentieth century visions of the shareholder, a monitoring role for shareholders would be paradoxical, if not absurd. Features of

---

[202] See Boros, n. 198 above.

[203] See F K Kubler, "Dual Loyalty of Labor Representatives" in Hopt and Teubner (eds.), n. 28 above, 429, 441–2.

[204] Corporations Law, s 243K.

[205] Corporations Law, s 243N.

[206] See Hanrahan, n. 196 above, 142–3, 152 ff; T Hadden, "The Regulation of Corporate Groups in Australia" (1992) 15 *UNSWLJ* 61, 75.

the corporate landscape regarded as inevitably fostering passivity were widely dispersed shareholdings (resulting in collective action difficulties),[207] free-rider problems,[208] centralised and strategically superior managerial power, the availability of the Wall Street Walk and the superior efficiency of the market for corporate control as a disciplinary mechanism.[209] On Easterbrook and Fischel's model of the rationally apathetic shareholder, the logical conclusion is that "none of the voters has the appropriate incentive at the margin to study the firm's affairs and vote intelligently".[210]

In the past, institutional investors were regarded as, if anything, more apathetic than widely dispersed natural shareholders, and treated as "short-term profligates",[211] a view echoed in some of the submissions to the Parliamentary Joint Committee on Corporations and Securities[212] inquiry into institutional investors in Australia. This disparaging image of institutional investors re-emerged in the Coles Myer affair, discussed below, when the then Prime Minister publicly attacked fund managers for shortsightedness in investment strategies.[213]

Such an image of shareholders and their relationship with the corporation makes reliance upon them, as effective corporate monitors, problematic to say the least. There is a tension between the assumption under collective action theory that a shareholder will only have the appropriate incentive to become adequately informed on proposals where the ultimate benefits outweigh the costs, and the fact that under, for example, the voting rules for shareholder approval of related party transactions those who stand to benefit from the proposal are prevented from voting.[214] If the traditional assumptions about shareholder passivity were correct, a guardianship role for shareholders would be largely ceremonial and ineffective as a regulatory tool.

---

[207] According to collective action theory, individual shareholders only initiate or oppose management where the ultimate benefits outweigh the costs of action. Since the ultimate benefits will be shared *pro rata* with other shareholders (enabling these to free-ride), the precondition of benefits outweighing costs is rarely satisfied. See, generally, E B Rock, "The Logic and (Uncertain) Significance of Institutional Shareholder Activism" (1991) 79 *Geo LJ* 445, 453–63.

[208] See Black, n. 5 above, 527–8.

[209] *Ibid.*, at 522.

[210] Easterbrook and Fischel, n. 133 above, 402.

[211] Buxbaum, n. 123 above, 28.

[212] Parliamentary Joint Committee on Corporations and Securities, Inquiry into the Role and Activities of Institutional Investors in Australia, Canberra, Nov. 1994. See, for example, the submission of the Australian Shareholders' Association, which blamed the lack of shareholder control over corporate management on institutional investors, "[t]he culprits . . . who have functioned as passive, short-term and self-interested investors who have abrogated their fiduciary responsibilities as trustees" (10).

[213] See D Shires, "PM blasts 'donkey' funds managers: The Coles Myer Affair", *Australian Financial Review*, 20 Oct. 1995, 14; B Toohey, "Labor's big business family", *Australian Financial Review*, 1 Mar. 1996, 25.

[214] C Hamilton, "A Touching Faith? Australian Regulatory Attitudes to Shareholder Democracy" (LLM research essay, 1993 (on file with the author)), 8.

The dominant assumptions about the role and conduct of shareholders have, however, been seriously questioned in recent times.[215] Institutional investors are taking greater interest in voting today, a matter which provides some hope that use of shareholder consent as a regulatory device may not be ineffectual. Voting of proxies has in the past been low for institutional investors, and there was often confusion as to whether the fund manager or trustee was empowered to exercise the relevant votes.[216] United States institutional investors are now required to cast their proxy votes on domestic shares and many are following suit as a matter of course on their international equity holdings. In Australia, Guideline 2 of the AIMA *Guide for Investment Managers and Corporations*[217] recommends that members "should vote on all material issues at all Australian company meetings where they have the voting authority and responsibility to do so". Guideline 3 recommends that AIMA members should have in place a clear written policy concerning the exercise of voting rights. These principles recognise that voting rights are a "valuable asset of the investor which should be managed with the same care and diligence as any other".[218] Another important development in the commercial arena in both Australia and the United States is the emergence of specialist proxy advisory services for institutional investors.

There has been a growing number of examples of institutional activism in Australia this decade.[219] The events in 1994 at Goodman Fielder and in 1995 at Coles Myer can be seen as watershed case studies in redefining the role of shareholders in corporate governance. The actions of the institutional investors in these companies exemplify the gap between commercial reality and traditional corporate theory. They also demonstrate some possible dangers of shareholders shifting from a role as monitor to one of full managerial partner.

The Goodman Fielder scenario, unlike some earlier instances of institutional investor activism which had been triggered by extreme circumstances,[220] arose as a result of continuing underperformance by the company, the market value of which had dropped more than 15 per cent to approximately $1.8 billion, as against a 35 per cent rise in the All Ordinaries Index.

---

[215] See, for example, Roe, n. 5 above; Black, n. 5 above.

[216] See S Griffin, "Institutional Investors in Australia: A Shareholder's Perspective", paper presented at the AIMG Conference on Corporate Governance and Australian Competitiveness: The Role of Institutional Investors, Sydney, Nov. 1993, 5.

[217] AIMA, *Corporate Governance: A Guide for Investment Managers and Corporations* (2nd edn., AIMA, July 1997).

[218] *Ibid.*, at 17.

[219] See, generally, J Hill, "Institutional Investors and Corporate Governance in Australia" in T Baums, R Buxbaum and K Hopt (eds.), *Institutional Investors and Corporate Governance* (Berlin, NY, de Gruyter, 1994), 583, 600 ff; G Stapledon, *Institutional Shareholders and Corporate Governance* (Oxford, Clarendon, 1996), 189 ff.

[220] Such an example was institutional investor pressure resulting in the removal of half the board and the managing director of Bennett & Fisher Ltd. in 1991 and 1992. See "MD gets the boot in big Bennett clean-out", *The Age*, 9 May 1992, 25.

Dissatisfied with the company's performance, Goodman's major institutional investors, AMP Society, Bankers Trust Australia, the NSW State Authorities Superannuation Board, together with Doug Shears' Agrifoods group, holding around 18 per cent of the company's shares, requisitioned a general meeting in October 1994 to remove certain members of the board and reconstitute it.[221]

An acrimonious proxy battle[222] was ultimately avoided when an agreement was reached, with the board yielding to the institutions' pressure. The events at Goodman Fielder, however, are fascinating in that they showed the fine line which can exist between monitoring through the re-assertion of standard shareholder rights (in this case appointment and removal of non-executive directors) and actual interference by shareholders in the management of a public corporation under a managerial partnership model. The institutions had been at pains to avoid the appearance of involvement in managerial matters, providing no blueprint of any particular strategy to lift the company's fortunes. In this they were strongly criticised by Goodman and by other shareholders as being "disruptive without offering any solutions".[223] In a last-minute turn of events, however, it was reported in the financial press that the institutions demanded that their three nominee directors (replacing resigning incumbents) should be granted a collective power of veto over all major board decisions.[224] This demand, branded by the Goodman board as "unworkable and illegal",[225] would have unambiguously shifted the institutional investors into a role as managerial partners, consistent with the re-emergence of an ownership model of the corporation. The demand was, however, swiftly retracted after AMP and Bankers Trust Australia threatened to withdraw their support for the other dissidents unless the power of veto was jettisoned.[226]

The events at Coles Myer demonstrated that institutional investor activism is not the fail-safe corporate panacea that some commentators would suggest; even when institutional investors become involved in issues of corporate governance, their victories can sometimes be Pyrrhic at best. In 1995, the same institutions who were responsible for the boardroom changes at Goodman Fielder[227] attempted to remove a number of directors from the Coles Myer

---

[221] See "Ganging Up On Goodman", *The Bulletin*, 6 Sept. 1994, 71–3.

[222] See "Goodman: the final showdown", *Australian Financial Review*, 17 Aug. 1994, 1; "Are institutions prepared to fight?", *Sydney Morning Herald*, 6 Sept. 1994, 47, describing as the critical factor in the likelihood of a compromise being reached, "whether any or all of the institutions have become uncomfortable with the option of a full frontal proxy attack . . .".

[223] N. 221 above, 72. This echoes the concern in academic literature as to "the competence of institutional investors as corporate decisionmakers": see Fisch, n. 153 above, 1036–7.

[224] See "It's high noon for agreement at Goodman" and "What the dissidents really want", *Sydney Morning Herald*, 7 Sept. 1994, 41.

[225] "It's high noon for agreement at Goodman", *Sydney Morning Herald*, 7 Sept. 1994, 41.

[226] "Goodman resolution like a Cambodian peace treaty", *Sydney Morning Herald*, 8 Sept. 1994, 33.

[227] Bankers Trust Australia Ltd., AMP, and the State Superannuation Board of NSW (now Exicom Ltd.) held a combined shareholding of 15% in Coles Myer and were supported by a number of smaller institutional shareholders.

board, following revelations in the financial press concerning the controversial Yannon transaction,[228] which had effectively resulted in an \$18 million loss for Coles Myer. They also attempted to reform corporate governance practices in the company.[229]

Coles Myer epitomised the type of situation where institutional investor monitoring can be most beneficial,[230] since the Yannon transaction raised conflict of interest and related party transaction issues with the outside commercial interests of the Coles Myer chairman, Mr Solomon Lew. The transaction resulted in loss to Coles Myer as a commercial entity, indirectly harming all stakeholders, not simply its shareholders.

Nonetheless, the ultimate outcome in Coles Myer was less than decisive and fell far short of the institutions' original goals. Although one financial commentator described the actions of the institutions as "a victory for the institutions, for good corporate governance and for Australia's reputation in the international capital markets",[231] the board-level changes accepted by the institutions at the time were a clear compromise position, accepted to avoid a major public struggle at the annual general meeting.[232] A number of institutions later chose to exercise the option of "exit" over "voice", which substantially weakened the continuing influence of the institutional bloc.[233]

Coles Myer subsequently recovered \$12 million of Coles Myer's losses, via a settlement with a number of parties including Solomon Lew. However, twelve months after the original boardroom coup there remained widespread dissatisfaction among the company's shareholders. The extant institutional

---

[228] The exact circumstances behind the Yannon transaction became the subject of a continuing ASC investigation (see T Allard, "Yannon probe going nicely", *Sydney Morning Herald*, 21 Apr. 1997, 37). Briefly, the transaction was as follows. In 1990, Coles Myer granted a guarantee covering a loss by Yannon Pty Ltd. Yannon had been acquired by CS First Boston for the purpose of acquiring \$25 million of convertible preference shares in Premier Investments, a company controlled by Coles Myer shareholder and chairman, Solomon Lew. The preference shares were issued by Premier as part of a refinancing following Premier's \$450 million purchase of Coles Myer shares. Coles Myer subsequently incurred an \$18 million loss under the guarantee. The Yannon transaction came to light following the dismissal of Coles Myer's finance director, Phillip Bowman, who raised questions about the propriety of the transaction. See generally B Frith, "Coles investors should move to reinstate Bowman", *The Australian*, 13 Sept. 1995; J Hurst, "Sacked director wins \$1.7m deal", *Australian Financial Review*, 30 May 1996, 26.

[229] See, for example, G Korporaal, "Coles must have independent chair", *Sydney Morning Herald*, 11 Sept. 1995, 21.

[230] An international adviser on pension funds stated at the time that Coles Myer was a classic example of how "pension fund capitalism" operates: see B Dunstan, "Coles Myer fight won't be the last", *Australian Financial Review*, 2 Nov. 1995, 8.

[231] B Frith, "Coles compromise is still a victory for the institutions", *The Australian*, 20 Oct. 1995, 36.

[232] Under this compromise, Solomon Lew was removed from the position of chairman, but was permitted to remain on the board. Lew was replaced by a non-executive independent chairman, Nobby Clark. 3 other board members, 2 of whom were closely aligned with Lew, resigned. An additional 5 non-executive directors were appointed increasing the number of board members from 10 to 13, and giving independent directors 6 out of 13 board seats: see n. 231 above.

[233] By late 1996, BT Australia had sold its stake in Coles Myer, while AMP had reduced its holding to around 2% and Axiom to around 1.33%: see J Hurst, "Big Coles investors back vote against Lew", *Australian Financial Review*, 13 Nov. 1996, 21.

investors were dissatisfied with the new board's handling of the Yannon trans-action and with the level of disclosure of the Yannon settlement.[234] Small shareholders were frustrated by continuing poor earnings performance by the company, its worst in ten years, coupled with a $1 million increase to the chief executive's remuneration package.[235] There was also the perception that, as a result of the emergence of a new power alliance within the firm,[236] the inde-pendent non-executive directors had become powerless and vulnerable to removal. As a result of a deal struck with major shareholders,[237] Solomon Lew successfully stood for re-election to the board at the 1996 annual general meet-ing,[238] withstanding a report of Independent Shareholder Services advising shareholders to vote against him and clear discord between different groups of shareholders.[239] Mr Lew's position and influence in Coles Myer have proved to be surprisingly resilient in the face of institutional investor activism.[240]

The events at Goodman Fielder and Coles Myer show that a greater par-ticipatory and monitoring role for institutional shareholders in corporate gov-ernance is not only feasible, but has the potential to enhance corporate accountability and to legitimate managerial decisions.[241] Nonetheless, these case studies also demonstrate that there are possible dangers in this and that institutional monitoring cannot be a complete solution to the problem of man-agerial accountability. One problem is the blurred boundary between share-holder monitoring and interference with managerial functions. Goodman Fielder suggests that a vision of institutions as reasserting ownership rights, and so bridging the gulf between ownership and control, is misguided as a model on which to base these new developments.[242] Full partnership rights in management would unjustifiably privilege the sectional interests of share-holders over other groups "enmeshed with corporate enterprise".[243]

It must also be remembered that as well as the rise of institutional investment, there has recently been a return to the market by many small

---

[234] Hurst, n. 233 above.

[235] Chanticleer, "Big boys show how it's done", *Australian Financial Review*, 20 Nov. 1996, 52; J Hurst, "Coles makes Bartels the $2.8m man", *Australian Financial Review*, 29 Oct. 1996, 1. Mr Bartels received a further 200,000 shares in Coles Myer worth $1 million as part of his exit package from the company at the end of 1996. See J Hurst, "Bartels received $1m shares", *Australian Financial Review*, 3 Feb. 1997, 19.

[236] This boardroom alliance was described by one financial commentator as "the Brierley-Myer-Lew Troika": see Chanticleer, n. 235 above.

[237] J Hurst, "Lew survives stormy Coles AGM", *Australian Financial Review*, 20 Nov. 1996, 1.

[238] R Stretton, "How Solly survived", *Australian Financial Review*, 24 Oct. 1996, 20; Hurst, n. 237 above.

[239] M Maiden, "Vic ASA members rebel over Lew", *Sydney Morning Herald*, 7 Nov. 1996, 29.

[240] See Stretton, n. 238 above; I Ries, "Lew may be set for a comeback", *Australian Financial Review*, 28 Feb. 1997, 80.

[241] See, for example, R Talbot-Stern, "The shortcut to better boards: Corporate governance—Keeping business honest", *Australian Financial Review*, 2 Jan. 1996, 13.

[242] Pound, n. 63 above; Pound, n. 75 above; Buxbaum, n. 123 above, 28.

[243] R Buxbaum, "Corporate Legitimacy, Economic Theory, and Legal Doctrine" (1984) 45 *Ohio St LJ* 515. See also Teubner, n. 141 above, stressing corporate autonomy to the exclusion of sectional interests within the corporation.

private investors, as a result of a series of high-profile floats.[244] It cannot be assumed that the institutional investors' interests will always be aligned with those of smaller shareholders.[245] Indeed, early in the Coles Myer saga, there was speculation that the institutional investors might not wish to enter the fray, given their own stake in the management rights to Coles Myer's $650m Super Fund.[246] The greater the role given to shareholders in corporate decision-making, the more likely it will be that doctrines such as oppression, traditionally confined to the close corporation context, will appear in the arena of public corporations where majority and minority interests are in conflict.[247]

IV CONCLUSION

A hundred years is a long time in corporate law. While the closely-held company of Mr Salomon still exists, the other end of the corporate spectrum has altered radically. The rise of institutional investors has displaced many of the assumptions about shareholders and the nature of corporate law itself. Whereas in the past, the corporate veil concealed natural persons, today it conceals an institutional veil, beyond which, in the case of superannuation funds, lies the majority of a country's working population. Indeed, the advent of the Superannuation Guarantee Charge has placed Australia firmly within Robert Clark's fourth and final stage of financial capitalism, with the government appropriating the savings-decision function itself.[248] This is a development that challenges even the "private" and "voluntary" characterisation of corporate investment.

It is not surprising that simple models of the past, such as the "shareholder as owner", are inadequate today. We need to re-examine the legitimate role of the shareholder, in the light of today's complex commercial world, to prevent a disjunction between law and reality.[249]

---

[244] Australian Stock Exchange, *1997 Australian Shareownership Survey*, 2–9.

[245] See generally Hill, n. 219 above, 602–3.

[246] E Mychasuk, "Coles super gags critics", *Sydney Morning Herald*, 23 Sept. 1995, 31.

[247] For recent examples of splits in shareholding ranks, see the rejection of executive options by small shareholders of St George Bank, despite the fact that the Australian Shareholders' Association (ASA) had approved the scheme as one of the fairest analysed. By contrast, option schemes for ANZ Banking Corporation and Westpac Banking Corporation, which were opposed by the ASA, were successfully proposed by the respective boards due to institutional investor support. See T Allard, "St George options blocked", *Sydney Morning Herald*, 31 Jan. 1996, 25. Ructions at a recent ANI annual general meeting also reflected major differences between small shareholders and institutional investors: see L Knight, "A big hand trumped by the big band", *Sydney Morning Herald*, 22 Oct. 1996, 25.

[248] Clark, n. 6 above, 565–6.

[249] "A law cannot afford, at least in the long run . . . to live with a contradiction between law and reality. This would undermine the credibility of the legal order as a whole": see K Hopt, in R Buxbaum, G Hertig, A Hirsch and K Hopt (eds.), *European Business Law: Legal and Economic Analyses on Integration and Harmonization* (Berlin, NY, de Gruyter, 1991), 243.

11

Commentary on Hill

ROBERT P AUSTIN*

For readers who are fascinated by corporate law for its own sake, as a set of principles about proper business organisation, Professor Hill's essay is bound to be intensely interesting. Drawing on extensive legal scholarship, she reviews the broad landscape of academic thinking about corporate governance and perceives some important contours and trails, as well as some rocky outcrops and some dead ends. She has carried out an ordnance survey of the law of corporate governance, providing us with an illuminating map.

Now that we have a map, the question is, how do we use it? Professor Hill identifies seven "visions" of the shareholder. These are paradigms of the shareholder/manager relationship, which assist us to understand the complete truth. As she says, her images of the role of the shareholder overlap and recur in different forms, giving rise to a richer and more complex picture of the shareholder's relationship with the company than that which emerged from nineteenth-century cases such as *Salomon* v. *A Salomon & Co. Ltd.*[1]

I propose to offer a few very brief observations about each of her seven visions, designed to show how they offer useful perspectives on the shareholder/manager relationship, and how these perspectives might be balanced or qualified to permit a complete account to emerge.

I THE SHAREHOLDER AS OWNER/PRINCIPAL

The vision of shareholders as the "owners" of the corporate enterprise has been qualified and refined since its articulation in cases such as *Isle of Wight Railway Co.* v. *Tahourdin*.[2] The notion that directors are merely the agents of shareholders has been abandoned. But the idea that the role of directors is to carry out the will and implement the interests of shareholders remains very potent. After all, shareholders are the contributors of the company's risk capital, and this fundamental fact affects the content of the duties of directors and management.

---

* Partner, Minter Ellison, Sydney.
[1] [1897] AC 22.
[2] (1884) 25 Ch D 320.

The decision of the High Court of Australia in *Gambotto* v. *WCP Ltd.*[3] is about the shareholder's "ownership" in a rather different sense, and may not in the end add much to the analysis of the shareholder as "owner". One could say consistently that shareholders are the "owners" of the corporate enterprise but their shares may be expropriated by majority decision; and, equally consistently, shareholders do not own the corporate enterprise but their shares are nevertheless property which cannot be expropriated by a mere majority decision. It may be better to see *Gambotto's* case as an example of a different policy conflict in corporate law, namely the conflict between individual rights and the interests of the majority.

II THE SHAREHOLDER AS BENEFICIARY

While the notion of shareholders as "beneficiaries"for whom managerial powers are held in trust is not supported by modern corporate law, the law nevertheless subjects directors and managers to fiduciary duties which, in typical contexts, can be every bit as strict as the trustee's duty. Consider, for example, the relative severity of the outcomes in the Australian cases *Advance Bank of Australia Ltd.* v. *FAI Insurances Ltd.*[4] and *Paul A Davies (Aust). Pty. Ltd.* v. *Davies.*[5]

III THE SHAREHOLDER AS BYSTANDER

Professor Hill points to some evidence that the "managerialist paradigm" of the large corporation may be retreating, and it may therefore no longer be appropriate to treat shareholders merely as bystanders. However, the proposition articulated in Australia in *NRMA Ltd.* v. *Parker,*[6] that shareholders in general meeting do not have the power to make managerial decisions—or even to express, formally, their views on management matters, remains an important, enduring and central proposition of corporate governance. There is a very good reason for it—how could it be sensible to regard the shareholders of a large corporation as equipped to take management decisions, given the confidentiality and complexity of modern business? The inability of shareholders to participate in management reinforces the view that managers should be subject to trustee-like duties in the exercise of their powers. This is the balance which the modern law seeks to achieve.

---

[3] (1995) 69 ALJR 266.
[4] (1987) 9 NSWLR 464.
[5] (1983) 8 ACLR 1.
[6] (1986) 11 ACLR 1.

IV SHAREHOLDERS AS PARTICIPANTS IN A POLITICAL ENTITY

Two basic propositions are crystal clear:

(a) at least in Australia, corporate management practice is in fact about as far away from the paradigm of participatory democracy as one could imagine; but

(b) the statutory power of shareholders to dismiss directors by ordinary resolution is of absolutely critical importance to the shareholder-director relationship in public companies.

Beyond this, the government analogy is not particularly illuminating. In legal terms, the key question is whether directors and managers owe duties directly or indirectly to non-shareholder stakeholders. If the corporation is a political entity, a "mini-democracy", then the answer to the question is obvious, and the problem then becomes one of finding mechanisms to balance the demands of stakeholders to whom inevitably inconsistent duties will be owed. So far the law, in Australia at any rate, has avoided this chaotic situation by denying the major premise of the argument, refusing to accept the analogy between corporate and political structures.

V THE SHAREHOLDER AS INVESTOR

What Professor Hill calls the contractual theory has the same sort of artificiality as Rousseau's social contract. But the corporate contractual theory has amazing explanatory power. It focuses attention on wealth maximisation and assesses corporate regulation by reference to its efficiency in contributing to the reduction of agency costs and hence to the maximisation of wealth. Some very important specific insights flow from the overall approach. Thus, corporate contractual theory recognises the fundamental importance of market forces and of the efficient operation of markets, provided that there is access to material information at an operational (if not necessarily at a regulatory) level. The ideas of rational apathy and the "Wall Street Walk", and of the market for corporate control as a constraint upon managers, are also important and valuable ideas.

We need to identify and preserve the insights of which these are just a few examples, while fitting them into a broader framework which will allow other criteria of fairness to be relevant to legal and regulatory policy. We must be careful not to take the notion of short-form bargaining between independent resource holders too uncritically or too far. It follows that there is no universal answer to proposals for the enhancement of shareholder participatory rights. Everything depends on the fairness of the proposal in specific circumstances.

VI THE SHAREHOLDER AS CERBERUS

The notion of the shareholder as guardian or monitor of managerial decision-making is deeply problematic. It implies that shareholders are able to monitor or review management decisions effectively. The assumption that this is so has led to a trend in Australian corporate regulation which Professor Hill properly identifies as an important one—namely, the trend to use "disinterested" shareholder consent, informed by an "independent" expert's report, as a central regulatory device.

What is the justification for referring management decisions to shareholders, or giving them the opportunity of review? As a group, shareholders cannot negotiate; they cannot keep secrets; they cannot fully understand; and they can only say "yes" or "no", without explication. The growing trend in Australia to use independent experts' reports to overcome some of the deficiencies of shareholder decision-making tends to shift effective decision-making from managers to a necessarily less expert team. However much proficiency the independent experts may have in business and finance generally, it is most unlikely that, in the course of a three- or four-week engagement, they could become as expert in the company's affairs as the company's own management team. Added to this is the problem that in a relatively small economy with a limited number of players, the notion of "independence" is a highly diluted one.

Coupled with the growing use of independent experts' reports is a growing tendency to exclude groups of shareholders from the vote on issues in which they are thought to be interested. One understands completely that directors and managers should be excluded from voting and otherwise influencing outcomes where they have a material personal interest in the matter for decision. They occupy a fiduciary position. Shareholders, in contrast, occupy their position because they have invested risk capital in the company, and the larger the shareholding the larger the investment. Their investment means that they necessarily have an "interest" in the proper management of the company. To exclude them from voting because of that interest would be preposterous. Voting exclusion is justified, if at all, only where there is a real risk that a shareholder will use voting power to extract unfair advantages for itself or its associates.

In the end, problems about independent experts' reports and voting exclusion demonstrate the unsatisfactoriness of referring management decisions to shareholders. Referring management matters to shareholders should be used by regulators and companies themselves only as a recourse of last resort.

VII THE INSTITUTIONAL SHAREHOLDER AS MANAGERIAL PARTNER

As to the "collectivisation" of institutional shareholder and management interests, I suspect that Australian institutions would recoil in horror at any idea that they should become partners with management in the control of corporations. While they are more or less willing to express their opinions on the management of Australian companies, the institutions by and large respect the principle that management is the responsibility of the corporation's managers.

However, there must be effective safety valves to deal with situations where it appears that management is failing. The examples of institutional activism which Professor Hill identifies are cases where, in the judgement of some institutional investors, they had no practical option but to act positively in order to resolve a crisis and restore value to their own and other shareholders' investments. There is room for debate as to whether those judgements were correct, though in fairness the debate should include an assessment of the subsequent management and share price performance of the companies concerned.

VIII CONCLUSION

All in all, Professor Hill's "visions of the role of shareholder" are insightful and useful components in thinking about modern corporate law. In some respects they evoke the work of J K Galbraith and Robert Clark. Professor Clark, for example, has identified four stages of capitalism, painting a picture of economies moving from earlier into later stages of capitalism in which the connection between investors and their money is more and more remote.[7] But Professor Hill's work is different in an important respect: her work is not to be taken as a "dynamic" analysis of the movement of economies or investment forces towards new patterns which inevitably require new regulatory responses. The trends which she identifies—for example, towards "disinterested" shareholder consent and the "collectivisation" of institutional shareholder and management interests—could be reversed at any moment.

The significance of Professor Hill's seven visions is, rather, that they give us a framework for identifying and accounting for many of the most important movements in the law and practice of corporate governance. The correct policy solutions will depend, nevertheless, on a detailed analysis in which all of the overlapping visions are appropriately brought into focus.

[7] "The Four Stages of Capitalism: Reflections on Investment Management Treatises" (1981) 94 *Harv L Rev* 561.

12

Models of Corporate Regulation: the Mandatory/Enabling Debate

IAN M RAMSAY*

I INTRODUCTION

Few corporate law judgments would be worthy of a major conference one hundred years after they are handed down. Yet the decision of the House of Lords in *Salomon* v. *Salomon & Co. Ltd.*[1] continues to generate much discussion. As noted in *Ford's Principles of Corporations Law*, a later judgment referred to the decision in *Salomon* as constituting "the foundation of our modern company" while one commentator refers to the decision as "calamitous".[2]

The decision in *Salomon* remains important today because a number of the matters considered by their Lordships are still being debated. For example, when is it appropriate to grant limited liability to an organisation? This was fundamental to the decision in *Salomon*, yet remains important today when we consider recent debates concerning whether or not certain professions such as solicitors and accountants should be able to incorporate and thereby gain the benefits of limited liability. Is it appropriate to grant limited liability to a company which, although having more than one shareholder, may in fact reasonably be described as a "one person" company because of the dominance of one particular shareholder? Again, this was fundamental to the decision in *Salomon* and we finally saw this debate resolved in Australia in late 1995 with the enactment of the First Corporate Law Simplification Act, which allows a proprietary company to be formed with only one shareholder.

What is the appropriate balance between protecting shareholders of a company by granting them limited liability and protecting unsecured creditors who will bear additional risk where shareholders have limited liability? In

---

* Harold Ford Professor of Commercial Law and Director of the Centre for Corporate Law and Securities Regulation, Faculty of Law, The University of Melbourne.

[1] [1897] AC 22.

[2] H A J Ford, R P Austin and I M Ramsay, *Ford's Principles of Corporations Law* (8th edn., Sydney, Butterworths, 1997), para 4.150, citing *MacLaine Watson and Co. Ltd.* v. *Department of Trade and Industry* [1988] 3 WLR 1033, 1098 (*per* Kerr LJ), and O Kahn-Freund, "Some Reflections on Company Law Reform" (1944) 7 *MLR* 54.

Salomon it was the unsecured creditors represented by the liquidator of Salomon & Co. Ltd. who lost. This issue remains central to a number of significant corporate law debates when we consider statutory provisions of the Australian Corporations Law which impose liability on the directors of a company which engages in insolvent trading and also the holding company of such a company.[3] These statutory provisions have as their objective the protection of unsecured creditors.

There is a further issue arising from the decision in *Salomon*. To what extent should corporate regulation be essentially mandatory or enabling? By enabling regulation I mean regulation that has as its objective the promotion of private agreements between participants in companies on the basis that they are typically in a better position to understand and contract for their own needs rather than the government. How did this issue arise in *Salomon*? The English Companies Act 1862 allowed companies to be incorporated with seven shareholders. The Act specifically granted shareholders limited liability. Aron Salomon had a company duly incorporated in accordance with the Act on 28 July 1892.[4] He held 20,001 shares in the company and his wife, daughter and four sons each held one share.

Once there was formal compliance with these provisions allowing for incorporation, was this sufficient to obtain limited liability? A negative reply was given by the Court of Appeal where the judges stated that more than formal compliance with the statutory provisions was required.[5] Lindley LJ stated that "the incorporation of the company cannot be disputed".[6] However, he, along with the other judges of the Court of Appeal, did not believe that the legislature intended to give "one person" companies limited liability.[7]

> "Although in the present case there were, and are, seven members, yet it is manifest that six of them are members simply in order to enable the seventh himself to carry on business with limited liability. . . .
>
> The company must, therefore, be regarded as a corporation, but as a corporation created for an illegitimate purpose. . . .
>
> If the legislature thinks it right to extend the principle of limited liability to sole traders it will no doubt do so, with such safeguards, if any, as it may think necessary. But until the law is changed such attempts as these ought to be defeated whenever they are brought to light. They do infinite mischief; they bring into disrepute one of the most useful statutes of modern times, by perverting its legitimate use, and making it an instrument for cheating honest creditors."

Even stronger language was used by Lopes LJ:[8]

---

[3] Corporations Law, ss 588G and 588V.

[4] For detailed background information about Aron Salomon and the *Salomon* litigation, see G R Rubin, "Aron Salomon and his Circle" in J Adams (ed.), *Essays for Clive Schmitthoff* (Abingdon, Professional Books, 1983), 99.

[5] *Broderip* v. *Salomon* [1895] 2 Ch 323.

[6] *Ibid.*, at 337.

[7] *Ibid.*, at 337 and 339.

[8] *Ibid.*, at 341.

"It would be lamentable if a scheme like this could not be defeated. If we were to permit it to succeed, we should be authorising a perversion of the Joint Stock Companies Acts. . . . It never was intended that the company to be constituted should consist of one substantial person and six mere dummies, the nominees of that person, without any real interest in the company. . . . To legalize such a transaction would be a scandal."

Lopes LJ stated that the Companies Act required the incorporation of companies by "seven independent *bona fide* members".[9] Kay LJ stated that the Act required shareholders who were "*bona fide* associated for the purpose of trade".[10] It can be seen that the Court of Appeal put in place additional mandatory requirements concerning the incorporation of companies.[11] Yet these additional requirements, going to the motivations and intentions of those who incorporate companies, necessitate difficult, if not impossible, enquiries.

As we know, the decision of the Court of Appeal was overturned by the House of Lords. Lord Halsbury stated:[12]

"The statute enacts nothing as to the extent or degree of interest which may be held by each of the seven [shareholders], or as to the proportion of interest or influence possessed by one or the majority of the shareholders over the others. One share is enough. Still less is it possible to contend that the motive of becoming shareholders or of making them shareholders is a field of inquiry which the statute itself recognizes as legitimate."

Lord Herschell stated:[13]

"If, then, in the present case all the requirements of the statute were complied with, and a company was effectually constituted, and this is the hypothesis of the judgment appealed from, what warrant is there for saying that what was done was contrary to the true intent and meaning of the Companies Act?"

In the remainder of this essay, I examine in greater detail issues relevant to the debate on whether corporate regulation should be mandatory or enabling. In Part II I look more closely at mandatory and enabling systems of

---

[9] *Ibid.*, at 341.

[10] *Ibid.*, at 345.

[11] It is interesting to consider how this argument continues to resonate today. In 1993 a judge of the Commercial Division of the New South Wales Supreme Court suggested that limited liability should be restricted to companies which have, as their purpose, legitimate trading and which have a sufficient degree of risk associated with them so as to justify being granted limited liability:

"Perhaps there ought to be two classes of companies. The risk-takers, who really need limited liability, and those that carry on ordinary trading activities and who should not require or receive the protection of limited liability. . . . Does limited liability serve a socially and economically useful purpose for 90% of incorporated companies? Should it not be restricted to public companies and such others as may be able to convince the regulatory authorities that they require that privilege for the purpose of their trade?"

A Rogers, "Reforming the Law Relating to Limited Liability" (1993) 3 *Aust J of Corp L* 136, 140.

[12] *Salomon* v. *A Salomon & Co. Ltd.* [1897] AC 22, 30.

[13] *Ibid.*, at 46.

regulation. In Part III I provide some examples, drawn from Australian corporate regulation, of mandatory rules which have had high costs associated with them. In Part IV I discuss mandatory corporate disclosure rules as a case study of the mandatory/enabling debate. In Part V I return to a key theme evident in *Salomon*—limited liability. Should we promote and facilitate limited liability or strictly regulate the circumstances where limited liability should be permitted? Finally, in Part VI I turn to examine the implications of two significant recent developments (the growth of institutional investors and electronic commerce) for the mandatory/enabling debate.

II CORPORATE REGULATION: THE MANDATORY/ENABLING DEBATE

This section has three objectives. First, I make some preliminary observations regarding regulation and identify some of the more important justifications which have been advanced for regulation. Secondly, I consider and evaluate various arguments relevant to the mandatory/enabling corporate regulation debate. Finally, I consider directors' liability in the United States as an example of enabling corporate law rules.

A Introductory Observations on Regulation

Regulation has been defined as the law which implements a system where the State seeks to direct or encourage behaviour which it is assumed would not occur without such intervention.[14] The objective is to correct perceived deficiencies in meeting collective or public interest goals.[15] As part of exploring the dimensions of regulation, Ogus identifies two general systems of economic organisation. The first, which he terms the market system, is where individuals and groups are generally left free to pursue their own goals subject to only certain basic restraints. Under this system or model, the law has a primarily enabling or facilitative function, in the sense that it offers certain rules which may be adopted by parties or displaced by agreement by parties if they are found to be inappropriate. Individuals play a prominent role in enforcing rights under this system. Ogus contrasts the market system with what he terms the collectivist system or model, where regulation is used by the State to correct perceived deficiencies in the market system. Regulation under the collectivist system has a strong mandatory or directive function and the State plays a prominent role in enforcing obligations which cannot be displaced by private agreement between parties.[16]

---

[14] A I Ogus, *Regulation: Legal Form and Economic Theory* (Oxford, Clarendon, 1994), 1–2.

[15] *Ibid.*

[16] *Ibid.* Ogus notes that the two systems he presents are, to some degree, oversimplified, in that the market system cannot be identified exclusively with private and facilitative law, and regulation in the collectivist system is not always mandatory and enforced by the State (3).

B Justifications for Regulation

Perhaps the most significant justification for regulation is market failure. This is particularly important when we consider justifications for corporate regulation. Much of our existing corporate regulation appears to be premised on the assumption that the market has failed to produce satisfactory outcomes. Two recent amendments of the Australian Corporations Law provide evidence of this. First, what is known as Part 3.2A of the Corporations Law, which regulates financial benefits between public companies and their related parties, is based on an assumption that the market has not adequately protected shareholders in such companies. It is stated in the Report of the Companies and Securities Advisory Committee, upon which the government reforms were based:[17]

"Following the corporate collapses of the 1980s, it has become evident that some corporate controllers abused their positions of trust by arranging for the shifting of assets around and away from companies and corporate groups, and into their own hands. They achieved this by various means, including remuneration payments, asset transfers or loan arrangements, on terms highly advantageous to themselves but to the detriment of these companies. In other instances, substantial inter-corporate loans were entered into with the apparent purpose or effect of disguising the true financial position of individual companies within a group. This was made easier by the lack of any general statutory requirement that shareholders either consent to, or be informed of, these transactions. These abuses generally involved significant losses of corporate funds, with adverse effects on investor and creditor returns and confidence. They also brought into question the integrity of Australian financial markets, with detrimental consequences for the national economy."

An even clearer use of the argument of market failure to justify corporate regulation is evident in the reforms to the Corporations Law that introduced a statutory regime of continuous disclosure. Once again, a Report of the Companies and Securities Advisory Committee formed the basis of the legislative reforms. In this Report, the Committee stated that:[18]

"A statutory-based system of continuous disclosure will promote investor confidence in the integrity of Australian capital markets and . . . will overcome the inability of general market forces to guarantee adequate and timely disclosure by disclosing entities."

There are justifications for regulation other than market failure. Francis lists several of these.[19] They include:

---

[17] Companies and Securities Advisory Committee, *Report on Reform of the Law Governing Corporate Financial Transactions* (Sydney, 1991), 1.

[18] Companies and Securities Advisory Committee, *Report on an Enhanced Statutory Disclosure System* (Sydney, 1991), 6–7.

[19] J Francis, *The Politics of Regulation: A Comparative Perspective* (Oxford, Clarendon, 1993). See also Ogus, n. 14 above, Chaps 2 and 3.

(a) *reducing risks*. This can include, for example, regulation of tobacco advertising, but may also be used as a justification for mandatory corporate disclosure rules.

(b) *fairness and justice*. This may be used, for example, as a justification for legislation regulating anti-competitive conduct. Indeed, Francis notes how much legislation has in its title the word "fair" such as fair trading legislation and fair employment legislation.

(c) *defining boundaries*. Regulation may be justified on the ground that it sets reasonable limits between prohibiting an activity and leaving it unfettered. According to Francis:[20]

> "by choosing regulation over prohibition, the state can reduce the risks associated with ill-monitored practices and secure the co-operation of many more members of the community in allowing the practice within generally accepted limits."

(d) *maintaining equilibrium*. Regulation is seen as a means of establishing stability and confidence. Francis states:[21]

> "confidence borne of equilibrium is the working assumption of much financial regulation. The cycles of panics characteristic of financial markets in the nineteenth and certainly through the first third of the twentieth century contributed to the successful demands for state regulation of stock markets and financial institutions to institutionalize stability over time."

C Corporate Regulation

An important part of corporate regulation is corporate law. What is the role of corporate law? At one level, the objective of corporate law is to provide a set of rules which "encourage profit-maximising business decisions, provide professional managers with adequate discretion and authority, and protect shareholders (and to some extent creditors) against opportunism by managers and other corporate insiders".[22] However, corporate law is also concerned with establishing rights among participants in companies. At the same time, it allocates among those participants the risk which is an inevitable part of conducting business.

(i) Definitions of Mandatory and Enabling Rules

A fundamental question is whether these functions or goals of corporate law are best achieved with a system of corporate regulation which is mostly enabling in nature, or mostly mandatory in nature. What do we mean by these

---

[20] Francis, n. 19 above, 20.
[21] *Ibid*.
[22] B Black and R Kraakman, "A Self-Enforcing Model of Corporate Law" (1996) 109 *Harv L Rev* 1911, 1920.

terms? Mandatory rules cannot be varied by the parties. Enabling rules can be.[23] One commentator describes the corporate law codes of the various United States jurisdictions in the following way:[24]

"Modern corporation codes tend to be enabling rather than mandatory statutes: they are standard form contracts specifying the rights and obligations of managers and shareholders, which can often be altered by private agreement to suit the circumstances of particular firms. The enabling approach is a function of the contractual nature of a corporation. Participation in a firm is voluntary; common stock is one of a vast array of available investment vehicles."

Those commentators who advocate a substantial role for enabling rules in corporate regulation essentially see corporate law as providing a set of default rules (which could be referred to as a standard form contract) which operate to reduce the transaction costs which would otherwise be incurred in continually negotiating new contracts.[25] This is not to say that there is no role for mandatory rules. Even the most fervent supporters of enabling rules see a role for mandatory rules which deter one-off instances of self-dealing by directors and managers which cannot be prevented by those market forces which would otherwise operate to ensure that directors and managers act in the interests of shareholders.

If a particular corporate law can be classified as a default rule which participants in companies are able to modify to suit their particular needs, then there is a question as to the appropriate standard to be used in formulating such a rule. In his overview of a number of the arguments relevant to the mandatory/enabling debate, Bebchuk notes that many corporate law scholars adopt the "hypothetical contracting" standard.[26] According to the hypothetical contracting model, the institution formulating the rule should identify and adopt the arrangement that parties would have adopted if they had full information. Bebchuk argues that such a standard is efficient because fully informed and rational parties would be expected to agree on arrangements which are value-maximising.[27]

---

[23] Eisenberg argues that it is possible to divide corporate rules into three categories: mandatory rules, enabling rules, and what he terms suppletory rules. Suppletory rules are those which govern defined issues unless corporate actors adopt other rules: M A Eisenberg, "The Mandatory Structure of Corporation Law" (1989) 89 *Columbia L Rev* 1461.

[24] R Romano, *The Genius of American Corporate Law* (AEI Press, Washington, DC, 1993), 85. For other contributions relevant to the mandatory/enabling debate, see R Campbell, "Opportunistic Amendment of the Corporate Governance Contract" (1996) 14 *CSLJ* 200; F Easterbrook and D Fischel, *The Economic Structure of Corporate Law* (Cambridge, Mass., Harvard University Press, 1991); L Bebchuk, "Limiting Contractual Freedom in Corporate Law: The Desirable Constraints on Charter Amendments" (1989) 102 *Harv L Rev* 1820; Symposium, "The Debate on Contractual Freedom in Corporate Law" (1989) 89 *Columbia L Rev* 1395–1774. For a thoughtful exposition in the context of Australian corporate law, see M Whincop, "Of Fault and Default: Contractarianism as a Theory of Anglo-Australian Corporate Law" (1997) 21 *Melb Univ L Rev* 187.

[25] Campbell, n. 24 above, 206.

[26] L Bebchuk, "The Debate on Contractual Freedom in Corporate Law" (1989) 89 *Columbia L Rev* 1395, 1410.

[27] *Ibid.*

(ii) The Australian Corporations Law

At first glance, the Australian Corporations Law, unlike the state corporations codes in the United States, appears to have a substantial mandatory core. In other words, the Australian Corporations Law cannot be classified as being essentially a standard form contract which stakeholders in companies are free to modify to suit their own particular needs. The mandatory rules cover a broad range of matters including disclosure requirements, requirements regarding meetings, requirements regarding the keeping of registers, directors' and officers' duties, requirements in the context of takeovers and requirements regarding the regulation of financial benefits to related parties of public companies.

Gordon argues that mandatory corporate rules or laws can be divided into four categories: procedural, power allocating, economic transformative and fiduciary standard setting.[28] Procedural mandatory rules include those rules in the Corporations Law which regulate meetings of shareholders, such as requirements imposing minimum periods of time for notice of a meeting of shareholders. For example, section 253 of the Corporations Law requires twenty-one days' written notice of a meeting of a company at which a special resolution is to be considered. Some meetings require twenty-eight days' notice: section 254. However, it is interesting to note that some procedural rules which appear to be mandatory may in fact be default rules which can be altered. Although section 253 requires twenty-one days' written notice of a meeting at which a special resolution is to be considered, where shareholders who together hold at least 95 per cent in value of the shares so decide, a resolution may be passed at a meeting of which less than twenty-one days' notice has been given: section 253(4).

An example of what Gordon terms a "power allocating" mandatory corporate rule is section 227 of the Corporations Law, which allows the shareholders of a public company to remove a director before the end of that director's period of office, notwithstanding anything in the articles of association of the company or in any agreement between the company and the director. Provisions of the Corporations Law which vest powers in either shareholders or directors and which cannot be altered by agreement can be regarded as power allocating mandatory rules. "Economic transformative" mandatory rules are mandatory rules which apply where the economic structure of the company is altered. Certain takeover provisions of the Corporations Law fall into this category. Finally, "fiduciary standard setting" mandatory rules refer to those aspects of directors' duties which cannot be altered by agreement of the parties.

Although it is relatively easy to identify mandatory rules which form part of Australian corporate law, it would not be true to say that Australian

---

[28] J N Gordon, "The Mandatory Structure of Corporate Law" (1989) 89 *Columbia L Rev* 1549, 1591.

corporate law is entirely mandatory, and this includes certain aspects of directors' duties. The High Court in *Whitehouse* v. *Carlton Hotel Pty. Ltd.*[29] stated that the shareholders of a company may agree to modify the duties owed by company directors. More particularly, the Court stated that the articles of a company may be drafted so that they "expressly or impliedly authorise the exercise of the power of allotment of unissued shares for what would otherwise be a vitiating purpose".[30] In other words, the duty imposed upon company directors to act for a proper purpose cannot be regarded as totally mandatory in the sense that it cannot be modified, to some degree, to suit the needs of participants in companies. Another example is the important area of conflicts of interest and duty. There is, of course, the basic common law principle that directors must not place themselves in a position of conflict whereby a personal interest or duty conflicts with their duty to the company. The general expectation is that the common law rule will be modified by the articles of association. In other words, the shareholders may agree that, provided full disclosure of the interest is made, the director may place him or herself in a position of conflict (for example, by contracting with the company of which he or she is a director).[31] Consequently, the basic common law prohibition on conflicts of interest and duty can be viewed as a default rule which shareholders in companies are free to modify and which they typically do modify.

Another example of default rules in Australian corporate law is the model Table A articles contained in the Corporations Law. Section 175(2) provides that the Table A articles automatically apply to a company limited by shares unless they are modified or excluded by shareholders. It is interesting to note that it is proposed in the Company Law Review Bill to introduce the concept of "replaceable rules" into the constitutions of companies. These replaceable rules dealing with the internal administration of companies will form part of the Corporations Law; they will be updated from time to time as the need arises; and they will apply as amended to companies unless precluded by the company's constitution. It is anticipated that some rules will be replaceable rules for proprietary companies and mandatory rules for public companies.

Other examples of default rules can be provided. Section 249 of the Corporations Law provides that in a company which has share capital, every member has one vote for each share unless the articles provide otherwise. It is, of course, very common in private companies to alter this default rule and to issue shares with different voting rights attached to them. Section 247 is another example of a default rule. It provides that two or more members of a company holding at least 5 per cent of the issued share capital of a company may convene a meeting of shareholders unless the articles make some

---

[29] (1987) 162 CLR 285, 291.

[30] *Ibid.*

[31] For analysis of the development of the law in this area, see Ford, Austin and Ramsay, n. 2 above, Chap 9.

other provision. There has been a certain amount of litigation regarding the precise meaning of the words in section 247 "so far as the articles do not make other provision".[32] However, the essential point is that section 247 allows for some form of contracting out by shareholders although the form that this contracting out must take has not been finally resolved by the courts.

Section 164 of the Corporations Law may also be regarded as a default rule. This section allows persons contracting with companies to make certain assumptions in regard to those agents and officers who execute contracts on behalf of companies. In particular, section 164(3) allows a person contracting with a company to assume that a person who is held out by the company to be its officer or agent has been duly appointed and has the authority to exercise the powers and perform the duties customarily exercised or performed by an officer of the kind concerned. Actual or imputed knowledge by the person contracting with the company that the assumption is not correct disentitles that person from making the assumption: section 164(4). Section 164 can be regarded as a default rule because it is possible for the company to vary what is regarded as the customary authority of an officer of the company, and provided the person contracting with the company knows, or ought to know, about this variation of customary authority, then the default assumptions in section 164(3) will not apply.

There are some enabling rules which cannot be classified as default rules. As we have seen, default rules are those which apply unless they are modified or varied by the parties. Some rules are simply enabling in the sense that they facilitate corporate transactions. An example is section 255 of the Corporations Law which allows members of a private company to pass resolutions "on paper" without requiring the formality of a meeting provided all the members of the company sign the document. Another example of a corporate rule which has the objective of facilitating corporate transactions is section 161 of the Corporations Law which grants to companies the legal capacity of a natural person. The informal corporate acts doctrine, or what is sometimes referred to as the doctrine of unanimous assent, may also come within this category. Although the boundaries of this doctrine are not clear, as a general rule, the doctrine allows members of a company expressly or impliedly to waive certain formalities.[33]

There is another category of enabling corporate rules. These are rules which allow the court to give effect to the intention of parties where that intention was thwarted because of some mistake or irregularity. For example, section 1322 of the Corporations Law provides that certain matters or proceedings

---

[32] *Vision Nominees Pty. Ltd.* v. *Pangea Resources Ltd.* (1988) 14 NSWLR 38; *L C O'Neil Enterprises Pty. Ltd.* v. *Toxic Treatments Ltd.* (1986) 4 NSWLR 660; *Re Totex-Adon Pty. Ltd.* (1980) 1 NSWLR 605.

[33] See the discussion in Ford, Austin and Ramsay, n. 2 above, para 7.590. As the authors of this book note, the doctrine of unanimous assent was explicitly recognised by Lord Davey in *Salomon* where he stated that "the company is bound in a matter intra vires by the unanimous agreement of its members" ([1987] AC 22, 57).

are not invalid because of irregularities. The court has a discretion whether or not to validate an irregularity. An irregularity can include a number of matters involving meetings such as a lack of quorum and a failure to notify all those entitled to receive notice of the meeting. Section 194 of the Corporations Law, which allows the court to validate an improper share issue, can be regarded as an enabling rule which operates to give effect to the intention of parties where the carrying out of that intention has been thwarted by an irregularity.

(iii) An Example of Enabling Corporate Rules: Directors' Liability in the United States

In 1986 Delaware amended its General Corporation Law to allow shareholders of Delaware companies to limit or eliminate the personal liability of directors for breach of their duty of care. A number of reasons were advanced in support of the amendment. These included: difficulties in obtaining directors' and officers' liability insurance; court decisions holding directors personally liable for duty of care violations; and perceived difficulties in obtaining and retaining directors of the required quality.[34] Since 1986, almost all American states have followed Delaware in limiting the liability of directors[35] although the approach among states is not consistent.[36]

While these legislative amendments have been criticised by a number of commentators,[37] the amendments have been supported by others on the basis that they provide efficient legal rules for corporate governance.[38] One study[39] examined the share prices of eighty-eight Delaware companies which amended their charters to limit or eliminate the liability of their directors and compared the findings with a control group of eighty-eight non-Delaware companies. The authors were able to conclude that the decision by the Delaware companies to limit the liability of their directors "did not have a significant impact

[34] I M Ramsay, "Liability of Directors for Breach of Duty and the Scope of Indemnification and Insurance" (1987) 5 *CSLJ* 129.

[35] J J Hanks and L P Scriggins, "Let Stockholders Decide: The Origins of the Maryland Director and Officer Liability Statute of 1988" (1989) 18 *Baltimore L Rev* 235, 237.

[36] D A DeMott, "Limiting Directors' Liability" (1988) 66 *Washington L Q* 295.

[37] T L Hazen, "Corporate Directors' Accountability: The Race to the Bottom—The Second Lap" (1987) 66 *North Carolina L Rev* 171; T C Lee, "Limiting Corporate Directors' Liability: Delaware's Section 102(b)(7) and the Erosion of the Directors' Duty of Care" (1987) 136 *Univ of Penn L Rev* 239; Note, "Limiting Directors' Duty of Care Liability: An Analysis of Delaware's Charter Amendment Approach" (1987) 20 *Univ of Mich J of Law Reform* 543; R B Titus, "Limiting Directors' Liability: The Case for a More Balanced Approach—the Corporate Governance Project Alternative" (1989) 11 *Western New England L Rev* 1.

[38] D S Schaffer, "Delaware's Limit on Director Liability: How the Market for Incorporation Shapes Corporate Law" (1987) 10 *Harv J of Law and Public Policy* 665. The author notes that Delaware increased the number of new incorporations by 28% in the six months following the enactment of the amendments (688).

[39] V Janjigian and P J Bolster, "The Elimination of Director Liability and Stockholder Returns: An Empirical Investigation" (1990) 13 *J of Fin Res* 53.

upon shareholder wealth" and therefore did not appear to harm share-holders.[40]

The important feature of these recent amendments limiting directors' liability is that they reject the notion that mandatory rules should regulate a director's duty of care. In the context of Australian law, this would mean that shareholders and directors would be permitted to modify section 232(4) of the Corporations Law, which provides that an officer of a corporation must at all times exercise the degree of care and diligence that a reasonable person in a like position in a corporation would exercise in the corporation's circumstances. No doubt some would find this objectionable. Yet it has been argued that not only should shareholders and directors be permitted to contract out of any duty of care which would otherwise be imposed upon directors, but the same principle should apply to the duty of loyalty.[41] In fact, the state of Maryland has enacted legislation which permits the shareholders of Maryland companies to eliminate the liability of directors for breaches of the duty of loyalty provided that the conduct in question does not constitute receipt of an improper benefit or profit or active and deliberate dishonesty.[42]

This can be seen as the logical application of the "contractual" theory of the corporation. Shareholders should be permitted to decide all of the terms of their contracts with managers and with other shareholders.[43] A number of commentators reject the notion that private ordering or contracting should be the underlying approach to an analysis of companies and should govern the relationships among participants in the corporate enterprise. For these commentators, there must be mandatory rules, the application of which is not eliminated by private contracting.[44]

(iv) Arguments Supporting and Opposing Mandatory Corporate Rules

We have seen that Australian corporate law consists of both mandatory and enabling rules. However, most commentators would agree that the mandatory core of Australian corporate law is significantly higher than that of some other countries, including the United States. What are some of the arguments

---

[40] Janjigian and Bolster, n. 39 above, 60.

[41] See D M Branson, "Assault on Another Citidel: Attempts to Curtail the Fiduciary Standard of Loyalty Applicable to Corporate Directors" (1988) 57 *Fordham L Rev* 375, who surveys the views of those who propose this idea and concludes that opting-out of the fiduciary duty of loyalty will result in "[e]xtreme moral hazard, self-enrichment, tolerance of extreme ineptitude, or nepotism" (392).

[42] Maryland Corporations and Associations Annotated Code, s 2–405.2(a) cited in M A Sargent, "Two Cheers for the Maryland Director and Officer Liability Statute" (1989) 18 *Baltimore L Rev* 278, 296. It has been argued that even these exceptions should be narrowed: H N Butler and L E Ribstein, "Free at Last? The Contractual Theory of the Corporation and the New Maryland Officer-Director Liability Provisions" (1989) 18 *Baltimore L Rev* 352, 363–4.

[43] Butler and Ribstein, n. 42 above.

[44] See, for example, Eisenberg, n. 23 above; Gordon, n. 28 above.

supporting and opposing mandatory corporate rules? A number of these arguments are taken up elsewhere in this essay in the context of specific examples. However, it is worthwhile summarising briefly some of the relevant arguments.[45] Those who support a strong core of mandatory corporate rules often argue that such rules are necessary because individuals cannot contract to protect their own interests. In addition, it can be argued that if there is a mandatory rule which reflects what all parties would always agree to, then such a rule can operate to reduce transaction costs by eliminating the need for individual parties to negotiate continually to have this rule incorporated into their contracts. Such a rule might be the duty of good faith owed by directors of companies.

It is not only mandatory rules which may operate to reduce transaction costs. This may also be the case with certain default rules. An example is section 164 of the Corporations Law which, as we have already seen, allows a person contracting with a company to make certain assumptions regarding the authority of officers and agents of the company. To the extent to which section 164 protects persons contracting with a company by allowing them to make certain assumptions which do not have to be the subject of individual negotiation, it can be regarded as reducing transaction costs. As Mason CJ noted in *Northside Developments Pty. Ltd.* v. *Registrar-General*,[46] business convenience would be put at risk if persons dealing with companies were put to the expense and inconvenience of investigating the authority of those acting for a company each time a transaction is undertaken. Another judge has observed that provisions such as section 164:[47]

> "recognize the fact that the innumerable business transactions with corporations, so fundamental to our economy and form of society, cannot ordinarily require the proof of formalities concerning compliance by the company with its own internal rules and requirements."

Those who oppose extensive use of mandatory rules point out that such rules preclude parties from reaching their own agreements, and this can inhibit efficient outcomes. It might be possible for parties to structure their particular transaction in a way which avoids the mandatory rule. However, costs are incurred in adopting this course of action. In addition, mandatory rules are difficult to apply to a broad range of situations given the diverse preferences of participants in companies.

Some of these arguments were taken up in the extensive debate which followed the proposal in 1993 by News Corporation Ltd. to issue shares with differential voting rights. We have already seen that section 249 of the Corporations Law, which provides that, unless the articles of a company

---

[45] For more detailed analysis of these arguments, see the contributions in the Symposium, n. 24 above.

[46] (1990) 170 CLR 146, 164.

[47] *Bank of New Zealand* v. *Fiberi Pty. Ltd.* (1993) 14 ACSR 736, 741 (*per* Kirby P).

otherwise provide, a member of a company has one vote for each share held, is a default rule. However, the Australian Stock Exchange (on which News Corporation is listed) provides in its Listing Rules for a mandatory rule of one share, one vote for ordinary shares. A number of arguments were made in the debate.[48] Those supporting the mandatory listing rule argued that it operated to protect minority shareholders who would be unable to protect themselves. In addition, allowing ordinary shares with differential voting rights would entrench incumbent managers by making takeovers more difficult. On the other hand, those who supported changing the mandatory listing rule argued that shareholders should be able to determine the acceptability of ordinary shares with such voting rights, and that differential voting rights may help encourage long-term investment and may also allow companies increased flexibility in raising equity capital. These arguments made by those on both sides of the debate are examples of arguments which are often made in the context of examining the desirability of mandatory corporate rules.

The final point to note is that it is not always possible neatly to categorise corporate rules as mandatory or enabling. First, some enabling or default rules may be difficult to contract out of (for example, by imposing high transaction costs such as a shareholders' meeting for public companies). The more difficult or costly it is to contract out of a default rule, the more such a rule starts to operate actually as a mandatory rule. Secondly, some rules which appear mandatory may in fact not be. In an influential contribution to the mandatory/enabling debate, Black has argued that some rules which appear to be mandatory may be trivial for any one of four reasons.[49] First, some mandatory rules would be universally adopted anyway, assuming that parties actually thought about these rules. An example of such a rule, according to Black, is the duty of loyalty imposed upon company directors. This is a mandatory rule, yet, if it was not in the law, parties would presumably contract to impose such a duty upon company directors. Black suggests that because the rule has remained central to corporate governance, this suggests that it is efficient. Secondly, what appears to be a mandatory rule may in fact be trivial if it can be avoided. For example, because corporate law is generally state-based law in the United States, a mandatory rule in one state can be avoided by companies re-incorporating in another state which does not have that mandatory rule. Thirdly, some mandatory rules may be susceptible to change by either Parliament or the courts. Finally, some mandatory corporate rules are trivial because they either involve situations that almost never occur, or can be complied with at nominal cost.

---

[48] For elaboration of some of these arguments, see *Report by Expert Panel of Inquiry into Desirability of Super Voting Shares for Listed Companies* (Canberra, 1994).

[49] B Black, "Is Corporate Law Trivial? A Political and Economic Analysis" (1990) 84 *Northwestern Univ L Rev* 542. For an application of Black's arguments to Australia, see M J Whincop, "Trivial Pursuit: A Theoretical Perspective on Simplification Initiatives" (1997) 7 *Aust J of Corp L* 250.

Consequently, one of the important conclusions that can be drawn from Black's analysis is that we need to be careful in trying to determine whether particular corporate rules are mandatory, since what may appear at first glance to be a mandatory rule may in fact, because of one or more of the reasons noted by Black, be what he terms a trivial rule.

D What Factors Determine Whether Corporate Regulation is Mandatory or Enabling?

A critical issue is the identification of the factors which determine the appropriate balance between mandatory and enabling corporate regulation. I suggest there are at least four critical factors. First, the balance depends upon the strength or bargaining power of those subject to the regulation. Secondly, the balance depends upon one's view of the effectiveness of market forces in protecting the interests of stakeholders in companies. Thirdly, the balance may depend upon whether corporate regulation is undertaken by the national government or by state governments. Fourthly, the balance may depend on the expertise of the institution making the rule.

(i) Bargaining Power as a Determining Factor

An important factor in determining the appropriate balance of mandatory and enabling regulation is the bargaining power or strength of those subject to the regulation. Do they have the strength to contract to protect themselves so that default rules are appropriate? An interesting case study in this respect is the growth of institutional investors. As I note in Part VI of this essay, life insurance and superannuation funds hold over 25 per cent of the shares of companies listed on the Australian Stock Exchange. Other financial institutions hold another 8.5 per cent. Because of the strength of institutional investors, it is appropriate to consider whether default rules should have more general application to these investors. This issue is addressed in Part VI.

Sometimes default rules will still be allowed even if there are doubts whether those subject to the rule are able fully to protect themselves. They may still be able to contract out of the rule subject to the protection of judicial review, review by a regulator such as the Australian Securities Commission, or an independent expert's report.

(ii) Market Forces as a Determining Factor

Much has been written in relation to whether or not various market forces operate to such a degree that they enable corporate regulation to be less mandatory and more enabling. The issue is whether these market forces effectively protect shareholders so that less mandatory regulation is required.

I do not intend to do more in this essay than outline briefly the main arguments.

First, management must ensure that the company competes effectively in the market for the company's goods or services and not attempt personally to profit at the expense of shareholders. This is because a lack of success in this market will not only be reflected in lower earnings, which will disadvantage the company in raising debt or equity capital, but will also result in the share price of the company declining.[50] This creates the threat of a takeover with the consequential replacement of management because those who might attempt to mount a takeover perceive that they can profit by managing the company more efficiently.

Secondly, the existence of a market for corporate capital means that potential investors of debt and equity capital must be convinced that the company is being managed efficiently.[51]

Thirdly, the market for corporate control, which operates by means of acquisitions and takeovers, will lead to the replacement of inefficient managers whose decisions lead to a decline in the price of the company's shares.[52]

Finally, it is argued that there is a labour market for managers and, because managers tend to monitor the performance of other managers, this directly results in individual managers being concerned with the price of their companies' shares.[53] In addition, managerial salaries and other types of compensation can align the interests of managers and shareholders where such compensation is tied to how well the company is performing.[54] Therefore, the combined effect of these market forces, it is argued, disciplines managers and operates to reduce costs that may eventuate because of a divergence between the interests of managers and shareholders. This minimises the need for mandatory regulation.

This view of the role that the markets play in disciplining managers has not been universally endorsed:[55]

---

[50] D R Fischel, "The Corporate Governance Movement" (1982) 35 *Vanderbilt L Rev* 1259, 1263.

[51] H N Butler, "The Contractual Theory of the Corporation" (1989) 11 *George Mason L Rev* 99.

[52] F Easterbrook and D R Fischel, "The Proper Role of a Target's Management in Responding to a Tender Offer" (1981) 94 *Harv L Rev* 1161.

[53] *Ibid.*

[54] Butler, n. 51 above, 115–16.

[55] V Brudney, "The Role of the Board of Directors: The ALI and its Critics" (1983) 37 *Univ of Miami L Rev* 223, 235. See also V Brudney, "Corporate Governance, Agency Costs, and the Rhetoric of Contract" (1985) 85 *Columbia L Rev* 1403. For further criticisms, see R M Buxbaum, "Corporate Legitimacy, Economic Theory, and Legal Doctrine" (1984) 45 *Ohio State L J* 515; R C Clark, "Agency Costs Versus Fiduciary Duties" in J W Pratt and R J Zeckhauser (eds.), *Principals and Agents: The Structure of Business* (Boston, Mass., Harvard Business School Press, 1985), 55; J C Coffee, "No Exit? Opting Out, the Contractual Theory of the Corporation, and the Special Case of Remedies" (1988) 53 *Brooklyn L Rev* 919; W B Bratton, "The 'Nexus of Contracts' Corporation: A Critical Appraisal" (1989) 74 *Cornell L Rev* 407.

"Notwithstanding the efforts of the academic free marketers and their associates in the business community, there has not yet been demonstration or acceptance of the proposition that the markets alone provide an adequate mechanism for narrowing managerial discretion so as to press management to improve its efficiency, much less to press management to perform optimally for the shareholders of their corporations."

Critiques of the effectiveness of the market forces which are important for those who argue for limited mandatory regulation of companies have been undertaken by several commentators. Thus, Coffee[56] has argued that the market for corporate control applies only within a limited range. Companies in which the degree of inefficiency is not extreme enough to create a sufficient reduction in the share price to cause a takeover and companies in which the degree of inefficiency is so extreme as to preclude a takeover because it is such a risky undertaking fall outside this range, and the market for corporate control may only weakly discipline these companies.[57]

Eisenberg[58] has also argued that the disciplining power of the product market has been overstated. Although a highly competitive product market may render insolvent a company that is not operating efficiently, an imperfectly competitive market will not necessarily have this effect.[59] In addition, Eisenberg surveys empirical studies in the United States which show that although management compensation does to some extent align the interests of managers and shareholders because such compensation is tied to shareholder gain, the relationship between management compensation and corporate performance is not economically significant.[60] A study of the largest eighty-nine Australian companies found no evidence of a significant relationship between remuneration paid to Chief Executive Officers and company performance.[61]

A number of the arguments about the effectiveness of market forces depend upon the existence of a capital market which efficiently transmits information in the form of share prices about the performance of a company. The efficiency of the capital market in transmitting information has not been resolved.[62] However, the implications of the efficiency of the capital market are significant for the mandatory/enabling debate. There can be no doubt that

---

[56] J C Coffee, "Regulating the Market for Corporate Control: A Critical Assessment of the Tender Offer's Role in Corporate Governance" (1984) 84 *Columbia L Rev* 1145.

[57] *Ibid.*, at 1203–4. See also E S Herman, "The Limits of the Market as a Discipline in Corporate Governance" (1984) 9 *Del J of Corp L* 530.

[58] Eisenberg, n. 23 above.

[59] *Ibid.*, at 1489.

[60] *Ibid.*, at 1489–95. See also M C Jensen and K J Murphy, "Performance Pay and Top-Management Incentives" (1990) 98 *J of Pol Econ* 225.

[61] A Defina, T C Harris and I M Ramsay, "What is Reasonable Remuneration for Corporate Officers? An Empirical Investigation into the Relationship Between Pay and Performance in the Largest Australian Companies" (1994) 12 *CSLJ* 341.

[62] R Gilson and R Kraakman, "The Mechanisms of Market Efficiency" (1984) 70 *Virginia L Rev* 549.

market forces affect the decisions of managers. The important question is the extent to which they override the tendency of management to place its own interests with respect to matters such as remuneration above those of shareholders. If the capital market transmits information inefficiently about a company's performance and, as part of this, the performance of management, it is clearly the case that management will be less inhibited in maximising its own benefits. In this situation, we must look to government intervention in order to enforce those standards of fiduciary responsibility expected of management. On the other hand, an efficient capital market, when combined with an effective product market and market for corporate control, undercuts the position of those who call for increased government intervention in the form of mandatory corporate regulation.

An extensive and influential debate is occurring with respect to what is termed the Efficient Capital Market Hypothesis ("ECMH"). The hypothesis asserts that the share market quickly reacts to publicly available information and, therefore, share prices fully reflect all publicly available information.[63] The ECMH is now part of an on-going debate in areas such as disclosure requirements imposed upon companies,[64] the liability of those persons involved in disclosure[65] and insider trading.[66] Although the hypothesis has clearly proved to be influential, it is not without its critics.[67]

Of course, should the conclusion be reached that the capital market is in fact inefficient in some respects, and there is evidence which tends to support this conclusion,[68] there are other factors which influence the mandatory/enabling debate.

---

[63] W K S Wang, "Some Arguments That the Stock Market is Not Efficient" (1986) 19 *Univ of Calif Davis L Rev* 341, 341–2. It is important to distinguish between informational efficiency (the ECMH) and allocative efficiency, which implies that the market allocates resources to their most efficient, or highly valued, users.

[64] Note, "The Efficient Capital Market Hypothesis, Economic Theory and the Regulation of the Financial Services Industry" (1977) 29 *Stan L Rev* 1031; Note, "Broker Investment Recommendations and the Efficient Capital Market Hypothesis: A Proposed Cautionary Legend" (1977) 29 *Stan L Rev* 1077.

[65] D R Fischel, "Use of Modern Finance Theory in Securities Fraud Cases Involving Actively Traded Securities" (1982) 38 *Bus Lawyer* 1; D R Fischel, "Efficient Capital Markets, the Crash, and the Fraud on the Market Theory" (1989) 74 *Cornell L Rev* 907; Note, "The Fraud on the Market Theory and the Efficient Capital Markets Hypothesis: Applying a Consistent Standard" (1988) 14 *J of Corp L* 443; B Cornell and R G Morgan, "Using Finance Theory to Measure Damages in Fraud on the Market Theory" (1990) 37 *Univ of Calif LA L Rev* 883.

[66] J F Barry, "The Economics of Outside Information and Rule 10b–5" (1981) 129 *Univ of Penn L Rev* 1307.

[67] Wang, n. 63 above; L Stout, "The Unimportance of Being Efficient: An Economic Analysis of Stock Market Pricing and Securities Regulation" (1988) 87 *Michigan L Rev* 613; R Sappideen, "Securities Market Efficiency Reconsidered" (1988) 9 *Univ of Tas L Rev* 132; L A Cunningham, "Capital Market Theory, Mandatory Disclosure, and Price Discovery" (1994) 51 *Washington and Lee L Rev* 843.

[68] J N Gordon and L A Kornhauser, "Efficient Markets, Costly Information, and Securities Research" (1985) 60 *NY Univ L Rev* 761. For a review of empirical tests of the ECMH in Australia, see S R Bishop, H R Crapp and G J Twite, *Corporate Finance* (3rd edn., Sydney, Holt, Rhinehart and Winston, 1993), 108–11; G Peirson, R Bird, R Brown and P Howard, *Business*

(iii) National or State Corporate Regulation as a Determining Factor

If it is believed that a key objective of corporate regulation is to facilitate choice by stakeholders in companies, and thereby support enabling regulation, it may be that this can be better promoted by state governments rather than by the federal or national government. Australian corporate regulation is essentially a national system of regulation. In this respect, Australian corporate regulation differs significantly from that of some other federal countries where corporate law is the responsibility of State governments and the legislation can differ in substantial ways from state to state.

There are of course arguments which favour national regulation of companies. For example, the transaction costs associated with companies doing business can be reduced if they have to deal with only one uniform national law rather than a series of different state laws. In addition, regulation by the national or federal government may overcome the incentive of state governments to externalise costs. This will occur where a state government does not bear all of the costs of action that it undertakes.

Yet there are arguments supporting state government regulation of companies. First, the federal government may be more insensitive than state governments to the needs of shareholders and other stakeholders in companies. Indeed, a fundamental principle of a federal system of government is that, because of the enormous variety of preferences in society (including the preferences of those who invest in companies), it is important to have governments with limited jurisdiction so that these preferences can more readily be satisfied.

The second argument favouring state government regulation is that a state government has less scope for enacting harmful legislation than the federal government. This is because the more local the jurisdiction of a government, the more readily people and businesses can move in order to find a more hospitable jurisdiction. In other words, each of these governments can be thought of as a substitute for the others. Thirdly, national regulation of companies means that it is difficult to determine whether this regulation is optimal because there is no competition for the provision of corporate regulation. Companies and their shareholders do not have a choice and cannot indicate their preference for alternative regulation by incorporating in another jurisdiction. Finally, allowing regulation by state governments can increase innovation and experimentation as each of these governments competes to attract business and employment by enacting corporate legislation which appeals to companies and their stakeholders.

Finance (3rd edn., London, McGraw-Hill, 1990), 530–50. In brief, these studies tend to support the view that the Australian share market is semi-strong form efficient in that new publicly released information (for example, announcements concerning profits, dividends, bonus issues and rights issues) is quickly and in an unbiased manner impounded into share prices. However, there is evidence of share market anomalies.

Consequently, although it is possible to have corporate regulation which is both enabling and enacted by a national government, there are arguments to support the conclusion that, in appropriate circumstances, where corporate regulation is undertaken by state governments, these state governments have greater incentives to enact enabling corporate regulation which facilitates choice by stakeholders in companies.

(iv) The Law-making Institution as a Determining Factor

Whether one believes in mandatory or enabling laws depends, to some degree, on the quality of the law. If there is uncertainty about how efficient the law is, then it is preferable for it to be an enabling law which parties are able to modify. At the same time, Bebchuk notes that our assessment of the quality of the law depends in part on an assessment regarding the expertise of the law-making institution.[69]

This raises for discussion the important issue of the comparative expertise of different law-making bodies. Although a detailed examination of the respective merits of law-making bodies such as courts and specialised regulators like the Australian Securities Commission must remain for another occasion, it is appropriate to refer briefly to a number of points. In particular, although courts play an important role in corporate law-making, courts do suffer several limitations.

First, litigation is typically an "after the event" means of regulation (an exception is the use of injunctions). Secondly, courts may adopt unnecessarily restrictive interpretations of statutory provisions. An example which is frequently given is section 260 (the anti-avoidance provision) of the Australian Income Tax Assessment Act (which was operative until 1981). This provision has been described as "a weapon aimed against devices used to thwart the objectives of the Act".[70] Yet, while this was the purpose of the provision, it has been said that the approach adopted by courts during the 1970s resulted in the "effective nullification" and "destruction" of section 260.[71]

A more recent example is the controversial judgment of Young J of the Supreme Court of New South Wales in *Mesenberg* v. *Cord Industrial Recruiters Pty. Ltd.*[72] This judgment concerned the interaction of section 1324 of the Corporations Law (which allows the Australian Securities Commission ("ASC") or a "person whose interests have been, are or would be affected by" conduct in contravention of the Corporations Law to apply to the court for an injunction) and the civil penalty provisions of the Corporations Law. In *Mesenberg*, the complaint of the plaintiff was that the second defendant had

---

[69] Bebchuk, n. 26 above, 1414.

[70] Y Grbich, "Section 260 Re-Examined: Posing Critical Questions About Tax Avoidance" (1976) 1 *UNSWL J* 211, 223.

[71] G Lehmann, "The Income Tax Judgments of Sir Garfield Barwick: A Study in the Failure of the New Legalism" (1983) 9 *Monash Univ L Rev* 115, 117 and 132.

[72] (1996) 19 ACSR 483.

breached section 232(2) of the Corporations Law in that the second defendant, while an officer of the company, had failed to act honestly in the exercise of her powers and the discharge of her duties. Section 232(2) has, since 1993, been a civil penalty provision. Young J considered whether contraventions of section 232(2) are dealt with exclusively by the civil penalty provisions of the Corporations Law, or whether section 1324 continues to apply to section 232(2). In the absence of any guidance in the legislation itself or previous authority, his Honour held that section 1324, in relation to breaches of section 232, is only available to be used by the ASC, its delegate or some other person authorised in writing by the Minister (i.e. those permitted to apply for a civil penalty order).

The judgment has been widely criticised.[73] One criticism is that the judgment of Young J would appear not to provide an appropriate balance of the roles of shareholders and the ASC in enforcing the civil penalty provisions of the Corporations Law. In particular, giving the ASC, its delegate or some other person authorised in writing by the Minister the sole power and authority to enforce the civil penalty provisions by way of an injunction under section 1324 results in exclusive public enforcement by injunction of these provisions, which may prove undesirable for several reasons:

(a) limits on the funding of corporate regulators mean they cannot pursue all breaches of the law;

(b) there is no reason to believe the priorities established by a corporate regulator for enforcement are necessarily the correct ones. This dictates a role for private enforcement; and

(c) it is generally undesirable when the government holds a monopoly on access to remedies.[74]

A third limitation of courts is that courts in different jurisdictions may adopt different interpretations of the same statutory provision resulting in considerable uncertainty for the business community. An example was section 592 of the Corporations Law (now section 588G), which deals with the problem of insolvent trading. For a period of time, courts in different states adopted fundamentally different interpretations with respect to this important provision.[75]

Fourthly, courts may be susceptible to what can be termed opportunistic behaviour by minority shareholders. This arises because shareholders who commence litigation may often have poor incentives to maximise the wealth

---

[73] See, for example, Ford, Austin and Ramsay, n. 2 above, para 11.365; H Bird, "A Spanner in the Works: The Impact of *Mesenberg* v. *Cord Industrial Recruiters* on Enforcement Rights Under the Corporations Law" (1997) 25 *ABLR* 179. Justice Einfeld of the Federal Court has disagreed with *Mesenberg* in a recent judgment : *Airpeak Pty. Ltd.* v. *Jetstream Aircraft Ltd.* (1997) 15 ACLC 715.

[74] These points are made in Ford, Austin and Ramsay, n. 2 above.

[75] I Trethowan, "Directors' Personal Liability for Insolvent Trading: At Last, a Degree of Consensus" (1993) 11 *CSLJ* 102.

of other shareholders and the value of the company. This point is emphasised by two commentators.[76] They observe that voting rules in corporate law ensure that shareholders with the largest economic stake have the greatest effect on corporate policy. Because shareholders with the largest stake will gain the most from good performance by the company and yet bear most of the costs of poor performance, these shareholders have the best incentives to maximise the value of the company. These commentators note that although minority shareholders with small shareholdings have little or no power to thwart the majority shareholders, generally speaking, this does not disadvantage the minority shareholders because they benefit from a voting system which ensures that shareholders with the largest shareholdings have the best incentives to maximise the value of the company. Yet they observe that shareholder derivative litigation is a notable exception to this fundamental principle of corporate law. Derivative litigation means that minority shareholders with small shareholdings can commence litigation on behalf of the company. However, because of the small shareholding, the shareholder bringing the litigation has very little incentive to consider the effect of the litigation on other shareholders who are the supposed beneficiaries.

Fifthly, more generally, there may be concerns about the abilities and expertise of courts. Some concerns have been noted by the former Chief Justice of the High Court of Australia, Sir Anthony Mason:[77]

> "Courts have been ill-equipped or reluctant to grapple with policy issues which often must be examined before one can decide that an existing rule is no longer serving a useful purpose and that it should be replaced by another and better rule. The inductive and analogical reasoning by which the courts have traditionally proceeded is not appropriate to the resolution of such questions. In a society in which community values change with great rapidity, the inability or the reluctance of the courts to bring about change in the substantive principles of judge-made law has been a catalyst to legislative action in some fields."

It has been argued that courts lack the flexibility, expertise, initiative and powers of co-ordination which are necessary to deal with complex regulatory problems when compared with specialist agencies.[78] It is also asserted that the fact-finding capacity and accountability of regulatory agencies are greater than those of courts.[79] The fact that courts have limitations is not itself a problem. However, costs are created if courts are assigned tasks for which they are not equipped in terms of expertise.

Discussion of these costs reveals only one side of the argument. Courts have been a very positive and constructive force in many areas of the law. They

---

[76] D R Fischel and M Bradley, "The Role of Liability Rules and the Derivative Suit in Corporate Law: A Theoretical and Empirical Analysis" (1986) 71 *Cornell L Rev* 261, 271–2.

[77] Sir Anthony Mason, "Australian Law for Australia", Address to the 27th Australian Legal Convention, Sept. 1991, reprinted (1991) 26 *Aust Law News* 14.

[78] C R Sunstein, "Law and Administration After *Chevron*" (1990) 90 *Columbia L Rev* 2071.

[79] *Ibid.*, at 2087.

also have a powerful advantage over Parliament in relation to corporate regulation. When Parliament enacts corporate law it does so with a broad-brush approach which often makes it difficult to distinguish between different types of companies or different types of corporate transactions. However, courts can examine specific situations on a case-by-case basis, and can provide remedies to fit particular circumstances. This is difficult for Parliament to do. Perhaps the best example is the development of the oppression remedy. There is little doubt that this is now the most effective remedy available to minority shareholders. The decided cases indicate a very broad range of circumstances in which the oppression remedy has been used by minority shareholders. These circumstances include: improper diversion of business; payment of excessive remuneration to a company controller; failure to prosecute an action; unfairly restricting dividends; making a share issue with the dominant purpose of reducing a shareholder's proportional stake in the company; denial of access to corporate information; decisions for the benefit of related companies rather than the shareholders in the company; and oppressive conduct of board meetings.

It is interesting to speculate why the oppression remedy forms such an important part of the corporate landscape for minority shareholders in private companies even though the remedy is available to shareholders in public companies. A review of these reasons indicates the valuable role that the courts can play. First, it is typically the case that minority shareholders in private companies require more protection than shareholders in public companies because they do not have a liquid market and are thereby denied a means of readily exiting the company if they are dissatisfied. Secondly, private companies have greater freedom to put in place different mechanisms for corporate governance. For example, they are not required to comply with the legal requirements contained in the Stock Exchange Listing Rules or to comply with particular parts of the Corporations Law, such as Part 3.2A which regulates financial benefits between public companies and their related parties. What this means is that there is a valuable role for the oppression remedy in filling the gaps left by broad legal rules implemented by Parliament, or by other law-making bodies such as the Stock Exchange.

An essential objective must therefore be to determine the tasks for which courts are best suited in corporate regulation. For example, while courts may be well suited to determining whether officers of a company have breached their fiduciary duties based upon loyalty and good faith (after all, courts have a lengthy tradition of considering fiduciary principles), they are poorly suited to reviewing managerial incompetence, under-performance or inefficiency. This point has been emphasised by Coffee in relation to the shareholder derivative action:[80]

---

[80] J C Coffee, "New Myths and Old Realties: The American Law Institute Faces the Derivative Action" (1993) 48 *Bus Lawyer* 1407, 1426–7.

"Clearly, when a business decision proves erroneous, multiple explanations for that failure are possible. It could be that the decisionmaker was negligent, but, conversely, the truth may be that a risk that was accepted knowingly and prudently simply came to an unfortunate fruition. Or, it could be that a new and unforeseeable risk arose and matured after the time the business decision was irrevocably made. Because business decisionmaking involves unavoidable trade-offs between risk and return, some prudent decisions will prove disastrous. Examining these decisions with the 20/20 vision of judicial hindsight, courts may be unable to distinguish accurately lack of care from statistical bad luck. If this risk of judicial error is considerable, then to the extent the derivative action is relied upon to enforce the duty of care, it may deter risk taking by management and service on the board, rather than negligence."

In summary, an analysis of whether corporate law should be mandatory or enabling involves, to some degree, an analysis of the quality of law-making institutions—whether they be the courts, the ASC or Parliament. This is because, if we are uncertain about how efficient a particular law is, then it is preferable for it to be an enabling law which parties may modify. An important task therefore is determining the comparative expertise of different law-making institutions. Some of the arguments relevant to this task have been reviewed in this section.

III THE COSTS OF MANDATORY RULES

In this section I identify three mandatory corporate rules which I suggest have had particularly high costs associated with them. These are the regulation of partial takeovers, the regulation of share buy-backs and the regulation of compulsory acquisition of minority shareholdings (the *Gambotto* judgment[81]).

A Partial Takeovers

The market for corporate control is often viewed as an important market for aligning the interests of managers and shareholders.[82] Legal regulation may play a significant role in determining how effective the market for corporate control is in achieving this objective. An illustration is the 1986 amendments to the Australian takeovers legislation. In brief, these amendments restricted the way in which an offeror could conduct a partial takeover.

---

[81] *Gambotto* v. *WCP Ltd.* (1995) 182 CLR 432.

[82] H Manne, "Mergers and the Market for Corporate Control" (1965) 73 *J of Pol Econ* 110; Easterbrook and Fischel, n. 24 above, Chap 7.

(i) Types of Partial Takeover

Prior to 1986, an offeror could conduct a partial takeover in Australia in one of two ways.[83] First, under section 16(2)(a)(i) of the Companies (Acquisition of Shares) Act (as it then was), an offeror could pro-rate the shares from each shareholder who accepted the offer so as to ensure that the desired objective was achieved. For example, if an offeror with no shareholding in the target company bid for 60 per cent of the target's shares then, assuming that some shareholders declined the offer, the offeror could take a greater percentage of shares from each of the accepting shareholders in order to ensure that the objective of 60 per cent was achieved.

The alternative method of conducting a partial takeover was to proceed via section 16(2)(a)(ii). In this case, the offeror would bid for a proportion of the shares held by each shareholder in the target company. The offeror could not pro-rate the shares from the accepting shareholders. Assume, once again, that an offeror with no shareholding in the target company desires 60 per cent of the target's shares. A bid under section 16(2)(a)(ii) for 60 per cent of each shareholder's holding would fail to achieve the desired objective if only one shareholder decided not to accept. Because pro-rating of shares is not permitted under this option, an offeror would, in order to achieve a holding of 60 per cent of the target's shares, need to bid for a higher proportion of each shareholder's holding in order to take account of the possibility that some shareholders will not accept the offer.

It is clear that the first alternative provides the most certainty to the offeror. At the same time, this alternative provides the least certainty to the target company shareholders. This is because the shares may be pro-rated, and therefore a target company shareholder will not know the number of shares that he or she will be selling to the offeror until the offer period closes and the offeror is in a position to calculate the level of acceptances. The Federal Government's Companies and Securities Law Review Committee ("CSLRC") recommended in its 1985 Report that the second alternative (namely, proportional bids) be the sole method for conducting a partial takeover, and this recommendation was enacted in 1986. It is now contained in section 635(b) of the Corporations Law. Consequently, if an offeror now wishes to undertake a partial takeover, it is mandatory for this to be implemented as a proportional bid.

(ii) Effect of Legal Amendments

The effect of the 1986 amendments was dramatic. Prior to the introduction of the Companies (Acquisition of Shares) Act, partial takeovers constituted

---

[83] I Ramsay, "Balancing Law and Economics: The Case of Partial Takeovers" [1992] *JBL* 369.

approximately 17 per cent of all takeovers undertaken in Australia.[84] By late 1982, this had increased to 40 per cent according to Gross.[85] However, the period since the 1986 amendments has witnessed the demise of partial takeovers in Australia, as Table 1 illustrates. In 1987, partial takeovers constituted 6 per cent of all takeovers of that year. In 1988, the percentage declined to 5 per cent and 1989 saw a further decline to less than 2 per cent. In the early 1990s, the percentage of partial takeovers varied between 1 per cent and 4 per cent of all takeovers each year.

Table 1. Bid Type and Bid Outcome 1988–1993

Bid Method	Successful			Unsuccessful			Total		
	1993	1992	1991	1993	1992	1991	1993	1992	1991
Full	37	30	52	22	24	33	59	54	85
Partial	2	0	1	0	1	0	2	1	1
Total	39	30	53	22	25	33	61	55	86

Bid Method	Successful			Unsuccessful			Total		
	1990	1989	1988	1990	1989	1988	1990	1989	1988
Full	67	113	169	26	63	105	93	176	274
Partial	1	—	5	3	3	10	4	3	15
Total	68	113	174	29	66	115	97	179	289

Source: Corporate Adviser, *Analysis of Takeover Activity.*

For those commentators who advocate an active market for corporate control on the basis that takeovers are a means of (i) allocating resources to their most valued users and (ii) aligning the interests of managers and shareholders, the 1986 amendments would be viewed as costly.

[84] D Gross, "Partial Takeovers—A Critique of the Provisions in the Companies (Acquisition) of Shares) Act and Codes" (1983) 1 *CSLJ* 251.

[85] There is some dispute concerning the exact percentage of all takeovers occurring during the 1980s in Australia which were partial takeovers. There is no doubt that the percentage of partial takeovers increased significantly during the first half of the 1980s as the following statistics indicate, although they may never have counted for 40% of all takeovers:

Year	Partial takeovers as a percentage of all takeovers
1980	5%
1981	8%
1982	23%
1983	13%
1984	20%
1985 (half year)	18%

Source: S Bishop, P Dodd and R Officer, *Australian Takeovers: The Evidence 1972–1985* (Centre for Independant Studies, Sydney, 1987), 69.

B Share Buy-backs

The regulation of share buy-backs in Australia has recently been eased by changes introduced in late 1995 in the First Corporate Law Simplification Act. However, it would be true to say that up until then, the Australian legislature had indicated a marked distrust of allowing companies to buy back their own shares. This was reflected in a blanket prohibition on share buy-backs until 1989 and then very rigid regulation of permitted share buy-backs between 1989 and late 1995. This "rigid regulation" consisted of thirty-seven pages of legislation and ninety-one sections regulating share buy-backs. Much of this was mandatory requirements to be followed in order to implement a share buy-back.

In some other countries, share buy-backs are a very common feature of the corporate landscape. For example, between 1977 and 1987, the amount of cash distributed to shareholders of United States companies by means of share buy-backs grew by over 800 per cent.[86] In 1987, $54 billion was distributed to shareholders of American companies by means of buy-backs. The importance of buy-backs is demonstrated by observing that the equivalent figure in 1987 for dividends was $83 billion.[87] In other words, out of the $137 billion distributed to shareholders of American companies in 1987 by means of buy-backs and dividends, almost 40 per cent of this total amount was distributed by means of buy-backs. In a study I undertook with a financial economist, we observed that between 1989 (when the prohibition on share buy-backs by Australian companies was removed) and late 1993, a total of only thirty-five buy-back announcements were reported by companies listed on the Australian Stock Exchange.[88]

There are substantial costs to mandatory corporate rules which make it difficult for companies to conduct share buy-backs. One cost is the denial to companies of opportunities to alter their capital structure by way of cost-effective share buy-backs. Another cost is the fact that there is very strong evidence that a major reason companies engage in share buy-backs is to signal the market. In other words, when a company buys back its shares, management gives an information signal to shareholders. The signal may, however, be ambiguous. On the one hand, it may be that the company has no profitable uses for its funds and therefore undertakes a buy-back as a means of returning these funds to shareholders. Alternatively, management may believe that the company is undervalued and a buy-back is undertaken at a significant premium above the current market price as a means by which management passes this information on to shareholders.

[86] L S Bagwell and J B Shoven, "Cash Distributions to Shareholders" (1989) 3 *J of Econ Perspectives* 129, 131.

[87] *Ibid.*

[88] T C Harris and I M Ramsay, "An Empirical Investigation of Australian Share Buy-Backs" (1995) 4 *Aust J of Corp L* 393.

The signalling theory of buy-backs can be tested empirically. In particular, the share price of companies undertaking buy-backs can be examined in order to determine whether or not any premium that is offered to shareholders by the company to acquire their shares is permanent. If it is, it is strong evidence that the buy-back signals that, at the time the buy-back occurs, the shares of the company are undervalued. Numerous studies undertaken in the United States have found support for the signalling explanation of buy-backs.[89]

Consequently, another cost of rules which make it difficult for companies to undertake share buy-backs is that these rules deny to companies the opportunity to disclose information to the market place by way of a buy-back.

C Compulsory Acquisition of the Shares of Minority Shareholders

In *Gambotto* v. *WCP Ltd.*,[90] the High Court of Australia refused to allow the expropriation of the shares of a minority shareholder against his will, even though a more than fair price was offered to the minority shareholder, and even though there were significant economic advantages in compulsorily acquiring the shares of the minority shareholder so that WCP Ltd. would be a wholly-owned subsidiary.

The judgment of the High Court has been much debated and it is not necessary for me to revisit these arguments.[91] However, *Gambotto* is relevant in terms of analysing the judgment as a mandatory rule which now applies to compulsory acquisition of the shares of minority shareholders where this is done by way of an amendment to the articles of association. The High Court put in place new tests or rules which have had the effect of rendering it virtually impossible to undertake compulsory acquisition of minority shareholdings in this way.[92] Are there costs to such a mandatory rule? If the views of commentators are anything to go by, the costs may be significant. One American commentator has offered the following view of the High Court's decision in *Gambotto*:[93]

"The High Court's opinion in *Gambotto* v. *WCP Ltd.* is a development that confounds robust visions of impending convergence among corporate law regimes. By

[89] See the study cited in Harris and Ramsay, n. 88 above.

[90] (1995) 182 CLR 432.

[91] See, for example, I M Ramsay (ed.), *Gambotto* v. *WCP Ltd.: Its Implications for Corporate Regulation* (Centre for Corporate Law and Securities Regulation, The University of Melbourne, 1996).

[92] The High Court held that the compulsory acquisition of the shares of a minority shareholder by means of an amendment to the articles of association of the company must: (a) be undertaken for a proper purpose (defined narrowly by the court to exclude the advancement of the interests of the company as a commercial entity or even the great majority of the shareholders and limited to situations where the purpose is to secure the company from significant detriment or harm); and (b) not operate oppressively in relation to minority shareholders.

[93] D DeMott, "Proprietary Norms in Corporate Law: An Essay on Reading *Gambotto* in the United States" in Ramsay (ed.), n. 91 above, 90.

treating a shareholder's interest as proprietary, the *Gambotto* court impeded transactions that eliminate the equity investment of minority shareholders. By comparison, corporate law in the United States, and particularly in Delaware, facilitates
such transactions."

The compulsory acquisition of minority shareholdings can produce considerable economic, administrative and taxation benefits including:

(a) facilitating financial restructuring;
(b) permitting the transfer of tax losses between wholly-owned grouped com-
    panies;
(c) reducing administrative and reporting costs; and
(d) protecting the confidentiality of commercial information and otherwise
    eliminating possible conflicts of interest in partially-owned companies.[94]

Mandatory rules that inhibit or make difficult the compulsory acquisition
of minority shareholdings, where the price offered is fair, deny to companies
these economic benefits.

IV MANDATORY CORPORATE DISCLOSURE RULES: A CASE STUDY

In this Part, and also in Part V, I examine two important corporate rules:
mandatory disclosure rules and limited liability (a default rule). The intention
is to identify the rationales underlying these rules and to examine the practical application of the rules.

Mandatory corporate disclosure rules form a reasonably significant portion
of the Australian Corporations Law. The following is a summary of some of
the circumstances where disclosure of information is mandated:

(a) on-going disclosure to shareholders required by Parts 3.6 to 3.8 of the
    Corporations Law (dealing with accounts, audits and annual returns);
(b) specific disclosure to shareholders, and in some circumstances creditors,
    in the context of changes to the capital structure of companies (for exam-
    ple, reduction of capital, alterations to the rights of classes of shares, cer-
    tain types of share buy-backs, and the giving of financial assistance in
    connection with the acquisition of shares);
(c) specific disclosure to investors in the form of a prospectus when raising
    capital;
(d) on-going disclosure by managers and trustees of prescribed interests (such
    as unit trusts) to unit holders;
(e) specific disclosure in the context of takeovers required by Part 6.3 of the
    Corporations Law (for example, Part A and Part B Statements which are

---

[94] Legal Committee of the Companies and Securities Advisory Committee, *Report on
Compulsory Acquisitions* (Sydney, 1996), para 1.11.

required to be given by the offerer and directors of the target company respectively).

(f) on-going disclosure to shareholders required by the Australian Stock Exchange listing rules.

Disclosure was an issue in *Salomon*, although the House of Lords was divided on whether there should be mandatory disclosure to unsecured creditors that debentures have been issued by a company. Lord Herschell stated that, where a company issues debentures to the vendor of a business the company is purchasing, "ample notice to all who may have dealings with the company should be secured".[95] However, Lord Watson stated:[96]

"The unpaid creditors of the company, whose unfortunate position has been attributed to the fraud of the appellant, if they had thought fit to avail themselves of the means of protecting their interests which the Act provides, could have informed themselves of the terms of purchase, by the company, of the issue of debentures to the appellant, and of the amount of shares held by each member. In my opinion, the statute casts upon them the duty of making inquiry in regard to these matters. Whatever may be the moral duty of a limited company and its shareholders, when the trade of the company is not thriving, the law does not lay any obligation upon them to warn those members of the public who deal with them on credit that they run the risk of not being paid. One of the learned judges asserts, and I see no reason to question the accuracy of his statement, that creditors never think of examining the register of debentures. But the apathy of a creditor cannot justify an imputation of fraud against a limited company or its members, who have provided all the means of information which the Act of 1862 requires; and, in my opinion, a creditor who will not take the trouble to use the means which the statute provides for enabling him to protect himself must bear the consequences of his own negligence."

A Possible Rationales for Mandatory Disclosure

The need for mandatory disclosure requirements has been the subject of considerable theoretical debate. Some commentators have questioned the value of mandatory disclosure rules, suggesting that market forces, if left unfettered, will produce optimal disclosure practices.[97] However, others have argued that mandatory disclosure is necessary to overcome "market failure" associated with the private production of securities information.[98] This is not to suggest

---

[95] [1897] AC 22, 47.

[96] *Ibid.*, at 40.

[97] See, for example, G J Stigler, "Public Regulation of the Securities Markets" (1964) 37 *J of Business* 117 and G Benston, "The Value of the SEC's Accounting Disclosure Requirements" (1969) 44 *Accounting Review* 515.

[98] See, for example, Securities and Exchange Commission Advisory Committee on Corporate Disclosure, *Report of the Advisory Committee on Corporate Disclosure to the Securities and Exchange Commission* (1977); J Seligman, "The Historical Need for a Mandatory Corporate Disclosure System" (1983) 9 *J of Corp L* 1; J C Coffee, "Market Failure and the Economic Case for a Mandatory Disclosure System" (1984) 70 *Virginia L Rev* 717.

that the arguments for and against mandatory disclosure should be regarded in absolute terms. Rather, the issue is what level of disclosure regulation is desirable.[99]

Dr Mark Blair and I have examined five main arguments that, individually or in combination, are potential rationales for a regulatory mechanism that explicitly mandates the nature of what must be disclosed.[100] These are:

(a) unequal possession of information among investors;
(b) reduction of social waste;
(c) monitoring of management;
(d) the public goods hypothesis; and
(e) public choice theory.

Mandatory disclosure requirements are sometimes also justified on the basis that managers have incentives to misinform the market in public disclosures. However, such incentives do not appear to provide a rationale for more frequent or detailed disclosures.[101] This problem has been addressed in a number of other ways. The most obvious of these has been to enact laws against fraud.[102] Such laws are commonplace, applying to the sale of a variety of commodities that have uncertain quality characteristics.[103] Another approach has been to develop generally accepted accounting standards.[104]

Our analysis found that no definitive conclusions can be reached regarding the extent to which the government should mandate the nature and amount of corporate financial disclosures. Nor do the justifications for mandatory

---

[99] See, for example, H Kripke, in a dissenting statement in the Report by the SEC Advisory Committee on Corporate Disclosure, argued that applying a "black-or-white, all-or-none approach" to the evaluation of mandatory disclosure is undesirable. See Securities and Exchange Commission Advisory Committee on Corporate Disclosure, n. 98 above, 49.

[100] See M Blair and I M Ramsay, "Mandatory Corporate Disclosure Rules and Securities Regulation" in G Walker, B Fisse and I Ramsay (eds.), *Securities Regulation Law* (forthcoming, LBC Information Services, Sydney, 1998). See also G Benston, *Corporate Financial Disclosure in the UK and the USA* (Farnborough, Saxton House, 1976) and C J Meier-Schatz, "Objectives of Financial Disclosure Regulation" (1986) 8 *J of Comp Bus and Capital Market Law* 219 for discussion of other possible rationales.

[101] The Securities and Exchange Commission Advisory Committee on Corporate Disclosure, n. 98 above, 622, queried whether making disclosure mandatory will deter or reduce such abuses. The Committee noted that "it is not clear that there has been a decline in the frequency of abuse over the last 44 years since the inception of the [US Securities and Exchange] Acts".

[102] For example, s 995 of the Corporations Law prohibits misleading or deceptive conduct in a variety of circumstances including the allotment or issue of securities and takeover offers or announcements, while s 996 prohibits false and misleading statements in prospectuses. Such provisions provide strong incentives for managers to provide the "whole truth" when disclosing. On the desirability of anti-fraud rules, see F H Easterbrook and D R Fischel, "Mandatory Disclosure and the Protection of Investors" (1984) 70 *Virginia L Rev* 669, 674–80. Section 299(1) of the Corporations Law also requires directors to ensure that annual financial statements provide such information and explanations as to convey a "true and fair" view of the profit or loss and state of affairs of the company.

[103] For example, Trade Practices Act 1974 (Cth), ss 52, 52A.

[104] Accounting standards in Australia, once approved by the Australian Accounting Standards Board, have the force of law and must be followed in company accounts: Corporations Law, s 298(1).

disclosure provide clear guidance concerning the desirable form and content of corporate reports.

A number of studies have attempted to assess the usefulness of mandatory disclosure rules by undertaking an analysis of the economic impact of these rules. The Australian Federal government has supported mandatory disclosure rules on the grounds that such rules reduce fraud by managers and improve investment decisions by investors.[105] If such arguments are correct, we might expect the results of these economic impact studies to show that returns to shareholders (measured in terms of share prices) increase with the introduction of mandatory disclosure rules (other factors remaining stable).

Important disclosure rules were introduced in the United States in 1933 and 1934.[106] Several studies have examined returns to shareholders both before and after the introduction of these rules.[107] Although Stigler, Jarrell and Benston did not find evidence of increased returns to shareholders (which suggests that the mandatory disclosure rules under consideration do not benefit shareholders), these studies have been criticised.[108] The most recent American study did find a significant increase in returns for initial public offerings not listed on the New York Stock Exchange but listed on regional exchanges in the United States following the introduction of the 1933 Act.[109] Simon also found that the dispersion of abnormal returns to shareholders declined after 1933. In other words, the variance of outcomes among companies issuing new securities was reduced, thereby exposing investors to less risk.

There is Australian evidence regarding the economic impact of the 1994 amendments to the continuous disclosure regime applying to companies. Prior to the amendments, a company listed on the Australian Stock Exchange had to disclose information that would be expected to have a material effect on the price or value of the company's securities, in accordance with Listing Rule 3A(1). The 1994 amendments gave statutory backing to the Listing Rule and also broadened the continuous disclosure obligation so that it applies to those companies and other entities which, although not listed on the stock exchange, raise funds from the public. A study of the economic effects of the amendments found that:

---

[105] Second Reading Speech, Corporate Law Reform Bill (No 2) 1992, 26 Nov. 1992.

[106] The Securities Act of 1933 (which regulates new issues of securities) and the Securities Exchange Act of 1934 (which regulates ongoing disclosure).

[107] Stigler, n. 97 above; G Benston, "Required Disclosure and the Stock Market: An Evaluation of the Securities Exchange Act of 1934" (1973) 63 *American Econ Rev* 132; G Jarrell, "The Economic Effects of Federal Regulation of the Market for New Security Issues" (1981) 24 *J of L and Econ* 613; C J Simon, "The Effect of the 1933 Securities Act on Investor Information and the Performance of New Issues" (1989) 79 *American Econ Rev* 295.

[108] See, for example, I Friend and R Herman, "The SEC Through a Glass Darkly" (1964) 37 *J of Bus* 382; I Friend and R Westerfield, "Required Disclosure and the Stock Market" (1975) 65 *American Econ Rev* 467; H Mendelson, "Economics and the Assessment of Disclosure Requirements" (1978) 1 *J of Comp Corp L and Sec Reg* 49.

[109] Simon, n. 107 above.

(a) continuous disclosure appeared to have provided the market with some additional price sensitive information for smaller listed disclosing entities. It did not appear to have made any significant change to the disclosure policies or disclosure levels of larger listed disclosing entities. This is consistent with their having already been adequately disclosing under Listing Rule 3A(1);

(b) the bulk of additional information provided to the market by small listed disclosing entities consisted mainly of "bad" news;

(c) there was an increase in both forward-looking and voluntary disclosures, though it was difficult to determine whether this increase resulted from continuous disclosure or wider macro-economic influences;

(d) there was an increased anticipation in share prices of the content of preliminary statements, though mainly for companies less relevant to larger investors; and

(e) there was a significant decrease in market and share price volatility, though it was difficult to confidently attribute this to the operation of continuous disclosure.[110]

The authors conclude that there is no strong evidence that the continuous disclosure reforms had any significant impact on the efficiency of the Australian share market or on the disclosure policies of listed companies.[111] The authors note that this may be because the reforms did not create any new disclosure obligations for listed companies, although they did introduce statutory criminal and civil liability for breach of the existing disclosure obligations.[112]

B Australian Stock Exchange Listing Rule 4.10.3

Some corporate law disclosure rules are less mandatory than others. One example is Australian Stock Exchange ("ASX") Listing Rule 4.10.3. This Listing Rule came into operation on 30 June 1996 and requires each listed company to include in its annual report a statement of the main corporate governance practices that the company had in place during the reporting period. When the ASX released a discussion paper in 1994 on disclosure of corporate governance practices, it canvassed a number of options. One of these options was mandatory disclosure of a list of corporate governance practices that would be set at what the ASX termed "best practice benchmarks".[113] However, as the ASX noted, such a mandatory rule presents

---

[110] Companies and Securities Advisory Committee, *Report on Continuous Disclosure* (Sydney, 1996), 9–10. The economic study, by P Brown, S L Taylor and T S Walter, is a series of appendices to the Report.

[111] *Ibid.*, Appendix 6 at 4.

[112] *Ibid.*, Appendix 7 at 19.

[113] Australian Stock Exchange, *Disclosure of Corporate Governance Practices by Listed Companies*, Discussion Paper, Sept. 1994.

difficulties for smaller companies as "best practice benchmarks" may only be appropriate for the largest ASX listed companies. Smaller companies may have neither the need nor the expertise to follow such best practice. Moreover, the costs of reviewing, formalising and adopting detailed corporate governance practices:[114]

> "may be proportionately larger for small companies either due to smaller companies having further to move to achieve compliance or because the cost of, say, forming and running an audit committee is not dependent on the size of the company. A cost which is approximately the same for all sizes of company will represent a larger proportion of sales revenue for a smaller company. If compliance brings less benefits and more costs as company size reduces, costs could begin to outweigh benefits for companies below a certain size."

Listing Rule 4.10.3 does not require compulsory or mandatory disclosure of particular corporate governance practices. Rather, there is "an indicative list of corporate governance matters" that a company make take into account contained in Appendix 4A of the Listing Rules. Appendix 4A covers matters such as board composition, appointment and retirement of non-executive directors, remuneration policies, procedures for directors seeking independent advice, audit review, business risk strategy and ethical standards.

How successful has the new Listing Rule been? It has certainly proved to be controversial. The ASX believes that listed companies have adequately complied with the Listing Rule. The Australian Investment Managers' Association (representing the largest institutional investors) disagrees and claims that only 10 per cent of the largest one hundred listed companies have provided appropriate disclosure of their corporate governance practices. I have recently completed a co-authored study of the corporate governance disclosure practices of almost three hundred companies listed on the ASX. We divided the companies into three groupings (large, medium and small) based on their market capitalisation. Industry classification of the companies was undertaken so that industry comparisons in relation to disclosure could be made.[115] We concluded that while there was scope for improvement, many companies are now disclosing detailed information about a range of corporate governance practices. Such disclosure may assist shareholders and other stakeholders in companies in monitoring directors and may also cause directors to reflect upon the appropriateness and adequacy of the corporate governance practices of their companies. There is significant variation in terms of disclosure, particularly between large and small companies. However, this is perhaps not surprising given that larger companies have greater resources available to prepare detailed disclosure statements.

---

[114] A Belcher, "Regulation by the Market: The Case of the Cadbury Code and Compliance Statement" [1995] *JBL* 321, 326.

[115] I Ramsay and R Hoad, "Disclosure of Corporate Governance Practices by Australian Companies", The *University of Melbourne* (1997) 15 *C & SLJ* 454.

Listing Rule 4.10.3 can be regarded as partly mandatory. It puts in place a requirement that companies must, in their annual reports, address their main corporate governance practices. However, the Rule does not mandate particular disclosure and enables companies to highlight particular practices. Although the Listing Rule has been in operation for only one year and it is therefore too early to draw definitive conclusions, by allowing this flexibility to companies, it may mean that the Listing Rule has the effect of providing more meaningful disclosure to shareholders and other stakeholders in the disclosing companies.

V LIMITED LIABILITY: A SECOND CASE STUDY

An important corporate law default rule is limited liability. It is a default rule because upon incorporation, shareholders of a company limited by shares have their liability limited to the amount, if any, unpaid on their shares: Corporations Law, section 516. However, shareholders can contract out of this default rule, for example, by giving a personal guarantee to a creditor.

Limited liability was at the heart of the decision of the House of Lords in *Salomon*. The question before their Lordships was whether Aron Salomon, as the dominant shareholder in A Salomon & Co. Ltd., would receive the benefit of limited liability and thereby not be personally liable for the claims of the company's unsecured trade creditors. In addition, Aron Salomon was a secured creditor of his company, and if he was to obtain the benefit of limited liability his secured debt would, in the usual course of events, receive priority over the claims of the unsecured creditors. As we know, the House of Lords decided that it would extend to Aron Salomon the benefit of limited liability, thereby overturning the judgment of the Court of Appeal.

However, some concern is expressed in the House of Lords about the effects upon the unsecured creditors of granting Aron Salomon limited liability. As Lord Macnaghten stated:[116]

> "I have long thought, and I believe some of your Lordships also think, that the ordinary trade creditors of a trading company ought to have a preferential claim on the assets in liquidation in respect of debts incurred within a certain limited time before the winding-up. But that is not the law at present. Everybody knows that when there is a winding-up debenture-holders generally step in and sweep off everything; and a great scandal it is."

Different views regarding limited liability were expressed long before the decision of the House of Lords in *Salomon*. It was an 1855 amendment to the Joint Stock Companies Act of 1844 that made limited liability widely available in the United Kingdom. Historians have documented the different views expressed in the first half of the nineteenth century regarding whether

---

[116] [1897] AC 22, 53.

Parliament should legislate to permit limited liability on a wide scale.[117] Even the English "captains of industry" were divided. A number of chambers of commerce opposed limited liability.[118] As one "captain of industry" stated:[119]

> "There is no way of preventing fraud unless 'the man with the money should be responsible for the character of the business'."

There is a historical connection between the development of limited liability and one of the factors mentioned earlier in this essay as a consideration in the mandatory/enabling debate; namely, whether corporate regulation should be undertaken by a national government or by state governments. Commentators who have examined the history of limited liability have noted that limited liability was accepted much more quickly in the United States than in England. A number of possible explanations have been advanced. It has been argued that American firms had larger capital requirements than English firms and thus were in greater need of limited liability.[120] In addition, the delay in the development of the corporation in England and also limited liability may partially be attributed to the general distrust of companies following the collapse of the South Sea Company and the consequent enactment of the Bubble Act of 1720.[121] Turning to the United States, Forbes argues that competition among states contributed to the adoption of limited liability:[122]

> "In England, the power to issue corporate charters was monopolized by the national government. On the other hand, each state in the United States had the power to issue corporate charters. This latter system of granting charters can be expected to produce more innovation in business organization as states compete against one another for charter revenue. For example, when [limited liability] was being considered in Massachusetts, one of the arguments employed in support of limited liability was that unlimited liability was causing capital to flee to states in which the limited form was sanctioned."

Consequently, it may be that the more rapid adoption of limited liability as a default rule available to shareholders in the United States, when compared to England, may partially be explained by the fact that State governments in the United States controlled the incorporation of companies rather than a national government.

Some of the concerns expressed in the judgments in *Salomon*, and also the division among industrialists in England regarding whether Parliament should legislate to allow limited liability broadly, show that there have always been ambivalent views in relation to limited liability. Should it be facilitated or

---

[117] See, most recently, R A Bryer, "The Mercantile Laws Commission of 1854 and the Political Economy of Limited Liability" (1997) 50 *Econ Hist Rev* 37.

[118] *Ibid.*, at 41.

[119] *Ibid.*

[120] K F Forbes, "Limited Liability and the Development of the Business Corporation" (1986) 2 *J of L, Econ and Organization* 163, 173.

[121] *Ibid.*, at 172.

[122] *Ibid.*, at 173.

should it be restricted? Should it be regarded as a standard rule that is generally available or should it be regarded as a privilege? This is obviously an important question in relation to the corporate regulation debate. In the remainder of this section, I first identify the economic justifications for limited liability, and then turn to consider several recent Australian developments regarding limited liability.

A Economic Justifications for Limited Liability

Why are companies granted limited liability? Five reasons, based upon principles of economic efficiency, can be provided.[123] First, limited liability decreases the need for shareholders to monitor the managers of companies in which they invest because the financial consequences of company failure are limited. Shareholders may have neither the incentive (particularly if they have only a small shareholding) nor the expertise to monitor the actions of managers. The potential costs of operating companies are reduced because limited liability makes shareholder diversification and passivity a more rational strategy.[124]

Secondly, limited liability provides incentives for managers to act efficiently and in the interests of shareholders by promoting the free transfer of shares. This argument has two parts to it. First, the free transfer of shares is promoted by limited liability because under this principle the wealth of other shareholders is irrelevant. If a principle of unlimited liability applied, the value of shares would be determined partly by the wealth of shareholders. In other words, the price at which an individual shareholder might purchase a share would be determined in part by the wealth of that shareholder which was now at risk because of unlimited liability. The second part of the argument (that limited liability provides managers with incentives to act efficiently and in the interests of shareholders) is derived from the fact that if a company is being managed inefficiently, shareholders can be expected to be selling their shares at a discount to the price which would exist if the company were being managed efficiently. This creates the possibility of a takeover of the company and the replacement of the incumbent management.

---

[123] These reasons are drawn from Easterbrook and Fischel, n. 24 above, 41–4.

[124] Easterbrook and Fischel also argue that limited liability reduces the costs of monitoring other shareholders. With unlimited liability, because any one shareholder could be responsible for all the debts of the company, it is necessary for that shareholder to ensure that other shareholders possess enough wealth to bear their share of any company debts. This requires costly monitoring of other shareholders according to Easterbrook and Fischel. This justification for limited liability has been criticised on the basis that if unlimited liability means that individual shareholders are liable for company debts only in the proportion which their investment bears to that of the total investment in the company, shareholders do not need to monitor other shareholders. This is because under proportional shareholder liability, the wealth of other shareholders is irrelevant: S B Presser, "Thwarting the Killing of the Corporation: Limited Liability, Democracy, and Economics" (1992) 87 *Northwestern Univ L Rev* 148, 160–1.

Thirdly, limited liability assists the efficient operation of the securities markets because, as was observed in the preceding paragraph, the prices at which shares trade does not depend upon an evaluation of the wealth of individual shareholders.

Fourthly, limited liability permits efficient diversification by shareholders, which in turn allows shareholders to reduce their individual risk. If a principle of unlimited liability applied and a shareholder could lose his or her entire wealth by reason of the failure of one company, shareholders would have an incentive to minimise the number of shares held in different companies and insist on a higher return from their investment because of the higher risk they face. Consequently, limited liability not only allows diversification but permits companies to raise capital at lower costs because of the reduced risk faced by shareholders.

Fifthly, limited liability facilitates optimal investment decisions by managers. As we have seen, limited liability provides incentives for shareholders to hold diversified portfolios. Under such circumstances, managers should invest in projects with positive net present values, and can do so without exposing each shareholder to the loss of his or her personal wealth. However, if a principle of unlimited liability applies, managers may reject some investments with positive present values on the basis that the risk to shareholders is thereby reduced. "By definition this would be a social loss, because projects with a positive net present value are beneficial uses of capital."[125]

Professor Blumberg has demonstrated that a number of these justifications for limited liability have either limited application or no application to holding companies and their wholly-owned subsidiaries.[126] First, the justification that limited liability decreases the need for shareholders to monitor managers does not apply because of the clear incentive of a holding company to monitor the activities of its wholly-owned subsidiary. Secondly, the justification that limited liability provides incentives for managers to act efficiently and in the interests of shareholders by promoting the free transfer of shares has less application to holding companies and wholly-owned subsidiaries, although limited liability may reduce transaction costs in sales of the shares of a subsidiary because it can assist the separation of liabilities between the holding company and its subsidiary.[127]

Thirdly, the fact that limited liability assists the operation of the securities markets is largely irrelevant in the case of a wholly-owned subsidiary, although this justification is still relevant in the case of a partially-owned subsidiary where there is a market in which the publicly held shares are traded.[128] Finally, the fact that limited liability permits efficient diversification by share-

---

[125] Easterbrook and Fischel, n. 24 above, 44.
[126] P I Blumberg, "Limited Liability and Corporate Groups" (1986) 11 *J of Corp L* 573, 623–6.
[127] K Hofstetter, "Multinational Enterprise Parent Liability: Efficient Legal Regimes in a World Market Environment" (1990) 15 *North Carolina J of Int L and Comm Reg* 299, 307.
[128] Blumberg, n. 126 above, 624.

holders, which in turn allows shareholders to reduce their individual risk, is less applicable to holding companies because they are less risk averse than individual shareholders. This follows from the fact that the individual shareholders of the holding company still receive the protection of limited liability, which means they can diversify their investments independently of the holding company's liability for the subsidiary.[129] This conclusion is not unqualified however. If companies are risk averse, they may forego investment opportunities with positive net present values if they are denied the avenue of isolating the risk of the investment in a subsidiary.[130]

It is therefore evident that a number of the justifications for why limited liability applies to companies are less relevant when the company is the holding company of a wholly-owned subsidiary. This provides general support for rethinking some aspects of limited liability in the context of corporate groups. Another reason for such a rethink is the significant tension between the legal principle that a company is a separate legal entity and therefore deserving of limited liability even if it is part of a corporate group, and the fact that many corporate groups operate as a single entity because of the economic benefits that result from the integration of activities.

B Developments Regarding Limited Liability

An important recent development is one I referred to in Part I of this essay. In late 1995, the Australian federal government permitted the incorporation of one-shareholder and one-director companies. This was done as part of the First Corporate Law Simplification Act. In other words, the government extended the benefits associated with limited liability (along with other benefits that attach to incorporation) to one-person companies. However, it would be far from true to say that we have, in recent years in Australia, witnessed a general expansion of limited liability, as this section demonstrates.

In this section, the developments regarding limited liability I examine are:

(a) holding company liability for the debts of an insolvent subsidiary; and
(b) lifting of the corporate veil by courts.

(i) Holding Company Liability for the Debts of an Insolvent Subsidiary

We have seen that a major issue in relation to limited liability is whether it provides an appropriate balance of the interests of shareholders and creditors. In this part of the essay, section 588V of the Corporations Law is examined.

---

[129] Hofstetter, n. 127 above, 307.
[130] G W Dent, "Limited Liability in Environmental Law" (1991) 26 *Wake Forest L Rev* 151, 167.

It came into operation in June 1993. This section has as its key objective the protection of unsecured creditors. It does this by imposing liability on a holding company of a subsidiary where the subsidiary trades while it is insolvent and certain other conditions are satisfied. However, there are other possible ways of protecting creditors. One alternative was in fact mentioned by Lord Herschell in *Salomon*. He raised for consideration whether Parliament should require companies to be established with a minimum amount of capital.[131]

Section 588V of the Corporations Law provides that a holding company contravenes the section if a subsidiary is insolvent when it incurs a debt or becomes insolvent by incurring the debt and at that time there are reasonable grounds for suspecting that the subsidiary is insolvent, or would so become insolvent, and:

(a) the holding company, or one or more of its directors, is or are aware at that time that there are grounds for so suspecting; or

(b) having regard to the nature and extent of the holding company's control over the affairs of the subsidiary and to any other relevant circumstances, it is reasonable to expect that either a holding company in the company's circumstances would be so aware or one or more of such a holding company's directors would be so aware.

Section 588W provides that where a holding company contravenes section 588V in relation to the incurring of a debt by a subsidiary and the person to whom the debt is owed has suffered loss or damage in relation to the debt because of the subsidiary's insolvency and the debt was wholly or partly unsecured when the loss or damage was suffered, the subsidiary's liquidator may seek to recover from the holding company an amount equal to the amount of the loss or damage.

A number of defences to proceedings under section 588W are provided in section 588X. It is a defence if it is proved that:

(a) At the time when the debt was incurred, the holding company, and each relevant director (if any), had reasonable grounds to expect, and did expect, that the subsidiary was solvent at that time and would remain solvent even if it incurred the debt.

(b) At the time when the debt was incurred, the holding company, and each relevant director (if any):

 (i)   had reasonable grounds to believe, and did believe that a competent and reliable person was responsible for providing to the holding company adequate information about whether the subsidiary was solvent and that the person was fulfilling that responsibility; and

 (ii) expected, on the basis of the information provided to the holding company by the person, that the subsidiary was solvent at that time and would remain solvent even if it incurred that debt.

---

[131] [1897] AC 22, 46.

(c) Because of illness or for some other good reason, a particular relevant director did not take part in the management of the holding company at the time when the subsidiary incurred the debt.

(d) The holding company took all reasonable steps to prevent the subsidiary from incurring the debt.

Where the court is satisfied that, at the time when the subsidiary incurred the debt, the creditor who suffered the loss or damage knew that the subsidiary was insolvent or would become insolvent by incurring the debt, section 588Y provides that the court may order that the compensation paid by the holding company is not available to pay the debt unless all the subsidiary's other unsecured debts have been paid in full.

The provisions outlined have their origin in a report of the Australian Law Reform Commission.[132] The recommendations of the Commission were broader than section 588V, in that liability for insolvent trading could attach under the recommendations of the Commission not just to a holding company but to any related company.[133] The Commission proposed that a court should be able to order a company to be liable for the debts of a related company if the court determined this to be just. Three criteria to which the court should have regard were proposed:

(a) the extent to which the related company took part in the management of the insolvent company;

(b) the conduct of the related company towards the creditors of the insolvent company; and

(c) the extent to which the circumstances that gave rise to the winding up of the company were attributable to the actions of the related company.[134]

Because section 588V is specifically designed to protect creditors, a critical question that must be addressed is whether creditors require protection or whether they should be expected to contract to protect themselves. The starting point is a recognition of the conflicts of interest that exist between a company's shareholders and its creditors. Smith and Warner[135] identify four major sources of conflict:

(a) the payment of excessive dividends;

(b) claim dilution (through taking on debt with similar or higher priority);

(c) asset substitution (for example, substituting saleable for non-saleable assets); and

(d) excessive risk taking.

---

[132] Australian Law Reform Commission, *General Insolvency Inquiry* (Canberra, 1988).

[133] *Ibid.*, at para 334.

[134] *Ibid.*, at para 335.

[135] C W Smith and J B Warner, "On Financial Contracting: An Analysis of Bond Covenants" (1979) 7 *J of Fin Econ* 177.

Although the first three conflicts are straightforward, the fourth warrants elaboration. A conflict arises because payment to a creditor may be jeopardised where the company engages in high-risk investments. Shareholders in a leveraged company have incentives to invest the company's resources in risky projects: if a project is successful, the excess returns will be distributed among the shareholders as dividends but will not be shared with the creditors, who are only entitled to a fixed return on their investment. Company losses, however, are shared among both creditors and shareholders.

Creditors can generally be expected to contract to protect themselves against actions that reduce the prospect of them being paid. This contracting has two parts to it. First, the interest rate on the loan that is negotiated between the creditor and the company can be expected to reflect the risks that the creditor faces. Secondly, the contract may contain restrictions on activities of the company. For example, there may be restrictions on the amount that the company can pay out as dividends. There may also be restrictions on the company incurring debt of a similar or higher priority. These types of restrictions are common in debenture trust deeds.[136]

However, this type of contracting may not always be possible. The theory that creditors charge different interest rates for different levels of risk does not work where the costs of the creditor acquiring adequate information about the level of risk are disproportionate to the amount of the transaction.[137] The theory also does not work in the case of involuntary creditors (such as tort claimants).[138] Moreover, dispersed creditors face a collective action problem and may therefore lack the appropriate incentives to undertake joint action to prevent opportunistic behaviour by the company that threatens payment to creditors.[139] Finally, even sophisticated creditors cannot foresee all contingencies and contract for protection against them. Significant corporate restructurings, such as leveraged buy-outs, have seen transfers of wealth from sophisticated creditors (namely some bondholders) to shareholders.[140] The

---

[136] R Sappideen, "Protecting Debenture Holder Interests: A Delicate Art" (1991) 4 *Corp and Bus L J* 36. For an empirical study of the restrictive covenants contained in Australian trust deeds, see G Whittred and I Zimmer, "Accounting Information in the Market for Debt" (1986) 26 *Accounting and Finance* 19.

[137] J M Landers, "Another Word on Parents, Subsidiaries and Affiliates in Bankruptcy" (1976) 43 *Univ of Chi L Rev* 527, 529. However, creditors are expected to "price protect" in this situation. In other words, they will require a higher interest rate as compensation for risk which they are unable to ascertain.

[138] *Ibid.*

[139] V Brudney, "Corporate Bondholders and Debtor Opportunism: In Bad Times and Good" (1992) 105 *Harv L Rev* 1821.

[140] This has mainly occurred in the United States: W W Bratton, "Corporate Debt Relationships: Legal Theory in a Time of Restructuring" [1989] *Duke L J* 92. A leveraged buy-out occurs where existing shareholders of a company transfer control of the company to an outsider. A high level of debt is used to fund the acquisition. Because this debt will be serviced by the acquired company (by cash flows of the business or by disposal of assets) this increases the risk of existing creditors of the company not being paid.

result has been a vigorous debate concerning whether directors should owe fiduciary duties to bondholders as a means of protection.[141]

In addition to contractual protections, there are constraints upon companies which operate to protect the interests of creditors. First, there is the maintenance of share capital doctrine. This doctrine has been described in the following way:[142]

> "Paid-up capital may be diminished or lost in the course of the company's trading; that is a result which no legislation can prevent; but persons who deal with and give credit to a limited company naturally rely upon the fact that the company is trading with a certain amount of capital already paid, as well as the responsibility of its members for the capital remaining at call; and they are entitled to assume that no part of the capital which has been paid into the coffers of the company has been subsequently paid out, except in the legitimate course of its business."

However, the effectiveness and relevance of the maintenance of share capital doctrine has been questioned by a number of commentators.[143]

A second constraint which operates to protect the interests of creditors is the reputations of the managers of the company with which the creditors are contracting. Managers will be reluctant to undertake actions which harm their reputations and which may make it difficult to raise capital in the future. However, as one commentator observes, this constraint applies only when the present value of maintaining the company as a going concern exceeds the value of the benefits derived from taking action that adversely affects creditors (for example, the payment of excessive dividends).[144]

A final constraint is that, although shareholders may want to take actions which adversely affect creditors, the shareholders may lack effective control

---

[141] M W McDaniel, "Bondholders and Stockholders" (1988) 13 *J of Corp L* 205 (arguing that directors should have a fiduciary duty to deal fairly with all investors in a company—bondholders as well as shareholders because "leveraged takeovers, buyouts and recapitalizations are having a devastating impact on existing bondholders. Stockholders are getting rich in part at bondholder expense"); L E Mitchell, "The Fairness Rights of Corporate Bondholders" (1990) 65 *NY Univ L Rev* 1165 (supporting fiduciary duties to bondholders on the basis that this would enhance corporate social responsibility); K Lehn and A Poulson, "The Economics of Event Risk: The Case of Bondholders in Leveraged Buyouts" (1990) 15 *J of Corp Law* 199 (arguing against fiduciary duties to bondholders for two reasons. First, such duties would induce additional litigation and more resources would be expended in redistributing wealth among holders of different securities, thereby reducing the documented wealth gains created by leveraged buyouts. Secondly, market forces compensate bondholders for the risk of leveraged buy-outs. If leveraged buy-outs increase the riskiness of bonds, then this is reflected in a higher interest rate for the bondholders. In addition, investors can mitigate risk by diversifying and holding both bonds and stocks in their portfolios); T R Hurst and L J McGuinness, "The Corporation, the Bondholder and Fiduciary Duties" (1991) 10 *J of L and Comm* 187 (arguing against fiduciary duties on the basis that directors would have the difficulty of serving two masters—bondholders and shareholders—which would undercut their existing fiduciary duty to maximize shareholder returns).

[142] *Trevor* v. *Whitworth* (1887) 12 App Cas 409, 423–4.

[143] See, for example, Ford, Austin and Ramsay, n. 2 above, para 24.360; J H Farrar, N E Furey and B M Hannigan, *Farrar's Company Law* (3rd edn., London, Butterworths, 1991), 169–77.

[144] W Frost, "Organizational Form, Misappropriation Risk, and the Substantive Consolidation of Corporate Groups" (1993) 44 *Hastings L J* 449, 483.

over the management of the company because of a separation of ownership and control.[145] However, whether the separation of ownership and control adequately protects creditors is open to question. First, as managers increase the percentage of shares that they own in the company, their incentive to act in the interests of shareholders increases. Secondly, there is evidence that the ownership concentration of Australian companies is increasing. One study of one hundred Australian companies found that the five largest shareholders held, on average, 54 per cent of the issued shares of these companies.[146] Consequently, the degree to which the separation of ownership and control in Australian companies operates to protect creditors of these companies is an open issue.[147]

It can, therefore, be seen that the debate on creditor protection is largely unresolved. However, it does not need to be resolved in order to evaluate the merits of section 588V. This is because section 588V does not provide unqualified protection to creditors. It operates only where the subsidiary is insolvent. Consequently, the question of creditor protection can be phrased in a more precise way for our purposes. Is creditor protection warranted where the company with which the creditor has contracted is insolvent?

Parliament and the courts have long recognised that insolvency presents special problems for creditors. Parliament has enacted section 588G (previously section 592) of the Corporations Law which imposes a duty upon every director to prevent insolvent trading by his or her company. Courts have also been active. While the vexed issue of directors' duties to creditors remains unresolved,[148] there is concensus that the onset of insolvency imposes special obligations upon directors with respect to the interests of creditors. This is best articulated in the judgment of Street CJ in *Kinsela* v. *Russell Kinsela Pty. Ltd.*:[149]

---

[145] "This separation of ownership from control redounds to the benefit of creditors. Because managers are heavily invested in the firm and are unable to diversify their firm-specific skills, they are likely to be risk-averse. Thus, while shareholders may desire to increase enterprise risk after the interest rate of debt is fixed, managers may be reluctant to do so. The shareholders' inability to have complete control over the management of the corporate group reduces their opportunity to engage in misappropriations.": Frost, n. 144 above, 484–5.

[146] I M Ramsay and M Blair, "Ownership Concentration, Institutional Investment and Corporate Governance: An Empirical Investigation of 100 Australian Companies" (1993) *19 Melb Univ L Rev* 153.

[147] Increasing ownership concentration of Australian companies may not result in a reduction of the separation of ownership and control if these few shareholders who have the potential to control the companies in which they invest do not actually exercise this control. These large shareholders are typically institutional investors and there are many reasons why such investors do not exercise control over the management of companies in which they invest: *ibid.*, 179–80. See also G P Stapledon, "Disincentives to Activism by Institutional Investors in Listed Australian Companies" (1996) 18 *Syd L Rev* 152.

[148] The cases and issues are evaluated in D A Wishart, "Models and Theories of Directors' Duties to Creditors" (1991) 14 *NZULR* 323 and V Finch, "Directors' Duties: Insolvency and the Unsecured Creditor" in A Clark (ed.), *Current Issues in Insolvency Law* (London, Sweet & Maxwell, 1991), 87.

[149] (1986) 4 NSWLR 722, 730.

"In a solvent company the proprietary interests of the shareholders entitle them as a general body to be regarded as the company when questions of the duty of directors arise. . . . But where a company is insolvent the interests of the creditors intrude. They become prospectively entitled, through the mechanism of liquidation, to displace the power of the shareholders and directors to deal with the company's assets. It is in a practical sense their assets and not the shareholders' assets that, through the medium of the company, are under the management of the directors pending either liquidation, return to solvency or the imposition of some alternative administration."

Kinsela provides a powerful justification for creditor protection upon corporate insolvency. Shareholders' funds have been dissipated and it is now the creditors' funds which are at risk. However, there is a further justification for creditor protection. I have already observed that one of the problems confronting creditors is excessive risk-taking by shareholders.[150] As insolvency approaches, this problem is exacerbated. This is because the shareholders now have an even more powerful incentive to engage in risky investments, given that most of their funds have been dissipated yet there is the possibility of a "bonanza payoff that will prevent insolvency".[151]

The existence of corporate groups may exacerbate these problems for creditors. Commentators have noted that the creation of complex group structures may be used to conceal the true financial position of individual companies from creditors. In addition, tort claimants may be uncompensated when their injuries are caused by under-capitalised subsidiaries of holding companies. Finally, it has been noted that, where a company in a corporate group is in financial difficulty, managers may move assets from that company to other companies in the group that have a better chance of survival.[152] This will be at the expense of the creditors of the company in financial difficulty.[153]

Consequently, some protection for creditors upon the onset of insolvency of the company with which they have contracted is warranted. This suggests that the default rule of limited liability should be replaced in this situation so that shareholders no longer have limited liability.

(ii) Lifting of the Corporate Veil by Courts

One way in which limited liability is denied to shareholders in a company is when courts decide to lift the corporate veil. The fact that the corporate veil of a limited liability company could be lifted by the court was acknowledged by Lord Halsbury in *Salomon* when he stated:[154]

---

[150] See n. 135 and accompanying text.

[151] R Grantham, "The Judicial Extension of Directors' Duties to Creditors" [1991] *JBL* 1, 3, quoting J Coffee "Shareholders Versus Managers: The Strain in the Corporate Web" (1986) 85 *Mich L Rev* 1, 61.

[152] Frost, n. 144 above, 485.

[153] An example is *Walker* v. *Wimborne* (1976) 137 CLR 1.

[154] [1897] AC 22, 33.

"If there was no fraud and no agency, and if the company was a real one and not a fiction or a myth, every one of the grounds upon which it is sought to support the judgment [of the Court of Appeal] is disposed of."

I have recently been engaged in a study which endeavours to ascertain, by examining Australian cases where an argument has been put to the court that it should lift the corporate veil, whether any trends can be detected in these cases. The preliminary results of this study are contained in Tables 2–10 of this essay. In total, fifty-five cases were found in which an argument had been made before an Australian court that the corporate veil should be lifted. It should be noted that excluded from analysis were those cases involving insolvent trading under the statutory provisions of the Corporations Law.

Table 3 indicates that there has been a substantial increase in the number of cases involving arguments about lifting of the corporate veil. In fact, thirty-

Table 2. Frequency of Australian Courts Piercing the Corporate Veil

Category	Total Number of Cases	Pierced	Not Pierced	Percentage Pierced
All	55	13	42	24

Table 3. Temporal Changes to Australian Courts' Willingness to Pierce the Corporate Veil

Category	Total Number of Cases	Pierced	Not Pierced	Percentage Pierced
Pre 1960s	2	0	2	0
1960s	3	1	2	33.3
1970s	4	1	3	25
1980s	15	6	7	40
1990s	31	5	26	16.1

Table 4. Level of Court in Which the Piercing Argument Was Raised

Category	Total Number of Cases	Pierced	Not Pierced	Percentage Pierced
Trial	38	11	27	28.9
First Appeal	14	0	14	0
Second Appeal	3	1	2	33.3

Table 5. Jurisdictional Variation in Willingness to Pierce

5A. *State v. Federal*

Category	Total Number of Cases	Pierced	Not Pierced	Percentage Pierced
State	38	10	28	26.3
Federal	17	3	13	17.6

5B. *Variation Among States*

Category	Total Number of Cases	Pierced	Not Pierced	Percentage Pierced
New South Wales	17	3	14	17.6
Victoria	4	2	2	50
South Australia	4	1	3	25
Queensland	5	2	3	40
Tasmania	0	0	0	0
Western Australia	8	2	6	25

Table 6. Characteristics of Plaintiff

Category	Total Number of Cases	Pierced	Not Pierced	Percentage Pierced
Government[155]	8	2	6	25
Company	26	5	21	19.2
Individual	13	4	9	30.8
Bank	3	0	3	0
Trustee Company	1	0	1	0
Trustee in Bankruptcy or Liquidator	4	2	2	50

one of the fifty-five cases have been brought in the 1990s. However, no trend over time is apparent in relation to whether or not courts are prepared to lift the corporate veil. Table 8 indicates that most of the companies in relation

[155] Director of Public Prosecutions, Trade Practices Commission, (twice), Crown Prosecutor, Australian Trade Commission, Brisbane City Council, Department of Social Security, Repatriation Commission.

Table 7. Characteristics of Defendant

Category	Total Number of Cases	Pierced	Not Pierced	Percentage Pierced
Government[156]	10	2	8	20
Company	20	5	15	25
Individual	19	4	15	21.1
Bank	2	1	1	50
Finance Company	1	0	1	0
Partnership	3	1	2	33.3

Table 8. Nature of the Company Sought to be Pierced

8A. Proprietary v. Public

Category	Total Number of Cases	Pierced	Not Pierced	Percentage Pierced
Proprietary	47	11	36	23.4
Public	8	2	6	25

8B. Number of Shareholders

Category	Total Number of Cases	Pierced	Not Pierced	Percentage Pierced
1	7	4	3	57.1
2–3	24	4	20	16.7
>3 but closely held	4	1	3	25
Not closely held (public)	8	2	6	25
Pty. Ltd., but not ascertainable	12	2	10	16.7

to which an argument is made about lifting the corporate veil are small proprietary companies. Table 9A indicates that the most common context in which the lifting of the corporate veil argument was made was a statutory context (twenty-six cases) followed by a contract context (eighteen cases) and

[156] For example, Commissioner of Land Tax, Victorian Road Corporation, Australian Trade Commission, Commissioner of Taxation (4 times).

Table 9. Context and Bases Advanced Justifying the Piercing of the Corporate Veil

9A. Context[157]

Category	Total Number of Cases	Pierced	Not Pierced	Percentage Pierced
Contract	18	5	13	27.8
Tort	5	2	3	40
Criminal	3	0	3	0
Statute	26	6	20	23.1
Procedural/ discovery	3	1	2	33.3
Solicitor/client	1	0	1	0

9B. Bases Advanced Justifying the Piercing of the Corporate Veil[158]

Category	Total Number of Cases	Pierced	Not Pierced	Percentage Pierced
Agency	34	8	26	23.5
Fraud	11	2	9	18.2
Group Enterprises	18	2	16	11.1
Trust	3	0	3	0
Unfairness/ Justice	10	5	5	50

a tort context (five cases). Table 9B indicates that the most common basis advanced in relation to why the court should lift the corporate veil was that of agency (thirty-four cases). This was followed by a group enterprises argument (eighteen cases) and an argument that the corporate veil should be lifted because of fraud (eleven cases).

In *Briggs* v. *James Hardie and Co. Pty. Ltd.*,[159] Rogers J suggested that different considerations should apply in deciding whether to pierce the corporate veil in actions in tort when compared to other actions such as contract:[160]

"Generally speaking, a person suffering injury as a result of the tortious act of a corporation has no choice in the selection of the tortfeasor. The victim of the neg-

[157] One case was both contract and tort.

[157] Some cases had more than one argument advanced to justify the lifting of the corporate veil. Hence the sum total of cases is more than 55.

[159] (1989) 7 ACLC 841.   [160] *Ibid.*, at 863.

ligent act has no choice as to the corporation which will do him harm. In contrast, a contracting party may readily choose not to enter into a contract with a subsidiary of a wealthy parent. The contracting entity may enquire as to the amount of paid up capital and, generally speaking, as to the capacity of the other party to pay the proposed contract debt and may guard against the possibility that the subsidiary may be unable to pay."

Are courts more willing to lift the veil in actions in negligence? Our study showed that in 40 per cent of the tort cases, the court was prepared to lift the corporate veil. This was the highest percentage of all categories. However, because there was a total of only five cases, the sample is too small to make any meaningful conclusions. We saw earlier that Professor Blumberg has demonstrated that a number of the economic justifications for limited liability have either limited application or no application to holding companies and their wholly-owned subsidiaries.[161] Are courts more prepared to lift the corporate veil where there is a corporate group? Although we need to do further analysis fully to answer this question, our preliminary results indicate that once again the question would be answered in the negative.

Overall, in 24 per cent of the fifty-five cases, courts were prepared to lift the corporate veil. These are only preliminary results. However, as previously indicated, the results do not indicate any significant themes or trends in relation to cases where an argument is made that the court should lift the corporate veil other than an increasing number of cases in recent years where this argument has been made.

VI SOME IMPLICATIONS OF INSTITUTIONAL INVESTMENT AND ELECTRONIC COMMERCE FOR MANDATORY RULES

In this section I consider some of the implications of two major developments—the increasing influence of institutional investors and electronic commerce—for mandatory legal rules.

A Institutional Investment[162]

As the following table demonstrates, institutional investors are major holders of the shares of companies listed on the Australian Stock Exchange ("ASX"). As at June 1996, life insurance companies and superannuation funds owned over 25 per cent of the shares of companies listed on the ASX. Other financial institutions held another 8.5 per cent.

---

[161] Blumberg, n. 126 above, 624.

[162] For detailed examination of a range of issues regarding institutional investors, see G Stapledon, *Institutional Shareholders and Corporate Governance* (Oxford, Clarendon, 1996).

Table 10. ASX Share Ownership by Sector. June 1996

Sector	$A billion	%
Companies	38.1	11.0
Banks	6.9	2.0
Non-bank financial intermediaries	3.1	0.9
Life insurance and superannuation funds	88.1	25.4
Other financial institutions	29.4	8.5
Government	4.5	1.3
Rest of world	111.5	32.1
Households	65.4	18.8
Total	347.0	100.0

Source: M Heffernan, "The Role of the Australian Stock Exchange" in G Walker, B Fisse, and I Ramsay *Securities Regulation Law* (LBC Information Services, Sydney, forthcoming, 1998).

What are some of the implications of the increasing importance of institutional investors? There is increasing evidence that the growth of institutional investors has improved the informational efficiency of the capital markets. This evidence suggests that a higher degree of institutional ownership is associated with more frequent information releases from companies and more intensive research activity by analysts. This results in an inverse relationship between the degree of institutional ownership and variance of share returns. Moreover, recent evidence concerning share issues supports the argument that the information acquisition activities of institutional investors reduce information differences or asymmetries between managers on the one hand and the capital markets on the other hand.[163] The authors of this study state that there may be a number of reasons for this:

(a) institutions typically have greater resources than individual investors to expend on obtaining and analysing corporate information;

(b) economies of scale and professional expertise give institutions lower marginal costs in acquiring information, as a result of which they can acquire more information of higher quality;

(c) some institutions (such as insurance companies and banks) may have business relationships with the company that provide them with information that is unavailable to other investors;

(d) institutions have greater incentives than individual shareholders to monitor the activities of companies because they typically have larger investments; and

[163] S H Szewczyk, G P Tsetsekos and R Varma, "Institutional Ownership and the Liquidity of Common Stock Offerings" (1992) 27 *Fin Rev* 211.

(e) because institutions typically trade more frequently than individual investors, this increases the likelihood of new information being rapidly incorporated into share prices.[164]

This evidence has implications for mandatory rules regarding disclosure. Institutional investors have a number of means of acquiring information independently of any information obtained by reason of mandatory corporate disclosure rules (such as annual reports and prospectuses). This is recognised in specific provisions of the Corporations Law that provide exemptions from mandatory disclosure requirements where the investor is an institutional investor. For example, where a company is raising capital, a prospectus is not required if the investor is a life insurance company, the trustee of a government superannuation fund, the trustee of any other superannuation fund that has net assets of at least $10 million or the manager of an investment fund that has at least $10 million in assets.[165]

The evidence that has been documented concerning the ways in which institutional investors improve the informational efficiency of the capital markets supports these exemptions. The exemptions are also appropriate given the high costs of mandatory disclosure requirements.[166] If institutional investors are instrumental in providing the informational efficiency of the capital markets, this necessitates consideration of whether the current exemptions from the mandatory disclosure requirements should be extended. In other words, is there merit in maintaining mandatory disclosure requirements for unsophisticated investors if these investors play an insignificant role in providing the informational efficiency of the capital markets? Of course, there may be other justifications for mandatory disclosure requirements designed to protect unsophisticated investors.[167]

B Electronic Commerce

There has been much discussion in recent times regarding the implications of electronic commerce for securities regulation.[168] Recent developments in electronic commerce and securities regulation have included the primary offer-

---

[164] Szewczyk, Tsetsekos and Varma, n. 163 above, 214.

[165] Corporations Regulations 7.12.05 and 7.12.06.

[166] Industry Commission, *Availability of Capital* (1991), Part 9.5.

[167] These are discussed in Blair and Ramsay, n. 100 above.

[168] See, for example, Parliamentary Joint Committee on Corporations and Securities, *Virtually No Liability? Securities Markets in an Electronic Age*, Issues Paper, 1997; R Robertson, "Personal Investing in Cyberspace and the Federal Securities Laws" (1996) 23 *Sec Reg L J* 347; J Seligman, "The Obsolescence of Wall Street: A Contextual Approach to the Evolving Structure of Federal Securities Regulation" (1995) 93 *Mich L Rev* 649; A C Gavis, "The Offering and Distribution of Securities in Cyberspace: A Review of Regulatory and Industry Initiatives" (1996) 52 *Bus Lawyer* 317; M McGregor-Lowndes, "Corporate Disclosure, the Internet and the Australian Securities Commission" (1996) 14 *CSLJ* 219. See also the papers presented at the Australian Securities

ing of securities via prospectuses on the Internet, and secondary trading of securities on the Internet. In the United States, over seventy mutual fund companies and over fifty broker-dealer firms have established sites on the Internet.[169]

The Chairman of the Australian Securities Commission has recently stated that electronic commerce raises key issues related to corporate law, securities markets and share trading that are currently governed by the Corporations Law. These issues include:

(a) *electronic markets*: the approval and subsequent regulation of electronic share and other securities markets;
(b) *initial offerings of securities*: ensuring compliance with the law regulating prospectuses and initial offers of securities by electronic means;
(c) *investment advice*: advice given by persons via the Internet without an appropriate licence or with no consideration of the needs of investors receiving the advice;
(d) *disclosure of interests*: non-disclosure of commissions and other relevant interests in securities by persons providing advice via the Internet;
(e) *false statements*: the capacity for dissemination of false and misleading information about securities on the Internet; and
(f) *market manipulation*: the potential for creation of false markets, manipulation of prices or volumes, and insider trading as a result of information disseminated about securities on the Internet.[170]

These are significant issues according to the ASC Chairman because, while electronic commerce may result in improved availability of information for regulatory or enforcement purposes, it also facilitates huge volumes of activity that entirely disregard traditional jurisdictional borders, and thus poses urgent questions about:

(a) the practical enforceability of currently existing national securities regimes;
(b) the need for international co-operation between regulators and market authorities; and
(c) the effectiveness of many of the traditional regulatory approaches and mechanisms that have been employed to date.[171]

Commission, *Electronic Commerce Conference*, 4–5 Feb. 1997, Sydney; and Washington University School of Law and John M Olin School of Business Conference, *Markets and Information Gathering in an Electronic Age: Securities Regulation in the 21st Century*, 14 Mar. 1997, Washington University.

[169] Gavis, n. 168 above, 363–4.
[170] A Cameron, "Electronic Commerce: The ASC's Experience", paper presented at the *Electronic Commerce Conference*, Sydney, 4–5 Feb. 1997.
[171] *Ibid.*

In 1996 the Australian Securities Commission issued Policy Statement 107 on Electronic Prospectuses. In this Policy Statement, the ASC states that it considers the use of electronic prospectuses should be allowed in cases where the policy underlying the prospectus provisions of the Australian Corporations Law is satisfied. The fundamental objective of these prospectus provisions is to ensure that investors are able to make informed investment decisions, on the basis of a prospectus containing all material information about the securities being offered and about the issuer. Consequently, the ASC will allow issuers to distribute electronic prospectuses if:

(a) the issuer lodges a paper prospectus containing an application form with the ASC;

(b) the issuer and any other person who passes on an application form takes reasonable steps to ensure that the investor receives an application form attached to or accompanied by an electronic prospectus, or a print-out of it;

(c) the issuer takes reasonable steps to ensure that the electronic prospectus received by the investor is complete and protected from alteration or tampering;

(d) the electronic prospectus contains the same information in the same sequence as the paper prospectus lodged with the ASC, except for differences allowed by the ASC;

(e) the issuer provides a free paper copy of the prospectus lodged, if requested;

(f) the electronic prospectus and any promotional material are made available in a way that encourages investors to make decisions on the basis of the prospectus, and not on the basis of promotional material or pressure selling; and

(g) the investor receives any necessary update in information before the investment decision is finalised.

What are some of the implications for regulation of developments in electronic commerce? Perhaps the most profound question is whether traditional regulation will actually work. How does the ASC regulate securities offered by the Internet when the posting on the Internet is made in some distant country yet the posting is read by potential investors in Australia?

What type of regulation is appropriate? Steven Wallman, a Commissioner of the United States Securities and Exchange Commission, believes that securities regulation in an era of electronic commerce should be as goal-oriented as possible, as opposed to dictating specific processes that must be followed.[172] In other words, rather than mandatory "command and control" type regulation, those who are subject to the regulation should be permitted

---

[172] S M Wallman, *Regulating in a World of Technological and Global Change*, paper presented at the Institute of International Bankers Annual Washington Conference, 4 Mar. 1996, Washington DC.

flexibility to allow their methods of complying with the regulation to evolve in accordance with changes in the markets. Commissioner Wallman provides as an example the SEC's policy regarding the use of electronic communications to fulfil the delivery requirements of the United States federal securities laws. The goal of the SEC was to encourage electronic delivery of information. However, instead of dictating specific formats that must be satisfied for electronic delivery of information (in other words, a "command and control" approach to regulation) the SEC focused on two goal oriented issues: whether the electronic communication provides investors with *notice* of and *access* to information similar to that which would be received by traditional paper delivery. Consequently, the SEC has encouraged the market to create particular ways to satisfy these two goals. As Commissioner Wallman states, "in this way, technological innovations in this area might best continue to flourish, instead of be constrained".[173]

VII CONCLUSION

The decision of the House of Lords in *Salomon* continues to be debated because the issues raised in the case one hundred years ago remain relevant. When should limited liability be granted to an organisation? What is the appropriate balance between protecting shareholders of a company by granting them limited liability and protecting unsecured creditors who will bear additional risk where shareholders have limited liability?

What is the appropriate balance in corporate regulation between mandatory rules which cannot be varied and enabling rules which can be varied by participants in companies? We have seen that this was relevant in *Salomon* because the critical issue before the House of Lords was whether to extend limited liability, a default rule, to Aron Salomon. The debate on the balance between mandatory and enabling corporate laws or rules did not end in 1897 and will continue for the foreseeable future. Yet it is important that we continually focus upon this issue. Particular laws have both costs and benefits. Part of my analysis has consisted of an examination of the costs and benefits of particular corporate rules such as limited liability, and the regulation of share buy-backs and takeovers. The corporate law regimes of all countries are a balance of mandatory and enabling rules. Not surprisingly, the balance differs among countries. Consequently, another challenge is to identify the factors that determine whether corporate law is mostly mandatory or enabling. Some of these factors will play a more important role in some countries than in other countries. Several of these factors were considered in Section II of this essay. They included the effectiveness of various market forces in protecting the interests of shareholders so that the need for mandatory rules to protect shareholders is reduced.

[173] *Ibid.*, at 7.

Finally, recent developments, such as the rise of institutional investors and the growth of electronic commerce, have implications for the type of regulation that we have. For example, the information-gathering activities of institutional investors undercuts some of the rationales for mandatory corporate disclosure rules in certain circumstances. The six members of the House of Lords who gave speeches in *Salomon* would have been unable to predict these developments. Yet the issues they considered continue to resonate in corporate law debates one hundred years later.

13

Commentary on Ramsay

TIM HAZLEDINE*

Faced with the task of commenting on a lengthy essay on a subject I had never before heard of I was briefly tempted to follow the advice of the Rev. Sidney Smith—Macaulay's "Smith of Smiths"—who once confided: "I never read a book before reviewing it—it does prejudice one so".[1]

But curiosity got the better of me and I did read, more than once, what is indeed a fine essay. Whether my personal profit from having done so can be turned to others' advantage is however moot. I must stress that I come to the task of commentator with no background in the law or even in "law and economics" to guide (or blinker) me. I do, however, share with Professor Ramsay a field of specialism within my discipline, namely the study of firms in their markets, known as Corporate Law to him, and industrial organisation ("IO") to me. Thus we must be concerned with the same phenomena, and I will take it as my role to indicate how Professor Ramsay's legal approach to these contrasts (or concords) in interesting ways with the IO economist's view of the world.

I will follow Professor Ramsay in moving beyond the *Salomon*[2] case to the broader issue of "regulation" of which *Salomon* is an (obviously) important example. At once we must acknowledge a substantial difference in usage. To the lawyer, regulation is the system of laws that constrain or facilitate business behaviour. To the economist, a system built only on such laws is an *unregulated* system, as found in the telecommunications sector in New Zealand, wherein very tricky and valuable disputes over access of a competitor to another's network have been left to the courts to resolve through the application of competition law.

True, the official Wellington name for this regime is "light-handed regulation", but I am not alone amongst economists[3] in dismissing this as a

---

* Professor of Economics, The University of Auckland.

[1] H Pearson, *The Smith of Smiths* (London, Hamilton, 1945), 54.

[2] *Salomon* v. *A Salomon & Co. Ltd.* [1897] AC 22.

[3] Nor politicians. A story in the *NZ Herald* in the week of the conference ("Govt in the spotlight", 21 July 1997, p. C1) quotes the leader of the political party ACT, Richard Prebble, who sold Telecom Corporation of NZas Minister in charge of privatisation in the Lange Labour administration of the 1980s, complaining that the current Minister of Telecommunications is adopting a "no hands" stance, to the detriment of both Clear Communications (Telecom's major competitor) and the telecommunications industry in general.

euphemism for *"no-hands"* regulation, or no regulation at all. What economists mean by regulation is the direct, day-to-day interference in the affairs and decisions of private firms by a government-appointed agency—a "regulator". Professor Ramsay mentions such "specialist agencies", but does not dwell on them.

Are economists thereby dismissing as unimportant what to corporate lawyers is the very stuff of their existence? No, but we do rather take it for granted. In mainstream economics—of the right or the centre (the left is in temporary abeyance)—*laissez-faire* does not mean anarchy. The most conservative or right-wing of economists are not true libertarians. Having peeled away all the economic policy meddling that they consider misguided at best and downright subversive at worst (macro-economic management, income redistribution, public enterprises, "regulation"), they always stop at a core, residual role for a coercive state in economic affairs, namely, to "define and protect property rights". But they—and economists in general—do not often trouble themselves with concerns about whether defining and protecting property rights could possibly be a teeny bit problematic in principle and in practice.

One line of defence for such an attitude could draw on the very useful principle of the division of labour. We economists will let lawyers look after property rights and, furthermore, we are confident that lawyers will do it well (otherwise they would choose to do something else). Of course we understand that issues must arise from time to time, but we expect that conferences like this will sort things out. After all, if lawyers are still chatting about a hundred-year old case, it does suggest that nothing of terrific importance has arisen since.

I actually think there is a lot of practical merit in this position. Few of us are smart enough to move confidently across paradigms. We have to concentrate our scarce resources of time and wit on those issues which are both pressing and susceptible to the analytical tools we are comfortable working with. Ask an economist or the citizenry in general where are the big problems of the day, and I expect few to finger the rule of law. Indeed, I would venture to place our legal system high on the short list of true successes of the liberal capitalist democracies, along with the international postal system, Keynesian financial management, the near-elimination of infant mortality and the perfection of the game of rugby.

So I suppose I could stop right there, wish the lawyers to carry on the good work and get back to my economic models. But I am troubled by what I have read in Professor Ramsay's essay. Economists may ignore the law, but lawyers clearly have not ignored economics. Professor Ramsay knows more economic theory than I have legal expertise. These property rights issues turn out (at least in the field of corporate law) to be economic matters; specifically, the economics of agency, in which someone ("the principal") seeks someone else ("the agent") to do their bidding under conditions of asymmetrically held private information. When either or both of the principal and the agent has private information about states or behaviour which it is costly for the other party to ferret out and verify, then all potential gains from exchange may not be realised, unless some suitable mechanism (which may involve a legal construct) can be devised so as to align the principal's and the agent's incentives to reveal or behave.

Classical examples of agency problems are generated by the insurance industry. If insurees can conceal how accident-prone they are (their type), then insurers will have to set their rates to cover the possibility of high-risk subjects being amongst their clients, which will mean that low-risk clients will not find it worthwhile to purchase insurance, so that in equilibrium only high-risk subjects will be insured. The market for low-risk people, who would love to buy suitably priced insurance which insurers would love to supply to them, will simply not exist. This inefficiency is called *adverse selection*. Another application is or was the American light aircraft industry, which, despite the wonderful utility of its product, was virtually driven out of existence by the inability of manufacturers to distinguish between those people who would make ridiculous damages claims if they crashed their aircraft and those who would not.

The other type of agency problem, known as *moral hazard*, is generated by the responsiveness of risk to the imperfectly observable behaviour of the agent, as when, having taken out theft insurance, the agent becomes careless about securing her property. "Solving" these problems is in general an imperfect trade-off, with resources diverted away from directly productive activities towards monitoring behaviour or states.

It is true that limited liability itself can be justified by risk, unadulterated by agency considerations. If bad outcomes are generated solely by unfavourable throws of God's die, as in crop failures due to drought or gold mines that turn out to have no gold in them, and if individuals are risk-averse, and if aggregations of small pieces of capital are needed to finance projects, then limiting individual liability for failure can result in more projects being undertaken which in the long-run will be on average wealth-increasing.

If, however, the likelihood of a bad outcome does partially depend on behaviour, it is easy to imagine how limited liability—which is a form of insurance—could exacerbate agency problems. Rather than a sensible, risk-reducing portfolio, the limited liability farmer could gamble all on a high-yield but drought-sensitive crop. The gold miners could drill willy-nilly, rather than take the trouble to carry out proper geological assays which would improve the probability of making a strike.

It is, I presume, for this reason that the extension of limited liability to sole proprietorships is controversial. But for the joint stock case, Professor Ramsay is able to show a list of agency-theoretical justifications for limited liability, generated by the principal–agent relationship between shareholders and managers; in particular, that managers will be constrained to act more efficiently if the share price is more sensitive to their company's performance, which in turn is more likely the more active is trading at the margin, which in its turn is more likely if the "free transfer of shares" is facilitated by individual share-holders not having to worry about the wealth of other shareholders—a nice point.

So much for limited liability. I follow Professor Ramsay now in turning to the broader issue of the command versus facilitation question. In the specific corporate law context, do regulations "enable" or "mandate" behaviour—a distinction that is very important to Professor Ramsay's essay?

There is a very large class of regulations, not all involving directly the legal system, for which the distinction may be of practical importance, but is not a matter of principle. This type is found when the regulation is a "standard"—what economists call a focal point—not necessarily of any special intrinsic merit, but enabling the parties to deal quickly and efficiently with each other when they judge it not worthwhile to invest the time in reaching some tailor-made agreement. In economists' terms, such regulations are designed to economise on transaction costs. Economists and others have not perhaps appreciated the pervasiveness and power of transaction costs—I will give some figures on these below.

Now, the interesting thing about standards is that they are nearly always wrong but are very useful. Take the example of petrol, which the four petrol companies that operate in New Zealand have agreed to supply for normal retail use at just two standard specifications: 91 and 96 octane ratings. There is of course some intrinsic merit in these standards: it would be awkward if octane ratings were set, say, at 50 and 150. But I expect that 92 and 97 octane petrol would do just about as well. In general, neither strength of petrol will be optimal for a particular car's engine, but nearly all engines can be tolera-bly well tuned for one or the other, and there are, presumably, worthwhile savings in transaction costs (distribution, number of pumps needed, etc.) that justify the standards on balance. However, the petrol companies are clearly "enabled" to offer other octane ratings if they wish to, and already do for spe-cial uses, such as rally cars.[4]

How many of the matters of corporate law considered by Professor Ramsay are like this? Does, the difference, say, between a mandatory corpo-rate code and a code requiring that the same rules be followed unless the par-ties can agree on something else just differ in the quantitative extent of its applicability: the first case applying to 100 per cent of situations, the second to that percentage of situations in which mutual agreement has not been reached? That is, is the mandatory/enabling distinction not fundamental here?

---

[4] There can be a sinister side to standards or focal points. In other jurisdictions motorists are in fact offered more than two octane standards to choose from. Petrol pricing may also be judged more competitive in these markets. It may be that the voluntary restriction by the New Zealand industry to just two ratings is one of the factors facilitating its (alleged) ability to collude to avoid passing on cost decreases into lower retail pump prices—it makes such collusion simpler.

Perhaps not, but perhaps it matters very much. It depends, it seems to me, on what was the justification of the original mandating regulation. If this was just a co-ordinating standard, then fair enough, the distinction is not qualitative. But not so if the mandatory-without-exceptions rule was enacted because it was believed by the legislator to be *right* in some absolute moral sense—i.e. beyond the domain of the cost-benefit calculus: *thou shalt not sell thyself into slavery*. Then, any exception-enabling amendment is fundamentally subversive of the integrity of the rule: *thou shalt not sell thyself into slavery, unless you're quite sure you want to.*

This is a very big issue in competition law. For a long time—nearly a century in the cases of Canada and the United States—antitrust was essentially mandatory: *thou shalt not act in such a way as to substantially lessen competition.* Ascertaining whether an act had or would perpetrate substantially lessened competition was up to the tribunals and the courts, a difficult job that they carried out, in my opinion, tolerably well, except in highly unusual or unprecedented situations, such as the interconnection dispute in New Zealand between Telecom NZ Ltd. and Clear Communications Ltd.[5]

But for a decade now in the Anglo-Saxon jurisdictions we have seen tacked on to antitrust law a rider variously known as the public benefit test or the efficiencies defence. Now, *thou shalt not act in such a way as substantially to lessen competition unless it is in the public interest that you do so.*

I have argued the subversiveness of this,[6] and that this is deliberate. The public benefit is measured according to the Benthamite calculus of the monetarised sum of gains and losses, so that consumer losses from higher prices can be outweighed by producer gains from higher profits. Gone, then, is the primacy of lessening of competition, with its justification rooted in the need to protect less powerful participants in the market (consumers, small firms, etc.) and in a quite fundamental belief in the desirability of competition as due economic process.

Indeed, it hardly seems possible to retain the traditional "substantially lessened competition" focus of antitrust alongside the modern efficiency trade-off mechanism, and it has been suggested (in New Zealand by the Business Roundtable[7]) that the term "competition policy" be dropped and replaced with "efficiency policy" as a more appropriate heading for the purpose of

---

[5] Major landmarks in the ongoing stream of litigation between Telecom Corporation of NZ Ltd. and Clear Communications Ltd. include: *Clear Communications Ltd.* v. *Telecom Corporation of New Zealand Ltd.* (1993) 4 NZBLC 103,340 (CA); *Telecom Corporation of New Zealand Ltd.* v. *Clear Communications Ltd.* [1995] 1 NZLR 385 (PC); and *Telecom Corporation of New Zealand Ltd.* v. *Clear Communications Ltd.* (1997) 6 NZBLC 102,325 (HC).

[6] T Hazledine, "The 'Public Interest' in Competition Policy: Due Process or Economic Rationalism?", The University of Auckland, Department of Economics, Working Paper 142, Dec. 1994; "Rationalism Rebuffed? Lessons from Modern Canadian and New Zealand Competition Policy" (1998) 13 *The Review of Industrial Organization* (forthcoming).

[7] The New Zealand Business Roundtable is an organisation of chief executives of major New Zealand businesses. The organisation's self-defined purpose is to contribute to the development of sound public policies that reflect overall New Zealand interests.

modern antitrust intervention. I think this makes logical sense, but also that it would not be the end of the story. I suspect that the addition of efficiencies defences to antitrust statutes (or at least to the guidelines that flesh out for practitioners the meaning of terms such as "public benefit") is in fact a Trojan horse, that once established within the portals of competition law and policy will issue an irresistible army of the right fighting for *laissez-faire*. This is because the calculus of (predicted) costs and benefits from, say, a proposed merger is so notoriously imprecise and unreliable that it would really be difficult for the courts or tribunals to use such calculations justly to impede private-sector parties from going about whatever business they agree with each other.

I should note that, with the usual exception of rationalist New Zealand, efficiencies defences have not so far in their first decade of use been determining (in the sense of overthrowing a judgment based on likely substantial lessening of competition)—not in Canada, not in the United States, nor, I believe, in Australia. Also, my view that the enabling efficiencies trade-off is, if taken seriously, fundamentally subversive of mandatory antitrust is not at all a mainstream view amongst my competition policy economist colleagues. I hope they are correct, but would leave on the table for discussion the suggestion that other moves towards enabling regulation, such as those discussed by Professor Ramsay, are intended to subvert rather than supplement the old mandatory regime.

But so what? Why isn't that a Good Thing? The economic issues here are those thrown up in the great debate between "freshwater" and "saltwater" economists that has dominated policy discourse in our subject for the past quarter century. Freshwater doctrine sprang from universities dotted around the shores of the Great Lakes: Chicago, Minnesota, Rochester and Carnegie-Mellon. Saltwater specialists live on or near the sea: Harvard, Yale, Massachusetts Institute of Technology, Princeton and the University of Pennsylvania. The groupings are not fortuitous. The salty schools are older, Ivy League, Anglo-Saxon establishments, tending to inculcate a patrician *de haut en bas* spirit that, in economics, leans towards government interventionism. The younger inland academies were peopled by later, less favoured immigrant groups—Jews and continental Europeans—who have struggled to escape from State oppression and see the free market as the great guarantor of freedom and opportunity.

In macro-economics the two schools are represented by Keynesians and monetarists. The monetarists enjoyed an ascendancy in the 1980s but seem now to be in retreat, though the new-Keynesian forces are not yet well enough organised to mount much of a pursuit. In micro-economics, which is what matters here, the key issue is the presence or absence of market power. Antitrust—the oldest and saltiest of interventionist microeconomic policies— is based on the presumption that individuals and firms can distort markets to achieve for themselves positions of privilege and wealth, so that government intervention is justified to correct these monopolistic abuses. But freshwater enthusiasts point to the endless opportunities for competition to deny the very possibility of entrenched monopoly positions, *unless these be sanctioned by the only power superior to the market—the State itself.*

Adept freshwater exponents are marvellously ingenious at turning any saltwater argument on its head, to the effect that public policy intervention, however well-meaning (and it might not be—policy may be captured by special interests), will in fact always make things worse, not better, because of its inevitable interference with efficient free market forces. Take as an example the forced disclosure by firms of the salaries of their top executives. This is, of course, a saltwater stratagem, designed to redress asymmetries in power between managers and shareholders, by at least giving the latter information on what their nominal agents are paying themselves.

That is, its desired effect is, on balance, to reduce top executive salaries. But a freshwater analyst can argue, presumably sincerely, that the actual effect of this disclosure rule will be to *increase*, not decrease, remuneration. How do they figure this? Well, start from the presumption that the market for executives, left to itself, is efficient. Then everyone is being paid the price that efficiently balances the supply and demand for their services. Add a disclosure rule that publicises top persons' pay, and these jobs will be made less attractive (because of vulgar publicity and the increased threat of extortion). The supply curve for executives will shift up, and so too must their pay, to compensate them for the additional unpleasantness.

The freshwater position (markets always work properly) is more extreme than the saltwater model (markets sometimes do not work properly) and so might be judged less plausible *a priori*. But in particular disputes of law and policy, including the disclosure and other issues addressed by Professor Ramsay, the balance of probabilities is difficult to assess, even empirically. These matters will remain contentious, and should do so.

A real problem is that economics has actually not taken markets (or co-ordination of production and exchange in general) seriously enough. In an economics textbook virtually all the analysis is of the production (supply) and consumption (demand) of goods and services, not of how supply and demand are brought together, both between and within firms and other organisations, apart from simple dynamics of price adjusting somehow to balance supply and demand. The "invisible auctioneer" is dimensionless as well as unseen. This neglect includes the blithe propensity of our discipline to assume a well functioning property rights system, as noted above.

Now this just has to be wrong. Recently I have replicated for New Zealand an American analysis by Wallis and North[8] that estimated the proportion of economic activity that is in fact devoted to transaction activities, rather than

---

[8] J J Wallis and D C North, "Measuring the Transaction Sector in the American Economy, 1870–1970" in S L Engerman and R Z Gallman (eds.), *Long-term Factors in American Economic Growth*, (NBER Studies in Income and Wealth, University of Chicago Press, 1986), vol. v.

the direct "transformation" of inputs into outputs. Transaction activities include all forms of monitoring and exchanging property rights, including business services, finance, insurance, clerical work and management. The results are startling. Twenty years ago, in 1976, there was about one transaction worker for every two transformation workers in New Zealand. The period of economic liberalisation since then has been associated with a sharp increase in the resources devoted to transactions. The number of lawyers, for example, has increased by about 50 per cent. Overall, movement from transformation into transaction activities has been such that, by 1995, *about as many New Zealanders in the workforce were involved with co-ordinating, monitoring, etc. (transacting) as were directly producing goods and services.* Free markets have not come free! These figures surely justify economists diverting more attention to transaction activities, including those discussed in Professor Ramsay's essay and in other essays presented in this book. If transacting is such an important part of everyday economic activity, then we can expect that changes in transaction technologies must be an important (though, outside economic history, neglected) source of economic growth.

Towards the end of his long and busy life (1771–1845) the dear old Rev. Sidney Smith marvelled at the improvements he had witnessed in his time on earth: gas, steam-boats, railways, McAdamised roads, wooden pavements, the police force, cabs (taxis), umbrellas, braces, quinine, carriage springs, (gentlemen's) clubs, the penny-post, plus "humane laws, the sobriety of the gentry and the safety of the streets".[9] Smith was "utterly surprised that all these changes and inventions did not occur two centuries ago",[10] which is an acute observation, since many of the items on his list depended on improvements in organisational and other transactional techniques, rather than advances in physical technologies depending on progress in the natural sciences. If Smith had lived a little longer he could have added the widespread adoption of limited liability as one of the great wealth-generating innovations of the modern world.

---

[9] Pearson, n. 1 above, 316.
[10] *Ibid.*

14

Financial Transparency and Corporate Governance: the United States as a Model?

LOUIS LOWENSTEIN*

In speaking of corporate governance, and how to make corporate boards and managements more effective and responsive to long-term shareholder interests, we usually look to board structures, compensation patterns, independent oversight and the like. The suggestion here is that good financial accounting, the the extensive disclosures mandated most often in the English-speaking world, and notably in the United States, is an often overlooked but powerful tool for enhancing corporate survival and efficiency.

I THREE ELEMENTS OF SHAREHOLDER OVERSIGHT

Insofar as they concern shareholder action or control, corporate structure and governance break down into three distinct factors:

(a) is there a shareholder or group that is motivated to take whatever affirmative action might be needed?
(b) does it have the means, by control of the board or some co-operative arrangement, to take remedial action? and
(c) does it have access to the financial and other information needed to know when and what action is called for?

In a private company, one with, say, ten to twenty shareholders, these issues would rarely be significant. The shareholders, boards and managers are rolled into one; they have the incentives, the means to act and all the necessary information.

For a public company, corporate governance is inherently complex. Will shareholders in fact select the board rather than merely bless management's choices, will they watch management closely, will they act if management slips or will they merely pass the bad coin, as Keynes put it?

---

* Professor Emeritus of Finance and Law, Columbia University.

II THE GERMAN AND JAPANESE STRUCTURES ARE INTUITIVELY SENSIBLE

All the major industrialised countries have implicitly relied on a relational model, where one or more investors have close ties to the company, own significant amounts of stock, have board representation and tend to take remedial action where required. All the major industrialised countries, that is, except the United States.

Consider these few facts about corporate control and power in Germany. (One could use, say, Japan or France to similar effect, but we will focus on Germany.) In 1986, the latest year for which good data are available, at thirty-three widely-held stock corporations, all among the one hundred largest in Germany, an average of 82 per cent of the votes were cast by banks and 45 per cent of the votes were cast just by the three largest banks, Deutsche Bank, Dresdner Bank and Commerzbank. This extraordinary voting power translates into direct representation in the boardroom, where we can be sure that managements listen carefully, oh so very carefully, to what the banks have to say. Of the one hundred largest firms in 1990, Deutsche Bank alone had managerial representation on thirty-five. As one would expect, the managements of German companies consult with their banks, not just at board meetings, but on a regular basis.

On the other hand, the German stock market is underdeveloped compared with the United States, so that the requirements for financial reporting and for disclosure of executive compensation, personal stockholdings and trading are predictably weak. The banks have private access to corporate data, and the public shareholder has no power to insist on financial transparency American-style.

The other two of our three tests for active shareholder monitoring have obviously been met in Germany. Banks have the necessary incentives, if for no other reason than that they own a substantial minority of the shares. One commonly cited example is the 28 per cent block of Daimler Benz owned directly by Deutsche Bank, a single block that is large even by German standards. A 10–12 per cent bank-held block would be more common. The third element, the means to act, also appears to be satisfied, perhaps by some form of implicitly concerted action.

This German main bank system is not without its strains. No system is. Do the banks and their industrial clients slip into cosy, old-boy relationships (where substantial sloth is tolerated)? Are banks able to compete on an equal footing in an age of global equity markets offering low-cost capital? The system has come under pressure to become more open and, for better or worse, more democratic.

Note that the German main bank and also the Japanese *keiretsu* structures make intuitive good sense. If the problem is how to correct for managerial failures when they are still no more than a nosebleed and not yet a hæmorrhage, then it greatly helps to have close at hand a doctor who can spot problems early on. It is no coincidence that these are two countries with remarkably homogeneous populations, educated and disciplined workforces, in which continuing relationships are what matter across the social spectrum.

The United States is a very different, far less structured, far less relational society. It is not just our racial and cultural diversity, but our social and geographic mobility, which goes back to colonial times. (A great uncle of mine who was a pedlar when he arrived in 1885 died as the founder of a major metals refining business.) One consequence is that shareholders typically have no continuing involvement with the companies in which they invest. None! Turnover of stocks listed on the New York Stock Exchange is about 75 per cent annually, compared with 14 per cent back in 1960. Of the three factors mentioned earlier, we in the United States are essentially missing the two that are most visible in Germany and Japan: the incentive for particular shareholders to intervene and the means to do so. Even more so than individual investors, the professional managers exhibit a persistent emphasis on momentary stock prices. Owning about half the stocks, they account for the bulk of the trading. Mutual funds own 16 per cent of the shares but they account for 23 per cent of the trading. The subtleties and nuances of a particular business utterly escape them.

III   THE UNITED STATES MODEL SEEMS TO BE INFERIOR, YET IT WORKS

One wonders, how can American industry hope to succeed? Yet succeed it does. Unemployment is below 5 per cent, lower than any of the other G–10 countries except Japan. Despite that low rate, manufacturing productivity has increased sharply since the end of the 1980s, matched only by countries such as Korea and Singapore. Norbert Walter, chief economist of the Deutsche Bank Group, recently reported that Japanese workers were only 53 per cent as productive as Americans, while Germans, whose wages are on average much higher, were but 90 per cent as productive as Americans.[1] And *Fortune* magazine noted with awe that returns on shareholder equity, traditionally the single most widely used benchmark of corporate performance, have risen to their highest level in United States history.

IV   THE AMERICAN MANDATED DISCLOSURE SYSTEM IS A CORNERSTONE

Having posed the puzzle, let us begin to find the answers. Fortunately, there are many roads to heaven, and each country, if it is to succeed, tends to find its own. To compensate for our shortcomings on factors one and two, the

---

[1] N Walter, "What Productivity Gap?", *New York Times*, 14 Aug. 1996, p A21, col 2.

United States has developed the third factor, the financial reporting and disclosure system, to a degree not known anywhere else, not even in England, which is the best of the other major industrialised nations. That should not surprise us. Given American history and mobility, we have developed a populist, decentralised solution, one that is market-based, highly impersonal, but wholly consistent with a culture in which sunshine laws and the Freedom of Information Act are implicitly and more broadly trusted more than old-boy networks of "boys" from Harvard or Columbia.

V THE CORPORATE CHIEFTAINS MANAGE WHAT WE MEASURE

The roots of this financial disclosure system lie in the securities laws of 1933–4, proposed by President Roosevelt and adopted by a Congress fearful of a loss of confidence in United States financial markets. The single most important act is the Securities Exchange Act 1934, which created the reporting and disclosure framework for the day-to-day trading markets and also created the Securities and Exchange Commission ("SEC"). There are in all eight statutes under which the SEC operates, but as has been said "the recurrent theme throughout [is] disclosure, again disclosure, and still more disclosure".[2]

Better markets have thus made for better managed companies. The financial disclosure system, while intended to permit investors and creditors to make rational decisions[3] and to make markets fair and efficient, in fact has the quite independent effect of forcing managers to confront disagreeable realities in detail and *early on*, even when those disclosures may have no immediate market consequences. There is nothing here that should surprise chief executive officers (CEOs). Financial accountability to the public requires of senior management no more than they routinely require of the divisional chiefs who in turn report to them.

The Business Roundtable, a CEO group, routinely objects on this or that issue, but compared to, say, France or Germany, the principle of full disclosure is simply not controversial.

Three factors significantly helped to bring about this result:

(a) Unlike some European countries, we are not burdened by a requirement that financial accounting follow tax accounting.[4] Unlike Japan, we do not confuse financial reporting goals with national fiscal policy. These are enormous advantages. One need only look at the undesignated, hidden

---

[2] L Loss, *Fundamentals of Securities Regulation* (2nd edn., Boston, Mass., Little, Brown, 1988), 3.

[3] D Kieso and J Weygandt, *Intermediate Accounting* (7th edn., New York, Harper and Row, 1992), 6.

[4] M J Lawrence, "The Where and Why of Transnational Listing From a Corporate Perspective" (IASC 20th Anniversary Conference, 29 June 1993), 6. Mr Lawrence is chairman of The Hundred Group of Finance Directors, United Kingdom.

reserves used by Germans and others to see the dilemma. Europeans like to say that these provisions or reserves are conservative, but look at the effect on the three Cs. Clarity and Consistency of disclosure suffer; one company's earnings cease to be Comparable with another's. And those reserves, which do "conservatively" understate earnings when they are created, will overstate them when reversed. Daimler Benz reversed provisions and reserves totalling DM1.8 billion in the first half of 1993, creating a German-style "profit" at a time when its operations otherwise showed a reality-style loss. Contrast with this the recent Financial Accounting Standards Board ("FASB") statement (No 115) that requires banks and others to mark to market on their books securities that have declined in value, even though the losses have not been realised and therefore cannot be recognised for tax purposes. If companies had been required to conform their financial reporting to the dictates of the Internal Revenue Code, many of those losses would have remained undisclosed for years to come.[5]

(b) Transparency is an eleventh commandment of American life generally, not just in financial markets. We insist on open hearings all through government; we open up to public scrutiny under the Freedom of Information Act the records that elsewhere would be kept confidential; we and the press relentlessly pursue the tax returns and business dealings of almost anyone seeking high public office. Much as those CEOs find it distasteful, their bonuses and stock options are the gist of many a story. We do all this as part of the public's unquestioned (if sometimes exaggerated) "right to know". It comes as no surprise that what is so ubiquitous in our society should affect the financial reporting of the country's major businesses. A recent piece in the *Harvard Business Review* suggests that this transparency be taken one step further, down to the factory floor, giving to hourly-paid workers the real picture of how their group is performing.[6]

(c) The SEC has the statutory right to prescribe, in whatever detail it chooses, the accounting practices and standards employed by publicly owned companies. Period. In practice, however, the Commission has long done what it has also done elsewhere, namely, allow a so-called self-regulatory organisation to write almost all the rules. In this case, it has relied on the FASB, a full-time group of seven, based in Norwalk, Connecticut, who have severed all ties with their firms. Unlike in many countries, the initiative remains, therefore, in the private sector, subject to sometimes intensive SEC oversight. Needless to say, the proceedings of the FASB are very open.

---

[5] In the case of FASB No 106, requiring companies to accrue currently the present value of retiree health benefits, the gap between financial and tax accounting is larger still because the tax deduction typically will not occur until many years hence.

[6] J Case, "Opening the Books", *Harvard Business Review*, Apr. 1997, 118.

Corporate managements manage what we measure. It is true, financial statements report on a performance that has already occurred, and (with minor exceptions) not on management's forecasts. Does that negate their value? Not at all. Security analysts, who are, after all, knee-deep in the market-place, have made it clear that they are looking for neither current-value-based financial statements nor projections from management. And for good reason: what they prefer are data that are objective, comparable and auditable.

VI HOW GOOD IS AMERICAN ACCOUNTING?

For the continuing shareholder, the one who is conscious of owning not just a tradeable stock but a part interest in a business, financial reports offer the most articulate and precise review of the stewardship of the enterprise. And this is just one of the several respects in which financial reporting American-style makes a unique contribution, not just to markets, but to corporate performance. Others include:

(a) disclosure obviates much of the need for substantive regulation or, in the words of Louis D Brandeis which so influenced President Roosevelt and Congress in 1933, "[s]unlight is said to be the best of disinfectants; electric light the most efficient policeman".[7]
(b) given the high turnover in United States stockholdings, disclosure compensates remarkably well for the absence of a body of large-stake, long-term, knowledgeable shareholders able to sit on boards of directors or otherwise to act as proxies for shareholders generally. The flow of reliable, textured financial data enables the larger, public world of security analysts, the financial press, and the body of generally passive institutional holders to do what no shareholders individually are likely to do.

Power without accountability invites abuse, in industry as in government. A free press stands guard in the political arena. Think of accountants and security analysts as the guardians of industry: despite all their shortcomings, they not only seek out the inevitable abuses but encourage more appropriate behaviour in the first place.

Accounting is inherently imprecise. There is no singly correct set of numbers. Will American Airlines' new aeroplanes be serviceable for thirty years or should they be depreciated over just twenty? Should research and development or software expenses be charged to earnings as they are incurred, or should some portion be capitalised and charged only over time? When the Dow Jones 30 Industrial Companies wrote off $49 billion of so-called restructuring charges in the five-year period 1991–5, did they outrageously inflate

---

[7] L Brandeis, *Other People's Money and How Bankers Use It* (New York, 1914), 92.

future earnings? And so on. The three Cs will remain a goal, one never fully achieved.

The progress has been remarkable. Here are a few illustrations of the high quality of disclosure in the United States:

(a) Ever since the 1970s, reporting companies (i.e. those required to file under the federal securities laws) have been required to disclose their operating results for each significant line of business and also by geographic areas. Almost every company of any size is an amalgam of different businesses operating in different places. General Electric, for one, which operates eleven industrial businesses and twenty-four financial service units, furnishes data for them in ten separate segments as varied as aircraft engines, broadcasting, power systems and financing. Looking at Gillette, we see that while its United States operations are highly profitable, over 60 per cent of its earnings come from overseas.

No requirement is so cordially disliked by industry or by European companies contemplating listing on the New York Stock Exchange. All for good reason, of course. Coca-Cola continually jiggles its overseas profit reporting. In 1994, for example, it lumped Canada with East Asia and Northeast Europe with the Middle East, presumably to obscure the results in areas where the profits were indeed outsized. (In 1996, the sector reporting was rearranged.) No one likes to get undressed in public.

But allowing for all that, it remains true that segment reporting provides a vast fund of information that the market and the press use to gain insights and to put pressure on those managers, of whom there are always too many, who would prefer to bask in the light of their triumphs than to confront their inevitable failures. They manage what we measure. The current stream of divisional sales and spin-offs—AT&T spinning off its equipment and computer divisions, Pepsico its restaurants—have been a predictable by-product.

(b) Accounting principles require that pension benefits for current employees be charged against current earnings, even though the payments will not be made until years hence. The theory is clear; those pay-later pensions are a cost of this year's production, and employers are required to fund plans to guarantee that the money will be there. Because private pension schemes play such a major role in the United States, the annual charges to income can be very large. In a down period, managers are tempted— very tempted!—to modify one or more of the actuarial assumptions on which the cost of these pension benefits is based in order to soften their impact. General Motors, for example, showed $22 billion of unfunded pension liabilities at the end of 1993. It is difficult to ignore a $22 billion shortfall, and of course General Motors did not. By dint of special contributions and other steps, it cut these unfunded liabilities by almost 90 per cent in two years'. Contrast this with Japan, where bad accounting has concealed major problems, even as they fester.

What is distinctive about the United States practice is: (i) the recalculation of plan benefits, assets and shortfalls (or surpluses) is required annually, not every five years as elsewhere; (ii) the FASB requires about as much detail as a shareholder/analyst could desire with respect to those pension funds and their impact on the income statement; and (iii) these detailed requirements are then policed by the SEC, which has made it pointedly clear that unrealistic assumptions will not be accepted.

(c)   At year-end 1993, when its shareholders' net worth was $5 billion, General Motors was also showing on its balance sheet, in addition to the just-mentioned $22 billion of unfunded pension obligations, an accrued liability for retirees' health care costs of $37 billion. General Motors, of course, was not alone. Many old industrial companies had guaranteed employees generous retirement medical benefits years earlier, when costs were far less. Eventually corporate America's aggregate liability for these once modest benefits mushroomed to hundreds of billions of dollars—too large to be ignored. Over the predictable objections of the business leaders, who said the sky would fall, the FASB issued an exposure draft of a new standard that would require corrective action, and at that point, and only then, did companies began to put their houses in order, for example by capping benefits and by putting these programmes on a contributory basis.

(d)   Many years ago, Con Edison, while tearing up the streets to lay new power lines, plastered the city with signs saying "Dig we must for a better New York". The SEC must have had the same thing in mind when, seeing Penn Central and other companies reporting good "earnings", only shortly thereafter to file for bankruptcy, it began to require a management discussion and analysis ("MD&A") section. Within the overall limit that confidential product and market plans need not be made public, the MD&A is intended to add a textual analysis of the numbers contained in the financial statements which, even if they technically comply with US-Generally Accepted Accounting Principles, may not provide an adequate picture of the quality and *sustainability* of a company's earnings or liquidity. At the simplest level, if a company has benefited in the past from a major contract which however is about to expire, or if it has shipped extra quantities of goods just before year-end, it must disclose that fact in its MD&A. On a more complex issue, that of derivatives, the SEC has recently been asking companies to disclose in the MD&A the extent of the risks and the impact of their trading.

As one group of analysts has said, other than the financial statements themselves, the MD&A is "perhaps the most useful single part of the annual report".[8]

[8] P Knutson, *Financial Reporting in the 1990s and Beyond* (New York, Association for Investment Management and Research, 1993), 75.

(e) If some managers would only put all the energy spent on manipulating their reported earnings to some modestly productive use, the effect would be wondrous. Be that as it may, just as European companies have used "hidden reserves" to manipulate earnings, so too have American companies "restructured" away large asset values and expenses by taking so-called special charges now, the effect of which is to enhance their earnings in the years to come. One recent survey found that among just the thirty Dow Jones Industrial Companies, twenty-six had "restructured" at least once in the years 1991–5, and twenty-two had done so at least twice. Over the five years, the thirty-company total was $49 billion. There is no FASB requirement, so why are companies so eager to record these large charges? A European investor might think it reassuring to be rich in the old-fashioned sense of owning large and valuable balance sheet assets. Not so in the United States, where large asset values are seen as burdensome. The actual assets, of course, remain the same; it is only the "cost" of them that disappears in these restructurings, thus increasing future earnings. Note that these restructurings are entirely voluntary on the part of management.

A case in point: in its 1991 annual report, AT&T announced that it had set as a financial goal a return on equity exceeding 20 per cent. Given its historically lower level of performance, that goal might have seemed ambitious, but a close reading of footnotes revealed that by then the company had "restructured" away over $14 billion of shareholders' equity, thus simplifying the task.[9]

After a time, the SEC's Division of Corporation Finance ("CorpFin") noticed from press releases and the like the growing number of companies announcing these "one-time" charges. They also noticed the enthusiasm with which these announcements were greeted in the stock market. A restructuring, it seems, would be ignored by security analysts in the year it was taken, because it was, after all, a "special" charge. It would also be ignored, as ancient history of sorts, in calculating earnings thereafter.

The staff took corrective action. The Chief Accountant of the Division and others made speeches and advised companies that these restructuring charges would trigger a specific review, then and for several years to come, in order to determine whether, for example, they were treating ordinary operating items as special charges or, perhaps, creating charges now for events which had not yet occurred. In the course of the review, the staff found charges for such "losses" as: start-up costs not yet incurred, inventory not yet purchased, advertising costs for a logo not yet adopted and the costs of terminating 20,000 employees, of whom 17,000 were still on the payroll two years later.

[9] AT&T *1991 Annual Report*, 18, 20–1. In 1995, in what by then seemed to be obsessive behaviour, the company wrote off an additional $5 billion.

Note that the thrust of the SEC's concern was not just to eliminate the outright deception, which after all might have been achieved with more detailed footnoting. Rather, the Commission was seeking more *consistency* in reported earnings from year to year—are the earnings *as reported* at Company X this year in fact better than last?—and *comparability* with other companies. It is a game of cat-and-mouse, and the corporate "mice" are energetic in their efforts to put the best possible face on their stewardship of the "cheese". But then the regulatory "cats" are also alert.

VII THE PROCESS BY WHICH THE PRESSURE IS APPLIED

Disclosure documents are not simply filed at the offices of the SEC. An array of services and mechanisms have sprung up to process, deliver and analyse the data. Sitting at my computer, I can dial up the reports of public companies filed as recently as twenty-four hours ago. The reports are promptly digested, repackaged and interpreted, not just by security analysts but by the financial press, a host of advisory services and others. The financial cable television station, CNBC, broadcasts interviews with analysts and even CEOs of major corporations. Why would the head of a powerful industrial company subject himself to detailed questioning in such a public format? But they do; the visibility is prized as a means of maintaining a good market in their stocks, just as the President of the United States appears on talk shows to maintain the price of his "stock".

The process runs deep. Within the SEC, there are one hundred and twenty accountants just within CorpFin—one-half of its review staff—reading annual reports and other filings. They are an integral part of what Linda Quinn, until recently the director of the Division, liked to call the Commission's "active oversight" function. Why wait, she argued, until losses have been suffered? Why let misrepresentations and errors fester until only the Division of Enforcement can act? Those one hundred and twenty accountants in CorpFin, who have no counterpart elsewhere, monitor routine filings and are likely to be the first to see emerging issues.

Does all this mandated disclosure seem excessive? Not to Quinn, who would argue that unlike many other major industrialised countries, we have no regulatory gatekeeper to decide which new stock issues may be floated and which must wait for bank sponsorship (as in Germany) or for government merit approval (as in Japan).

VIII DRAWBACKS OF THE AMERICAN SYSTEM

Financial accounting attempts to reduce a complex reality to a single, or at least a modest, set of numbers. Whatever the theory, there is enormous emphasis in the market-place on a single number, the earnings per share. It is inevitable, therefore, that managements will often manage not for what is the economically better outcome but for the *measured* outcome, or will simply manipulate the reported numbers.

Critics like to argue that our financial reports can also be jiggled. True enough, although they can be jiggled far less than those elsewhere. Still the jiggle is not trivial. For example, General Motors was for many years an icon of American industrial leadership. Yet during much of the 1980s, while Roger Smith was chairman and CEO, the company repeatedly manipulated such items as its inventory values and its depreciation and pension expenses, all with the consistent effect of reporting better "earnings". I am always saddened at the extent to which these disingenuous games are played by respectable companies, but managers like to believe they are deceiving impersonal markets, not real owners. And accountants, for whom auditing has tended to become the access to lucrative consultancies, increasingly cheerlead the process.

The two criticisms most often heard about the American system are:

(a) the fear of a competitive injury through the disclosure of otherwise confidential information; and
(b) the risk that it imposes excessive costs.

I think both have been overstated.

A short answer to these fears is first that the International Accounting Standards Committee, although under exquisite pressure to accommodate European corporate interests, is in the process of developing a provision for segment data which in these respects would be essentially similar to US–GAAP.[10] Also, the reality is that there are few secrets in industry; Pepsi Cola knows how well Coca Cola is doing in Tokyo. And beyond that, lead times have shrunk all over the industrial landscape; a new product may literally be obsolete within months.

And the so-called high "cost" of mandated financial disclosure American-style needs to be measured against the gains, not just to shareholders but to the company itself. Senior officers of Ciba-Geigy Limited and The Holderbank Group report a long list of managerial gains from improved financial disclosure. Divisions now report on a consistent basis, there is a more rational allocation of costs, and expenses are no longer charged directly to surplus.

IX AN INTERNATIONAL PERSPECTIVE

It is easy to speak in bland generalities about accounting and disclosure requirements abroad. Japan and Germany are hardly primitive societies. What

---

[10] United States—Generally Accepted Accounting Principles.

could be so awful if we mimicked their practices instead of stubbornly insisting on our own? A lot.

Financial reporting in some countries, notably Germany, is said to be conservative. It is, as a senior official at the Bonn Ministry of Justice admonished, based on the principle of a prudent understatement of profits, unlike the United States—United Kingdom system, which he said "give[s] the short-term interests of speculative investors greater importance than safeguarding the companies on a long-term basis".[11] Damn the gnomes of Wall Street and the City! It is true that Germany has a system under which voting control is concentrated in the hands of a few banks and insurance companies that are able to provide oversight privately. In practice, however, conservative becomes a code word for concealment, as if disclosure were somehow the enemy of prudence. In practice, management behind a veil becomes management without accountability, and what eventually emerges may look less prudent than pungent. Examining just three of the issues discussed above suggests that the reporting elsewhere is not as open, not as conservative and indeed not as prudent as in the United States:

(a) Foreign accounting for defined-benefit pension plans and other post-employment benefits is markedly inferior to ours. The failure to mark to market threatens a major fiscal crisis in Japan, and German pension accounting is said to be woeful.

(b) Mark to market accounting for portfolio gains and losses and derivatives. As Dennis Beresford, the then head of FASB, said recently, the most relevant picture of a company's derivative portfolio is probably fair value, but it is certainly not zero, as is presently the practice.[12]

(c) Segment reporting, which Americans regard as one of the most useful tools of financial analysis, but one rarely seen elsewhere.

Managers everywhere behave better earlier when people are watching. And that has become increasingly important not just for the United States, but for all the industrialised nations. Four reasons for this are:

(a) the growing internationalisation of markets;
(b) the increased emphasis on deregulation and privatisation;
(c) the shift from tangible-asset based to knowledge-based wealth; and
(d) the intensity of technological change and the rapid obsolescence of products.

In Silicon Valley, Silicon Hills and Silicon Alley, competitive advantage is measured in months, not years. Wealth and capital are painfully unstable. The United States service sector is now twice as large as the manufacturing sector. Some of that service sector consists simply of hamburger stands, but the

---

[11] J Kelly, "Signalling the Advance on Global Harmonization", *Financial Times*, 25 May 1995, 13, col 2.
[12] Letter to the Editor, *Wall Street Journal*, 17 Mar. 1997.

important part is the increasingly significant knowledge-based industries, such as computing and bioscience. As the Royal Bank of Canada, for one, has noted, it is increasingly necessary to finance *ideas*, as opposed to conventional assets—bricks and mortar and machinery. And that requires an entirely different mindset. A steel plant cannot be replicated except at a comparable cost. But the next copy of my Windows 95 programme costs next to nothing, and your use of it does not interfere with mine.

Paul Romer, the Stanford economist, asks: is the recipe now more valuable than the oven? Consider that accountants consider the oven an asset, while the recipe often is not. Microsoft's financial reports do not show most software programs as assets; the costs are expensed as they are incurred. The company has a market capitalisation of $120 billion, supported by a mere $8 billion of tangible asset values. And of that about $7 billion are simply cash and receivables. With 21,000 employees, Microsoft has a market capitalisation over three times that of Ford Motor Company, which has 345,000 employees. And roughly the same would be true of Intel, Cisco Systems and Oracle, to name but a few.

In this emerging world of knowledge-based wealth, successful companies are able to generate huge amounts of the cash flow that we discussed a few moments ago. A copy of Windows 95 costs pennies to produce and sells at retail for US$200. The successes are dramatic and, compared with those of fifty years ago, they often need neither huge capital investments nor many years of lead time. But it is also true that the wheel can turn with remarkable rapidity. We have all seen various hi-tech companies slip far and fast, once they lose momentum. Compared to the steel and auto companies that once dominated the industrial scene, the road downhill has few resting places.

Once upon a time, when I was young, companies could coast on the sustaining power of their entrenched market position, in cold rolled steel or whatever. Managers could play golf on Fridays, and none would care. But in the emerging knowledge-based markets, that comfort factor has dried up. As the head of Sun Microsystems said not long ago, he is training at Sun his competitors of five years hence. If Sun and othes do not keep a prompt and accurate tally on how they are doing, if we do not *insist* on it, they may have run aground before their fans—the shareholders, the employees, the community—realise what went wrong.

X CONCLUSION

Why is financial transparency important for others as well as the United States? According to a proverb that was popular in America when I was a child, "a stitch in time saves nine". My mother darned my socks, as most mothers did in those days, and as few, if any, mothers do today. (The socks are now cheap, and the mothers have become mutual fund managers.) But my mother would have understood corporate governance in those same terms: it is better to act before more damage is done.

The conclusion seems clear. For an industrialised country, corporate accountability and transparency were always important, but they have become vital as the society becomes more diverse and the economy becomes more complex and rapidly evolving. Otherwise the necessary stitches will not be taken in time.

Index